First
San Salvador Conference
Columbus And His World

Compiled by Donald T. Gerace

PROCEEDINGS

held
October 30 — November 3, 1986

at
The College Center of the Finger Lakes
Bahamian Field Station
San Salvador Island, Bahamas

Library of Congress Catalog Card Number   87-70948

ISBN 0-935909-23-0

Typeset by Summit Technical Associates, Inc.
     Coral Springs, Florida

Printed by Technical Communications Services
     North Kansas City, Missouri

Published by College Center of the Finger Lakes
     Bahamian Field Station
     270 Southwest 34 Street
     Fort Lauderdale, Florida 33315

Table of Contents

Preface

The College Center of the Finger Lakes, a consortium of Alfred University, Corning Community College, Elmira College, Empire College, Hartwick College, Keuka College, and Mansfield State University, operates a research and educational field station on San Salvador Island in the Bahamas. Since this island is believed by many to be the one Columbus first landed upon in 1492, the Board of Trustees of the College Center of the Finger Lakes wished to pursue a greater role in the rising scholarly interest in Columbus as the quincentennary of his first landfall approached. Their interest and financial support was further sparked by the archaeological investigations of Dr. Charles Hoffman, who located Spanish contact period artifacts while excavating on San Salvador under the auspices of the CCFL.

The Ohio State University and the Institute for Early Contact Period Studies of the University of Florida, both deeply involved in research related to Columbus and that time period, expressed interest in cooperatively organizing and sponsoring a conference focused on Columbus and his first voyage to the New World. Charles Hoffman also showed a keen desire to bring together various archaeologists and historians of the Spanish contact period.

Dr. Christian Zacher, Director of Ohio State University's Center for Medieval and Renaissance Studies, provided numerous contacts with European scholars, specifically those from Italy. Dr. Zacher's unending assistance, the international coordination of Dr. Luciano Farina, and the generous financial support from Ohio State University provided the framework within which the First San Salvador Conference could develop.

The Institute for Early Contact Period Studies of the University of Florida, under the direction of Dr. Michael Gannon, is involved in several ongoing projects related to Columbus, specifically the studies by Eugene Lyon of one of Columbus' ships, the Niña, and the archaeological research for La Navidad by Dr. Kathleen Deagan. Dr. Gannon's valuable guidance and financial support greatly assisted in successfully organizing this conference.

With the exception of Turks and Caicos, it is generally agreed that Columbus first landed somewhere in the Bahamas on that historic first voyage in 1492, although the exact island may always be in question. The Commonwealth of the Bahamas was actively involved in planning the First San Salvador Conference, specifically, Dr. Gail Saunders, Director of the Department of Archives, Neil Sealey from the College of the Bahamas, and

Philip Smith, Member of Parliament for San Salvador and head of the Bahamas National Commission for Celebrations of the Quincentennial of the Discovery of the New World.

The success of the First San Salvador Conference: Columbus and His World, is reflected in the papers making up this volume, all of which were fully presented and discussed during the symposium. The original presentations were divided into four panels, and these proceedings follow the same format.

The first panel emphasized Columbus, the man; the personal and intellectual heritage which provided the compelling drive to devote the major part of his adult life to a dream of discovering a new route to Asia. Chaired jointly by Drs. Zacher and Gannon, the papers presented are the first five of this volume, those by Taviani, Wolper, Varela, West and Provost.

The panel entitled Columbus' Ships, Crew and Navigation was admirably chaired by Dr. David Buisseret of the Newberry Library. The papers by Phillips, Ferro, Kelley and Charlier were presented during this session and reflect the 1492 voyage of Columbus and the maritime advancements which made the voyage possible.

Stimulated by strong public interest, the third panel in which the various landfall theories were presented and discussed became the focus of the conference, especially by those who did not attend. Most adequately monitored by Louis DeVorsey, those papers presented by Molander, Fuson, Obregón and Taviani, as well as the data related by Gerace during this session, are found in the third section of this volume.

The people Columbus met on his first voyage in the New World were the topic of the final panel, chaired by Dr. Saunders. Papers by Rouse, Winter and Rose provide background information on the original inhabitants of the Caribbean and their environment, while those by Hoffman, Brill and Deagan give us an idea of that first contact between the Indians and the early Spanish.

It is with pleasure that I, along with the Program Chairman, the Conference Committee, and the Sponsors, present these Proceedings of the First San Salvador Conference, Columbus and His World.

Donald T. Gerace
Conference Organizer

Conference Participants

Conference Organizer

Dr. Donald T. Gerace, Director
CCFL Bahamian Field Station
270 Southwest 34 Street
Fort Lauderdale, FL 33315

Program Chairman

Dr. Charles A. Hoffman
Department of Anthropology
Northern Arizona University
Flagstaff, AZ 86011

International Coordinator

Dr. Luciano Farina
Romance Languages
Ohio State University
248 Cunz Hall
Columbus, OH 43210

Sponsors

Bahamas Ministry of Education
  College of the Bahamas and
  Department of Archives

Bahamas National Commission
  for Celebrations of the
  Quincentennial of the
  Discovery of the New World

College Center of the Finger
  Lakes

Institute for Early Contact
  Period Studies of the
  University of Florida

The Ohio State University

Panel Chairpeople

Dr. David Buisseret
The Newberry Library
60 West Walton
Chicago, IL 60610

Dr. Louis DeVorsey
Department of Geography
University of Georgia
Athens, GA 30602

Dr. Michael Gannon
Institute for Early Contact
  Period Studies
University of Florida
2121 Turlington Hall
Gainesville, FL 32611

Dr. Gail Saunders, Director
Department of Archives
P. O. Box SS 6341
Nassau, Bahamas

Dr. Christian Zacher, Director
Center for Medieval &
  Renaissance Studies
Ohio State University
230 West 17 Avenue
Columbus, OH 43210

Conference Committee

Prof. Mary Jane Berman
Director, Museum of Man
Wake Forest University
P. O. Box 7267
Winston-Salem, NC 27106

Dr. Michael V. Gannon, Director
Institute for Early Contact
    Period Studies
University of Florida
2121 Turlington Hall
Gainesville, FL 32611

Dr. Donald T. Gerace, Director
CCFL Bahamian Field Station
270 Southwest 34 Street
Fort Lauderdale, FL 33315

Dr. Perry Gnivecki
Department of Anthropology
Hartwick College
Oneonta, NY 13820

Dr. Charles Hoffman
Department of Anthropology
Northern Arizona University
Flagstaff, AZ 86011

Dr. D. Gail Saunders, Director
Department of Archives
P. O. Box SS 6341
Nassau, Bahamas

Prof. Neil Sealey, Chairman
Social Science Division
College of the Bahamas
P. O. Box N 4912
Nassau, Bahamas

Prof. John Winter
Science Department
Molloy College
Rockville Center, NY 11570

Dr. Christian K. Zacher, Director
Center for Medieval &
    Renaissance Studies
Ohio State University
230 West 17 Avenue
Columbus, OH 43210

Contributors

Dr. Robert Brill
Research Scientist
Corning Museum of Glass
Corning, NY 14830

Mr. George Charlier
244, Boulevard d'Avroy
B4000 Liège
Belgique

Dr. Kathleen Deagan
Florida State Museum
University of Florida
Gainesville, FL 32611

Prof. Gaetano Ferro
Universita degli Studi di Genova
Facolta di Scienxe Politiche
Genova, Italia

Dr. Robert H. Fuson
Prof. Emeritus, Univ. of So. Florida
11405 Gibraltar Place
Temple Terrace, FL 33617

Dr. Donald T. Gerace, Director
CCFL Bahamian Field Station
270 Southwest 34 Street
Fort Lauderdale, FL 33315

Dr. Charles Hoffman
Department of Anthropology
Northern Arizona University
Flagstaff, AZ 86011

Mr. James E. Kelley, Jr.
7602 Spring Avenue
Melrose Park, PA 19126

Mr. Arne Molander
19131 Roman Way
Gaithersburg, MD 20879

Mr. Mauricio Obregón
Ambassador to the Caribbean
Apartado Aereo 3529
Bogota, 1 Columbia

Dr. Carla Rahn Phillips
4066 Caminito Espejo
San Diego, CA 92107

Dr. Foster Provost
Department of English
Duquesne University
Pittsburgh, PA 15282

Dr. Richard Rose
Curator of Anthropology
Rochester Museum & Science
   Center
657 East Avenue
Rochester, NY 14607

Dr. Irving Rouse
Department of Anthropology
Yale University
Box 2114, Yale Station
New Haven, CT 06520

Dr. Paolo Emilio Taviani
Ministero Per 1 Beni
   Culturali E. Ambientali
Via. DiS. Michaele, 22
00153 Roma
Italia

Consuelo Varela
San Vicente, 32
Sevilla — 41002
Spain

Dr. Delno C. West
Department of History
Box 6023
Northern Arizona University
Flagstaff, AZ 86011

Prof. John Winter
Molloy College
Rockville Centre, NY 11570

Ms. Ruth Durlacher Wolper
7811 North Shore Road
Norfolk, VA 23505

Columbus The Man:
A Psychologically Modern Man
of the Middle Ages

Paolo Emilio Taviani
Senato della Repubblica
Roma, Italia

INTRODUCTION

During the last five centuries, thousands of books, essays and articles, as well as novels, plays and even operas, have been written about Christopher Columbus and his life. Two works stand out from among the latter that, because they are not tied to historiography, depend exclusively on poetic inspiration. These are *Le livre de Christophe Colomb* by Paul Claudel, and *El Harpa y la sombra* by Alejo Carpentier.

The authors interpret truth in a completely distorted fashion, altering historical data, that, at times, they respect thoroughly. Both Claudel's and Carpentier's books are unparalleled works of art, so that they can stand as jewels of world literature.

Each describes his own version of the "truth": Claudel depicts Columbus as though he were Saint Joan of Arc, hearing voices; Carpentier depicts Columbus as a swindler, a thief and a rogue. The knowledge of Columbus's true personality is irrelevant in the reading of these two artistic interpretations of events. However, in the conclusive chapters of this work, which seeks to be rigorously historiographic, the problems are analyzed on a purely historical level.

Could we say, historically, that Columbus has been a saint? The answer to that is no. And we gave incontrovertible evidence elsewhere to prove that. Nor was Columbus a farsighted politician.

His mishaps cannot possibly be blamed on bad luck, on his enemies, spite, or on those who envied him for the fact that a low-born foreigner could have achieved such honor and privileges.

As we have often pointed out, Columbus's life is fraught with errors and contradictions, although at times he did act properly and with timely cunning; but we cannot say we judge positively Columbus's political qualities on the whole. He was neither a stupid nor an inefficient person, but he

1

lacked the two qualities that make a man into a true politician: the capacity to make firm decisions for the long run and a profound psychological knowledge of his fellows, which is indispensable for appointing the right man to the right position.

Some have said that Columbus was a man come from the Middle Ages. Others claim that his soul was superior to that of the century in which he lived (Cladera), maintaining that he was a child of Renaissance. In reality, he stood astride the two ages: his theoretical approach to philosophy, theology, and even his scientific concepts were medieval. His eagerness for scientific investigation and keen interest in nature as well as his capacity for accepting facts and phenomena so far unknown were peculiar of the Renaissance.

Psychologically, he was a modern man, practical and concrete to the point of being over-meticulous. His projects were elaborated only after he had acquired direct experience — and his great design was born along those lines.

In conclusion, a psychologically modern man of the Middle Ages.

NOT A SAINT, BUT A DEFENDER OF THE FAITH

The same can be said about his spirituality. He was a Christian and a Catholic in the modern sense, influenced by medieval teachings. His faith was strong, sincere, inexhaustible, free from superstition and hypocrisy, whatever might befall him. Convincing some recalcitrant Indian tribes that a natural event such as an eclipse was instead a sign from God represents the sole exception in the complex and incredible string of adventures that accompanied Columbus's life. Columbus received a rigorously modern and profoundly religious education, which was reflected in his frequent reference to God.

Sometimes he gave into fanaticism, or, as they say today, he was a "fundamentalist". However, his fanaticism never trampled over the principles of both the Christian and Catholic *Weltanshaüung* that Columbus always held in high consideration.

He was never particularly fond of the clergy. He did not hesitate to fight against priests, friars and bishops in defense of true Christianity, although throughout his life a few friars and bishops gave him their friendship. The Franciscan Father Antonio Marchena was one of his friends among the clergy. Marchena can be certainly considered, after Columbus, another outstanding leading figure in the history of discoveries.

Unlike Dante Alighieri, when Columbus was faced with the incredible mystery of a fourth continent, he thought better than placing the transcendent Purgatory into the immanent southern hemisphere. He resorted to his idea of an earthly Paradise. Even Amerigo Vespucci, who was very much inclined to skepticism, had to admit that, "if it ever existed, it must have been in those places".

During the terrible storms at sea, Columbus would turn to the Virgin Mary and to the Saints, as Catholics have always done throughout the ages, even in present times.

When he fell victim to men's envy, spite, avarice, wickedness, and, above all, to the King's injustice, Columbus always reacted with Christian humility, with the submission of those who have faith in life after death.

Columbus was particularly devoted to the Virgin Mary and to Saint Francis. He knew by heart all of the New Testament and long passages from the Old. In his never-ending struggle against the Ocean, Columbus — and we have already pointed this out — never asked for miracles of Jesus Christ, but he would look to the Original Source of Christian Truth: "In the beginning there was the Word, and the Word was with God and the Word was God".

This is important in that it proves that Columbus's devotion to the Virgin Mary, which derives directly from his being Genoese, and to Saint Francis, linked to the fact that he was Italian, was not a result of superstition, but fitted in well with his systematic and rigorous spirituality.

We shall point out again that Columbus's continuous and obsessive search for gold and riches had to him a precise purpose: to launch a crusade in order to recover the Holy Land. Such a crusading spirit had nothing to do with that prevailing during the Middle Ages. It had been renewed and revived by the psychological effects of the fall of Constantinople which, with Rome, was the great capital of Christendom. A renewed urge for a crusade did not underlie only an aspiration for the recovery of the Holy Land. It aimed at uniting again what had been split, at bringing the world back to unity. It had been united under the legions of Rome and stayed so, rather consolidated, under the Cross of Jesus Christ. All the barbarians —Germans, Slavs, even Vikings and Tartars — had found a place in Christianity — but Islam had disrupted the world by splitting Christianity.

During Columbus's wanderings in the entourage of the Spanish king, an event occurred that could help to demonstrate the existing link between the war waged against the Moors and the destiny of the Holy Land. In July 1489, two Franciscan friars arrived at the Catholic Royal Court from Jerusalem. They acted as envoys of the Great Sultan of Egypt to the Pope who, in turn, sent them to the King and Queen of Spain. The friars were bearers of a threatening message. The Sultan demanded that the war against the Moors in Spain be interrupted, that all the Muslims of Andalusia be given back their property and freedom — or else he would retaliate against the Christians living in Palestine. Columbus, who was at Court, must have learned of the message and may even have met the two envoys, one of whom was Italian. Some historians note that Columbus probably began to plan a recovery of the Holy Land on that occasion. That idea would never fade from his mind.

We believe that episode certainly affected Columbus, but the link between his projects and his religious plan for a crusade must have had far deeper roots. His profound religiousness which developed in Genoa, explains those roots. The feeling for the necessity of a new crusade originated in Genoa, around the 1450s, in particular when Genoa came into contact with Christians who had escaped from Islam's oppression.

To conclude our analysis of Columbus's religious sentiments, we could say that his personality was primarily based on the Christian-Catholic conception of the world. There is no contradiction between such a statement and the other statement that he was not a saint. To be one, faith, humility and generosity are not enough. We have sufficient proof that indicates his being proud, attached to money and privileges. He was partial to his family and relatives and showed indifference to slavery. The stronger Columbus's "faith" was, the weaker his "charity". Therefore, he was neither a great nor a small saint. He always defended the faith in a convinced, tenacious and profound manner — and that is not to be overlooked: he was a "defensor fidei".

HE WAS NO ADVENTURER

The image of Columbus as an adventurer is false. He never refused to embark on an adventure. He lived through adventures with courage and indifference to dangers, which is peculiar of those who are aware of their own abilities and the helping hand of God.

His first crossing of the Atlantic was certainly a great adventure: but, in a way, his early voyages to Chios, Iceland and Guinea had been adventures. And his third crossing, which saw him through the torturously hot and becalmed waters of the tropics, was an adventure. However, his fourth voyage was certainly his greatest and most daring feat. He undertook it when his fame was already on the wane, with the precise intention of circumnavigating the globe. It ended with just two vessels left, and those all but devoured by ship worms and caught in the shallow waters of Santa Maria of Jamaica for one entire year, on the most open shores found along the entire world's numerous coasts.

However, his adventures did not only take place on the seas. Was it not an adventure to flee from Portugal to reach Spain, where for seven years he incessantly pursued his great design? Even the foundation of San Tomaso, during his land expedition in the Vega Real, a land as unknown as the ocean was, had been a daring feat.

Columbus's whole life was a wonderful adventure, albeit sorrowful at times. But those who accuse him of adventurism do that to belittle his merits, trying to credit sheer luck and chance for the success of a man. In this sense Columbus was other than an adventurer. Columbus's merits are certainly to be measured in relation to his success — but they are its cause, not its effect.

HE WAS A GREAT SAILOR

History would be distorted if we were to deny one particular aspect of Columbus's character. He was an exceptionally gifted sailor. We have already demonstrated that in our previous work (*The Genesis of the Great Discovery*); however, we felt it should be pointed out again in our second work, *The Great Discovery*, throughout which we have often offered facts and episodes to support our assertion.

Not only did Columbus discover America, he discovered the route from Europe to the Gulf of Mexico, and vice versa. Until the invention of motor-propelled vessels, any ship sailing from Spain, Portugal, France, or Italy, headed for Mexico, for the mouth of the Mississippi, the Caribbean, Columbia or Venezuela, followed Columbus's routes. On the voyage back, they passed through the Sargasso Sea on the Azores parallel. Even today, those who want to sail through the Atlantic pick the same route as Columbus laid out in his second voyage, that from the Canary Islands to Guadalupe.

The discovery of routes is connected to that of the trade winds. We have already noted that Columbus was the first man who crossed the Sargasso Sea, without fear, who perceived the existence of the Gulf Stream, who discovered the westerly magnetic declination. But, above all, he was the initiator of open sea navigation in the modern era — the first man who had enough courage to navigate with no sight of the coast-line.

He had the exceptional physical fitness of a sailor, his sight and hearing were perfect, his sense of smell was unparalleled. That is easily deduced from all of his writings. Many of those who personally knew him praised his sense of smell and noted his ability to distinguish various perfumes. Some viewed that as an indication of affectedness — it was, instead, an uncommon inborn gift that represented the fundamental component of his sixth sense, the seafaring sense.

Michele da Cuneo wrote: "By a simple look at the night sky, he would know what route to follow or what weather to expect; he took the helm and once the storm was over, he would hoist the sails, while the others were asleep".

Andrés Bernàldez wrote: "He does not consider himself a good navigator and a master who, having to sail from one land to another, with no sight of the coast-line, makes a mistake of ten leagues, even in a voyage of one thousand leagues, unless a very violent storm forced him into erring, preventing him from proving his skill".

The most renowned experts on Columbus — Thacher, Harrisse, Caddeo, Revelli, Morison, Madariaga, Nunn, and Bradford — fully confirmed Las Casas's judgment: "Christopher Columbus surpassed all of his contemporaries in the art of navigation".

Contrasting opinions on this issue are very scarce. Vignaud was the most drastic critic of Columbus's sailing skills — but, it seems that the former's experiences on a body of water are limited to sight-seeing tours on the river Seine.

The great French explorer Charcot defined Columbus: "A sailor who had 'le sens marin': that mysterious and inborn gift that allows you to pick the right route in the middle of the ocean". "Dogs bark and will continue to bark, but the caravels have sailed past. Christopher Columbus's feat is so great as to arouse all people's enthusiasm". This is a great sailor's judgment of a man, who, with Cook, can be considered the greatest sailor in history.

HE WAS A GREAT SELF-TAUGHT GEOGRAPHER

Columbus was also a great geographer, and, partly, he had taught himself to be one. The fact that he was born in Genoa is not irrelevant, as some say quite thoughtlessly. As a child in Genoa and later in Savona, he had got to know, and become familiar with, the problems of navigation and its techniques, which were traditional in Genoa. Genoa's sea supremacy was unquestioned not only in the Mediterranean but in the whole of Christendom. Later, with the beginning of voyages and the long crossings of the Ocean, geography became very important to good navigation and geographical problems came to be tackled for the first time. Columbus demonstrated in his writings how inclined he was toward geography and how cleverly he often solved problems related to it.

Among Columbus's various traits and personality features, Humboldt points out the cleverness with which Columbus would observe the surrounding environment. Once in a new world and under a new sky, he began to study the land, the local vegetation, the behavior of animals, the variations in temperature and in earth's magnetism. The entries logged in his Journal touch upon the whole range of scientific research that was carried out during the last part of the 15th and throughout the 16th centuries. Although he lacked a solid preparation in natural history, Columbus became a great geographer.

HE WAS A GENIUS

To consider Columbus just a great sailor and geographer would be reductive. He was a genius in the true and full meaning of this term. Not only did he have a seafaring sense and an acute sensitivity for geography, but his faith was indestructible and his hunger for fame bottomless. He was strong-willed, tenacious and almost mulish, as is typical of people from Liguria. He was courageous, patient, imaginative and possessed of an excellent memory. In the decisive moments of his countless adventures, he nearly always managed to mould his intuitions and manifold qualities into effective action which only geniuses can eventually carry out.

This explains how he could conceive of his great design, "buscar el Levante por el Ponente". This explains how he could give up his family, his money, and his most cherished dream, the sea, for years, his best years: from the age of 34 to 42. This explains how he could manage to fulfill his four Atlantic feats: to lead, order, resist, and keep a lucid mind before both the force of the elements and his mutinous men.

Firmly determined and with unshakable convictions, Columbus had dealt, almost as a peer, with the King of Portugal, the King and Queen of Spain, with Genoese, Florentine and Jewish bankers. He was not conceited. He was perfectly aware of his valor and merits, of the strength of his ideas. If conceited, he would never have won either Father Antonio Marchena's or Father Juan Pérez's friendship. If conceited, he would never have had so many friends, protectors and supports within the Spanish Court. Queen Isabel, an exceptionally intelligent woman, would never have given him her sympathy and her trust. If conceited, he would never have convinced that skilled and shrewd captain Martín Alonso Pinzón, the man who shared the merit and glory of the Great Voyage. It was thanks to this man that Columbus managed to enlist the majority of his crew. And, if he had shown conceit, he would never have always had the prestige and respect from even the most cunning and difficult sailors whom he knew how to make obey and respect him, even when the event of the Santa Gloria turned into a tragedy.

Columbus's intellectual insight has been confirmed despite the fact that his foot-notes on *Milione* were ingenuous. By way of contrast, the foot-notes on *Imago Mundi* show how much the seaman had learned in a few years, perhaps even months. Even if his Latin had a few errors, it is important to recognize all the same the talent of his quasi-classical style of writing, at time reminiscent of Seneca. His skillful memory emerges in the metric faults of Seneca's transcription. It's important to realize that he chose those topics which interested him the most and wrote by sheer memory.

All these aspects confirm the man was an indisputable genius. Christopher Columbus was not a fortunate traveller who became a discoverer over night. He was a discoverer because he was an inventor with his own idea of a new horizon. The man was a genius.

NOTES

On Columbus, man of the Middle Ages and of the Renaissance, see:

C. Cladera, *Investigaciones históricas sobre los principales descubrimientos de los españoles en el Mar Océano* (Madrid, 1794), p. 34.

S. Ruge, *Geschichte des Zeitalters der Entdeckungen* (Berlin, 1881), pp. 314-320.

C. Manfroni, "Di una presunta carta di Colombo," in *Atti del Real Istituto Veneto di scienze, lettere ed arti*, Tome XXXIV (Venezia, 1925).

A. Magnaghi, "I presunti errori che vengono attribuiti a Colombo nella determinazione delle latitudini," in *Bollettino della Società Geografica Italiana* (Roma, 1928).

A. Magnaghi, "Colombo," item of *Enciclopedia italiana*, Vol. X, (Roma, 1931), p. 810.

A. Ballesteros Beretta, *Cristóbal Colón y el descubrimiento de América*, Vol. II (Barcelona-Buenos Aires, 1945), pp. 760-761.

F. Morales Padrón, *Historia del descubrimiento y conquista de América* (Madrid, 1963), p. 48.

F. Fernández Armesto, *Columbus and the Conquest of the Impossible* (London, 1974), p. 213.

A. Gerbi, *La natura delle Indie nuove* (Milan-Naples, 1975), pp. 15-29.

G. Gliozzi, *Adamo e il nuovo mondo*, pp. 272-282.

J. Heers, *Christophe Colomb* (Paris, 1981), pp. 570-648.

T. Todorov, *La conquête de l'Amérique. La question de l'autre* (Paris, 1982), Part. I, Ch. 2.

L. Weckmann, *La herencia medieval de México* (Mexico, 1984), T. I, pp. 263 et seq.

On "Columbus the Saint", see:

A. F. F. Roselly de Lorgues, *Histoire posthume de Christophe Colomb* (Paris, 1885), pp. 213-225.

A. F. F. Roselly de Lorgues, *Les calomniateurs de Christophe Colomb* (Paris, 1898).

G. A. Dondero, *L'onestà di Cristoforo Colombo* (Genova, 1877).

L. Bloy, *Le révélateur du globe* (Paris, 1884), p. 197.

M. Ricard, *Christophe Colomb* (Tours, 1891), pp. 340-343.

Without going into the subject at great length, the following writers definitely side with Roselly de Lorgues in wishing to canonize the Admiral, and accuse as slanderers those who suggest Columbus engaged in an "amorous intrigue": L. Bloy, *Le révélateur du globe* (Paris, 1884), p. 197; and M. Ricard, *Christophe Colomb* (Tours, 1891), pp. 340-343. This absurd theory has been coherently contested by the Genoese canon Msgr. Sanguineti. See A. Sanguineti, *La canonizzazione di Cristoforo Colomb* (Genoa, 1875). In favour of canonization, however, was G. Baldi, *Degli avviamenti alla causa di beatificazione di Cristoforo Colombo* (Genoa, 1877).

On the subject of Columbus's instruments of navigation, see:

A. Antheaume-G. Sottas, *L'Astrolabe quadrant du Musée des antiquités de Rouen* (Paris, 1910).

G. Clerc-Rampal, "L'évolution des méthodes et des instruments de navigation," in *Révue maritime* (Paris, June-July 1921).

J. B. Charcot, *Christophe Colomb vu par un marin* (Paris, 1928), pp. 85-104.

E. De Gandia, "Viajes marítimos anteriores a Colón," in *Historia de la Nación Argentina* (Buenos Aires, 1939), pp. 237-238.

H. R. Ratto, "Las ciencias geográficas y las experiencias marítimas," in *Historia de la Nación Argentina* (Buenos Aires, 1939), pp. 94-97.

S. Crinò, *Come fu scoperta l'America* (Milan, 1943), pp. 63-67.

S. E. Morison, *Admiral of the Ocean Sea. A Life of Christopher Columbus* (Boston, 1949), pp. 183-196.

B. Landström, *Knaurs Buch der frühen Entdeckungsreisen* (Munich, 1969), pp. 147-151.

J. M. Martínez Hidalgo, *Las naves de Colón* (Barcelona, 1969), pp. 119-126.

The most thorough and exhaustive work underlining the discovery of the two Atlantic routes is that of G. E. Nunn, *The Geographical Conceptions of Columbus* (New York, 1924).

See, also, on this subject:

J. B. Charcot, *Christophe Colomb vu par un marin*, pp. 85, 136, 174, 313-314.

S. E. Morison, *Admiral of the Ocean Sea. A Life of Christopher Columbus*, pp. 213-214, 404-405, 670-671.

I. O. Bignardelli, *Con le caravelle di Cristoforo Colombo alla scoperta del Nuovo Mondo* (Turin, 1959), p. 155.

E. Bradford, *Christopher Columbus* (New York, 1973), p. 89.

On the subject of the Sargasso Sea and Columbus's experiences there, see:

Raccolta Colombiana, Part I, Vol. I, *Scritti di Cristoforo Colombo*, published and illustrated by C. De Lollis, *Giornale di bordo* (Rome, 1892), pp. 6-8, 14.

W. H. Babcock, *The Legendary Islands of the Atlantic* (New York, 1922).

G. E. Nunn, *The Geographical Conceptions of Columbus*, p. 28.

J. B. Charcot, *Christophe Colomb vu par un marin*, pp. 117-128.

S. E. Morison, *Admiral of the Ocean Sea. A Life of Christopher Columbus*, pp. 202-203.

G. Caraci, "Colombo e i Sargassi", in *Memorie Geografiche*, IX (Rome, 1964), pp. 197-272.

On the discovery of magnetic variation, with particular regard to Columbus's role, see:

A. Humboldt, *Cosmos*, Vol. II, trans. Span. (Madrid, 1853), pp. 348-356.

Raccolta Colombiana, Part VI, Vol. II: T. Bertelli, *La declinazione magnetica e la sua variazione nello spazio scoperte da Cristoforo Colombo* (Rome, 1893).

J. B. Charcot, *Christophe Colomb vu par un marin*, pp. 109-116.

A. Magnaghi, "I presunti errori che vengono attribuiti a Colombo nella determinazione delle latitudini," in *Bollettino della Società Geografica Italiana*, LXIV (Rome, 1928), pp. 459-494.

A. Magnaghi, "Incertezze e contrasti delle fonti tradizionali sulle osservazioni attribuite a C. Colombo intorno ai fenomeni della declinazione magnetica," in *Bollettino della Società Geografica Italiana*, LXIX (Rome, 1933), pp. 595-641.

S. E. Morison, *Admiral of the Ocean Sea. A Life of Christopher Columbus*, pp. 200-204.

Concerning the seafaring genius of Columbus, see the opinions of historians past and present:

M. Da Cuneo, "Lettera a Gerolamo Annari," in *Raccolta Colombiana*, Part III, Vol. II, *Fonti italiane per la storia della scoperta del nuovo mondo*, collected by G. Berchet (Rome, 1892), p. 107.

B. De Las Casas, *Historia de las Indias*, Tome I, Cap. III (Madrid, 1875), p. 49.

G. F. De Oviedo, *Historia general y natural de las Indias*, Vol. I, Cap. IV (Madrid, 1851), p. 18.

A. Humboldt, *Kritishe Untersuchungen* (Berlin, 1852), Vol. II, pp. 9, 14.

A. Humboldt, *Cosmos*, Vol. II, trans. Span., pp. 328-331, 344, 348-350, 359-379.

F. Duro, *Colón y Pinzón* (Madrid, 1883).

H. Harrisse, *Christophe Colomb* (Paris, 1884), p. 91.

E. Gelcich, "Kolumbus als Nautiker und als Seemann," in *Leitschrift der Berliner Gesellschaft*, XX (Berlin, 1885), pp. 281-287.

K. Kretschmer, *Die Entdeckung Amerikas* (Berlin, 1892), p. 267.

C. Markham, *The Journal of Christopher Columbus During his First Voyage, 1492-93* (London, 1893).

Raccolta Colombiana, Part IV, Vol. I: E. A. D'Albertis, *Le costruzioni navali e l'arte della navigazione al tempo di Cristoforo Colombo* (Rome, 1893).

J. B. Thacher, *Christopher Columbus, his Life, his Work, his Remians*, I (New York, 1903), pp. 163-186.

H. Vignaud, *Le vrai Christophe Colomb et la légende* (Paris, 1921), passim.

G. E. Nunn, *The Geographical Conceptions of Columbus*, p. 53 and passim.

M. André, *La véridique aventure de Christophe Colomb* (Paris, 1927), p. 109.

J. B. Charcot, *Christophe Colomb vu par un marin*, pp. 20, 85, 133, 174, 313, 316.

R. Caddeo, "Appendix L" to F. Colombo, *Historie di Cristoforo Colombo*, Vol. II (Milan, 1930), pp. 379-84.

G. Doria, "Introduction" to J. B. Charcot, *Cristoforo Colombo visto da un marinaio*, trans. Ital. (Florence, 1932), pp. XV-XX.

P. Revelli, *Cristoforo Colombo e la scuola cartografica genovese*, Vol. II (Genoa, 1937), pp. 389-390.

H. Henning, *Columbus und seine Tat* (Bremen, 1940), pp. 164-169.

S. De Madariaga, *Christopher Columbus* (London-New York, 1940), pp. 88, 111-112, 197.

S. Crinò, *Come fu scoperta l'America*, pp. 128-129.

A. Ballesteros Beretta, *Cristóbal Colón y el descubrimiento de América*, Vol. II (Barcelona-Buenos Aires, 1945), pp. 762-767.

S. E. Morison, *Admiral of the Ocean Sea. A Life of Christopher Columbus*, pp. 669-671 and passim.

S. E. Morison, *Christopher Columbus Mariner* (Boston, 1955), pp. 198-199.

I. O. Bignardelli, *Con le caravelle di Cristoforo Colombo alla scoperta del Nuovo Mondo*, pp. 154-158.

P. E. Taviani, "Cristoforo Colombo e la tradizione marinara di Genova," in *La Caravella* (Rome, 1972), pp. 11-18.

E. Bradford, *Christopher Columbus*, p. 280.

F. Fernández Armesto, *Columbus and the Conquest of the Impossible* (London, 1974), pp. 212-215.

D. G. Martini, *L'uomo dagli zigomi rossi* (Genova, 1974), pp. 423-433.

P. E. Taviani, *Christopher Columbus, the Grand Design*, V ed. (London, 1985), pp. 211-214; 526-535.

The Identity of Christopher Columbus

Ruth G. Durlacher-Wolper
Director
New World Museum, San Salvador

ABSTRACT

This treatise has been prepared to unravel the mystery that veils the identity of the great Admiral of exploration and discovery, Christopher Columbus. Historians wonder how he became so knowledgeable in many subjects; why his passionate mysticism and curiosity never failed. After studying the writings of Columbus and reconstructing some of his journeys, I concluded that the Discoverer was Byzantine, from the Royal Palaeologus family, and that he came from the island of Chios in Greece.

INTRODUCTION

Many books have been written about the illustrious navigator, Columbus. Each writer interpreted words or theories which were copied from historians who preceded him; many mistakes in history books, as well as on maps, were made and repeated through centuries by armchair historians and cartographers. It is time to solve this mystery as the quincentennial draws near.

Thirty-two years have passed since my research began. Columbus' *Logs*, Ferdinand's *Life of the Admiral* and Morison's translations from Las Casas' famous *Historia de las Indies* were the beginnings of my research. The countries that have claimed Columbus as coming from them are now participating to unveil the mystery of his life before he reached Portugal in 1476. Who was this man? Was he the Colombo from Genoa or another person by the name of Colón from a different place under the rule of Genoa? The research for this answer was conducted in the Bahamas, France, Greece, Italy, Portugal, Spain and the United States.

I believe the following paper provides the answers to questions asked for almost five hundred years. However, more investigations should continue to unravel the misty details of the identity of the Discoverer. Columbus' spiritual vision gave him the strength to continue his persistency after sixteen years of rejection until he finally received the support from Spain for his dream — the Great Enterprise!

COLUMBUS' BACKGROUND

The Prevailing Theory

The conclusions made in this paper about the identity of Christopher Columbus have been derived from the precise meaning of his writings. Ferdinand wrote a biography which was filled with a son's admiration for his father, and Bishop Bartolomé Las Casas, the eminent historian, wrote that he "copied the exact words of the Admiral." Las Casas and Ferdinand agreed on important issues of events, descriptions, and sayings of the illustrious Discoverer of the New World. An analysis of Columbus' writings, as presented by Las Casas and Ferdinand, is the foundation of this investigation into Columbus' true identity.

Many historians have written that his origin was from several cities, islands, and countries. They did not believe Columbus when he wrote that he and his ancestors always followed the sea.[1] They called Columbus vain, boastful, and filled with fancy ideas. Perhaps Columbus' ancestors did follow the sea!

History states that Columbus was Genoese, and this is well accepted as fact. But, did he come from Genoa or did he come from an island governed by Genoa?

Unresolved Questions Concerning The Prevailing Theory

Records reveal that Cristoforo Colombo, son of a poor woolweaver's family, Domenico Colombo and Susanna Fontanarossa, had a little house in Genoa now marked as CASA DI COLOMBO. In Paolo Emilio Taviani's book, *Christopher Columbus*, the brilliant Italian author wrote, "By 1451, the probable year of Christopher's birth, Domenico must have been married, although there is no documented record of this event and the first mention of his wife was in 1471."[2] Taviani is considered one of the greatest living scholars on Columbus, and even Taviani shows doubt.

Colombo family records also indicate additional family members: Giovanni Pellegrino, another son Giacoma, and a sister, Bianchinetta. Where were they when Ferdinand searched endlessly in Genoa and wrote, ". . . I have not been able to find out how or where he (my father) lived."[3] Why?

The eminent late Admiral Samuel Eliot Morison, USNR, wrote that the Colombos were illiterate, and when a dispute was settled or when they had business transactions, they went to a public notary who wrote down the essential facts, and whose word was accepted in any court. It seems unlikely that this Colombo and the intellectual, brilliant navigator are the same person. How could Columbus suddenly become knowledgeable about navigation, science, astrology, psychology, and nature? How could Columbus suddenly become an extremely educated man who knew Latin, Catalan, Castilian, and some Greek?

Columbus' strong religious beliefs as a Franciscan helped him to realize his ultimate dream: to sail west to meet the east and to prove the world was round. Columbus wore monk's robes even when he died. His closest friends were men of the cloth. It seems probable that Columbus wrote the truth.

Lionel Cecil Jane, historian, wrote that "Columbus never used Italian even when corresponding with those of his own nationality."[4] Taviani wrote that Columbus used the Castilian tongue and mistakes he made when writing in Latin were typically Spanish. "While none of his writings is in Italian . . . to the end of his days, he wrote in Castilian . . ."[5] Historians have been puzzled. Is it possible that Columbus was not the same Colombo from Genoa?

Columbus had two brothers: Bartholomew and Diego. None spent time in Italy. Bartholmew was a chartmaker, knew Latin and was well informed in seamanship. Where did he learn these things? Columbus sent Bartholomew with his "Map of the World" to present Columbus' plan to the King of England, Henry VII, hoping for support; Columbus had been struggling for sixteen years to get ships for his dream. On this map were verses in Latin and Columbus signed it; "Columbus de Terra Rubra" or Columbus of the red earth.[6] Although the King of England accepted the Admiral's project, by the time he summoned Columbus to come to court, Bartholomew was in the service of King Charles VIII of France, who informed him that Columbus had returned from discovering a New World. Bartholomew was later sent to Espagnola with three ships, and Columbus appointed him Governor.

Columbus' youngest brother, Diego, was "virtuous, wise and peaceful." Diego sailed with Columbus on his second voyage in 1493 and arriving in the New World, Columbus appointed him President of the Council of Isabella.[7] All three brothers were well educated, cultured, and brilliant. This implies a background rooted in royalty because of the life style of the time.

How did an ignorant woolweaver marry into one of the noble families of Portugal? Columbus married Doña Filippa Moniz de Perestrello; this was a mystery to all historians. In 1480, they had a son, Diego, at Santo Porto, Portugal, where Columbus' father-in-law was colonizer and Governor. They lived in Santo Porto until Columbus' wife died. In 1484, Columbus left Portugal (after his friend King John II refused his project to keep all discoveries for Portugal's explorers) and went to Spain, leaving his son Diego, at the monastery, La Rábida, at Palos.

In 1488, Columbus fell in love with Beatrix Enriquez de Harana in Cordova and had a son, Ferdinand, who accompanied his father on his fourth voyage. Before Ferdinand wrote the biography of his father, he searched in Italy for his family, but could find no relatives anywhere, and wrote, ". . . although (my father) endowed with all qualities that his great task required, chose to leave in obscurity all that related to his birthplace and family."[8] His father never married Beatrix, a peasant girl, but provided for her in his will. Was this because he was from a family of nobility?

Although Columbus never mentioned the family of *Genoa* in his will, he did mention his sons, and Spinola, Di Negro, and Centurione families related to the Palaeologi.[9]

Columbus read profusely; his scientific research included Plato, Aristotle, Ptolemy, Strabo, Pliny, Alfragan, Eratosthenes, and Marco Polo. His vast interest showed in his book collection: Seneca, Pierre D'Ailly and his *Imago Mundi*, in which Columbus wrote remarks in the margins. Ferdinand also had documents which implied that only Fra Machena and Toscanelli knew Columbus' secret. One letter written in 1474 from Toscanelli reveals that Columbus told him his plan to sail west to meet the east.[10] Columbus also knew about the globe of Martin Behaim and had heard about Lief Erikson.

NEW THEORY OF THE IDENTITY OF COLUMBUS

Columbus' Identity

Logic argues for another Genoese who claimed that he was not the first Admiral of his family, that he had devoted himself to the sea since he was fourteen, and that he sailed with his kinsman, a renowned man of his name and family, who was "Colón-the-Younger," the Greek corsair in the service of the King of France.[11] Las Casas, historian, confirmed this and wrote that they sailed together for a long time. "Colón-the-Younger" was George Palaeologus Dishypatos, from an old illustrious family, who was a friend of King John II of Portugal and the King's father, Alphonso V, whom he accompanied from France to Portugal. King John II was the nephew of "Henry the Navigator" under whom great voyages of western discovery began early in the 15th century. Columbus or "Colón" and "Colón-the-Younger" sailed for twenty-three years under France.

Research reveals that the experiences of these two men enabled them to know the Kings of France, England and Portugal. If they were not of royal background, they would not have had their positions and ships. Another person from the same family was Bishop Las Casas (Fig. 1), and perhaps this was the reason why Las Casas had possession of the original Journal, also used by Ferdinand. The Palaeologus Crest (Fig. 2) is Las Casas' Crest of 1552. According to the biographer, Ilorente, a man from a French prominent family, Casuas, accompanied Columbus on his first voyage; his name appears as an alias on the title page of some of his writings.[12] He was Antoine Las Casas, father of the magnificent historian Bartolomé de Las Casas.

The last Palaeologus Emperor, Constantine Palaeologus XV, sailed to Constantinople in a Catalonian ship in 1449. In 1453, many men changed their names in fear of being captured by the Turks and killed, and consequently fled to France, England, Magna Graeco and to the Kingdom of Majorca. The Palaeologus Dynasty with the Crest of the Two-Headed Eagle came to an end with the fall of Constantinople in 1453.

16

The Byzantine Empire of the Graeco-Roman civilization was divided into two parts: the west spoke Latin, the east spoke Greek, a Hellenistic civilization. This empire had existed for eleven centuries. As early as the 14th century, a large band of Spanish adventurers known as the Grand Catalan Co., overran many provinces of the Byzantine Empire and settled in Greece. During the 15th century, several Catalan families lived on the island of Chios, Greece, during the time when Columbus wrote that he was there. Is this where he learned to speak the Catala language? Is this why his *La Carte de Colón* to Luis Santangel, treasurer to Their Royal Sovereignties, was written in the Catalan language?[13] Is this why he signed his name "Colom" which is Catalan, on all his letters? No letters were ever signed "Colombo". (Borromeo)

Christopher Columbus, Discoverer of the New World signed legal documents with Xpo-Ferens (Fig. 3), in the Graeco-Latin form which is Byzantine for Christophorus. He instructed his heirs to sign in this way and the late Don Cristobal Colon XVII stated that legal documents are signed in this way and always have been. The old Byzantine aristocracy and the new aristocracy of the Genoese families have been intermarried for over 600 years since the Genoese overtook Chios. (Fig. 4)

Navigation

Admiral Morison described Columbus' navigation as follows: ". . . negotiating the difficult currents in the D'Orso Channel (in Greece) between Andros and Euboea, and then with luck catching a fresh norther for the last leg to Cape Mastika, Chios . . . Colón (Columbus) learned to 'Hand reef and steer, to estimate distances by eye,' to let go and weigh anchors properly, and all the other elements of seamanship."[14] However, an examination of the methods used before and during Columbus' time indicates the accuracy of Columbus' measure of distance. It is assumed that sailing directions were written several hundred years before Christ, because it was more difficult to *explain* how to get to a place than it was to *draw* a diagram. The first charts known are relatively accurate and cover large areas, and therefore, it seems logical that these served as guides for cartographers.

The size of the earth was measured at least as early as the third century B.C., by Eratosthenes, who is believed to have been the first person to measure latitude by using the degree.[15] From his own discoveries and from information contained in manuscripts of mariners, explorers, historians, and philosophers, he wrote an outstanding description of the known world, which helped elevate geography to the status of a science.

Later cartographers built on this knowledge and constructed charts with latitude and longitude, and in 1409, Ptolemy's map of the world fixed north at the top.[16]

The first recorded attempt to establish a tangible standard length of measurement was made by the Greeks, who used the Olympic stadium as a unit called a *stadium*. A stadium was 600 Greek feet (607.9 modern U. S. feet) or almost one tenth of a modern nautical mile. The Romans adopted this unit, but extended it to 625 Roman feet, after the Roman Stadium.[17]

Columbus wrote that he kept two logs: one for his men, and the other was his "secret accurate reckoning." Columbus' knowledge of the various methods of measuring distance becomes obvious when one analyzes his logs, although many historians assumed his measurement was inaccurate. Morison stated that Columbus overestimated the distance by 9 percent. It seems logical that Columbus must have used a different length mile: four miles to the league. The origin of the *Mediterranean* mile of 4,035.42 U. S. feet is attributed to the Greeks. The Roman mile of 4,858.59 U. S. feet was also used. The statute mile is now established as 5,280 feet in the U. S.; and in 1730, a longer nautical mile gradually became established. The Wolper-Landfall Expedition of 1959 utilized the Mediterranean mile, which appears to have been Columbus' "secret accurate reckoning."[18] By utilizing the Mediterranean mile, Columbus' Journal is accurate.

XIOS

Xios was under Genoese rule from 1346-1566 and during Colón's time by the Genoese firm of Giustiniani.[19] Xios was actually under the sovereignty of Genoa, but was administered by a Chartered company called Mahona or Maona. Although trade exports of mastics, silks, cotton and wool were extremely active, money was kept in the Bank of St. George *in Genoa*, which was a State Institution. Genoa had jurisdiction over all Genoese colonies, of which Xios was one.

Colón knew much about the mastic of Xios. He knew how easily it grew, its use, and for how much it sold. In the 1493 letter of Colón on his first voyage, he wrote "... besides spice and cotton, as much as Their Highnesses shall command, and gum mastic, as much as they shall order shipped, and which up to now, has been found only in Greece, in the island of Xios, and the Seignory sell it for what it pleases, and aloe wood, as much as they shall order shipped and slaves, as many as they shall order who will be idolaters."[20]

These were the Admiral's words when he landed on October 12, 1492, on the first island, called Guanahani, which he renamed San Salvador after the Saviour who guided them to safety. Ponce de Leon, remembering the mastic, stopped in 1513 to restore his ships with mastic. Mastic can be found on the island today.

Columbus also mentioned slavery in his letter. Although slavery was illegal in Spain, the main industry in Xios was the making of wine and many slaves were used. There were 100,000 slaves to 30,000 freemen in Greece. In the same letter, Columbus has mentioned the spices, cotton and aloe wood found on San Salvador, and these too grow on the island today.

Under the sovereignty of Genoa, the Genoese influence was far reaching, affecting customs (Fig. 4), language, folklore, and architecture (Fig. 5) as well as the costumes (Fig. 6) of the Chians. Garments worn by the men looked similar to the Italian costumes of the 15th century in Europe known as Genoese Fashion. Is it any wonder when Peter Martyr, the Italian writer of his time, called Colón "Genoese" that this caused a mistake in identification? (Fig. 7) Is this why historians thought he came from Genoa?

The originator of the Genoese legend, Peter Martyr of Anghiera (1455-1526), was the first Italian historian who wrote about Colón and his discovery.[21] In 1487, Martyr went to Spain and was employed as a teacher to the youthful noblemen of the Spanish Court, served as Ambassador of the Spanish Sovereignties, and later was made Court Treasurer by the Queen. He had met Colón and before Columbus' discoveries, were intimate friends.[22] However, Peter Martyr never fulfilled his promise to inform friends about Colón's voyages. Why did this prolific Italian writer, who reported events, cease to mention his illustrious friend, even to praise him for the glory of Genoa? Did his silence have meaning? Peter Martyr left over 813 letters and in only 12 letters does he mention the great Discoverer of the New World![23]

In a recent book about Chios island, John Haniotis states: "In 1492 Christopher Columbus disembarked on the beach of Daskalopetra before setting off for America. He was hospitably received at Villa Homerica by the famous Genoese, Andrea Banka (Bianco)."[24] Did he return to invite his cartographer friend to sail with him?

The Name COLÓN

Ferdinand wrote that the ". . . surname of Colón which he (Columbus) revived was a fitting one, because in Greek it means "member," and by his proper name Christopher, men might know that he was a member of Christ, by Whom he was sent for the salvation of those people. And if we give his name its Latin form, which is Christophorus Colonus, we may say that just as St. Christopher is reported to have gotten that name because he carried Christ over deep waters with great danger to himself, and just as he conveyed over people whom no other could have carried, so the Admiral Christophorus Colonus, asking Christ's aid and protection in that perilous pass, crossed over with his company that the Indian nations might become dwellers in the triumphant Church of Heaven."[25]

In Martyr's letters, he called Colón "Colonus." History tells us that Columbus was a good friend of Giovanni Borromeus, Count of Maggiore, Milan. The concealed secret Peter Martyr knew was revealed in 1929, when a document known as "Ex Libris Borrome" was found in the Borrome library in Milan in an old book belong1ng to the noble family of Borromei.

This newly found document (Fig. 8) was sent to the University of Barcelona to Dr. Manual Rubio Borras, the paleographer, and upon examination, was determined to be genuine. His son, Don Manual Rubio Borras, directed Don Renato Lianas de Niubo, a lawyer in Barcelona, to send a photostatic copy of the original to the New World Museum on San Salvador Island in the Bahamas in 1959.

"I, Giovan de Borromei, although lacking authority to reveal a secret declaration made by Signor Pedro de Angliere, treasurer to their Catholic Majesties of Spain, but at the same time not wishing to deprive history of the truth herewith states Christophorens Colonus is a native of Majorca (an island close to and forming part of Catalonia) and not of Liguria. The said Pedro de Angliera judged it expedient to counsel Giovani Colón for political and religious reasons to represent himself as Christopherens Colón in demanding aid and ships from the King of Spain.

I must add that Colóm is not the name of Colombo, for the navigator of the West Indies must not be confused with a certain Christoporo Colombo Canajole, son of Domenico and Susanna Fontanarossa who, I know, lives in Genoa. BERGAMO A.D. 1494"

In the analysis of the document, it was found that the name COLÓN was changed to COLOM with the N changed to an M, which made this name Catalan.

Columbus' sophistication in letter of 1501.[26]

In a letter that Columbus sent in 1501 to the most Serene Catholic Sovereigns, he wrote the following:

"Very High Kings:

From a very young age I began to follow the sea and have continued to do so to this day. This art of navigation incites those who pursue it to inquire into the secrets of this world. I have passed more than forty years in this business and have travelled to every place where there is navigation up to the present time. I have had dealings and conversation with learned men, priests, and laymen, Latins and Greeks, Jews and Moors, and many others of other sects. I found our Lord very favorable to this my desire, and to further it He granted me the gift of knowledge. He made me skilled in seamanship, equipped me abundantly with the sciences of astronomy, geometry, and arithmetic, and taught my mind and hand to draw this sphere and upon it the cities, rivers, mountains, islands, and ports, each in its proper place. During this time I have made it my business to read all that has been written on geography, history, philosophy, and other sciences. Thus Our Lord revealed to me that it was feasible to sail from here to the Indies, and placed in me a burning desire to carry out this plan. Filled with this fire, I come to Your Highnesses. All who knew of my enterprise rejected it with laughter and mockery. They would not heed the arguments I set forth or the authorities I cited. Only Your Highnesses had faith and confidence in me."

UNANSWERED QUESTIONS

1. Why did Columbus sign his letter "Colom," and legal documents with a Byzantine signature "Xpo-Ferens" which is Christophoros in Greek-Latin?

2. Why did Columbus spell Chios with a Greek X in Chios-Xios?

3. Why didn't Columbus speak or write in Italian?

4. Why didn't Columbus ask the King of Italy for ships?

5. Why didn't Columbus reveal his "secret accurate reckoning" used in his log?

6. Why didn't Columbus mention the Colombo family in his will?

7. Why did Columbus mix easily with royalty, marrying into the first family of Portugal?

8. Why did Columbus use Greek words in places he named and often in margins of books?

9. Why did Columbus say that he was not the first Admiral of his family?

10. Why did Columbus use the Catalan language in *First Letter of Discovery* to Santangel?

11. Why did Columbus say he sailed with his kinsman, the Greek corsair to the King of France? Why did Ferdinand and Las Casas agree with this statement?

12. Columbus was brilliant. How could he have been illiterate as historians wrote?

13. Why did the measurements of an experienced sailor seem inaccurate?

CONCLUSION

Assuming arguendo that Columbus was Genoese, and that he came from the island of Chios, which was under Genoese Rule, then logic dictates that Columbus was not illiterate but chose to conceal his true identity.

Indeed, the questions which were previously unanswered have perfectly logical answers. Further research of Columbus' identity, such as the "First International Convention for the History and Culture of the Island of Chios: Chios-Genova 1326-1566" to be held June 1987 on the island of Chios will reveal more evidence. I believe historians will soon acknowledge that the Admiral of the Ocean Sea had the knowledge, skill and courage of an experienced navigator, who came from one of the royal families of Chios.

CHRONOLOGY

1346-1566 Chios was under the Genoese sovereignty.

1439 . . . It is possible that Columbus was born on Chios, Greece. As a youth, he learned to sail around the Aegean islands and the Peloponnesus. Chios led in navigation. It is no wonder his interest began at an early age by the sea.

1453 . . . Fall of Constantinople. Columbus wrote that he began to follow the sea at fourteen. Columbus (Colón) and Colón-the-Younger fled to France where they were under King Charles VIII. Ships were given by him to fight off the Turks, Venetians, and Infidels. This was the end of the Palaeologus Dynasty.

1456 . . . Portugal was granted exclusive jurisdiction by the Pope over the coast of Guinea "and past the southern shore all the way to the Indies" meaning the real India. While on the seas, Columbus could have heard about this in Guinea (Ferdinand, p. 12).

1459-1461 Columbus wrote that he was once a Captain of King René when he made a voyage from Marseilles to Tunis to capture the galley Fernandina. It was here Columbus sailed to Cape Carthage instead of returning to Marseilles by "changing the point of the compass" to fool his men (Ferdinand, p. 11). Columbus was twenty-two in 1461. Mediterranean nations were at war.

1467 . . . Columbus had sailed a hundred leagues beyond Thule and to the Fort of St. George de la Mira, belonging to the King of Portugal (Canoutas, p. 21).

1469 . . . The King of Portugal continued to seek a southern route to India. In Portugal maps were made of the World since 1457 and 1460. The cartographer, Andrea Bianco, was a close friend to Columbus and his brother.

1470 . . . Columbus sailed to Chios many times with Genoese of the Palaeologi family.

1471 . . . There were two Greeks called "Colón." The Venetian Government tried to safeguard the Flanders Galleys against the attacks of Giovanni Griego and Giorgio Griego. The latter is George, known as "Colón-the-Younger," and it is certainly possible that Giovanni, John, could be the person in the Borromeo Letter. (Descriptions of the Colóns in Canoutas, pp. 63, 64, 65). The name of "Dishypatos" was Byzantine, and both Colóns had this name also.

1474 . . . Columbus was thirty-five. The two Colóns are still at sea. "Colón-the-Younger" became Commander of the French Fleet sailing between the English Channel and the Bay of Biscay. Columbus made many voyages here too, and his knowledge of winds and tides prepared him for his "Great Enterprise," (Canoutas, p. 117, n. 32).

1476 . . . Columbus was thirty-seven. The two Colóns were together in a fierce sea battle against four Venetian Galleys which they intercepted between Lisbon and Cape St. Vincent at Portugal. There was confusion with much fire, and as the story is reported,

Columbus grabbed an oar, jumped into the sea, and swam a distance of about two leagues to a place near Lisbon, where his younger brother Bartholomew lived. Later that year, they went into chartmaking.

1477 . . . The two Colóns were close friends with the King of Portugal. When Alphonso V was brought by them from France to Portugal, his son, John II, wrote Columbus was his "special friend." King John II preferred to keep all secrets of discovery for Portugal and not for outsiders.

1479 . . . Columbus, forty years old, married into an illustrious family. An intellectual of aristocratic roots, he married a lady of noble birth, Doña Felippa Moniz Perestrello. No one understood how he married into an old distinguished family of Portugal.

1480 . . . A son, Diego, was born at Santo Porto, Portugal.

1484 . . . Columbus had been refused ships, his wife died, and so he departed from Portugal to Spain. He left his son, Diego, at La Rábida, the monastery at Palos. Columbus sent his brother, Bartholomew, to England to King Henry VII, with his Map of the World, who accepted his proposal and summoned him to court. This map was stolen from a Spanish ship, copied later by Piri Reis, 1513, the Turkish cartographer. Bartholomew went to France where he stayed and drew charts until King Charles VIII told him that Columbus had already gone and returned from the New World, receiving the news from England too late. Bartholomew joined Columbus on his second voyage and from this point on most historians agree with the historical facts.

1488 . . . Columbus forty-nine years old, fell in love with Beatrix Enriquez de Harana, peasant girl, whom he did not marry. Is this because there was a law in Spain that royalty could not marry outside of its class? A son, Ferdinand, was born at Cordova, Spain.

1492 . . . Columbus, refused for many years for his enterprise, continued believing in God. Finally, Luis de Santangel, an Aragonese gentleman, secretary and treasurer to Their Royal Majesties, was extremely influential, and loaned Columbus funds for his dream. Meetings were arranged, and Columbus was given three ships and letters from Their Royal Majesties to take to the New World, to the Great Khan and to other kings. The Great Khan was from the House of the Palaeologi with the Crest of the Two-Headed Eagle.

1506 . . . Columbus died on May 20, 1506 in the city of Valladolid . . . 67 years old.

1513 . . . The Admiral's remains were brought to Seville where they are now.

23

It is universally accepted that Columbus made four voyages to the New World, but it is disputed where the remains of the Admiral are at rest. Don Cristobál Colón XVII gave me 182 documents from the Veragua Library (Madrid) in 1962. These documents prove that the great Discoverer's remains are in Seville, Spain.

NOTES

1. Ferdinand Columbus, *The Life of The Admiral Christopher Columbus* (New Jersey, 1959), p. 5.

2. Senatore Paolo Emilio Taviani, *Christopher Columbus* (London, 1985), p. 24.

3. Ferdinand Columbus, op. cit., pp. 4-5.

4. Lionel Cecil Jane, *Select Documents Illustrating the Four Voyages of Columbus* (London, 1932), p. xxxvi.

5. Sen. Paolo Emilio Taviani, op. cit., p. 30.

6. Ferdinand Columbus, op. cit., p. 36.

7. Seraphim G. Canoutas, *Christopher Columbus* (New York, 1943), p. 45.

8. Ferdinand Columbus, op. cit., p. 3.

9. Seraphim G. Canoutas, op. cit., p. 134.

10. Ferdinand Columbus, op. cit., pp. 19-22.

11. *Ibid.*, pp. 8, 12.

12. Justin Winsor, *Narrative and Critical History of America* (New York, 1889), p. 304, n. 1.

13. Admiral Samuel Morison, *Letter of Columbus* (Madrid, 1959), p. 1.

14. Admiral Morison, *Admiral of the Ocean Sea* (Boston, 1942), p. 31.

15. Justin Winsor, *Christopher Columbus* (Cambridge, 1892), p. 118.

16. Nathaniel Bowditch, *American Practical Navigator* (Washington, 1958), p. 19.

17. *Ibid.*, p. 26.

18. Ruth Durlacher-Wolper, *The Identity of Christophoros Columbus* (Virginia, 1982), p. 25.

19. Ferdinand Columbus, op. cit., pp. 6-8.

20. Ruth Durlacher-Wolper, *Light, Landfall, and Landing* (Smithsonian, 1964), p. 5, n. 4.

21. Justin Winsor, op. cit., p. 34.

22. Seraphim G. Canoutas, op. cit., pp. 3, 4.

23. *Ibid.*, p. 4.

24. John Haniotis, *Chios Island* (Athens, Greece, 1971), p. 77.

25. Ferdinand Columbus, op. cit., p. 4.

26. *Ibid.*, p. 10.

Fig. 1. Bishop Bartholomé de las Casas Authored Historia de las Indias

(courtesy Winsor)

Fig 2. The Palaeologi Crest of the Two-Headed Eagle that Belonged to Las Casas (courtesy Winsor)

Christophoros Columbus, discoverer of the New World, signed his name, *Xρō-Ferens*, (Christophoros) in the Graeco-Latin form, which is Byzantine.

Fig. 3. Columbus's Byzantine Signature

"KoλomboΣ" (Columbus)

Over many doors in Pyrghi and Cimbori the name "KoλomboΣ" appears carved in stone. A priest named Columbus said that his family was there for over·600 years, and that the Genoese had intermarried with the Greeks. The old Byzantine aristocracy and the new aristocracy of the Genoese families were bound by the same interests. They were intermarried since 1346.

Fig. 4. The Priest "KoλombuΣ" in Pyrghi on Chios (M. Mamounas Interpreted Conversations Between Him and the Author 1979)

Fig. 5. Italian Sgraffiti on Buildings in Chios

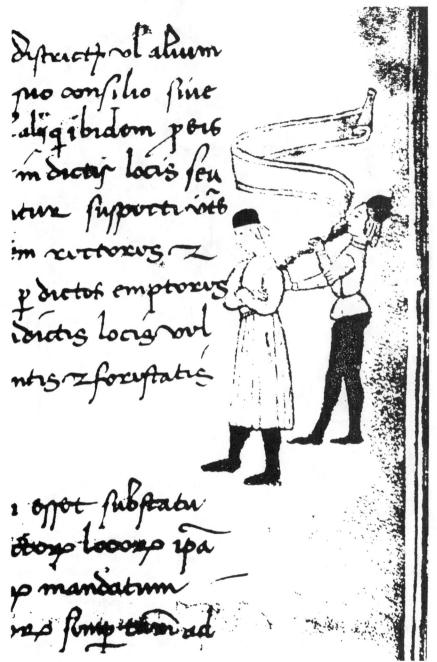

Fig. 6. Genoese Fashion of the 15th Century in Chios   (courtesy Argenti)

Fig. 7. Peter Martyr de Anghiera, Historian, was the Originator of the Genoese Legend   (courtesy Bettman Archives)

Christophorus Columbus was called "Genoese." Did the myth that surrounded this legend mean he came from Genoa?

The originator of this Genoese legend, Peter Martyr of Anghiera (1455-1526), was the first Italian historian who wrote about Columbus and his discovery.

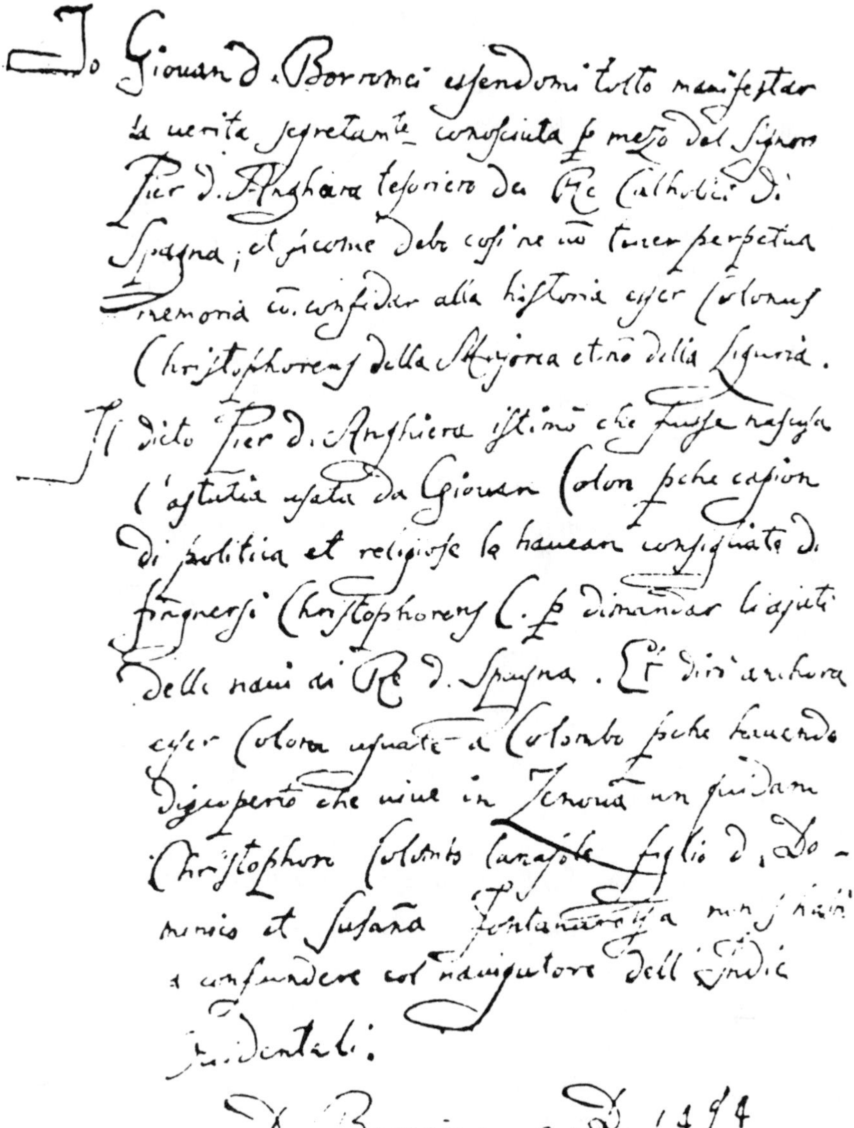
Io Giouan d. Borromei essendomi tolto manifestar
la verità segretamente conosciuta per mezzo del Signor
Pier d. Anghiara tesoriero del Re Catholici di
Spagna; et siccome debo così ne mio tener perpetua
memoria cu. considerar alla historia esser Colonus
Christophorens della Majorca et no della Liguria.
Il dicto Pier d. Anghiera estimò che fusse nascosta
l'astutia usata da Giouan Colon perche cagion
di politica et religiose le hauean consigliate di
fingersi Christophorens C. per dimandar li ajuti
delli navi di Re d. Spagna. Et dirò anchora
esser Colom usuate a Colombo perche hauendo
discoperto che vive in Zenova un quidam
Christophoro Colombo lanajolo figlio di Domenico et Susana Fontanarossa non si havè
a confundere col navigatore dell'Indie
Occidentali.
Di Bercimo, a. D. 1494

Fig. 8. The Borromeo Letter of 1494

BIBLIOGRAPHY

Argenti, Phillip P. *The Costumes of Chios*. London: B. T. Batsford Ltd., 1953.

Bowditch, Nathaniel. *American Practical Navigator*. Washington: U. S. Navy Hydrographic Office, 1958.

Columbus, Ferdinand. *The Life of The Admiral Christopher Columbus By His Son Ferdinand*. Translated by Benjamin Keen. New Brunswick, New Jersey: University Press, 1959.

Canoutas, Seraphim G. *Christopher Columbus — A Greek Nobleman*. New York: St. Marks Printing Corp., 1943.

Haniotis, John. *Chios Island*. Athens, Greece, 1971.

Jane, Lionel Cecil. *Select Documents Illustrating the Four Voyages of Columbus*. London: The Hakluyt Society, 1932.

Morison, Samuel Eliot. *Admiral of the Ocean Sea*. Boston: Atlantic Monthly Press, Little Brown and Co., 42.
Letter of Columbus Announcing the Discovery of America (translation). Madrid, Spain: Carlos Sanz, 1959.
The Caribbean As Columbus Saw It (with Obregón). Boston: Atlantic Monthly Press, Little Brown and Co., 1964.
Personal Correspondence. 1954-1976.

Nunn, George E. *The Geographical Conceptions of Columbus*. New York: The American Geographical Society, 1924.

Obregón, Mauricio. *The Caribbean As Columbus Saw It* (with Morison). Boston: Atlantic Monthly Press, Little, Brown and Co., 1964.

Runciman, Steven. *Byzantine Civilization*. New York: Meridian Books, 1956.

Taviani, Paolo Emilio. *Christopher Columbus, The Grand Design*. London: Orbis Publishing Ltd., 1985.

Winsor, Justin. *Narrative and Critical History of America* (8 volumes). Boston and New York: Riverside Press, 1889.

Wolper-Ruth G. Durlacher. *A New Theory Identifying the Locale of Columbus' Light, Landfall and Landing*. Washington, DC: Smithsonian Institution, 1964.
The Identity of Christophoros Columbus. Norfolk, Virginia: New World Museum, 1982.
The Identity and First Landfall of Columbus 1492.

Florentine's Friendship and Kinship with Christopher Columbus

Consuelo Varela
San Vicente, 32
Sevilla, Spain

INTRODUCTION

Famous people are always subject to a variety of interpretations, interpretations that, with repetition and the passing of time, become indisputable doctrine. To question such doctrines entails the risk of being labeled a nut or a snob. This is the case with Christopher Columbus, a historical figure who has been studied from many different perspectives. His numerous ailments and illness are obscured; a great man, even for his detractors, cannot be chronically sick. It is likewise repeated that he died a poor man, which is nonsense in the extreme.

There exists today a wealth of information on Christopher Columbus as well as something of a void in regard to many facets of his life. Columbus himself forged the image that he wished to leave for posterity. His first major biographers, his son Hernando and Fray Bartolomé de las Casas, quite tamely aided in the advancing of that image, either through omission, embellishment, or the plain falsification of facts. This assertion does not mean that the account of either the dominican or the bibliophile is worthless; indeed they both are valuable, but one must compare and contrast them.

This introduction is meant to serve as a frame of reference for the theme developed in this paper: the friendship and influence of a selected group of Florentines closely associated with Columbus and his family, heretofore not studied. This group of people is hardly mentioned in the Colombian sources par excellence — the Admiral himself, his son Hernando, or Las Casas. Yet, its influence deserves greater attention than it has received up to the present.

Both Fray Bartolomé and Hernando omit any mention of Columbus' non-Spanish friends. Neither biographer cites any Italian close to the Admiral, not Pinelo, not Riberol, nor even Juanoto Berardi. Only Bartolome Fiesco is mentioned in passing as if the Italian facet of Columbus' life were to be intentionally avoided.

33

A look at the Italians mentioned by the Admiral in his writings, not counting his family — his brothers Bartolome and Diego, his sons Diego and Hernando, and his relatives Juan Antonio and Andrea Columbo — yields a scant two dozen names in the ninety-three documents (memorials and letters) that have been preserved. It is commonplace in the historical treatment of the Discoverer, that upon his arrival in Castile, he surrounded himself with an important group of Genoese who eventually became his close friends. And in fact, of the twenty-five individuals mentioned, twenty-three are Genoese, seemingly confirming the opinion commonly held. The other two are a Novaran, Fray Gaspar de Gorricio, and a Florentine, Amerigo Vespucci.[1]

In order to examine the Italian surroundings of the Admiral, the present paper shall consist of three parts: *Columbus and his bankers, Columbus and his propaganda, and Columbus and his personal life.* Each, on the one hand, shall contrast the facts about these individuals as supplied by the Discoverer himself with those provided by other sources. On the other hand, each part shall point out the profound differences that existed between the Genoese and the Florentines. Because of this line of approach, one case, that of Fray Gaspar de Gorricio, shall be omitted.

COLUMBUS AND HIS BANKERS

Of the sixteen Genoese residing in Seville mentioned by Columbus in his accounts, eleven were bankers — much in keeping with the Admiral's obsession with money! Some of these individuals appear exclusively as royal bankers, as in the case of the Centurions, Martin, Agustin and Pantaleon. They were the ones who supplied the two million "maravedies" that the crown invested in the third voyage. The head of the firm was Martin who, from Sevilla, went to settle permanently in Granada, where he ran an important business concern.[2] It was this concern that Columbus approached to satisfy the financial needs of his sons, Diego and Hernando, when they found themselves part of the royal entourage in Granada. The Centurions, however, did not trust the Admiral and, in the end, the personal bankers of the Genoeses, Francisco Doria and Francisco de Riberol, were the ones to supply the necessary letters of credit.[3] Duardo Escaja and Bernardo De Grimaldo were simply agents of the Centurions in Sevilla and, as such, refused to pay the "albala" sent by Columbus, via Ximeno de Briviesca, in April of 1498.[4]

The Admiral mentions Francisco Pinelo twice, in two consecutive letters to his son, Diego, in December of 1504. He asks Diego to look after the bearer of the letters, Pinelo's son, for his father is doing for him "all that he can, with much affection and good will".[5] This friendship has been stressed because Pinelo was, along with Luis de Santangel, co-director of the Santa Hermandad's treasury, the entity responsible for financing, in part, the voyage of discovery, with Pinelo having an active hand in the affair. Also, in

1493, in the capacity of royal banquer, Pinelo administrated the funds invested by the crown in the fleet of that year. Nevertheless, from then on there is no written mention of this banker either in regard to Columbus' personal life or his business affairs. It is within the realm of probability that they remained in contact and were even friends, but not to the point of Pinelo being a frequent caller at the Admiral's home. This banker never lent any money to or honored any letter of credit for any of Columbus relatives and, furthermore, he never was the Admiral's personal banker. With Francisco's brother, Bernardo, Columbus' relationship was acrimonious to say the least, ever since Bernardo, as royal factor, had been placed in charge of organizing the fleets destined to the Indies.[6]

Other sources shed light on the financial activities of the Discoverer of the Indies. Juanoto Berardi's active part in the first two Columbian fleets is well known and indisputable. Also well known is that this Florentine was the Admiral's first factor and the one responsible for organizing the convoy sent by the crown in answer to the Genoese's call for help in February, 1492. What has not received enough attention is that Columbus formed a business partnership with the Florentine to handle the traffic of the Indies. It was this concern that Bartolomé Columbus approached on his arrival from France and it was Berardi who advanced him the monies and supplies for his first trip to the New World.[7] In fact, Berardi over-extended himself financially to the point that, after Columbus' first voyage, he was unable to enter into a single business contract of his own, save for the traffic to the Indies, and proceeded to liquidate his debts. His broad business interests, about which there is ample documentation, were automatically cancelled. Berardi abandoned everything and worked only with Columbus, investing in this new venture his last maravedi.[8] This, in fact, became the first instance of an American-related bankruptcy, since this costly fleet sank in January of 1496, barely a month after Berardi's death.[9]

Berardi's demise resulted in a professional advance for Vespucci.[10] As he himself stated, from a mere employee of the company, he became patron and factor to Columbus[11] and, in fact, the liquidation of a bankrupt business, rather than separating them, brought Amerigo and Columbus closer together. This is supported by the fact that an outstanding bill owed by the Admiral to Berardi[12] and dating back to 1495, had disappeared from the books by Berardi's death, no doubt owing to Amerigo's good offices. Yet, Berardi's heirs still owed 144,000 maravedies as late as 1511![13]

Before closing this section, mention must be made of a third Florentine factor, Columbus' brother-in-law, Francisco de Bardi, who will be discussed in the section dealing with the Admiral's personal life. The first two factors, then, as well as the last one, were Florentines. No Genoese ever occupied that spot, the factors between Vespucci and Bardi being all Sevillian.

COLUMBUS AND HIS PROPAGANDA

Little attention has been given to the propaganda that Columbus manufactured and spread abroad about his person and his voyages. Whereas the Admiral's letter to Luis de Santangel — the first best-seller of American historiography — was widely known, the news from ambassadorial desks in Spain to their respective countries, were quite meager. The only exception was the case of the Sigoría di Firenze, which received news of the Discoverer's doings by letter. The only account of the contents of this missive — author unknown — that has survived is a resume by Tribaldo de Rossi. It is surprising that this resume, which might well have been treated to embellishment by Rossi, came to be the longest and most complete version of Columbus' first voyage to reach the European courts. If the news came from Sevilla, one must ask whether Juanoto or Amerigo — closest to the Medici — were the ones to write it. If not them, who could it have been? The Florentine orator does not seem a probable choice because in this case the message would have been sent to the X of Bailia. On the other hand, a Medici employee or someone within this circle and, given the time factor, close to Columbus, seems to be a more plausible choice. For example, Donato Nicolini, who often corresponded with his patrons, could fit the bill. All things considered, the first option seems to be more logical given Vespucci's love of letter-writing and the fact that no letter to Florence in Berardi's hand has been discovered.

Of the Admiral's other voyages there are several synchronistic accounts. Only one came by the hand of a Genoese, Michele de Cuneo. The Florentines, Simon Verde and Juan Bardi, sent parallel accounts.[14] Verde wrote to Pedro Nicoli the accounts of the second voyage from Valladolid, and of the third, from Cadiz. Juan Bardi wrote from Seville to the court at Mantua the first news of the second trip.

Columbian propaganda, as was mentioned above, was directed for the most part by the Admiral himself. It is interesting to note, then, that as soon as Columbus came in contact with Pedro Martir de Angleria, a man from Milan, the Florentines ceased being the conveyers of his news. J. Gil has pointed out that from the third voyage on, Columbus reported directly to Angleria who then engaged in building up his compatriot's public image.[15] Thereafter, fallen in disgrace, the Admiral used other means of distribution; the letter from Simon Vede, an obscure businessman, holding no interest for him anymore. Instead, aiming at the publication of the account of the fourth voyage in Venice, Columbus availed himself of the good offices of an Oderigo or a Trevisan, this being the only Genoese having a hand in Columbian propaganda.

COLUMBUS' PERSONAL LIFE

The Admiral's personal life, as gleaned from his letters, shows the existence of a banker, Francisco Sobranis de Riberol, a diplomat, Nicolo Oderigo;

three servants, Marco de Bargali, Bartolome de Fiesco and Geronimo Santiesteban; a cleric, fray Gaspar de Gorricio; and a businessman Amerigo Vespucci.

Among the Genoese bankers of the Admiral, Francisco Sobranis is without a doubt the one with whom Columbus maintained, not only a business relationship, but a strong intimate friendship. From April, 1492, when they met in Santa Fe, until the death of Columbus, they remained close. Riberol had in his possession a copy of the Admiral's *Libro de los privilegios*, which he sent to the bank of Saint Georgi in Genoa for safekeeping and the information of the directors who had been empowered to look after the affairs of Columbus in Spain; it was in their interest to do so adequately.[16] Franco Cataneo, a Genoese from Cádiz, was Riberol's emissary in the matter of giving the document to the Republica.[17] Also in Riberol's charge were copies of the monarchs' letters, letters that Columbus needed to safeguard at all costs. When in May, 1502, the Admiral decided to appeal to the new Pope in Rome, it was again Riberol who took upon himself the arrangements for the frustrating trip.[18] Finally, it was he, as mentioned earlier, who provided don Diego and don Hernando with letters of credit. Riberol, then, moved within Columbus' personal circle as if he were a member of the family, presenting quite a contrast to the other bankers.

An important figure in the courts of the Catholic Monarchs was Nicolo Oderigo, the Genoese ambassador. Oderigo came to Castille with instructions signed by the Canciller Benito del Porto himself — the same one mentioned in Columbus' will and whose father had been engaged in litigation with the Columbus family. Firstly, because of this position, Oderigo had to come in contact with his fellow countryman. Later, and at Columbus' request, he handled through the Genoese bank some testamentary instructions, a fact that appears in two letters by the Admiral in 1502 and 1504.[19] Their relationship seems to have been limited to business affairs. And it is apparent that Oderigo did not live up to the trust that Columbus had placed in him, for the Admiral complained bitterly of not having received in two years' time, a single word, written or otherwise, from him. Nevertheless, Columbus sent him a copy of the last voyage's account.[20]

The three remaining Genoese who appear in Columbus' writings were all in his personal service. Marco de Bargali, his squire in the third voyage, must have remained in the Admiral's service for a while for he also appears as his emissary. Bartolome de Fiesco, captain of one of the vessels during the fourth voyage, was, together with Diego Mendez, the rescuer of the explorer.[21] Geronimo de Santiesteban, who can be identified as the same Girolomo de Santo Stefano who travelled to India in 1499, arrived in Castille during the fourth voyage.[22] The relationship must be traced back to Portugal, where they both resided prior to 1485. It is not known whether they ever met in Spain. The Florentine environment of the Genoese, at this time embodied by Amerigo Vespucci, was mentioned only once by Columbus, in a letter to his son Diego, then at court.[23]

Columbus never referred to anyone else with the same fondness and it is timely to remember that his relationship with Vespucci went beyond the financial one. Vespucci, in fact, was the Admiral's representative to the King, when through his son's contacts at Court, Columbus tried to obtain an appointment; little did he know the new metier that was to be Vespucci's![24] Their respective trips impeded continuous contacts with one another, never even travelling to the Indias together. The Admiral never recriminated the Florentine about his voyage for the Portuguese even though he did attack Hojeda, a fellow traveller of Vespucci, and never had any but kind words for his friend. In the end, after Columbus' death, it was Vespucci who came forward, in aid to the family, to testify to the authenticity of Columbus' signature on a document ordering the settlement of landmarks in the name of Diego, on a tract of land in Hispaniola.[25]

In the Archives of the Cuevas de Seville, there appears a letter described as "a letter from the first Admiral to the second admiral, his son, dated May 10, in which he asked him to look carefully after Simon Verde".[26] The relationship between the Florentine businessman, Simon Verde, and the Columbus family was of a permanent nature. When, on 2 January, 1498, Simon Verde told Mateo Cini about the third voyage of the Genoese, he admitted having used an account by Columbus himself, which indicates that by that time theirs must have been a close friendship.[27] As the Admiral's agent, Verde received the printed Papal Bull of Julius II on 15 November 1504. As a close family friend, Verde travelled to Valladolid to take charge of Columbus' remains and escort them to the monastery of the Cuevas de Sevilla.[28] It was Verde, who in Castille and acting as Bartolome Columbus' agent, made the necessary purchases for his home in Santo Domingo.[29] He also appears as executor to the wills of Columbus' brothers and heir to a legacy of 40,000 mrs. assigned to him by don Diego.[30] And, at least on two occasions, Verde acted as banker to don Diego and don Hernando,[31] and for the latter was instrumental in 1509, in securing Savonarola's *Triumphus Crucis*, published in Venice in 1505.[32]

It is logical to assume Verde's participation in the more or less learned gatherings hosted by Columbus. A couple of years ago, Taviani advanced the hypothesis of a possible intervention by Vespucci in determining the route of the third voyage, encouraging Columbus to try out a new route, viable under the Tordesillas treaty,[33] and suggested by the cosmographer Jaime Ferrer. Verde, too, gave Columbus advice on "How to deal kindly with the residents of the Indies", advice obviously highly priced by the Admiral, for he ordered a copy made of the Florentine's document.[34]

One last Florentine formed part of the personal circle of the Admiral, Francisco de Bardi. Married to Bripolanja Muñiz, the most influential woman in the Columbus' Clan. Bardi's was a much felt presence during the last two years of the Discoverer's life. In August of 1505 Bardi sent him from Seville two personal letters from Miguel Ballester and Vasco de San Martín, recounting the rumors of Nicolas de Ovando's bad government in the Indies and informing him of the arrival of a consignment of seven or eight thousands pesos in gold.[35] Francisco played an active part in the negotiations between Columbus and the duke of Medina Sidonia when the Genoese tried to arrange the marriage of his first son to a daughter of the Andalusian aristocrat.[36] In December of the same year, while in Salamanca, Columbus granted Bardi his last power of attorney "To receive the gold and jewels that should come from the Indies" and to act for him in all his affairs, thus making him in fact his third Florentine factor.[37] It was he who, upon Columbus' death on 20 May 1506, secured the necessary sum of money for the burial, obtaining from Tomas Calvo and Gaspar Centurion's Genoese banking firm 50,000 mrs.[38]

CONCLUSION

Several conclusions can be reached from the facts presented above. The Seville of Columbus' time had an active and restless colony of Genoese whose members, for the most part, belonged to branches of large commercial firms based in Genoa and Lisbon. This is why Columbus went directly to Seville on his arrival in Spain — whether he was or was not at la Rabida beforehand is irrelevant to this argument — to meet with his compatriots for whose firms he had worked in Portugal: The Negros, the Centurions, the Spinolas. All these people are remembered in his will, always in reference to debts acquired prior to his sojourn in Spain.[39] Undoubtedly, he approached them first, but did they extend to him the aid and protection he sought? Absolutely not. Whether they had no faith in his geographic theories or whether they did not see the matter clearly, the fact is that they never supported him. Columbus, then, was forced to appeal to the Andalusian noblemen who spoke kind words but contributed few maravedies. Always after the Court, his last recourse, the Admiral spent more time between 1485 and 1492 away than in Sevilla. He lived in Cordoba two or three years, returned to Portugal, travelled to Murcia, Malaga and Granada, and only after 1492 did he spend a few spells in Seville. By this time, his Sevillan friends were of no use to him, for the monarchs, as was logical, imposed their own Genoese bankers, not because of coincidence or because they were his compatriots, but because these bankers were the official royal money lenders. The future Admiral then forgot the Negroes and Company and became associated with a Florentine, Berardi. On Berardi's death he used the services of an old friend, Riberol, who had little to do with his old Lisboan friends. Columbus' constant dealings with the Genoese, whether or not to his liking, were the only alternative left to him. He never severed his relationship with them; he could not, and it would not have been wise. Though unskillful in many facets of his life, Columbus knew that he needed them and so they used each other to their mutual benefit. The difference between this and a closer relationship is far and wide. The only Genoese friend he had was Riberol, his intimate circle having been formed by other compatriots. This group, in the beginning, had also come from Portugal where they had formed part of the influential commercial firm of Marchioni, for whom they all worked.

Columbus' choice is at first surprising because the Genoese colony in Sevilla was rich and powerful, whereas that of the Florentines was infinitely weaker. Then, he surrounded himself with a group of people with meager resources who needed him as much as he needed them. The Admiral, an immigrant of doubtful social status, arriving in Castille without money, was not welcomed by his compatriots who saw in him a hapless adventurer. By contrast, Berardi, a Florentine of rising status due to the slave trade and his appointments as factor to the Andalusian Medicis, was the one who came to Columbus' aid, willing to make a bet since he held all the winning cards. The Admiral, proud as a good Genoese, never forgave the affront, and when intending to safeguard his interests he made his move, he did so not through his compatriot bankers in Sevilla, but instead, in a typical gesture of haughtiness, he approached the Banca de San Georgi. The Centurions, the Grimaldos and Company had lost a most worthy client.

NOTES

1. Por orden alfabético son los siguientes: Marco de Bargali; Franco Cataneo; Luis y Martín Centurión; Francisco Doria; Batista, Gaspar y Nicolás Spinola; Bartolomé Fiesco; Gaspar de Gorricio; Bernaldo y Francisco Grimaldo; Agustín y Pantaleón Italian (Centurión); Paolo del Negro; Nicolò Oderigo; Francisco Pinelo; Benito y Gerónimo del Porto; Micer Ribera; Francisco de Riberol; Gerónimo Santiesteban; Antonio Vazo y Amerigo Vespucci.

2. Y en Granada murió en 1534. Sobre estos banqueros of. A. Boscolo "Il genovese Francesco Pinelli, amico a Siviglia di Cristoforo Colombo" *Saggi su Cristoforo Colombo* (Roma, 1986), 7-13.

3. Cf. las cratas de Colón a su hijo Diego en C. Varela, *Cristóbal Colón, textos y documentos completos* (Madrid, 2ª edic., 1984), pp. 345 y 342.

4. *Ibidem* p. 199.

5. *Ibidem* p. 340 y 341. Para las relaciones de Pinelo y Colón véase el artículo citado de A. Boscolo en la nota 2.

6. Basta para ello consultar las numerosas notas marginales que colocó Bernardo Pinelo en los *Libros de Armadas*, que conserva el Archivo General de Indias de Sevilla, quejándose del almirante.

7. La intervención de Berardi fue estudiada en detalle por J. Manzano y Manzano *Cristóbal Colón siete años decisivos de su vida 1485-1492* (Madrid, 1964), p. 326 y ss.

8. Como comprueban p.e., los documentos del *Registro General del Sello* del Archivo General de Simancas de fechas; 10, julio; 23, octubre y 29 de marzo de 1495.

9. Para todas las incidencias de esta flota véase A. B. Gould, *Nueva lista documentada de los tripulantes de Colón* (Madrid, 2ª edic., 1984), pp 316 y ss.

10. Murió en sevilla el 16 de diciembre de 1495; un día antes efectuó su patético testamento, que publicó la Duquesa de Berwick y Alba *Nuevos autógrafos de Cristóbal Colón y Relaciones de Ultramar* (Madrid, 1902), p. 7.

11. El día 11 de julio de 1510; puede verse la transcripción de su deposición en R. Ezquerra "Los primeros contactos entre Colón y Vespucci" *Revista de Indias* (XLVI), p. 38-39.

12. Así lo declaraba Berardi en su testamento, citado en la n. 10: "El señor Almirante don Cristóbal Colón me deve e es obligado a dar e pagar por su cuenta corriente, ciento y ochenta mill maravedíes".

13. Como declaró Vespucci en su testamento de 9 de abril de 1511; texto que tengo entregado a la imprenta y que aparecerá en breve en *Historiografía y Bibliografía Americanista*.

14. Los tres textos, traduciods al castellano, pueden consultarse en J. Gil — C. Varela *Cartas de particulares a Colón y relaciones coetáneas* (Madrid, 1984), docs. IX, X Y X.

15. En la introducción al doc. I del libro citado en la nota anterior, p. 25.

16. Como indica Colón en su carta a Oderigo del 21 de marzo de 1502, *Cristóbal Colón, textos*, p. 313.

17. Carta a Juan Luis de Mayo, *Cristóbal Colón, textos*, p. 348.

18. Carta a fray gaspar de Gorricio de 25 de mayo de 1502, *Cristóbal Colón, textos*, p. 316.

19. *Cristóbal Colón, textos*, p. 313 y 347.

20. Así en J. Gil "El rol del tercerviaje colombino" *Historiografía y Bibliografía Americanista* (XXIX), p. 107.

21. De ellos habla Colón en una carta a N. Ovando en marzo de 1504, *Cristóbal Colón, textos*, p. 332. Firmó tambien como testigo en el testamento del almirante, *ibidem*, p. 360 y 363.

22. Véase la carta a oderigo del 21 de marzo de 1502, *Cristóbal Colón, textos*, p. 313.

23. En carta a su hijo Diego de 5 de febrero de 1505, *Cristóbal Colón, textos*, p. 353.

24. Tras este viaje Amerigo se convirtió en funcionario real, al ser encargado junto con Vicente Yañez Pinzón, de preparar una expedición a las islas de la Especiería. el 22 de mayo de 1508 fue nombrado primer piloto mayor de la Casa de la Contratación.

25. Es la deposición citada en la n. 2.

26. M. Serrano y Sanz, "El Archivo Colombino de la Cartuja de las Cuevas" *Boletein de la Real Academia de la Historia* (XCVII) p. 542.

27. *Ibidem* (XVVI), p. 185.

28. B. Cartero y Huerta, *Historia de la Cartuja de Santa María de las Cuevas* (Madrid, 1950), t. I, pp. 309-310.

29. M. Serrano y Sanz, *o.c.* (XCVII), p. 545 y 586.

30. "Véase el testamento de don Diego," en *Roccolta de documenti colombiani* (Roma, 1892), II, 1, p. 183 y ss.

31. Como demostró J. Gil, "Pleitos y clientelas colombinas," *Scritti in onore del prof. P. E. Taviani* (Génova, 1986), p. 182-199.

32. Así en S. Arbolí y S. de la Rosa, *Biblioteca Colombina, Catálogo de los libros impresos* (Sevilla, 1886), t. 1, p. 63.

33. P. E. Taviani, *I viaggi di Colombo* (2ª edic. Novara, 1986), p. 381-388.

34. M. Serrano y Sanz, *o.c.* (XCVI), p. 254.

35. La carta de Bardi a Colón fue publicada por J. Gil — C. Varela, *o.c.*, p. 346 y ss.

36. Para lo refernte al casamiento de don Diego Colón véase L. Arranz, *Don Diego Colón* (Madrid, 1982), p. 73 y ss.

37. Poder publicado por primera ves por A. Altolaguirre, *"Algunos documentos inéditos relativos a Cristóbal Colón y su familia" Boletín de la Real Academia de la Historia* (XCII), II, p. 513 y ss; y recientemente en *Cristóbal Colón, textos*, p. 355.

38. El documento que lo demuestra y el estudio del mismo, lo publiqué en "El entorno florentino de Cristóbal Colón," *La presenza italiana in andalusia nel basso Medioevo, Roma 1984* (Roma, 1986), p. 132-134.

39. Véase el testamento en *Cristóbal Colón, textos*, p. 359-364.

BIBLIOGRAPHY

Altolaguirre, A. "Algunos dovcumentos inéditors relativos a don Cristóbal Colón y su familia." *Boletín de la Real Academia de la Historia* XCII II, p. 513 y ss.

Arbólí, S y de la Rose, S. *Biblioteca Colombina Catálogo de los libros impresos*. Sevilla, 1886, t, 1 p. 63.

Arranz, L. *Don Diego Colón*. Madrid, 1982.

Berwick y Alba, duquesa de. *Nuevos autógrafos de Cristóbal Colón y Relaciones de Ultaramar*. Madrid, 1902, p. 7.

Boscolo, A. "Il genovese Francesco Pinelli, amico a Siviglia di Cristoforo Columbo." *Saggi su Cristoforo Colombo*. Roma, 1986.

Cartero y Huerta, B. *Historia de la Cartuja de Santa María de las Cuevas*. Madrid, 1950, p. 309-310.

Ezquerra, R. "Los primeros contactos entre Colón y Vespucci." *Revista de Indias* XLVI, p. 38-39.

Gil, J. "El rol del tercer viaje colombino." *Historiografía y Bibliografía Americanistas* XXIX, p. 107.

Gil, J. "Pleitos y clientelas colombinas." *Scritti in onore del prof. P. E. Taviani*. Génova, 1986.

Gil, J. y C. Varela. *Cartas de particulares a Colón y Relaciones Coetáneas*. Madrid, 1984.

Gould, A. B. *Nueva lista documentada de los tripulantes de Colón*. Madrid, 2 edic., 1984, p. 316.

Manzano y Manzano, J. *Cristóbal Colón, siete años decisivos de su vida 1485-1492*. Madrid, 1964, p. 326.

Serrano y Sanz, M. "El archivo colombino de la Cartuja de las Cuevas." *Boletín de la Real Academia de la Historia* XCVI y XCVII.

Taviani, P. E. *I viaggi di Colombo*. Novara, 2ª edic., 1986, p. 381-388.

Varela, C. *Cristóbal Colón, textos y documentos Completos* Madrid, 2ª edic., 1984.

Varela, C. "El entorno florentino de Cristóbal Colón." *La presenza italiana in Andalusia nel basso Medioevo, Roma maggio 1984*. Roma, 1986, p. 131-134.

Wallowing in a Theological Stupor or a Steadfast and Consuming Faith: Scholarly Encounters with Columbus' Libro de las Profecías

Delno C. West
Northern Arizona University
Flagstaff, Arizona

ABSTRACT

The *Libro de las profecías* was drafted in 1501 and remains the only work written by Christopher Columbus which has not been thoroughly studied. This paper describes the document and argues that the persuasive rhetorical power of noted nineteenth and twentieth century historians convinced scholars that the treatise was the ravings of a troubled mind. Only recently have historians begun to understand the importance of this work as it relates to Columbus' mentality and Enterprise of the Indies.

INTRODUCTION

Christopher Columbus is the first American hero with all the rights and privileges, myths and legends, and criticisms the title carries. He has been portrayed as imaginative, persistent, courageous, intelligent, ignorant, audacious, lucky, egotistical, humble, avaricious, generous, single-minded, tenacious, Spanish, Italian, Greek, Jewish, a Tertiery of the Third Order of St. Francis, a scientist, a mystic, a merchant, and a member of the Masonic Lodge.

In 1882, the largest American Catholic fraternity was founded at New Haven, Connecticut, and took the name of Columbus because, as the founders said, his first act was to plant the cross of Christ on the New World shores, "a symbol of his sacred commission."[1] In the same decade, a movement was mobilized by Count Antoine Roselly de Lorgues to canonize the discoverer on the grounds that he had brought the "Christian faith to half the world."[2]

Five hundred years of reports, chronicles and scholarship has investigated every aspect about Columbus and his "Enterprise of the Indies." New light is shed on old topics from time to time as a new document surfaces or our thinking is revised. As we approach the quincentennial of Columbus' discovery, mainframe computers are crunching important data in order to advance our knowledge and accessibility to the sources, life, thought and achievements of the Genoese explorer.

Such abundant attention to the subject has left us a significant corpus of literature about Christopher Columbus and his accomplishments. But even so, one major source about him and his enterprise, written by the Admiral himself, has remained generally unstudied. In the summer and fall of 1501 he drafted a manuscript titled, *Libro de las profecías*. Scholars have known of it but have not used it, and it was not put into modern print until 1892 when Césare de Lollis included it in the *Raccolta Columbiana*.[3] Even with a printed critical edition, scholars continued to ignore it for another sixty years.

The problem scholars have had with the *Libro de las profecías* has been one of misunderstanding and credibility. Historiographically, when Columbus scholars have been confronted with the *Libro de las profecías*, they have looked the other way. Our model of Columbus as Renaissance scientist, adventurer and mariner does not include an obsession with eschatology. Nevertheless, he believed that God had called him for a special mission of apocalyptic importance. As he carefully reminded his sovereigns in a letter dated 7 July 1503, he had received a vision while yet a young man in which the Holy Spirit spoke directly to him in these words:

> God . . . will cause your name to be wonderfully proclaimed throughout the world . . . and give you the keys of the gates to the ocean which are closed with strong chains.[4]

The driving motivational force in his life was ultimately his role in God's scheme for history:

> Who doubts that this light was from the Holy Spirit . . . whom with rays of marvelous clarity it consoled . . . with forty-four books of the Old Testament and four Evangelists, with twenty-three epistles of those blessed apostles, encouraging me to proceed, and continuously, without stopping a moment, they encouraged me with great haste.[5]

Columbus' spiritual desire was to spread the Gospel and initiate a new crusade to recapture the Holy site of Solomon's Temple. It is impossible to calculate when this mission became incorporated into a broader eschatological framework, but he implies that such thinking occurred early in his career and that these dreams were a part of his arguments before the king and queen.[6] Compiling the *Libro de las profecías* must have been on his mind for several years as elements of it appear in isolated passages in his early letters, the diary and reports. The adoption of Xpo Ferrers for his signature in 1502 confirms a specially perceived relationship and calling from God.[7]

Written between the third and fourth voyages, the timing of the *Libro de las profecías* was unfortunate due to the stress caused by losing favor at court. Later, scholars would come to the conclusion that this apocalyptic treatise was the product of a discouraged and troubled mind. To Columbus, however, it was the framework in which he wished the world to view his accomplishments. The central theme of the book is that an important stage of prophecy had been fulfilled, in time, by his discoveries. The eschatological clock was ticking away and the next steps, he tells his monarchs, must begin. First, the Gospel message must be spread on a global scale beginning with lands he has discovered and brought under the Spanish flag. Second, the riches of the New World should be dedicated to the recapture of Jerusalem thereby securing the most important site in Christendom so that other events of the last days could begin.

THE DOCUMENT

The *Libro de las profecías* presents an array of prophetic texts, commentaries by ancient and medieval authors, fragments of Spanish poetry and Columbus' own interpretations of these writings to prove his theses. Columbus finished the basic draft in the fall of 1501 and gave it to his friend the Carthusian monk, Gaspar Gorricio, to read and add more references where appropriate. On 23 March 1502, as Columbus left Seville to start his fourth voyage, Father Gorricio returned the draft manuscript to him with his additions. The Gorricio additions were minor as he indicated in his letter accompanying the manuscript.[8] This is the form in which we still have the treatise, a rough draft with notations and additions to be incorporated. The *Libro de las profecías* was first found when the library of Don Diego was inventoried. Ferdinand catalogued it with other books owned by his father and used it in writing his biography. Bartolomé de las Casas mentions it, and it was catalogued by De la Rosa y Copes in his *Biblioteca Colombina*.[9]

With the exception of some tutoring from his brother, Columbus was self-taught. Despite the hours he spent pouring over the theories of experts, the years at sea accumulating practical experience, and the long discussions with scholars, churchmen and old sailors in many ports, he believed the key to his success was the gift of knowledge given to him by the Holy Spirit. The gift of understanding, *spiritualis intellectus*, enables the recipient to penetrate revealed truth, and it intensifies one's faith so that all things ultimately are seen through faith.[10] Columbus never claimed to be a prophet and only recorded two visions in which he believed God communicated directly with him. Neither of these visions were revelations; rather they were words of comfort and encouragement. He believed that he had received the charismatic gift of *spiritualis intellectus* which enlightened his mind to enable him to understand the hidden mysteries of prophetic texts, to gain practical and intuitive abilities in navigation, and to comprehend cosmography and related sciences intellectually. As he put it,

I have met and I have had discussions with wise people, ecclesiastics and laymen, Latins and Greeks, Jews and Moors and with many others of other sects. To this I found our Lord very favorable to my desire and I received from Him the spirit of intelligence: in seamanship he made me abundant, of astrology he gave what was needed, and so of geometry and arithmetic and ingeniousness in the soul and hands to draw the sphere . . .[11]

Virgil Milani has argued that Columbus was attempting to stress a deeper meaning for "intelligence" at this point, and that he could have meant "entelequia," a term utilized by St. Augustine when referring to intelligence of or from God.[12]

The draft structure of the *Libro de las profecías* is composed of 84 folios (10 pages are missing) divided into an introduction and four parts. Although he gives credit to Joachim of Fiore, the Sybils, Merlin and the pseudo-Methodius, Columbus limited his citations, with very few exceptions, to the most impeccable authorities: the Church Fathers and well respected medieval and contemporary theologians. The only instance in which he interpreted an event without supporting authority was when he proclaimed that his discoveries fulfilled Isaiah's prophecy about a new heaven and a new earth. Columbus' exegetical method was orthodox and his conclusions conservative. He did not criticize the church, state or society nor did he even hint at any kind of *renovatio ecclesiae* or *reformatio mundi*. His interpretations accomplish the opposite in that they strengthen the established order by advocating the strongest possible apocalyptic role for the Church, Spain and its Catholic monarchs.

The introduction (ff. lv-6r) includes an unfinished letter to the Spanish monarchs which explains his purpose for writing the book and lists some of the authorities upon whom he relies, his general themes, and the scope and character of the treatise. He particularly calls attention to the prophet Isaiah who foretold his two principal themes (the salvation of all people and their gathering on Mt. Zion in the last days) and reminds his readers that Isaiah was the preferred prophet of St. Jerome and St. Augustine because the Church Fathers believed him to be the clearest herald of the Gospel preached to all people.[13]

Part I (ff. 6v-30v) begins with several quotations from Psalms announcing the "peoples of the world" and the capture of Jerusalem, St. Isadore's summary of types of prophecy and how to interpret them, and the prophecies announcing the triumph of Christianity when all men will join the faith and history will culminate in the heavenly Jerusalem. Part II (ff. 30v-53v) explores prophecies fulfilled in the past and includes the famous prophecy of Abdias foretelling lands in the southern hemisphere. Part III (ff. 54v-67r) is devoted to the present and immediate future and relates Columbus' discoveries to selected scripture. The key scripture upon which he builds his case is John 10: "I am the Good Shepherd and I know my sheep . . . and I have other sheep which are not of this flock and I must bring them in, and they will hear my voice, and there will be one flock and one shepherd." [14] This is then supported by quotations from Christian authors, especially St. Augustine, and includes the famous passage from Seneca's Medea. The final part (ff. 67r-84v) is devoted to the more distant future and contains many Biblical quotations about mythical islands and their treasures which Columbus argued should be donated to the greater cause of worldwide missionary activity and the recapture of Jerusalem. Attached to the end are lists of Biblical quotations to be incorporated into the text at a later date.

COLUMBUS SCHOLARS AND THE *LIBRO DE LAS PROFECÍAS*

The evidence of Columbus' strong spirituality has never been seriously questioned although that spirituality needs more detailed definition. He was closely tied to Franciscan Observantine reformers who had deep roots in Spiritual Franciscanism. [15] His reputation has been that of a man whose deep religious faith showed a special devotion to the Virgin and the Trinity. For the past two hundred years, however, scholars have been reluctant to incorporate his eschatological beliefs or his religious treatise on prophecy into his other writings.

Contemporaries noticed immediately the eschatological significance Columbus attached to his discoveries. Agostino Giustiniani, Bishop of Nebbio, in annotating his *Polyglot Psalter* left us what is probably the first biography of the Admiral. In the margin next to Psalms 19: 4, "their message reaches out to all the world," the bishop gives us a brief summary of Columbus' life and notes that the Admiral frequently claimed to have fulfilled this prophecy. [16] Bartolomé de las Casas recognized the providential role of Columbus in these words:

> But since it is obvious that at that time God gave this man the keys to the awesome seas, he and no other unlocked the darkness, to him and to no other is owed forever and ever all that exists beyond those doors. [17]

Early biographers down through Washington Irving generally accepted Columbus' apocalyptic faith and the *Libro de las profecías* as normal fare for fifteenth century Christians. Irving eloquently summarized:

> It . . . filled his mind with solemn and visionary meditations on mystic passages of the Scriptures, and the shadowy portents of the prophecies. It exalted his office in his eyes and made him conceive himself an agent sent forth upon a sublime and awful mission, subject to impulses and supernatural intimations from the Deity . . . [18]

Scholars in the middle and later nineteenth century and throughout much of the twentieth century have been curiously reluctant to admit that the first American hero was influenced by prophetic ideas. Ironically it is doubtful that many of these influential scholars bothered to read the treatise, but their persuasive rhetorical power convinced subsequent historians that the *Libro de las profecías* was simply the ravings of a troubled and senile mind. At best the document was an embarrassment to be avoided and it thus fell from favor as an historical source.

In his signal work, *Ferdinand and Isabella*, W. H. Prescott describes Columbus' *Libro de las profecías* as "dark and mysterious annunciations of sacred prophecy" and "visionary fancies." Henri Harrisse called the treatise a "deplorable lucubration which we sincerely hope will never be published ..." and Alexander von Humboldt, who accepted Columbus' apocalypticism up to a point, concluded finally that the treatise was the product of "melancholy and morbid enthusiasm." By 1891, Justin Winsor described the hero of the quatracentennial as having "mental hallucinations" in his later years. At the turn of the century, Filson Young grieved deeply at the state of the Admiral's mental health and lamented about the *Libro de las profecías*,

> Good Heavens! In what an entirely dark and sordid stupor is our Christopher now sunk — a veritable slough and quag of stupor out of which, if he does not manage to flounder himself, no human hand can pull him.[19]

In the early and mid-twentieth century, scholars have adopted Freudian explanations, tied the work to other social or political forces at work in the fifteenth century, or ignored the *Libro de las profecías* entirely. Bernardini-Sjcestedt placed the book in the genre of romantic crusade literature while both Jaques Heers and Felipe Ximénez de Sandoval believed it to be an attempt by Columbus to restore luster to his voyages by arousing Christian enthusiasm through the device of eschatological forecasting.[20]

Cecil Jane called Columbus a mystic and describes that mysticism as "an exaggeration of that of most of his contemporaries." Samuel Eliot Morison recognized Columbus' Christian faith as "genuine and sincere" and goes on to credit him "that his frequent communion with forces unseen was a vital element in his achievement." But the *Libro de las profecías*, Morison concluded, was simply a ploy to appeal to the Queen's mysticism "and convince her that he was the chosen man of destiny to conquer an Other World and bring home treasure wherewith to recover the Holy Sepulchre." Morison only mentions the *Libro de las profecías* once, did not bother to consult it, and proceeded to ignore it for the rest of his studies. A few years later Ballesteros y Beretta stated that the prophecies "bordered . . . on the ridiculous."[21]

One late nineteenth century study, specifically focused on Columbus' religious nature, is ambivalent about the depth of his conviction. William and Charles Gillett, in their paper before the American Society of Church History in 1892 titled, "The Religious Motives of Christopher Columbus," chose the tone of nineteenth century Protestant rhetoric to portray the discoverer's piety. Phrases such as ". . . Columbus and the sovereigns, having succumbed to dastardly motives of sordid gain . . . lost their pristine missionary zeal," or "in this, as almost everywhere, the first cry is 'gold,' and the second is 'Christianize' — but with a suspiciously intimate connection with *more gold.*" And, in summary, "but in these extracts [from the sources] we fail to find anything which necessitates or justifies the suppositions of those who imagine that we must incorporate religious motives with those of material advantage . . ."[22] Not only did the Gilletts miss the point, they failed to include the *Libro de las profecías* in their survey of the sources!

On the other hand, Francis Steck in his speculative essay, "Christopher Columbus and the Franciscans," goes in the opposite direction and almost canonizes the Admiral when he states:

> Christopher Columbus and the Franciscans . . . Christ-bearers they were . . . by unbroken and brave loyalty to Christian ideals and principles . . . traversing boldly the uncharted Sea of Darkness and carrying the Crib of Bethlehem, the Sermon on the Mount, and the Cross of Calvary to a degraded and down-trodden race . . . in the love of their Savior, and in the healing power of their Sanctifier . . .[23]

It has been only in the past thirty years that scholars have sought to find a definition for Columbus' apocalypticism. Marcel Bataillon examined Columbus' interpretations from the *Libro de las profecías* within the context of general millennialism of the times, and his efforts were followed by an excellent chapter in John Phelan's book devoted to apocalypticism in the Age of Discovery. Professor Phelan was not surprised at Columbus' eschatological conclusions about spreading the Gospel to the lands he had discovered

> Little wonder that he was obsessed by the image of himself as the instrument of Divine Providence. Little wonder that he was convinced that the mission of fulfilling the other apocalyptical prophecy had also been reserved for him [the capture of Jerusalem].[24]

Phelan stressed that Columbus must be taken seriously in his prophetic statements,

> Columbus' unique historical perspective must not be forgotten. He was looking back through fifteen hundred years of Christianity. It seemed to him that his discoveries represented the grandiose climax of Christian history. His opening of the 'door of the Western Sea' promised the speedy fulfillment . . . of the words of Mark 16:15 . . .[25]

James Cummins analyzed Columbus' scheme to liberate Jerusalem in a *festschrift* contribution published in 1976. Cummins advocated the provocative idea that the Admiral set about to fulfill the medieval ideal of freeing the Holy Sepulcher and saw himself as the new David. Just as David had provided the wealth for Solomon to build the original temple on Mt. Zion, Columbus would provide the gold for the Spanish monarchs to recapture the sacred site and usher in the apocalypse: "In his mind, the whole *empresa de Indias'* was only a memo to that predestined end: the New World was to redeem the Old City."[26]

The scholarly work by Phelan and Cummins legitimized Columbus' eschatological ideas, but they have been received by a mixed audience. Mario Góngora, for example, incorporated Phelan's conclusions into his history of colonial Spanish America as did Luis Weckmann in his study of medieval influences upon Mexico.[27]

Paolo Taviani in his important and comprehensive recent biography about Columbus utilizes the *Libro de las profecías* as an important source and calls the Admiral a man with a "sincere profession of religious faith" who could not remain indifferent to divine mystery and believed that his Christian faith gave meaning to his life,

> The reconquest of the Holy Sepulchre was a mission in which he felt privileged to participate . . . It was thus a vital element in his personal philosophy of existence. It gave him purpose, and for that purpose he worked, for that purpose he lived.[28]

Other biographers, however, have not followed suit. As recently as 1985, Gianni Granzotto declared that the *Libro de las profecías* indicates that Columbus,

> . . . drifted... away from reality . . . because of his advancing age, his infirmity, and his continual disappointments . . . turned [to] mad ravings . . . mild delirium . . . came to believe that he had been chosen by God for his exploits . . . attributed his successes to the divine mission for which he had been destined . . . projected . . . delusions into the future . . . [by] compiling a Book of Prophecy.[29]

The first in-depth study to focus on Columbus' eschatological ideas was published by Alain Milhou in 1983. This was followed in 1985 by Pauline Moffett Watts' article on Columbus' sources for the *Libro de las profecías*. Milhou attempted to give exhaustive explanations of Columbus' messianic mentality and its relationship to his apocalyptic ideas. The author has investigated almost every aspect of Columbus' eschatological statements even to the point that Milhou sees the Admiral's preoccupation with gold as symbolic Christian iconography. Many of Milhou's conclusions are sound and his book now provides a foundation from which scholars may comfortably investigate the Admiral's religious motives.[30]

Pauline Watts has improved our understanding of the *Libro de las profecías* by showing that Columbus' "Enterprise of the Indies" was part of a larger scheme to restore the Holy Lands to Christendom and that "his apocalypticism must be recognized as inseparable from his geography and cosmology . . ." She has clearly pointed out the extensive use the Admiral made of a wide range of ancient and medieval authors in composing the treatise.

Watts' most important contribution is her thorough analysis of Columbus' use of Pierre d'Ailly's *opuscula*, the *Imago mundi*, and Pope Pius II's *Historia rerum ubique gestarum* in developing his apocalyptic theories.[31]

CONCLUSION

We have just begun to incorporate the *Libro de las profecías* into our understanding of Columbus, fifteenth and sixteenth century apocalypticism, and the treatise's place in the history of ideas. Critical translations at least into Spanish, Italian and English need to be made so that the source is available to a wider audience. Columbus' knowledge and use of the Bible, the Church Fathers, and important medieval theologians, should be analyzed. The *Libro de las profecías* demonstrates that the Admiral was much better read and familiar with a wider range of literature than is usually assumed. Astrology also was important to Columbus, and he refers to it throughout his diary and letters. The most complete account of his knowledge on this subject is to be found in his eschatological treatise. Last, the *Libro de las profecías* should be compared with and placed into the larger body of apocalyptic literature from the late middle ages in Europe, especially its relation to Spanish and Spanish American eschatology.

The *Libro de las profecías* is an important treatise which gives us insight into the mind of Christopher Columbus. It is not the ravings of a psychotic or reflective of an old man's senility. It is a standard and rather ordinary apocalyptic text which displays some urgency for action but no hint for revolution. There is nothing radical in the treatise, and in fact, the Admiral limits himself to exploring the meaning of his discoveries without predicting any forthcoming cataclysmic events.

Columbus had an unshakable sense of calling which for him translated into prophetic destiny. Prophecy was the bridge between cosmological theory and fifteenth century science and God's plan for the world. The secret of the Sea of Darkness to the Admiral had not been penetrated because God wanted it hidden until He was ready. Columbus firmly believed that God had selected him to uncover its mystery and to reveal new lands to gain for Christ. Christoferrens, the Christ Bearer, believed that God had given him a special spiritual intelligence to understand the mysteries of prophetic Scripture relating to unknown regions of the earth and then he set out to accumulate the intellectual abilities necessary to achieve his mission. Thus, faith and reason became wedded in his mind and created an unshakable resolve to reach his goal.

NOTES

1. C. J. Caufman, *Faith and Fraternity: The History of the Knights of Columbus, 1882-1982* (New York, 1982), p. 81. By 1899, the ceremony for members of the fourth degree included a long discourse on the theme of

Columbus' prophetic name which translated as "Christ-Bearer Dove and symbolized the baptism of the New World," p. 139. Thomas Cummings, writing in *Donahoe's Magazine*, xxxiii (November, 1895), p. 1243, stated that Columbus inspired the Knights of Columbus because he was "a prophet and seer, an instrument of Divine Providence, a mystic of the very highest order . . ."

2. A. Roselly de Lorgues, *Histoire posthume de Christophe Colomb, per le cᵗᵉ Roselly de Lorgues* (Paris, 1885), p. 381. Despite widespread support, the effort toward canonization failed.

3. *Raccolta di documenti e studi pubblicati della R. Commissione Colombiana per quarto centenario dalla scoperta dell'America* (Scritti di Christofono Colombo, ed., C. de Lollis, Roma, 1894) II, pt. 1, *Libro de las profecías*, pp. 76-106. It is described briefly in Consuelo Varela, *Cristóbal Colón: Textos y documentos completos Relaciones de viages, cartas y memoriales* (Alianza Universidad, Madrid, 1982), pp. 262-266. The actual incipit (Biblioteca Colombina, Seville, No. 2091, Registro de Hernando Colón) reads: "Liber seu manipulus de actoritatibus, dictis ac sententliis et prophetiis circa materiam recuperande sancte ciuitatis et montis Dei Syon ac inuentionis et conversionis insularum Indie et omnium gentium atque nationum ad reges nostros Hispanos."

4. *Raccolta Colombiana*, II, pt. 1, *Relazione del quarto viaggio*, Letter to king and queen dated 7 July 1592, p. 192.

5. *Libro de las profecías*, p. 79.

6. *Ibid.*, p. 79. "And with this *fire*, I came to your Highnesses." [italics are mine] He is speaking here of Divine inspiration using the word "fire" in its typical medieval symbol for the Holy Spirit as derived from the fire which came down at Pentecost.

7. C. Varela, *Christóbal Colón*, p. 305, for the date of Columbus' adoption of Xpo Ferrens.

8. *Ibid.*, p. 75-76 for Gorricio's attached letter. In the *Raccolta Colombiana*, III, pt. 1, *Autografi de Cristoforo Colombo*, pp. xviii-xxii, de Lollis identifies four handwritings in the treatise, Christopher Columbus, Bartholome Columbus, Ferdinand Columbus and Father Gorricio.

9. *Biblioteca Colombina. Catálogo de sus libros impressos* (Seville, 1888), pp. 51-52.

10. P. F. Mulhern, "Gifts of the Holy Spirit," in *New Catholic Encyclopedia* (New York, 1967) VII, pp. 99-100. *Spiritualis intellectus* was promised in Isaiah 11: 1-3 and given to the Apostles at Pentecost. The Church Fathers saw this and other gifts as special aids for Christians to use against evil. St. Thomas Aquinas believed that all gifts from the Holy Spirit were supernatural aids to enable the receiver to achieve natural perfection. In the later Middle Ages, *spiritualis intellectus* was claimed by many individuals and groups. The importance of *spiritualis intellectus* to the Spiritual Franciscans, for example, who greatly affected Columbus' ideas through their influence upon the Observantine reform movement, was primary as it

validated their claims to be the new spiritual men predicted by Joachim of Fiore. The Spiritual Franciscans believed that the age into which the world was entering would be illuminated with a true form of *spiritualis intellectus*. See M. Reeves, *Prophecy in the Later Middle Ages*, (Oxford, 1969), p. 210.

11. *Libro de las profecías*, p. 79 and p. 82 where he proclaims that his self-education in all fields was secondary to the insights and knowledge given to him by the Holy Spirit.

12. V. Milani, *The Written Language of Christopher Columbus* (Buffalo, New York, 1973), pp. 129-132.

13. *Libro de las profecías*, p. 98.

14. *Ibid.*, p. 143. He thoroughly glossed this from St. Augustine, St. Gregory, St. John Chrysostom, and Nicholas of Lyra.

15. A. Bernaldez, *Historia de los Reyes Catholicos D. Fernando y Doña Isabel* (Sociedad de bibófilos andaluces, Sevilla, 1890) I, ser. 1, pt. 2, p. 78 clearly states that Columbus appeared in the streets of Castile "wearing the habit of an *Observantine Friar* . . ." [italics are mine]. His ties to the Observantine reformers has been shown most recently by A. Milhou, see note 29.

16. Agostino Giustiniani, *Polyglot Psalter* (Genoa, 1516), note D.

17. Bartolomé de las Casas, *History of the Indies*, trs. A. Collard (New York, 1971), p. 35.

18. W. Irving, *The Life and Voyages of Christopher Columbus* (New York, 1849) II, pp. 491-492.

19. W. H. Prescott, *Ferdinand and Isabella* (Boston, 1837) III, pp. 243-244. H. Harrisse, *Notes on Columbus* (New York, 1866), p. 84. A. von Humboldt, *Cosmos: A Sketch of a Physical Description of the Universe*, trs. E. C. Otté (New York, 1858), p. 65. J. Winsor, *Christopher Columbus and How He Imparted the Spirit of Discovery* (New York, 1891), p. 504. F. Young, *Christopher Columbus and the New World of His Discoveries* (London, 1906), p. 146. Similar wording of Columbus' condition can be found in many late nineteenth and early twentieth century writers. Three more prominent writers will serve as examples: J. Wassermann, *Christoph Columbus, der Don Quichote des Ozeans* (Berlin, 1926), p. 206 ". . . die ihn möglich machte, und der wie die meisten Elaborate des Verfassers den Beveis liefert, dass sein Bildungsniveau selbst für das Zeitalter auffallend niedrig war. Spanisch Finsternis." M. André, *La Véridique Aventure de Christophe Colomb* (Paris, 1927), p. 259 calls him "quite mad" and a "possessed and hallucinated being." And in the famous volumes by J. Thacher, *Christopher Columbus: His Life, His Work, His Remains* (New York, 1904) II, p. 566 "Fancy was disordering his brain." III, p. 461, the *Libro de las profecías* was written when the ". . . aged Admiral was broken in mind and body . . ."

20. A. Bernardini-Sjcestedt, *Christophe Colomb* (Paris, 1961), p. 275. J. Heers, *Christophe Colomb* (Bienne, 1981), p. 579. F. Ximénez de Sandoval, *Cristóbal Colón: evocación del Almirante de la mar Océana* (Madrid,

1968), pp. 277-279. Ramon Iglesias, however, seems to have misread the *Libro de las profecías* when he interpreted it only in light of Columbus' building a new argument to convince the court to restore his titles and privileges. Iglesias ignores the consistency of eschatological remarks made by Columbus in his earlier writings. See. R. Iglesias, "The Man Columbus," in *Columbus, Cortés, and Other Essays* ed. L. Simpson (Berkeley and Los Angeles, 1969), pp. 31-32. A reprint of Iglesia's original article published in 1920.

21. C. Jane, *The Voyages of Christopher Columbus* (New York, 1970), p. 27. S. E. Morison, *Admiral of the Ocean Seas: A Life of Christopher Columbus* (Boston, 1942), p. 577-578. A. Ballesteros y Beretta, *Cristóbal Colón y il discubrimiento de América* (Barcelona, 1945) II, p. 692.

22. W. Gillett & C. Gillett, "The Religious Motives of Christopher Columbus," *Papers of the American Society of Church History*, IV (1892), pp. 14, 18-19.

23. F. Steck, "Christopher Columbus and the Franciscans," *The Americas*, III, no. 3 (1947), p. 337.

24. M. Bataillon, "Evangélisme et millénarisme au Nouveau Monde," *Courants religieux et humanisme a la fin de xve et au début de xvie siècle* (Colloque de Strasbourg, May 9-11, 1957), pp. 25-36. J. Phelan, *The Millennial Kingdom of the Franciscans in the New World* (Berkeley and Los Angeles, 1970), p. 23.

25. *Ibid,.* p. 21.

26. J. S. Cummins, "Christopher Columbus: Crusader, Visionary and *Servus Dei*," *Medieval Hispanic Studies Presented to Rita Hamilton* ed. A. D. Deyermond (London, 1976), p. 45.

27. M. Góngora, *Studies in the Colonial History of Spanish America*, trs. R. Southern (London, 1975), pp. 206-209. L. Weckmann, *La herencia medieval de México* (El Colegio de México 1984) I, pp. 263-265.

28. P. Taviani, *Christopher Columbus: The Grand Design* (London, 1985), p. 113.

29. G. Grazotto, *Christopher Columbus*, trs. S. Sarterelli (New York, 1985), p. 246.

30. A. Milhou,*Colón y su mentalidad mesíanica en el ambiente franciscanista Españ*ol (Cuadernos Colombinos, XI, Valladolid, 1983).

31. P. Watts, "Prophecy and Discovery: On the Spiritual Origins of Christopher Columbus's 'Enterprise of the Indies'," *American Historical Review* 90, no. 1 (1985), p. 74.

Columbus's Seven Years in Spain Prior to 1492

Foster Provost
Duquesne University
Pittsburgh, PA

ABSTRACT

One of the most conspicuous facts in Columbus' biography is the prominence of unverifiable assertions in major scholarly treatments. The common practice of such "creative non-fiction" has caused widespread confusion about the most crucial and decisive period in the mariner's career, the seven years in Spain prior to the 1492 embarkation.

It appears that we cannot date or even place in sequential order various events that have been reported in the mariner's life in these years. The attempt to date and order these events has led biographers to create and describe unverifiable scenarios as if they really happened. Probably the only hope for establishing sounder points of reference for the events of this period lies in the Spanish archives, which the Spanish government is now putting in order.

This situation in Columbus scholarship raises important questions about the philosophy of historical biography. It invites speculation on necessary distinctions between the domain of the historian and the domain of the creative artist, and suggests that the analytical approach to the sources practiced by Jacques Heers in *Christophe Columb* might be a proper approach for future biographers.

One of the most conspicuous facts in Columbus biography is the presence of unverifiable assertions and incidents in major scholarly treatments. Such assertions and incidents, often quite clearly fictional, have been a traditional ingredient in lives of Christopher Columbus both in his own time and in the nineteenth and twentieth century. The most likely reason for the practice is simply the frustrating gaps in the available documentary evidence, gaps where little or nothing is known for certain about the activities of the subject. These fictional insertions are sometimes styled "creative non-fiction."

Those who favor this fleshing-out of scholarly biographies with imagined events contend that this is the only way to make biography palatable to prospective readers. These proponents sometimes hold that the practice is not unscholarly so long as the imagined events fall within the bounds of probability and do not violate the spirit and personality evoked by the events and activities which *are* authentic.

The best argument I can think of for opposing the practice of this "creative non-fiction" is the confusion that biography-padding has caused in the available biographies of Columbus. Nowadays everyone laughs at Washington Irving's sentimental imaginings in his account of a conflict between the pedantic scholars of Salamanca and the brilliant navigator.[1] But when we look at the most recent major biographies both in English and in Spanish, we find that neither Morison nor Ballesteros seems to have had any qualms about including in his narrative, without *caveat* of any kind, events for which there is no documentary proof.

The classic instance of this is the insertion into Columbus biography of the wreck of the ship *Bechalla* off Cape St. Vincent in August, 1476. The ship did indeed sink at that time in a fight between a Genoese convoy (in which the *Bechalla* was sailing) and a squadron of French marauders; but researchers have never found lists of the crews of the ships and so we do not in fact know that Columbus was aboard that ship or any other ship in the Genoese convoy. Yet in their biographies neither Morison (1942) nor Ballesteros (1945) shows any doubts that Columbus was aboard some ship in the convoy, and both name the *Bechalla* as the ship he was probably on.[2] As a consequence, generations of readers in the Spanish and English-speaking worlds have grown up thinking that Columbus was wrecked at the time the *Bechalla* went down and entered Portugal by swimming ashore near Lagoe at that time.

The extensive research that produced information about the attack on the Genoese convoy[3] was mounted in an attempt to ascertain the truth of the statement by Columbus's son Ferdinand, in his life of his father, that the navigator was aboard a ship that was wreckèd off Portugal and swam ashore.[4] It is true that Columbus was associated through a large part of his life with the firms which sponsored this convoy, and also true that Columbus arrived in Portugal about 1476; but these facts do not of themselves make it true that Columbus was aboard a ship in that convoy. The relatively careful Ballesteros, sensing that the case is not made, buttresses it by citing Columbus's 1505 letter to King Ferdinand claiming that his arrival on the peninsula was miraculous;[5] but Columbus's letter mentions no shipwreck at all, and his assertion might mean only that he had been under the miraculous direction of God throughout his life. Certainly there is no duty to prove or disprove Ferdinand's assertion that his father reached Portugal initially by swimming ashore after a shipwreck, for his biography is full of exaggerations and inaccuracies, and the wreck of the *Bechalla* and other ships in the seafight in question do not of themselves prove that Columbus was aboard a ship in the convoy in question.

The biographies of Morison and Ballesteros contain various less spectacular fictional incidents and imagined assertions which allow the reader to feel that a substantial amount is known about the discoverer's life at every period. This feeling, of course, is no less fanciful than the various examples of wishful thinking in Ferdinand's biography. In fact, there are still extensive periods in the life of the discoverer about which we know almost nothing.

Of the period in the biographies which are distinctively flavored by fictional inserts, the most crucial and decisive is the period of seven year in Spain, 1485-1492, just prior to the embarkation of the first fleet of discovery. A quote from the early paragraphs in Morison's account of this period in *Admiral of the Ocean Sea* will establish the flavor of the fiction I am speaking of:

> Columbus knew nobody in Spain except his Molyart brother- and sister-in law, who lived at Huelva, but they were in no position to do anything for him.
>
> When his ship rounded the promontory at the entrance to the Rio Tinto, Columbus noted on a bluff the buildings of the Franciscan friary of La Rabida. These suggested a solution of his first problem, what to do with Diego while he sought friends and ways and means. The Minorites were noted for their hospitality, and often conducted schools for young boys; perhaps this house would take charge of his son.[6]

This is fiction because no one knows whether the Molyarts could or could not have cared for Diego; and we do not even know whether Diego divided his time between the friars and the Molyarts or spent it exclusively with the friars. We do know that Columbus later gave Molyart employment, lent him money, and obtained some confiscated furniture from the sovereigns for the Molyarts.[7] Obviously he felt some obligation to the family — although this may have simply been the obligation which any Italian would feel to members of his family. At any rate, it is impossible to know whether Columbus's first thought of leaving Diego with the Franciscans came when he spied La Rábida from the river Tinto; we do not know whether he had inquired ahead of time about this possibility. And we do not know whether he had heard that the Franciscans might help him with his Enterprise. Morison is making the narrative readable, not overly concerned about sticking strictly to the documented facts.

The fourth centennial celebration and the increased availability of documents at that time[8] stimulated much new scholarship, including a new synthesis of known and presumed facts about the period in the life of Columbus between his departure from Portugal and his embarkation on the 1492 voyage. This synthesis was carried out by Henry Vignaud in his *Histoire Critique de la Grande Entreprise de Christophe Colomb.*[9] It is full of gaps during which nothing certain is known about Columbus, but it accommodates most of the known facts, and it dominated this portion of Columbus biography at least until the appearance in 1964 of Juan Manzano Manzano's study of these same years in Columbus's life. Morison pointed out in 1942 that nothing substantial had since been added to the facts in Vignaud's synthesis except the monograph of D. José de la Torre on Beatriz Enriquez de Harana and the work of Fr. Angel Ortega on La Rábida.[10]

In 1964 Manzano introduced a radically altered sequence of events in his *Cristóbal Colón: siete años decisivos de su vida, 1485-1492*.[11] Some of Manzano's sequence appears more cogent than Vignaud's, because his analysis of the movements of the Spanish court during these years makes it hard to see how some of the known events in Columbus's life could have happened at the times indicated in Vignaud's sequence, such as Columbus's initial acquaintance with Medinaceli.

Thus we have two radically contradictory accounts, both synthesized by conscientious scholars, of the sequence of the events which Columbus probably engaged in. I shall spend the rest of this paper comparing these two accounts and commenting on them.

The older account is presented succinctly by Morison in *AOS*, I, 107-138. Columbus arrived in Palos about the middle of 1485 and leaves his son Diego with the Franciscans at the friary, La Rábida. The prior, Fray Juan Pérez, may have sent Columbus to Seville with a letter to a notable Franciscan astronomer, Fray Antonio de Marchena. Alternatively, Marchena may have been visiting at La Rábida when Columbus got there.

At any rate, Marchena was impressed with Columbus's ideas and sent him to the wealthiest grandee in Castile, the Duke of Medina Sidonia, to seek support. Morison says Medina Sidonia was interested, and in a piece of fiction which I shall glance at below, "was at the point of promising to equip a fleet for Columbus when, owing to an unseemly brawl with the Duke of Cádiz, the Sovereigns ordered him to leave Seville and the negotiations were broken off. Columbus then turned to . . . (the) Count of Medina Celi, who had a large establishment at Puerto Santa Maria and owned a merchant fleet" (*AOS*, I. 110).

Medinaceli intended to sponsor the voyage, but when he asked permission of the queen she took the whole project over for the Crown and invited Columbus to court. He arrived in Córdoba on 20 January 1486. By then the sovereigns had departed on one of their frequent peregrinations, and so Columbus had to wait until the sovereigns returned in April. In the mean time he became acquainted with the Genoese in town and through them met the Haranas, including an orphan niece named Beatriz Enriquez de Harana, who became Columbus's mistress and in 1488 bore him his second child, the illegitimate son Ferdinand.

Columbus was first presented to Isabel in the Alcázar of Córdoba on about 1 May 1486 (*AOS*, I. 115). The queen "placed Columbus in the charge of her comptroller of finances, Alonso de Quintanilla, who put him up at his house, and introduced him to the very magnificent Don Pedro Gonzales de Mendoza . . . Grand cardinal of Spain . . ." (I. 115). This same summer she appointed a commission headed by Fray Hernando de Talavera to study the Enterprise and make recommendations (I. 116). The commission began deliberations at Córdoba in this same summer of 1486 (I. 116), and held some crucial sessions at the College of St. Stephen in Salamanca about Christmas, 1486. Columbus met the prior of St. Stephen, the Dominican priest Diego de Deza, at this time (I. 116-117). In spite of this activity the deliberations dragged on interminably and the commission did not report until four or five years later, perhaps in late 1490.

Columbus's activities in the mean time are shadowy. For awhile he was paid meager stipends by the crown, but these ceased in the summer of 1488 (I. 118). He reopened negotiations with Portugal in this same year, 1488, but these fell through (I. 118). At the invitation of the Spanish sovereigns he visited them at their siege camp near Baza in the summer of 1489 (I. 130). He may have sold books and maps in Seville, and it may have been at this time that he acquired and annotated a number of books on cosmology and history which survive to this day.

When the Talavera commission reported unfavorably, probably in Seville in 1490 (I. 131), the sovereigns neither accepted nor rejected the report, and let Columbus know that when the war with Granada was over they might be interested in his Enterprise. He waited awhile but in the summer of 1491 he decided to try his luck in France and went to La Rábida for his son, Diego (I. 132).

The rest of the account is not in question; with the aid of Fray Juan Pérez, who was at La Rábida when he got there, he reopened negotiations with the Spanish crown, and after the fall of Granada on January 2, 1492, the monarchs' resistance gradually diminished. Though the negotiations nearly broke down more than once, Ferdinand and Isabel agreed not only to sponsor the Enterprise but to do so on terms astonishingly favorable to Columbus.

In this narrative by Morison we frequently encounter his tendency to humanize a story with a bit of fiction, as when he says that Medina Sidonia became interested in the enterprise and was on the point of sponsoring a fleet when the sovereigns made him leave Seville. There are no documents to support the assertion that Medina Sidonia was about to sponsor a fleet for Columbus at this time, or even any documents to show that he met Columbus at this time. We encounter fiction again when Morison tells us that Quintanilla put Columbus up at his own house in Córdoba in 1486 following the mariner's introduction to the Queen about May 1. This is an extrapolation from a 1493 letter from Medinaceli to the Queen via Cardinal Mendoza;[12] no one knows whether Medinaceli means 1486 or 1488-9. If he means 1488-9, Morison's remark about Quintanilla vis-a-vis Columbus in 1486 are all fiction, but Morison gives no hint of this.

The key matters are the date of the Talavera Commission's report and the time of Columbus's encounter with the Medinas, although the date of his relationship with Quintanilla is of interest too. The account related by Morison, inherited from Vignaud[13] in substantially the order in which he tells it, suggests that Columbus had to give up the active sponsorship of

Medinaceli, who had the resources to mount the fleet, in favor of a half-hearted royal consideration which dragged on for five years or more without any report from the commission of inquiry for more than four years and without any real result until after Granada surrendered. This sequence has been called into question, as we shall see.

The biography of Antonio Ballesteros y Beretta (1945) follows the same traditional order and asserts the same excruciating slowness on the part of the commission, but adds in considerable detail an account of the movements of the court of Ferdinand and Isabel.[14] This addition makes little difference in the total impression we get of Columbus's life during these critical seven year, but it did inspire a younger scholar, Juan Manzano Manzano, to explore the implications of the itinerary of the royal court. Manzano examined the movements of the court in even greater detail and studied with care the laws governing presentation of petitions to the monarchs and laws governing the formation of commissions of inquiry like the Talavera Commission. This enabled Manzano to infer with some cogency a completely different sequence of events which does much to eliminate the almost total vacuum in the middle of the story as told by Morison. Manzano also adopts numerous corrections, both from his own scholarship and from contributions by Ballesteros and others. One reflection of his success is the fact that Paolo Emilio Taviani, in his elaborate study *Cristoforo Colombo: la genesi della grande scoperta* (1972), follows Manzano in a number of his revisions in the accepted sequence of Columbus's life at this point.[15]

Manzano reports his findings in his 1964 book *Cristóbal Colón*, mentioned above. In summary, his synthesis of the story is this (I have omitted a few points on which he and Morison do not differ substantially):

When Columbus arrived at La Rábida in March 1485, he met Fray Antonio de Marchena, who proved to be his firmest and most useful supporter during the next seven year. Fray Juan Pérez was probably not at La Rábida at this time (pp. 30-32).

From 18 March until 3 September 1485, the monarchs and the royal court were in or near Córdoba (pp. 38-39). Columbus went to Córdoba during this period, probably bearing an introduction from Marchena to Talavera, who may be the person who brought him to the sovereigns' attention. By custom and law the sovereigns would have referred him to their Royal Council, who heard Columbus's proposal at this time and rejected it (pp. 49-52). Columbus then took his only recourse and made a direct appeal to the sovereigns seeking a special commission to study his project (p. 50).

The sovereigns granted him an audience, which took place in the archbishop's palace in Alcalá de Henares on 20 January 1486 (p. 56). As a result of this audience Marchena appeared before the sovereigns in Madrid, probably on 24 February 1486, and warmly defended the navigator's proposal (p. 63). Subsequently the monarchs appointed a commission of scholars, of specialists in geography, and of specialists in navigation, headed by Talavera, to study the proposal (p. 64).

From 20 through 24 April 1486, Columbus was with the court in Guadalupe, and probably formed his famous attachment to the Virgin of Guadalupe at this time (pp. 73-74). During the rest of 1486 he may have been with the court in its wanderings (documented on a daily basis), or simply living in Córdoba (pp. 74-76). He may have met Beatriz Enriquez de Harana at this time. The first sessions of the commission took place in Salamanca at the College of St. Stephen in the period 7 November 1486 to 30 January 1487 (p. 79). Columbus probably appeared at some of these sessions and probably stayed at the Dominican convent with Father Diego de Deza, tutor of the royal prince Don Juan (p. 79).

On 3 March 1487 the court returned to Córdoba and instituted the final long crescendo of assaults on the kingdom of Granada which continued until the Moors surrendered in January 1492. On 5 May 1487, Columbus received a subvention from the crown (pp. 80-81), apparently to reimburse his expenses while testifying before the commission.

According to Manzano, the Talavera commission almost certainly reported to the monarchs before the fall of Málaga on 18 August 1487 (pp. 108-09), more than three years earlier than in the scenario followed by Morison and Ballesteros. On the day the city fell, Columbus received a further subvention at Córdoba to go to the royal camp at Málaga, where he learned from the monarchs that they could not undertake the Enterprise now but might consider it after the conquest of the Moors (pp. 108-111).

Before 17 October 1487, Columbus received what was apparently intended as a final subvention to cover expenses (p. 111). From then until late March 1488 he apparently lived in Córdoba and Seville, probably as a bookseller. This is the most likely time for his acquisition and annotation of the many books of his in the Columbian Library in Seville. By late October 1487 be had formed the liaison with Beatriz Enriquez, who gave birth to Ferdinand Columbus the following August (p. 122).

In the spring of 1488 Columbus received a letter dated 20 March from John II of Portugal inviting him to return to Lisbon to confer (pp. 148-49). Columbus went to see the sovereigns in Valencia or Murcia to try to get a decisive response about his enterprise (pp. 151-157). The war was not progressing, and the sovereigns apparently let him go on to Portugal without much concern (p. 157). On 16 June 1488 be received a gift of money from the court, perhaps solicited by Columbus himself in order to get to Lisbon (p. 150).

Whatever the tenor of the presumed talks with King John, Columbus was back in Seville in October, 1488 (pp. 160-162). Probably he was in touch with Fray Antonio de Marchena, custodian at this time of Los Observantes de Sevilla (p. 167). Marchena introduced him between October 1488 and May 1489 first to the Duke of Medina Sidonia and then to the Duke of Medinaceli (pp. 167-169). Medinaceli listened to Columbus, intervened with the queen through Cardinal Mendoza in an effort to get the Enterprise reconsidered, and provided Columbus with lodging and sustenance at various times from 1489 to 1491 (pp. 172-175). It is essential to note this: Manzano insists that Medinaceli's assertion to the Queen in his 1493 letter that he met Columbus when the latter first came from Portugal means the mariner's return from visiting King John in 1488. Since Medinaceli says Columbus was talking of going on to France at this time, Manzano's conclusion is an attractive one.[16]

By now the court was ready to try again to bring the Moors to their knees by taking Baza; and when in May 1489 the queen summoned Columbus to court in response to the appeals of Medinaceli she issued a proclamation (pp. 187-188) which would permit the navigator to follow the army to Jaen, the base of the campaign against Baza. Columbus arrived at Jaen after 22 May 1489 (p. 188) and had an interview with the queen (p. 193). He was still in Jaen when the influential Alonso de Quintanilla, treasurer for the king and queen, arrived there in August, 1489, and he was put under Quintanilla's protection (p. 197). (Morison, we remember, places this event in 1486.)

Baza fell on 4 December 1489, and then with a quick and hazardous march through the mountains the sovereigns attacked Guadix, which fell on the day it was attacked, 30 December 1489 (pp. 200-202). By 3 January 1490, Ferdinand and Isabel were back in Jaen, confident that the Moors were finished. Manzano thinks that Columbus stayed right with the court during these heady days in order to be present when the surrender came and, hopefully, beneficiary of the sovereigns' triumphant high spirits.

But when the triumph proved illusory he probably returned to Medinaceli's seat in Puerto de Santa Maria (p. 210) and finally, in 1491, became disgusted and returned to La Rábida intending to remove Diego and set out for France (pp. 221-224). It was now that he met Fray Juan Pérez, the former confessor of the queen (p. 229), who intervened successfully for Columbus as described in all accounts.

Manzano's synthesis, based on the day-to-day movement of the court, is attractive because, given the known facts of the mariner's stay in Spain during the period, it is hard to see any other arrangement that would match up with the known locations and activities of the monarchs and the court.

As for the key matters identified above in the description of Morison's account, Manzano asserts a credible dating for Columbus's encounter with Medinaceli and his residence with this nobleman, supporting the assertions of Ferdinand and Las Casas; and he advances a quite credible sequence and dating for the report of the Talavera commission and the royally ordered trip by Columbus to Málaga to receive the verdict from the sovereigns. Manzano's refusal to concede that Columbus probably was in Lisbon to see the Bartholomew Diaz fleet return to the Tagus in December 1488 is on the side of scholarly caution, for opinion is divided on whether Diaz returned in December 1488 or December 1487 and because opinion is also divided on whether Christopher or Bartholomew Columbus wrote the postil in which the writer claims to have been present when Diaz returned to Lisbon. [17]

Even so, Manzano frequently slips into fiction in the course of his narrative. A few examples must serve, among many. There is no documentation to show that Columbus was with the court at Guadalupe in April of 1486; he does appear to have been with the court in Alcalá de Henares on 20 January and in Madrid with them on 24 February; but this by no means shows that he was still with the court when it got to Guadalupe. He might have visited the shrine by himself in the intervening months, or at various other times when there are gaps in our knowledge of him.

Again, there is no documentation to show that Columbus was introduced to Medina Sidonia and Medinaceli by Marchena or by anyone else in the period between October 1488 and March 1489. There is no way to show that Medinaceli's crucial reference to Columbus's coming from Portugal (in his 1493 letter to the queen) actually means Columbus's return from a 1488 visit to Portugal. This is an important weakness, because much of Manzano's case depends on the reader's acceptance of the proposition that Medinaceli is referring to 1488 and not 1485. In justice we must acknowledge that if Medinaceli *did* mean 1488, then the case for Manzano's sequence is infinitely stronger than the one presented by Morison and Ballesteros.

Further, there is also no documentation to show that Talavera reported to the sovereigns prior to Columbus's visit to Málaga, as Manzano contends, although the cessation of regular stipends to Columbus shortly thereafter might indeed suggest that the crown felt the reason for the stipends had ceased — i.e., to enable CC to cooperate with the Talavera commission.

This last defect in Manzano's synthesis would perhaps be fatal except that no one can document any other date for the Talavera report, so that Ballesteros' otherwise cogent account of the Vignaud sequence lacks any strong or persuasive evidence that Talavera reported at all, as does Morison's account and that of Vignaud himself. Manzano's attitude that the punctual and demanding sovereigns would not have put up with year after year of interminable indecision speaks very loudly against a three- to four-year delay before a report.

On balance, Manzano's sequence is stronger than Vignaud's; but this must not blind us to the fact that he cannot prove that Medinaceli's phrase "when he first came from Portugal" means 1488 rather than 1485, just as Morison and Ballesteros do not cite any evidence at all that Columbus met the Medinas in 1485 or that Talavera reported late or early.

What is the inference to be made from this comparison of the two cases? The inference I make is that neither case is really very strong; we still simply do not know what the sequence of Columbus's activities in the period 1485-1492 was, except for the very few instances when he is recorded as receiving a stipend on a certain date in a certain place, or is otherwise clearly pinpointed in the few known documents.

Thus it all comes down to the philosophy of historical biography: what is it that the historical biographer is supposed to do? To the degree that he is a teacher, it is doubtless his duty to entertain. But we must ask, with Socrates in Plato's *Republic*, whether the teacher's first task is not to ascertain that what he is teaching is the truth, and to avoid teaching what he does not know to be the truth.

The only answer to Socrates is not a historian's answer. It is the poet and novelist's answer advanced by Philip Sidney, that a fiction writer cannot lie because he does not affirm that anything is literally true; he is simply writing fiction. The historian does not have this refuge, for his chief duty is to ascertain and promulgate the historical facts. What I am saying is that in the absence of much more documentary evidence, a large proportion of what passes for Columbus biography is simply fiction.

The research in the files of Genoa which led up to and followed the celebration of the fourth centenary of the Columbus landfall removed a great deal of the mystery from the early life of the mariner, though by no means all of it. What we have to hope is that the Spanish government's projects to catalogue, edit, and promulgate the voluminous document in the Spanish archives, and the parallel project of the American scholar Charles Polzer, the New World Archive, will ultimately bear fruit in extensive further discoveries of the sort that Alicia Bache Gould achieved in naming the crews of Columbus's ships in the 1492 fleet.[18] Eugene Lyons' recent discovery of the details of the *Niña's* construction in the Casa de Contratacion[19] is an example of what we must hope for. Until that time, this most critical period in Columbus's life is a period where extreme caution must be observed by historical biographers.

Perhaps the true future of historical study of Columbus — in the absence of many more Alicia Goulds — is mapped out by Jacques Heers' landmark study *Christophe Colomb*.[20] Heers' book is not a narrative at all but simply an analysis of the primary documents, carried out in roughly chronological order, made on the basis of Heers' profound knowledge of Genoa and of Genoese activity in Spain and the Atlantic islands. If the Heers approach is followed, then the shady areas of Columbus's life can safely be left to the poets, dramatists, and novelists, whose imaginary worlds are governed only by their duty to be true to the *spirit* of human society, and not by the letter of historical fact.

NOTES

1. *The Life and Voyages of Christopher Columbus*, ed. John Harmon McElroy (Boston: Twayne, 1986), pp. 47-53.

2. Samuel Eliot Morison, *Admiral of the Ocean Sea* (Boston: Little. Brown. 1942), I, 34; Antonio Ballesteros Beretta, *Cristóbal Colón y el descubrimiento de América* (Barcelona and Buenos Aires: Salvat Editore, 1945), I, 274.

3. A. Salvagnini, *Cristoforo Colombo e i corsari Colombo*, in *Raccolta Colombiana*, II.iii, 137-154; G. Pessagno, "Questioni colombiane," *Atti della Società Lioure di Storia Patria*, 3 (1926), 565-67, 603, 607.

4. Ferdinand Columbus, *The Life of the Admiral Christopher Columbus by his Son Ferdinand*, tr. Benjamin Keen. (New Brunswick, N.J.: Rutgers Univ. Press, 1959), pp. 13-14.

5. Ballesteros, I, 264, 274. The letter appears on p. 357 of Consuelo Varela's *Cristóbal Colón: Textos y documentos completos*, 2nd ed. (Madrid: Alianza Editorial, 1984).

6. Morison, *Admiral of the Ocean Sea*, I, 108.

7. Paolo Emilio Taviani draws this information together in *Cristoforo Colombo: la genesi della grande scoperta* (1972), paperbound rpt. (Novara, Italy: Istituto Geografico de Agostini, 1982), pp. 396-397.

8. Especially in the *Raccolta di documenti e studi pubblicate della R. Commissione pel Quarto Centenario dalla Scoperta dell'America* (Rome: Ministero della Publica Istruzione, 1892-1896). 14 vols.

9. (Paris: Welter, 1911), I, 399-730 and II, 9-134.

10. Morison, *AOS*, I, 125, note 1. The references are to José de la Torre y del Cerro, *Beatriz Enriguez de Harana y Cristóbal Colón* (Madrid: Compañia iberoamericana de publicaciones, 1933) and Angel de Ortega, *La Rábida, historia documental critica* (Madrid: Librería católica de Gregorio del Amo, 1925-26).

11. (Madrid: Ediciones Cultura Hispánica, 1964), pp. 30-229.

12. Duke of Medinaceli to the Cardinal of Spain, Collogado, 19 Mar. 1493. Vignaud, *Histoire Critique*, I, 528.

13. *AOS*, I, 107-129; Vignaud's account. *Histoire Critique,* I, 399-730.

14. Ballesteros, I, 393-556.

15. Paperbound rpt. (Novara, Italy: Istituto Geografico de Agostini, 1982), pp. 147-153. 170-175; 392-405, 430-443. English edition, *Christopher Columbus: The Grand Design* (London: Orbie, 1985), pp. 168-173, 189-194, 433-447, 474-487.

16. See note 12, above. The letter is addressed to Cardinal Mendoza.

17. The only evidence we have that Christopher Columbus was in Portugal in these years, except for the testimony of Juan Moreno in *Los Pleitos de Colón* (ed. Duro, II, 75) is Postil 24 in the discoverer's copy of D'Ailly's *Imago Mundi*, which says, or seems to say, that the writer was in Lisbon in Dec. 1488, at the return of the Diaz expedition which had rounded the Cape of Good Hope. Las Casas says this Postil 24 is in Bartholomew Columbus's hand (*Historia de las Indias, Biblioteca de Autores Españoles*, Vol 95 (Madrid: Real Academia Española, 1957), Chap. 27, I, 102-104), while Diego Luis Molinari (*La Empresa Colombina* (Buenos Aires: Impr. de la Universidad, 1938) and Morison (AOS, I, 106, note 29) identify the hand as Christopher's.

Respecting the date of Diaz's return, Las Casas (following the Portuguese chronicler Hernando Lopez de Castaneda) places the return of the Diaz expedition in Dec. 1487 at a time prior to King John's letter of 20 March 1488, inviting Christopher to come to Lisbon. Las Casas points out that at the time some persons started counting the new year from Christmas day, so that Bartholomew (who on this assumption must have written the postil, because Christopher was in Spain at the time; the return of Diaz occurred in the first week of 1488, i.e., between Christmas and New Year's of 1487. Morison, however, points out (*AOS*, I, 106, note 29) that some of the historical evidence strongly supports Dec. 1488, not 1487, for Diaz's return. We must conclude that the issue of whether Christopher went to Portugal in 1488 is right where it was in the early 16th century, when Moreno said yes and Las Casas said no: not proved either way.

18. *Nueva lista documentada de los tripulantes de Colón en 1492* (Madrid: Real Academia de la Historia, 1984).

19. *National Geographic,* 70, no. 5 (Nov., 1985), 600-605.

20. (Paris: Hachette, 1981).

Sizes and Configurations of Spanish Ships in the Age of Discovery*

Carla Rahn Phillips
University of Minnesota
Minneapolis/St. Paul, Minnesota

ABSTRACT

What little we know about ship dimensions during the Age of Discovery is speculative at best. The documentary evidence has not yet been studied in detail, and there are very few physical remains to guide us. As nautical archeology discovers more shipwrecks, we can look forward to a vast improvement in this state of affairs. Until then, documentary evidence about ideal and real ships for Mediterranean, Atlantic, and Pacific waters can serve a useful purpose, providing us with a range of common ship dimensions.

This paper discusses the meaning of the five measurements used to define Spanish ships in the Columbian period and thereafter. It then analyzes the common formulas used to calculate ship tonnages based on those five measurements. Tables listing more than 100 real and ideal ships accompany the paper. They include small vessels as well as large warships and merchantmen. The best estimates we have for Columbus's ships are examined in light of the previous discussion of measurements and tonnages. In conclusion, I develop a new set of estimates for Columbus's ships and a method for estimating the measurements of other historical ships.

INTRODUCTION

As the quincentenary of the first voyage of Christopher Columbus approaches, we can hope for an outpouring of scholarly research on many topics surrounding the man himself and the world in which he lived. High on the list of topics are the ships that carried Columbus and his men on that first voyage. Those ships still capture our imagination, symbolizing the breathtaking audacity of the voyage, however we define its purpose and its results. They also represent something much broader, a nexus of the technological development of the period. I would hope, as research for the quincentenary proceeds, that the study of Columbus's ships keep this broader context in mind, because in understanding his world as a whole, we can best understand Columbus and his place in it.

---

* Eugene Lyon, Harry Kelsey, Norman Rubin, and José María Martínez-Hidalgo Terán each gave this paper a careful reading and suggested points for clarification and further research. I am very grateful for their time and for their continuing contributions to nautical history.

We know very little about Columbus's ships, despite the lively interest of scholars over the centuries. For that matter, we know very little about any European ships before the late sixteenth century. Sketches and plans are exceedingly rare, as is the evidence about shipwrecks from nautical archeology. For the moment, our best sources are documents describing the ships and pictorial evidence of varying plausibility. Happily, the documentary evidence is mounting steadily, as scholars discover the astounding wealth and variety of information in the archives in Seville, Simancas, Madrid, and port cities around the Iberian Peninsula. That makes it possible to develop a range of ship sizes and configurations that were commonly found in Spain.

In the course of other research, I have collected data on numerous ships that were proposed or actually built in the fifteenth, sixteenth, and seventeenth centuries. Mine is not a scientific sample, by any means. It is simply a collection of ships that left fairly detailed records in the documents I was consulting. Nonetheless, they exhibit surprising similarities, encouraging the hope that they represent the range of sailing ships in Columbus's time and thereafter.

First I will deal with the measurement conventions used for Spanish ships. Then I will discuss the official rules for figuring tonnages based on those measurements. Finally, I will examine the data I have collected for more than 100 ships, both ideal and real, including the best estimates we have for Columbus's ships.

MEASUREMENT CONVENTIONS

Among those who study sixteenth and seventeenth century maritime history, it is generally known that the Spanish used five principal measures to define their ships: beam, keel, length, floor, and depth. Unfortunately, it would appear that we have missed important variations in the meaning of these terms, particularly depth. The problem becomes clear by examining the definitions of each of the terms and by taking a fresh look at one of the most famous early nautical treatises, the *Instrucción náutica* of Diego García de Palacio.

Official Spanish regulations for calculating ship tonnages (by the process called *arqueamiento*) ordinarily specified where to take the measures. For example, the regulations published in 1590 assumed that the decks had not yet been planked, and established procedures for measuring with lines stretched from point to point inside the hull.[1] Rejecting this approach, the 1607 regulations called for taking measurements at the lower deck, "and not in the air as heretofore has been done."[2] When historical documents or nautical treatises provide us with some or all of the measures, it is an easy matter to calculate ratios and compare them with similar ratios for other ships, both ideal and real. First, however, we must know exactly what was meant by the measures, and which set of regulations governed them.

The beam (*manga*), defined as the widest point of the hull, was enclosed by the master ribs. At times the beam would correspond to the breadth at the lower deck. At other times it would be situated above or below the lower deck, though its official measurement would normally be taken on the deck itself. Apart from that, the definition of the beam was straightforward, with more or less exact counterparts in other nations. (See Figures 1 and 2 for ship diagrams.)

The keel (*quilla*) or spine of the ship included only the straight portion of the timbers forming it, measured from the outside. The sloping stempost (*roda*) and sternpost (*codaste*) were not included. The definition of the keel did not change over time, and, like the beam, it had more or less exact equivalents in other nations.

Length (*esloria*) was another matter. In Spanish usage, the length of the ship was generally measured on the lower deck, from stem to stern. The length and the keel had a relationship customarily defined in two parts. The so-called *lanzamiento a proa* was the forward extension of the lower deck beyond the keel. The *lanzamiento a popa* was the aft extension. Adding both *lanzamientos* to the keel gave the length or *esloria*. For Spanish galleons of the early seventeenth century, the forward extension was generally about double the aft extension, giving the ships a pronounced forward rake.[3] There is no English equivalent of the *esloria*, as those in the field know well.[4] The English "length overall," as described in a document from 1637, included the distance from the fore-end of the beakhead to the aft end of the stern,[5] a considerably longer measure than the *esloria*. Continental nations seem to have used a measure of length closer to Spanish than to English usage,[6] and any comparisons of ship lengths and the ratios of length to beam must take these varying definitions into account.

The floor (*plan*) in Spanish usage was measured at the bottom curves of the master ribs, as if the distance between them were flat. Like the other measures, the floor was best measured before the ship was finished. Once planking was in place above the bilge, it was much more difficult to gauge precisely.

The definitions of these four measures changed little over the centuries, though the formulas for deriving tonnage from them were revised several times.[7] Thus, historians studying the evolution of ship design in the sixteenth and seventeenth centuries can confidently compare ratios of keel to beam or length to beam from one period to another.

Quite a different conclusion emerges from a close examination of the fifth measure — the depth (*puntal*) — and what it meant to Diego García de Palacio and others. García de Palacio published the first full-blown treatise on shipbuilding — his *Instrucción náutica* — in Mexico City in 1587.[8] The Portuguese manuscript of Fernando de Oliveira, evidently written in about 1565, was not published until the late nineteenth century,[9] and the 1575 manuscript of Juan Escalante de Mendoza[10] was far less detailed about ships than García's analysis. The *Instrucción náutica* remains an invaluable guide to a wide range of topics in early modern maritime history, from the design of ships to the duties of officers and crew members.

In the course of his analysis, García shared his notions of ideal ship proportions. Dealing with a merchant vessel (*nao*) of 400 *toneladas*,[11] he presented four of the five principal measures in turn, accompanying his text with illustrations drawn to scale. (See Figures 1 and 2.) For a beam of 16 Spanish *codos* (each one 22 inches or about 565 mm), the ship should have a keel of 34 *codos*, a length of 51.33 *codos*, and a depth of 11.5 *codos*.[12] This meant the ship would have had a keel to beam ratio of 2.13, a length to beam ratio of 3.21, and a depth to beam ratio of 0.72. The first two ratios follow closely the traditional proportions for merchant shipping in the Mediterranean of "as, dos, tres," in which every unit of beam was matched by two units of keel and three units of length on deck.[13] Such typical merchant "round" ships contrasted quite sharply with the other famous Mediterranean vessel — the galley — which could have length to beam ratios as high as 6 or 8 to one.[14]

The third ratio derived from García's figures, that of depth to beam (0.72 to one), supports the general assumption that merchant ships in the late sixteenth century were quite deep in the hold, much deeper than Spanish ships would be just a few decades later. If this were true, a major revolution in design must have occurred between the time García wrote and the appearance of the first official regulations for Indies ships in 1607, which called for ratios of depth to beam of about 0.54 to 1. (See Table 1.) Instead, we are dealing with a discrepancy in the definition of depth, not with a revolution in design.

García stated explicitly how he had derived his figure for depth. Starting from the floor, he divided the hold into three parts. The first division ended with unplanked braces called empty bows, placed at 4.5 *codos* above the floor, equivalent to the height of three pipes (large barrels) of wine. The second division ended with the lower deck (*primera cubierta*), placed 3 *codos* above the empty bows, equivalent to the height of two pipes of wine. The third division ended with the upper deck or bridge (*puente*), 3 *codos* above the lower deck. The total of 10.5 *codos* rose to 11.5 with the thickness of the braces and planking included. Ships that carried a grating (*jareta*) above the bridge to enclose additional deck space would add another 3 *codos* to the depth.

It is obvious from this that García included in his depth measurement all the enclosed area of the hull. Just over a decade earlier, in contrast, Escalante de Mendoza had defined the depth as the distance between the floor above the keel and the first fixed deck.[15] Though Escalante did not provide a figure for depth in the ideal ship mentioned in his treatise, there is no question that his definition would be the one preferred in later Spanish usage. The 1590 regulations called for measuring the depth at about the point where the first deck would be placed, and the 1607 rules explicitly defined the depth as the distance from the floor to the top of the first deck. All of the later rules for ship measurement would follow this definition of *puntal* as the depth in the hold alone.

Some shipbuilders in the late sixteenth century may have used the inclusive definition of depth favored by García, rather than the more limited depth in the hold of Escalante. Contracts for 25 Basque *naos* built from 1545 to 1611 included specifications for the depth at the second deck, as well as at the location of the maximum breadth (beam). In many cases, however, the depth at the first deck was not even mentioned. Depth to beam ratios figured at the maximum beam ranged from 0.66 to 0.73.[16] Where the data are sufficiently complete to figure depth at the first deck, the ratios are much lower. Only seven of the *naos* had complete data. I include them in Table 2, listing their depth at the first deck. Another 12 ships that entered Spanish service ca. 1580, built by Neapolitans, Venetians, and Ragusans, show depth to beam ratios ranging from 0.52 to 0.73.[17] It is possible that more than one definition of depth was used in their measurement as well.

Without knowing the bases for individual ship measurements, we can do no more than recognize possible discrepancies in their figures for depth. We can, however, correct the figures commonly attributed to García de Palacio. In order to bring García's ideal merchant ship into line with other treatises and with official regulations, we must use his figures for depth from the floor to the top of the first deck only, rather than the full amount that he called the depth. This means 4.5 *codos*, plus 3 *codos* for the space between the floor and the deck, plus an estimate for the planking. I propose using the figure 7.75 *codos* in all. This reduces the ratio of depth to beam in García's ship from 0.72 to 0.48. It also has the merit of reconciling García's measurements with the 400 *toneladas* he attributed to the ship.[18] (See Table 1.)

The corrected depth of García's ideal merchant ship comes quite close to the figures proposed in official regulations for the Indies trade in 1607, 1613, and 1618, in which the depth to beam ratios ranged from 0.46 to 0.55 for variously sized ships. (See Table 1.) Where the government's regulations and later treatises would diverge greatly from García's *Instrucción* was in increasing the ratio of keel to beam. The seventeenth century would continue this trend, both public and private, toward lengthening the hull in all types of ships. That much we have known for some time. What is new in taking a fresh look at García's treatise is that his ideal merchant ship was not particularly deep in the hold. Nor, if we accept that the Basque *naos* and some of the Mediterranean ships mentioned above used García's definition of depth, were they particularly deep in the hold, either. In light of this, we must revise some of our notions about the configurations of ships used in sixteenth century Spain and its Indies trade. The traditional merchant "round" ship was not quite as round as we thought.

TONNAGE CALCULATIONS

There has been considerable controversy over the definition of the Spanish *tonelada*, but, according to the official regulations in 1590, it was worth

8 cubic *codos* in capacity, equal to what is sometimes called the *tonel macho* of Vizcaya, and to the old French *tonneau de mer*.[19] Thus, in the formulas developed to calculate ship tonnage, a figure for cubic *codos* was divided by 8 to yield *toneladas*.

The *tonel macho*, which could be called a ship *tonelada*, was 1.2 times larger than the merchandise *tonelada* used for the Indies trade in Seville, so that 12 merchandise *toneladas* equalled 10 ship *toneladas*. Many historians have assumed that contemporary writers such as Escalante and García used the merchandise *tonelada*, whether describing ships in general or their merchandise capacity. I would argue that this is mistaken. García clearly had the larger ship *tonelada* in mind in describing ships. Escalante seems to have used the ship *tonelada* as well, when referring generally to ships. The passage in his *Itinerario* has given rise to much confusion, as he mentions both sorts of *tonelada* together, but he differentiates their use for ships and for merchandise capacity.[20] Tonnage measures had their roots in the wine trade, and the ability of a ship to carry a certain number of wine barrels of more or less known weight. As it evolved, Spanish tonnage continued to refer to both volume and weight, as the formulas to calculate it demonstrate.

Two formulas for calculating tonnage generally held sway in Spain in the sixteenth and seventeenth centuries, and perhaps earlier as well. The version for merchant ships can be expressed as (depth times beam) divided by 2; the result times length on deck; the product divided by 8. For warships, the formula was (depth times beam) divided by 2; the result times length on deck; minus 5%; the result divided by 8; plus 20%. All measurements were in linear *codos* equal to 22 inches or 565 mm, and the final figure for both formulas was in *toneladas*. When the same ship was gauged by both formulas, it measured about 14% larger as a warship than as a merchant ship. This was not the same as the difference between the ship *tonelada* and the merchandise *tonelada*, however. The version of the formula for merchant ships (Method 1 on Tables 1 and 2) was already in *toneles machos* or ship *toneladas*. The version for warships (Method 2 on Tables 1 and 2) resulted in an additional 14%.

Both formulas attempted to solve the problem of finding a cubic measurement for something other than a cube. The first part of each formula calculated the square measure of a cross section of the ship. Beginning with the product of the depth times the beam, it halved the result to account for the shape of the hull, which narrowed progressively fore and aft of the master ribs along the length. Because warships were thought to lose more capacity than merchant ships, from more sharply narrowing hulls and more internal bracing, an additional 5% was subtracted from the square measure of their cross-sections. A fraction could also be subtracted from certain merchant ships, if their shape justified it. The square measure for the average cross section was then multiplied by the length on the first deck, giving a total measure for the hold in cubic *codos*, which was divided by 8 to yield *toneladas*.

The Spanish government instituted a new set of formulas in 1613, rescinded it in 1618, and reinstituted it in 1633. The calculations varied depending on whether the floor was equal to, greater than, or less than half the beam. The simplest version, which could be applied regardless of the ratio of floor to beam, can be expressed as: .5 depth, times (.75 beam + .5 floor), times .5 (length + keel); the result divided by 8. This gave a tonnage about 12-14% smaller than the standard method for merchant ships just mentioned, which would have favored the crown in renting ships by the *tonelada*. In other words, it marked a return to the merchandise *tonelada*. Though the new set of formulas had the merit of trying to account more accurately for the capacity of the hull, it took quite a while to be widely used. Tonnages given in the tables appended to this paper all seem to have been calculated from the earlier formulas, even the government regulations issued after the new formulas became official. Eventually, however, the new formulas would prevail.[21]

ANALYSIS OF TABLES

Keeping in mind the customary meanings of ship measurements and the methods used to calculate tonnage, we can turn to the ideal and real ships listed in Tables 1, 2, and 3. For all of the ships, the tables include their measurements in *codos*, a calculation of their tonnages as merchant (Method 1) or military (Method 2) vessels, and a set of ratios defining their overall configurations. In proposing ideal ship proportions in 1575, Juan Escalante de Mendoza started with the proportions of keel, length, and beam and derived measures for variously sized ships from those proportions.[22] Other authors began with proportions, then adjusted them incrementally according to the size of the ship. All of the ideal ship proportions presented in table 1 followed one of these two approaches. The author of the "Diálogo" written ca. 1635, for example, seems to have begun with firm ratios in mind for keel to beam and floor to beam, varying the other measures for different sized ships.

The depth measure differentiates the treatises and government regulations in Table 1 from one another. Once we have adjusted García's measures to conform to the rest, all used a depth measure for the hold alone. Everyone dealing with the problem of ideal ship proportions was well aware that a ship would vary in speed and handling, depending upon the relationship of depth to beam. Tomé Cano (1611) and the author of the "Diálogo" (ca. 1635) both favored greater depth in the hold than government regulations called for. This was due in part to the larger capacity for trade goods that a deeper hold would provide, but the authors also argued that ships would handle better with a deeper hold.[23] The government regulations of 1607 evidently shared that opinion, but later versions would require a depth equal to less than half the beam.

Tonnages calculated according to Methods 1 and 2 provide useful comparisons with tonnage figures given in the source. García (1587) was describing merchant ships, and the close correspondence of his tonnage figures and the results calculated according to Method 1 confirms this. Equally clearly, the tonnages given in the 1607 regulations had warships in mind, as many of their critics claimed. Cano applied both methods to the same ideal ship, which was common practice in reality as well, when merchant ships sailed for the crown. The 1618 regulations seem to have used a modified version of Method 2, perhaps subtracting more than the customary 5% from the square measure of the average cross section.

The ideal ships listed in Table 1 may or may not have had counterparts in the real world. The ships listed in Tables 2 and 3, on the other hand, actually existed, though we do not know all of the five principal measures for some of them. Looking over both lists, from the early fifteenth to the late seventeenth century, there are striking similarities in the shapes of the larger ships, whether they sailed as merchantmen or as warships. Over time, there was a lengthening of the keel to beam ratio, measureable from about the 1570s to the 1670s. A Basque *nao* in 1577 had a ratio of 1.94, and a galleon built in Basoanaga in the Basque region in 1668 had a ratio of 2.86. We might assume that warships were always sleeker than ordinary merchant *naos*, but the documents do not support such an assumption. The list of 21 ships being repaired in Seville in 1625 had an average keel to beam ratio higher than that of six galleons built for the crown for military duty and measured in 1627.

The ratio of length to beam did not show any clear trend. Though the Basoanaga galleon of 1668 was longer on deck than all but a few of the other ships on the list, there was not a clear trend toward a general lengthening over time. The 12 ships built by Venetians, Neapolitans, and Ragusans, measured in 1580 for Spanish service, showed higher length to beam ratios than many later ships, including the warships measured in 1603 and 1627. The 12 foreign ships had shorter keel to beam ratios than those same ships, however, and a narrower floor, suggesting design differences between Spain and areas farther east in the Mediterranean. Even omitting them from consideration, there was no clear trend in the length to beam ratio.

It is difficult to compare the total tonnages and cargo space among all the ships listed, due to possible variations in the definition of depth, as discussed above. I suspect that any ship with a depth to beam ratio much over 0.60 included all the space in the hull as the depth. We must be very careful, therefore, not to assume that ships are directly comparable, unless we can know, or infer, the basis of their measurements.

The persons figuring tonnages in the sources used fractions, not decimals, and they had some discretion in deciding whether or not to apply the full formula. That explains a certain variation between my calculations and the figures given in the sources. Most of the given figures fall much closer to one method than the other, however. Bertendona's warships were undoubtedly measured by Method 2 in 1603; the 21 ships listed in Seville in 1625 were undoubtedly measured by Method 1, as merchant ships. How the source measured it is not a foolproof guide to a ship's function, however. The six galleons measured in 1627, though warships, had their tonnage calculated by the formula for merchant ships.

The foreign ships measured in 1580 raise different but related questions. Some of the figures given in the source are quite close to either Method 1 or 2. Others diverge from the nearest calculation by greater or lesser amounts (all but one positive), ranging from - 3.7% to + 24.8%. A certain tendency of given tonnages to cluster at even 100s suggests that some of the ships were roughly estimated rather than calculated. There is no consistency in the variations, so it is unlikely that a different formula was being used. The problem is the same with the Italian ships listed in Table 3, for which I converted Venetian feet to *codos* and Venetian *botte* to *toneladas*.[24] If my conversions are correct, the *nave* listed for 1420 fits plausibly within the same range as the Spanish ships. The *nave* listed for 1608 does not. It seems to have far too little depth and length to supply the tonnage given in the source. Similar doubts apply to the Venetian *naves* listed for 1550, 1591, 1597, and 1599, though there is not enough information to know for certain what caused the variations.

Used with caution, the formulas I have called Method 1 and 2 can serve as preliminary tests of the accuracy of a set of ship measures, if we assume that they can apply not only to Spanish ships, but to others as well. Calculated from trustworthy figures for known ships, they can also provide clues for estimating the configurations of unknown ships. For example, *La Couronne*, a French warship in service in 1636, was considered enormous, widely reported to have a capacity of 2,000 *toneladas*.[25] One Spanish naval commander remarked that a ship of such size was "never before seen on the sea."[26] Unfortunately, we lack precise measurements for *La Couronne*, and the estimates commonly accepted[27] seem too small to describe a ship of such magnitude. Comparing those figures with the proportions in contemporary Spanish warships suggests that *La Couronne* should be given more depth. As an experiment, if we take *La Couronne's* beam and assign other measurements according to Spanish warship proportions, its estimated tonnage is much more plausible. In fact, it is very close to the 2,000 *toneladas* that justified the vessel's reputation.

A similar process can be applied to estimate much earlier ships, comparing theoretical reconstructions of their proportions and tonnages with those of known ships, official regulations, and tonnage formulas. Despite the unquestionable changes in ship design during these centuries, the similarities outweigh the differences and encourage confidence in this comparative method, at least as an approximation. The measures of the *San Esteban* in Table 2, wrecked in 1554 off the Texas coast, have been estimated using quite fragmentary remains. The result is not very satisfactory.

The tonnage calculated by Method 1, based on those estimates, seems far too small for the contents the ship carried on that final voyage.[28] It is also much smaller than the tonnage listed in contemporary sources.[29] Based on this preliminary test, the estimated measures for the *San Esteban* need to be revised.

Which brings me back full circle to Columbus's ships. Two well-known modern estimates for the ships' configurations come from Carlos Etayo Elizondo and José María Martínez-Hidalgo Terán, revising the estimates of several other scholars from the late nineteenth century onward.[30] Etayo claims there were two different *Niñas* on Columbus's first two voyages. He also calculated the measures of all three ships on the first voyage as considerably smaller than previous authors had argued. Etayo based his estimates on a close and careful reading of contemporary sources, including Escalante's remark that Columbus's ships were small, with the largest "very little larger than 100 *toneladas*."[31] Assuming that Escalante's figures were in the *toneladas* used in Seville for merchandise, and not the *toneles machos* of Vizcaya that Measured 1.2 times larger, he adjusted his figures accordingly. Etayo also assumed that García de Palacio used the *tonelada* of Seville. His final figures are provided in Table 2, and he believed so strongly in them that he sailed the Atlantic in a reconstruction of the *Niña* he envisioned.[32] The verdict thus far, however, is that there was only one *Niña* and that Etayo's estimates are too small, for a variety of reasons.

Martínez-Hidalgo's reconstructions have generally been preferred. His estimates for the *Santa María*, based on the conclusion that the ship was a *nao*, fall well within the range for *naos*, both real and ideal, in Tables 1 and 2. He accepted Escalante's estimate for the tonnage of the *Santa María* without revision. The result is a *nao* supposedly measuring 105.9 *toneladas*.[33] By Method 1, however, it measures nearly 2.4 times that size, as Table 2 demonstrates. I would agree with Etayo that Martínez-Hidalgo's figures for the *Santa María* are too high. Martínez-Hidalgo's estimates for the *Pinta* and the *Niña* were based on proportions for caravels in the Portuguese *Livro nautico*.[34] That is certainly plausible, and the tonnages he gives are plausible as well — about 61 *toneladas* for the *Pinta* and 53 for the *Niña*. The problem, however, is that his measurements indicate far larger tonnages, when calculated by Method 1.

How can we solve the dilemmas presented by every estimate of Columbus's ships so far? The answer, it seems to me, lies in the use of contemporary methods of measuring ship tonnages and in the study of contemporary ship configurations. Surprisingly, neither Etayo nor Martínez-Hidalgo made use of what I have called Method 1, which was the official method of gauging Spanish ships from 1590 on, and was undoubtedly in use much earlier. García de Palacio used Method 1 for the ideal ships in his treatise. The correspondence between the figures he gave and calculations by Method 1 are too close to permit another interpretation. And Method 1, as we know from the discussion above, calculated tonnage in the *tonel macho* of Vizcaya. That is an important point. Etayo was mistaken in thinking García used the smaller merchandise *tonelada*.

Furthermore, as I maintain above, Escalante used the *tonel macho* as well, which had become standard for gauging ships by the time he wrote. The smaller *tonelada* of Seville seems to have been used when merchandise capacity was the central concern Though the same ship could be described by several different measures, contemporaries knew the difference. After the passage of several centuries, we no longer have that knowledge and are forced to reconstruct it. With that accomplished, we can take Escalante's "very little larger than 100 *toneladas*" and proceed to a new set of estimates for Columbus's ships.

The most trustworthy information we have concerns the number of crew members on Columbus's first voyage. The late Alice Bache Gould painstakingly researched the lives of every man on the voyage and was able to confirm identification for 87 of them. With 90 as a usable minimum, she concluded that 40 men would have been on the *Santa María*, 30 on the *Pinta*, and 20 on the *Niña*, which agrees well with other estimates of the relative sizes of the three ships.[35] With the *Santa María* at just over 100 *toneladas*, the resulting manning ratio is 2.5 *toneladas* per man, a figure somewhat high but still consonant with many others for the sixteenth and seventeenth centuries.[36] Applying the same ratio to the two caravels gives us estimates of 75 *toneladas* for the *Pinta* and 50 for the *Niña*. Michele de Cuneo, who accompanied Columbus on his second voyage, wrote that the *Niña* was about 60 *toneladas*.[37] If, despite Etayo's claim, the same *Niña* sailed on both the first and second voyages, we should estimate the smallest of Columbus's three ships at somewhere between 50 and 60 *toneladas*. For the sake of argument, I will estimate it at 55.

The proportions of *naos* and caravels provide the next piece in the puzzle. A plausible set of figures for the *nao Santa María* is the simple "as, dos, tres" described above, so that the keel would be twice the beam, and the length three times the beam. The depth can be estimated at half the beam. Or, we can use Martínez-Hidalgo's proportions, which are nearly identical. We can assume that the caravels were somewhat slimmer and shallower than the *nao*, but we cannot be sure how much. To provide a range of possibilities, I will calculate three separate sets of figures: one based on the Portuguese configurations used by Martínez-Hidalgo, a second based on the 1624 corsairing frigate listed in Table 2, and a third based on the proportions that *don* Diego Brochero recommended for dispatch boats in 1608. As more information becomes available from documents and wrecks of the period, those estimates can easily be adjusted.

The final step is to insert the estimated tonnages and configurations into the formula for Method 1, using "X" as the beam, and proportions of "X" as the other measures, in *codos*. It is important that the measures all be in *codos*, because the formula depends upon the value of the *tonelada* as 8 cubic *codos*. For example, using Martínez-Hidalgo's proportions for the

Santa María, X is the beam, .49X is the depth, and 2.98X is the length on deck, with the total tonnage at 105.9 *toneladas*. The formula is then:

$$\frac{\dfrac{(0.49X)\,(X)}{2}\,(2.98X)}{8} = 105.9$$

The value of X, representing the beam, works out to 10.51 *codos*. The other dimensions come from their value in proportion to the beam. This gives a keel of 21.02, a length on deck of 31.32, and a depth in the hold of 5.15 *codos*, for the estimated tonnage of 105.9 *toneladas*. We could just as easily use the classic proportions of "as, dos, tres" and 100 *toneladas*, which would vary the final measurements slightly. My own choice is for a ship 10.5 *codos* in the beam, 21 in the keel, 31.5 in length, and 5.25 in depth, with a total of 108.5 *toneladas*.

Applying the same procedure to the two caravels, with three possible sets of measurements for each, gives the results entered on Table 2 as Phillips-1, 2, and 3, for which I used the estimate of 75 *toneladas* for the *Pinta*, and 55 *toneladas* for the *Niña*. The method works equally well for the *San Esteban* (1554), using proportions midway between "as, dos, tres" and those for García's 1587 *nao*, with the tonnage estimated by Chaunu as 200 *toneladas*. (See Table 2.)

The method I have described has the merit of estimating ships that conform to the tonnage definitions understood by contemporaries, based on the proportions of ships common at the time. Most important, it uses the calculation of tonnage that was current for Spanish ships. Much of the confusion and wildly differing estimates we have for Columbus's ships to date can be traced directly to the use of modern measures, rather than contemporary ones. Martínez-Hidalgo, Etayo, and the many other scholars who have labored over this problem have done a great service for scholarship. Their specialized knowledge of rigging and other nautical matters has made invaluable contributions to our knowledge of seafaring in the past. Yet they left nagging doubts in two of the key questions regarding Columbus's ships: how large were they and what were their configurations? By taking a closer look at the pertinent documents, I hope to have clarified those questions. If my findings are borne out by further study, they will have important implications for reconstructions of Columbus's ships now under way. They will also provide a method and comparative data for scholarly work on other historical ships as the quincentenary approaches.

NOTES

1. Cesáreo Fernández Duro, ed., *Disquisiciones náuticas*, 6 vols. (Madrid, 1876-81), 5, pp. 150-54, regulations of August 20, 1590.

2. Martín Fernández de Navarrete, comp., *Colección de documentos y manuscriptos compilados*, ed. by Julio Guillén Tato, 32 vols. (Nendeln, Lichtenstein, 1971), 23(1), doc. 47, pp. 575-93.

3. See the official regulations from 1618 in the Archivo General de Marina, Museo Naval, Madrid (hereafter AGM), Caja Fuerte 134. The regulations are reprinted in *Recopilación de leyes de los reynos de las Indias, mandadas imprimir y publicar por el Magestad católica del rey don Carlos II*, 3 vols. (Madrid, 1681; repr. Madrid: Consejo de la Hispanidad, 1943), libro 9, título 28, ley 22, 3, pp. 340-62.

4. L. G. Carṛ-Laughton, "English and Spanish Tonnage in 1588," *Mariner's Mirror* 44 (1958), 151-154.

5. Thomas Heywood, *A True Description of His Majesties Royall Ship, Built this Yeare 1637 at Wooll-witch in Kent* (London, 1637), pp. 44-48.

6. Frederic C. Lane, *Venetian Ships and Shipbuilders of the Renaissance* (Baltimore, 1934), pp. 235-37, tables giving the measurements of various European ships.

7. See the discussion of tonnage calculations below.

8. Diego García de Palacio, *Instrucción náutica para navegar* (Mexico, 1587; repr. Madrid, 1944).

9. Fernando de Oliveira, *Livro da fabrica das naos*, ed. by Henrique Lopes de Mendonca, as *O padre Fernando Oliveira e a sua obra nautica* (Lisbon, 1898).

10. Juan Escalante de Mendoza, *Itinerario de navegación de los mares y tierras occidentales* (Madrid, 1575), in Fernández Duro, *Disquisiciones náuticas*, 5, pp. 413-515. The original manuscript is in the Biblioteca Nacional, Madrid.

11. See the discussion of tonnage calculations below.

12. García de Palacio, *Instrucción náutica*, fols. 90-92. The *codo* was the standard linear measure for Spanish ships. The printed 1618 regulations in AGM, Caja Fuerte 134, contain an exact scale for a quarter-*codo*, equal to 5.5 inches. Unfortunately, the 1943 reprinted edition is photographically reduced, so that the quarter-*codo* appears shorter than it should. *Recopilación de leyes de Indias*, libro 9, título 28, ley 22, 3, p. 362.

13. This is sometimes interpreted as one unit of depth for two units of beam, and three of length, but that is less plausible.

14. G. P. B. Naish, "Ships and Shipbuilding," in *A History of Technology*, ed. Charles Singer, et al, 7 vols. (Oxford, 1954-78), 3, p. 472; Lane, *Venetian Ships and Shipbuilders*, p. 236.

15. Escalante de Mendoza, *Itinerario*, in Fernández Duro, *Disquisiciones náuticas*, 5, p. 457.

16. Michael Barkham, "Sixteenth Century Spanish Basque Ships and Shipbuilding: The Multipurpose *nao*," in *Postmedieval Boat and Ship Archeology*, ed. Carl Olof Cederlund (Stockholm, 1985), pp. 114-116.

17. AGM, Colección Navarrete, IX, doc. 27, fols. 309-10. See Table 2.

18. Applying the formula for tonnage in merchant ships (Method 1 in Table 1) to the revised measurements from García gives a result of 397.81 *toneladas*.

19. See Michel Morineau, *Jauges et méthodes de jauge anciennes et modernes* (Paris, 1966), pp. 31-34, 64, 115-16, for a useful discussion of the *tonelada*, including critiques of other interpretations of its value, and a bibliography. Morineau mentions the *tonneau de mer* as 1.42 cubic meters. Horace Doursther, *Dictionnaire universel des poids et mesures* (1840; repr. Amsterdam, 1965), p. 541, lists it as 1.4396 cubic meters. Although I agree with Morineau on the approximate value of the *tonelada*, I disagree with several other points in his argument. I plan to write a brief article on the *tonelada* soon.

20. Escalante de Mendoza, *Itinerario*, in Fernández Duro, *Disquisiciones náuticas*, 5, pp. 461-62.

21. *Recopilación de leyes de Indias*, libro 9, título 28, ley 25, 3, pp. 363-369, contains the 1613 rules. A document from 1742 repeated the formula, mentioning that 14% more should be added to warships. AGM, ms. 439, doc. 1, fols. 1-3. This was the same net difference between merchant and war vessels as in the earlier formulas.

22. Escalante de Mendoza, *Itinerario*, in Fernández Duro, *Disquisiciones náuticas*, 5, p. 457. He wrote that for every 5 *codos* of keel, a ship should have 2-1/5 *codos* of beam and 7 *codos* of length on deck.

23. Tomé Cano, *Arte para fabricar y aparejar naos (1611)*, ed. Enrique Marco Dorta (La Laguna, Canary Islands, 1964), p. 67; "Diálogo entre un vizcaíno y un montañés," (ca. 1635), in Fernández Duro, *Disquisiciones náuticas*, 6, pp. 115-16.

24. The Venetin foot, at 13.691 English inches, was equivalent to .62 *codos*. Doursther, *Dictionnaire universel*, p. 418. The Venetian *botta*, calculated by Lane at 25.51 cubic English feet in capacity, was equivalent to 1.65 *toneladas*. Lane, *Venetian Ships and Shipbuilders*, p. 246.

25. Auguste Jal, *Abraham du Quesne et la marine de son temps*, 2 vols. (Paris, 1873), 1, pp. 87-88; Cesáreo Fernández Duro, *Armada española desde la unión de los reinos de Castilla y de León*, 9 vols. (Madrid, 1895-1903), 4, p. 173.

26. From a document printed in Rafael Estrada y Arnáiz, *El Almirante don Antonio de Oquendo* (Madrid, 1943), pp. 128-30.

27. Edmond Pâris, *Souvenirs de marine*, 6 vols. (Paris, 1886-1910), 3, plates 122-24. A selection of 26 plates published in 1882 also included the *Couronne*.

28. David McDonald and J. Barto Arnold, III, eds. *Documentary Sources for the Wreck of the New Spain Fleet of 1554* (Austin, 1979), pp. 151-58, 164-68.

29. Pierre Chaunu and Huguette Chaunu, *Séville et l'Atlantique*, 8 vols. in 12 (Paris, 1955-59), 2, pp. 484-85, 520-21. The *San Esteban*, master Francisco del Huerto, was listed at an estimated 200 *toneladas*. Though Chaunu included it among the ships in the 1555 outbound fleet to New Spain, it is highly probable that this was the same ship that sank in 1554. See n. 28 above for its salvage records.

30. Carlos Etayo Elizondo, *La expedición de la "Niña II"* (Barcelona, 1963), and the same author's *Naos y carabelas de los descubrimientos y las naves de Colón* (Pamplona, 1971). José María Martínez-Hidalgo Terán, *Columbus's Ships*, ed. Howard I. Chapelle (Barre, Mass., 1966). Etayo presents an extensive analysis and critique of earlier estimates in *Naos*, pp. 217-41.

31. Escalante de Mendoza, *Itinerario*, in Fernández Duro, *Disquisiciones náuticas*, 5, p. 445.

32. Etayo, *Naos*, pp. 165, 217-18, 230, 235.

33. Martínez-Hidalgo, *Columbus's Ships*, pp. 40-42. The author argued that Escalante used the Seville "tun," but he considered that worth 8 cubic *codos* (1. 4 cubic meters). The Vizcaya ton he considered worth 1.683 cubic meters. I disagree with both these points. See n. 19 above.

34. *Ibid.*, pp. 96-100. *Livro nautico* is a common variant for the name of Fernando de Oliveira's *Livro da fabrica das naus* (ca. 1565). See n. 9 above.

35. Alicia B. Gould, *Nueva lista documentada de los tripulantes de Colón en 1492* (Madrid, 1984), pp. 53-56. This welcome volume is a compilation of articles published by Gould between 1924 and 1944. She died in 1953.

36. Carla Rahn Phillips, *Six Galleons for the King of Spain: Imperial Defense in the Early Seventeenth Century* (Baltimore, 1986), pp. 42-43, 140, and notes.

37. *Raccolta di documenti e studi pubblicati dalla Reale Commissione Colombiana* (Rome, 1892-96), III, ii, p. 103.

38. Escalante de Mendoza, *Itinerario*, 5, pp. 456-58.

39. García de Palacio, *Instrucción náutica*, fols. 90-97v.

40. Navarrete *Colección de documentos*, 23 (1), doc. 47, pp. 575-93.

41. AGM, Marqués de la Victoria, "Diccionario demonstrativo, con la configuración o anathomía de toda la architectura naval moderna," plate 5.

42. Fernández Duro, *Disquisiciones náuticas*, 5, p. 54.

43. Cano, *Arte para fabricar y aparejar naos*, pp. 66-69.

44. Gervasio Artiñano y de Galdácano, *La arquitectura naval española (en madera)* (Madrid, 1920), pp. 128-29.

45. Navarrete, *Colección de documentos*, 24 (1), doc. 15, pp. 133-42.

46. AGM, Caja Fuerte 134, printed in *Recopilación de leyes de Indias*, libro 9, título 28, ley 22, 3, pp. 340-62.

47. "Diálogo" in Fernández Duro, *Disquisiciones náuticas*, 6, pp. 111-129.

48. José Pérez Vidal, *Díaz Pimienta y la construcción naval española en el siglo XVII* (Las Palmas, 1936), pp. 24-28.

49. Artiñano, *Arquitectura naval*, pp. 128-29; *Recopilación de leyes de Indias*, libro 9, título 28, ley 23, 3, pp. 362-63, undated.

50. Artiñano, *Arquitectura naval*, pp. 128-29; *Recopilación de leyes de Indias*, libro 9, note following título 28, 3, pp. 371-72.

51. Artiñano, *Arquitectura naval*, pp. 128-29.

52. Martínez-Hidalgo, *Columbus's Ships*, p. 42.

53. Etayo, *Naos*, p. 165.

54. Calculated using Method 1, and estimated proportions and tonnages. Sources for the tonnage estimates are as follows: *Santa María*, n. 31; *Niña*, n. 37; *Pinta*, n. 35; *San Esteban*, n. 29; *La Couronne*, n. 25.

55. Institute for Nautical Archeology (INA) exhibit, Museum of Texan Cultures, San Antonio, Texas, April 1984.

56. Barkham, "Basque Ships," p. 114.

57. AGM, Colección Navarrete, IX, doc. 27, fols. 309-310.

58. Archivo General de Simancas (AGS), Contaduría Mayor de Cuentas, 3a Época, leg. 2214, no. 7.

59. AGS, Guerra Antigua, leg. 3150.

60. Archivo General de Indias, Seville (AGI), Contratación, 41-1-2/13, cited in Abbott Payson Usher, "Spanish Ships and Shipping in the Sixteenth and Seventeenth Centuries," in *Facts and Factors in Economic History: For Edwin Francis Gay* (Cambridge, Mass., 1932; repr. New York, 1967), p. 201.

61. AGS, Guerra Antigua, leg. 3149, no. 2.

62. AGM, ms. 1311, fol. 86.

63. AGM, Colección Vargas Ponce, XVII, doc. 262, fol. 454.

64. Lane, *Venetian Ships and Shipbuilders*, pp. 235-37. All but the 1608 Venetian figures list length on the second deck, not the first. The 1420 figure for beam is on the second deck as well, and there is some confusion as to where the depth was measured on all the ships.

65. Oliveira, *Livro da fabrica das naus*, pp. 178-206. The Portuguese measures have been reduced to Spanish ones, based on 1 *palmo de goa* being equal to about 250 mm or 9.8425 inches, and 1 Portuguese *tonel* being equal to 2.0754 cubic meters. The latter figure comes from Doursther, *Dictionnaire universel*, p. 541.

66. Pâris, *Souvenirs de marine*. The second set of figures results from taking the beam measurement from Pâris, then assigning the other measures according to proportions in Spanish warships of the time.

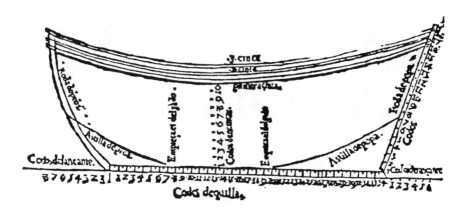

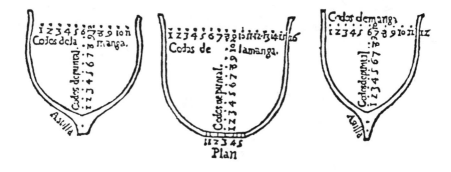

Fig. 1. Ship of 400 *toneladas*, showing its profile (top) and cross-sections of its hull at the prow, master ribs, and poop.

(García de Palacio, *Instrucción náutica*, fols. 93v-94.)

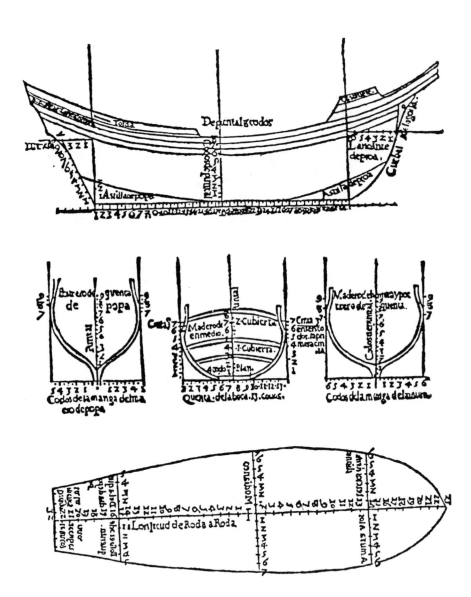

Fig. 2. Ship of 150 *toneladas*, showing its profile (top) cross-sections of the hull at the poop, master ribs, and prow (middle); and lower deck (bottom). Note that some of the labels on the lower deck illustration have been printed backwards. (García de Palacio, *Instrucción náutica*, fols. 96-97.)

Table 1
Ideal Measures and Estimated Tonnages of Ships According to Spanish Nautical Treatises and Memoranda
(linear measures in codos of 22 inches)

	Beam	Keel	Length on Deck	Depth in Hold Floor	Toneladas Method 1	Toneladas Method 2	Given in Source	Keel to Beam	Depth to Beam	Length to Beam	Floor to Beam	Source
Escalante de Mendoza (1575)	19.4	44	61.60					2.27		3.18		38
	18.5	42	58.80					2.27		3.18		
	16.7	38	53.20					2.27		3.18		
García de Palacio (1587)	16.0	34	51.33	7.75	397.81	453.50	400.00	2.13	0.48	3.21		39
	12.0	34	45.00	4.50	152.19	173.50	150.00	2.83	0.37	3.74		
Ordenanzas (1607)	19.0	47	65.00	10.00	771.88	879.94	897.38	2.47	0.53	3.42		40
	18.0	44	62.00	9.50	662.63	755.39	755.00	2.44	0.53	3.44		
	17.0	43	60.00	9.25	589.69	672.24	669.38	2.53	0.54	3.53		
	16.0	42	57.00	8.75	498.75	568.58	567.88	2.63	0.55	3.56		
	15.0	40	52.00	8.00	390.00	444.60	487.13	2.67	0.53	3.47		
	14.0	39	50.00	7.50	328.13	374.06	373.38	2.79	0.54	3.57		
Juan de Veas (ca. 1608)	15.0	42						2.80				41
	14.0	40						2.86				
	13.0	38						2.92				
	12.0	36		6.00				3.00	0.50			

87

Table 1 (continued)

Source												
Beltrán and Echevarrí (ca. 1608)	18.5	45	60.00	11.10	6.00	770.06	877.87	1000.00	2.43	0.60	3.24	42
Tomé Cano (1611)	18.0	48	46.50	7.00		244.13	278.30	232.00	2.67	0.58	3.88	43
	17.0	46						278.42	2.71			
	16.0	44							2.75			
	15.0	42							2.80			
	14.0	40							2.86			
	13.0	38							2.92			
	12.0	36							3.00			
Ordenanzas (1613)	20.0	51	66.00	10.00		825.00	940.50	833.63	2.55	0.50	3.30	44
	18.0	48	61.50	9.00		622.69	709.86	539.25	2.67	0.50	3.42	
	17.0	46	58.75	8.50		530.59	604.87		2.71	0.50	3.46	
Urquiola (ca. 1613)	14.5	36	47.00	7.00	7.00	298.16	339.90	360.00	2.48	0.48	3.24	45
Ordenanzas (1618)	20.0	49	63.00	9.50	10.00	748.13	852.86	821.88	2.45	0.48	3.15	46
	19.0	48	61.50	9.00	9.50	657.28	749.30	721.75	2.53	0.47	3.24	
	18.0	46	59.00	8.50	9.00	564.19	643.17	624.50	2.56	0.47	3.28	
	17.0	44	56.00	8.00	8.50	476.00	542.64	530.00	2.59	0.47	3.29	
	16.0	42	53.00	7.50	8.00	397.50	453.15	444.50	2.63	0.47	3.31	
	15.0	40	50.50	7.00	7.50	331.41	377.80	371.50	2.67	0.47	3.37	
	14.0	38	48.00	6.50	7.00	273.00	311.22	309.50	2.71	0.46	3.43	

Table 1 (continued)

													No.
Basque nao (1611)	14.8	30	46.00	7.67		325.26	370.79		2.00	0.52	3.12		56
Corsairing frigates (1624)	9.0	30	34.00	4.00		76.50	87.21		3.33	0.44	3.78		59
Ships Being Repaired in Seville (1625)	19.5	47	59.57	9.04	8.99	655.30	747.05	656.00	2.43	0.46	3.06	0.46	60
	19.5	49	60.11	8.78	8.99	642.23	732.14	655.00	2.53	0.45	3.09	0.46	
	19.5	46	58.24	8.78	8.99	622.25	709.36	619.50	2.38	0.45	2.99	0.46	
	19.3	48	60.74	10.00	8.99	731.16	833.52	736.00	2.51	0.52	3.15	0.47	
	19.2	45	57.82	8.88	8.51	614.53	700.56	605.00	2.34	0.46	3.02	0.44	
	18.8	47	59.57	9.04	8.99	633.76	722.49	642.00	2.49	0.48	3.16	0.48	
	18.5	47	59.04	8.88	8.99	606.52	691.43	615.00	2.56	0.48	3.19	0.49	
	18.5	47	59.04	8.78	8.51	599.69	683.65	604.00	2.56	0.47	3.19	0.46	
	17.6	45	57.45	9.04	8.51	569.66	649.41	584.00	2.56	0.52	3.27	0.48	
	17.2	44	54.79	9.20	7.98	542.82	618.81	551.50	2.46	0.53	3.18	0.46	
	17.2	42	50.00	8.51	7.98	456.88	520.84	456.00	2.53	0.50	2.91	0.46	
	16.5	42	51.86	8.19	7.50	437.74	499.02	441.00	2.55	0.53	3.14	0.45	
	16.2	41	50.69	8.51	7.23	435.96	496.99	442.00	2.38	0.46	3.13	0.45	
	16.0	38	47.98	7.29	6.97	349.99	398.99	338.50	2.60	0.51	3.00	0.44	
	15.7	41	50.85	8.03	6.97	400.41	456.47	404.75	2.77	0.58	3.24	0.44	
	15.5	43	53.35	9.04	6.97	466.61	531.94	470.00	2.54	0.48	3.45	0.45	
	15.4	39	49.47	7.34	6.49	350.17	399.20	347.00	2.71	0.58	3.21	0.42	
	15.0	41	52.39	8.67	6.97	425.83	485.45	437.50	2.58	0.51	3.49	0.46	
	14.8	38	48.30	7.50	6.49	334.85	381.73	341.50	2.74	0.55	3.27	0.44	
	14.7	40	50.32	8.03	6.97	372.00	424.08	346.00	2.85	0.54	3.42	0.47	
	14.5	41	50.53	7.82	6.49	357.36	407.39	357.75			3.49	0.45	
Average of 21 ships	17.1	43	54.39	8.54	7.83	505.03	575.74	507.14	2.55	0.50	3.19	0.46	

Table 1 (continued)

"Diálogo" (ca. 1635)												
22.0	66	80.67	12.00	11.00	1331.06	1517.40		3.00	0.54	3.67	0.50	47
21.0	63	77.00	11.50	10.50	1162.22	1324.93		3.00	0.55	3.67	0.50	
20.0	60	73.50	11.00	10.00	1010.63	1152.11		3.00	0.55	3.68	0.50	
19.0	57	69.67	10.50	9.50	868.70	990.32		3.00	0.55	3.67	0.50	
18.0	54	66.00	10.00	9.00	742.50	846.45		3.00	0.56	3.67	0.50	
17.0	51	62.50	9.50	8.50	630.86	719.18		3.00	0.56	3.68	0.50	
16.0	48	58.67	9.00	8.00	528.03	601.95		3.00	0.56	3.67	0.50	
15.0	45	55.00	8.50	7.50	438.28	499.64		3.00	0.57	3.67	0.50	
14.0	42	51.00	8.00	7.00	357.00	406.98		3.00	0.57	3.64	0.50	
Díaz Pimienta (ca. 1645)												
18.5	55	67.00	9.50	9.50	735.95	838.99		2.97	0.51	3.62	0.51	48
Ordenanzas (1666)												
18.5	53	65.00	8.75	9.58	657.62	749.68	700.00	2.86	0.47	3.51	0.52	49
17.5	50	62.00	8.25	9.00	559.45	637.78	500.00	2.86	0.47	3.54	0.51	
Ordenanzas (1679)												
19.0	56	67.50	9.25	9.75	741.45	845.25	800.00	2.92	0.49	3.55	0.51	50
Garrote (1691)												
22.0	66	75.62	8.69		903.56	1030.06	894.25	3.00	0.40	3.44	0.51	51
18.0	54	61.80	7.14		496.41	565.91	487.88	3.00	0.40			

Table 2
Measures and Estimated Tonnage of Real Ships Using Spanish Measuring Conventions
(linear measures in codos of 22 inches)

	Beam	Keel	Length on Deck	Depth in Hold	Floor	Toneladas# Method 1	Toneladas# Method 2	# Given in Source	Keel to Beam	Depth to Beam	Length to Beam	Floor to Beam	Source
SANTA MARÍA (1492)													
Martínez-H	14.0	28	41.84	6.82		250.39	285.45	105.90	2.00	0.49	2.98		52
Etayo	10.2	18	25.05	7.64		122.01	139.09		1.79	0.75	2.46		53
Phillips	10.5	21	31.50	5.25		108.53	123.72		2.00	0.50	3.00		54
PINTA (1492)													
Martínez-H	12.0	29	37.32	5.18		144.63	164.87	60.91	2.39	0.43	3.12		52
Etayo	7.3	17	22.37	3.94		40.38	46.03		2.29	0.54	3.05		53
Phillips-1	9.6	23	30.08	4.14		75.03	85.53		2.39	0.43	3.12		54
Phillips-2	9.0	30	33.91	3.95		75.09	85.61		3.33	0.44	3.78		54
Phillips-3	8.5	30	35.70	3.98		75.13	85.65		3.50	0.47	4.22		54
NIÑA (1492)													
Martínez-H	11.4	27	35.63	4.96		126.14	143.80	52.72	2.40	0.43	3.12		52
Etayo	6.0	15	20.85	3.51		27.49	31.34		2.56	0.58	3.47		53
Phillips-1	8.7	21	27.14	3.74		55.19	62.92		2.40	0.43	3.12		54
Phillips-2	8.1	26	30.58	3.56		55.04	62.75		3.21	0.44	3.78		54
Phillips-3	7.6	27	32.16	3.58		54.83	62.51		3.50	0.47	4.22		54
SAN ESTEBAN (1554)													
	10.8	23	36.60	5.18		127.97	145.89	200.00	2.13	0.48	3.39		55
Phillips	12.8	26	39.78	6.28		200.17	228.19		2.06	0.49	3.10		54
Basque nao (1577)	16.8	33	57.00	9.50		566.88	646.25		1.94	0.57	3.40		56

Table 2 (continued)

SANTIAGO* (ca. 1580)	20.5	45	64.00	13.50	7.25	1107.00	1261.98	1050.00	2.17	0.66	3.12	0.35	57
SANTÍSSIMA TRINIDAD Y SAN VICENTE* (ca. 1580)	19.0	44	63.00	10.50	6.30	785.53	895.51	1000.00	2.29	0.55	3.32	0.33	57
SAN GERÓNIMO* (ca. 1580)	19.8	47	65.50	13.50	7.50	1091.50	1244.31	1200.00	2.38	0.68	3.32	0.38	57
SAN PEDRO* (ca. 1580)	19.5	46	65.00	13.25	7.25	1049.65	1196.60	1060.00	2.33	0.68	3.33	0.37	57
SAN MATEO Y SAN FRANCISCO* (ca. 1580)	19.0	42	62.00	10.50	6.30	773.06	881.29	900.00	2.23	0.55	3.26	0.33	57
SANTA MARÍA LA ANUNCIADA* (ca. 1580)	18.8	41	60.00	10.00	6.00	703.13	801.56	900.00	2.19	0.53	3.20	0.32	57
SAN SALVADOR* (ca. 1580)	18.5	40	60.50	10.30	6.20	720.52	821.39	900.00	2.16	0.56	3.27	0.34	57
SAN PEDRO Y PABLO+ (ca. 1580)	18.5	41	59.75	10.00	6.00	690.86	787.58	900.00	2.20	0.54	3.23	0.32	57
SANTA MARÍA DE LORETO* (ca. 1580)	18.3	39	53.50	11.00	5.75	673.10	767.33	800.00	2.13	0.60	2.92	0.31	57
SANTO ESPÍRITO* (ca. 1580)	17.8	38	51.00	9.30	5.50	526.18	599.84	700.00	2.14	0.52	2.87	0.31	57

Table 2 (continued)

SANTÍSSIMA TRINIDAD+ (ca. 1580)	15.0	38	53.50	11.00	5.75	551.72	628.96	700.00	2.50	0.73	3.57	0.38	57
SANTA MARÍA Y SAN JUAN BAPTISTA++ (ca. 1580)	15.0	33	52.50	8.00	5.30	393.75	448.88	560.00	2.17	0.53	3.50	0.35	57
Basque nao (1584)	15.0	28	46.00	8.75		377.34	430.17		1.87	0.58	3.07		56
Basque nao (1585)	16.5	30	53.00	7.75		423.59	482.89		1.82	0.47	3.21		56
Basque nao (1596)	15.0	27	47.00	7.00		308.44	351.62		1.80	0.47	3.13		56
Basque nao (1600)	14.0	28	43.00	8.50		319.81	364.59		2.00	0.61	3.07		56
Basque nao (1601)	16.0	31	51.00	9.50		484.50	552.33		1.94	0.59	3.19		56
Bertendona's warships (1603)	18.8		60.50	10.90		774.85	883.33	889.63		0.58	3.12		58
	17.4		55.25	8.80		528.74	602.77	605.67		0.50	3.18		
	16.6		53.30	8.75		483.86	551.61	551.50		0.53	3.21		
	16.3		52.50	9.00		481.36	548.75	549.86		0.55	3.22		
	16.2		53.67	8.50		461.90	526.56	535.75		0.52	3.31		
	15.6		48.50	8.25		390.12	444.74	444.33		0.53	3.12		
	15.3		47.30	8.00		361.85	412.50	413.75		0.52	3.09		
	10.2		36.30	5.33		123.34	140.61	140.50		0.52	3.56		
	10.1		37.20	4.75		111.54	127.16	127.40		0.47	3.68		

Table 2 (continued)

N.S. BEGOÑA (1627)	18.0	44	56.75	8.50	8.50	542.67	618.65	541.50	2.44	0.47	3.15	0.47	61
SAN FELIPE (1627)	18.0	44	56.00	8.50	8.50	535.50	610.47	537.38	2.47	0.47	3.11	0.47	61
SAN JUAN BAPTISTA (1627)	17.0	42	53.50	8.00	8.00	454.75	518.42	455.75	2.47	0.47	3.15	0.47	61
LOS TRES REYES (1627)	17.0	42	53.33	8.00	8.00	453.31	516.77	455.00	2.47	0.47	3.14	0.47	61
SANTIAGO (1627)	15.2	38	49.50	7.12	7.00	334.82	381.69	338.50	2.50	0.47	3.26	0.46	61
SAN SEBASTIÁN (1627)	15.0	38	48.67	7.17	7.00	327.15	372.96	330.25	2.53	0.48	3.24	0.47	61
ENCARNACIÓN (1646)	17.1	47	58.00	8.75	8.56	542.39	618.33	557.00	2.75	0.51	3.39	0.50	62
Basoanaga galleon (1668)	18.5	53	66.00	8.25	9.67	629.58	717.72		2.86	0.45	3.57	0.52	63

Table 3

Measures of Selected Ships from Non-Spanish Sources

Ship												
Mediterranean Cog, c. 1410								2.50	0.49	3.60		64
Venice nave (1420)	16.7	40	58.90	5.42		333.20	379.85	303.00	2.41	0.32	3.53		64
Venice round ship, 1450	15.5	45		6.82	5.58			303.00	2.92	0.44		0.36	64
Venice nave (1550)	12.4	31		4.03	4.34				2.50	0.33		0.35	64
Venice galleon (ca. 1550)									2.70	0.45	3.60		64
Portugal nau (ca. 1565)	21.5	48	64.42	9.84	8.05	850.60	969.69	864.99	2.25	0.46	3.00	0.37	65
Burlioni nave (1591)	14.3	34		4.34	3.72			504.24	2.39	0.30		0.26	64
Steffano nave (1597)	12.4	33		3.72	4.03			363.64	2.63	0.30		0.27	64
Casotti nave (1599)	15.5	33		4.96				424.24	2.12	0.32			64
Steffano nave (1608)	13.0		40.92	3.72		141.32	161.11	300.00		0.29	3.14		64

Table 3 (continued)

LA COURONNE
(Fr. warship)
(ca. 1636)

26.4	69	87.75	9.69		1402.99	1599.41	2000.00	2.62	0.37	3.32	66
26.4	69	86.62	12.41	12.41	1773.67	2022.75	2000.00	2.62	0.47	3.28	0.47	54

---

*   Built by a Neapolitan
+   Built by a Venetian
++   Built by a Ragusan
#   Tonnages are calculated using two decimal places for each of the linear measures. Some of these are rounded off to conserve space in the table.

BIBLIOGRAPHY

Artiñano y de Galdácano, Gervasio. *La arquitectura naval española (en madera)*. Madrid, 1920.

Barkham, Michael. "Sixteenth Century Spanish Basque Ships and Shipbuilding: The Multipurpose *nao*." In *Postmedieval Boat and Ship Archeology*. Edited by Carl Olof Cederlund. Stockholm: Swedish National Maritime Museum, Report No. 20, 1985.

Cano, Tomé. *Arte para fabricar y aparejar naos (1611)*. Edited by Enrique Marco Dorta. La Laguna, Canary Islands: Instituto de Estudios Canarios, 1964.

Carr-Laughton, L. G. "English and Spanish Tonnage in 1588," *Mariner's Mirror* 44 (1958), 151-154.

Chaunu, Pierre, and Huguette Chaunu, *Séville et l'Atlantique*. 8 vols. in 12. Paris: A. Colin, 1955-59.

"Diálogo entre un vizcaíno y un montañés," (ca. 1635). In Fernández Duro, *Disquisiciones náuticas*, 6, pp. 115-16.

Doursther, Horace. *Dictionnaire universel des poids et mesures* (1840). Reprinted Amsterdam: Meridian Publishing Co., 1965.

Escalante de Mendoza, Juan. *Itinerario de navegación de los mares y tierras occidentales* (Madrid, 1575), in Fernández Duro, *Disquisiciones náuticas*, 5, pp. 413-515.

Estrada y Arnáiz, Rafael. *El Almirante don Antonio de Oquendo*. Madrid: Espasa Calpe, 1943.

Etayo Elizondo, Carlos. *La expedición de la "Niña II"*. Barcelona: Plaza y Janes, 1963.

——————. *Naos y carabelas de los descubrimientos y las naves de Colón*. Pamplona, 1971.

Fernández Duro, Cesáreo. *Armada española desde la unión de los reinos de Castilla y de León*. 9 vols. Madrid, 1895-1903.

Fernández Duro, Cesáreo, ed., *Disquisiciones náuticas*. 6 vols. Madrid: Sucesores de Rivadeneyra, 1876-81.

Fernández de Navarrete, Martín. See Navarrete.

García de Palacio, Diego. *Instrucción náutica para navegar*. Mexico, 1587; repr. Madrid: Cultura Hispánica, 1944.

Gould, Alicia B. *Nueva lista documentada de los tripulantes de Colón en 1492*. Madrid: Real Academia de la Historia, 1984.

Heywood, Thomas. *A True Description of His Majesties Royall Ship, Built this Yeare 1637 at Wooll-witch in Kent.* London, 1637.

Jal, Auguste. *Abraham du Quesne et la marine de son temps.* 2 vols. Paris: H. Plon, 1873.

Lane, Frederic C. *Venetian Ships and Shipbuilders of the Renaissance.* Baltimore: Johns Hopkins University Press, 1934.

McDonald, David, and J. Barto Arnold, III, eds. *Documentary Sources for the Wreck of the New Spain Fleet of 1554.* Austin: Texas Antiquities Committee, 1979.

Martínez-Hidalgo Terán, José María. *Columbus's Ships.* Edited by Howard I. Chapelle. Barre, Mass.: Barre Publishing Co., 1966.

Morineau, Michel. *Jauges et méthodes de jauge anciennes et modernes.* Paris: Armand Colin, 1966.

Naish, G. P. B. "Ships and Shipbuilding." In *A History of Technology.* Edited by Charles Singer, et al. 7 vols. Oxford: Oxford University Press, 1954-78, 3, p. 472.

Navarrete, Martín Fernández de. *Colección de documentos y manuscriptos compilados.* Edited by Julio Guillén Tato, 32 vols. Nendeln, Lichtenstein: Kraus Thompson Organization, 1971.

Oliveira, Fernando de. *Livro da fabrica das naos.* Edited by Henrique Lopes de Mendonca, as *O padre Fernando Oliveira e a sua obra nautica.* Lisbon: Academia Real das Sciencias, 1898.

Pâris, Edmond. *Souvenirs de marine.* 6 vols. Paris: Gautiers Villars, 1886-1910. A selection of 26 plates with the same title was published in 1882.

Pérez Vidal, José. *Díaz Pimienta y la construcción naval española en el siglo XVII.* Las Palmas: Ediciones Canarias, 1936.

Phillips, Carla Rahn. *Six Galleons for the King of Spain. Imperial Defense in the Early Seventeenth Century.* Baltimore: The Johns Hopkins University Press, 1986.

Raccolta di documenti e studi pubblicati dalla Reale Commissione Colombiana. Rome: Ministerio della pubblica istruzione, 1892-96.

Recopilación de leyes de los reynos de las Indias, mandadas imprimir y publicar por el Magestad católica del rey don Carlos II. 3 vols. Madrid, 1681; repr. Madrid: Consejo de la Hispanidad, 1943.

Usher, Abbott Payson. "Spanish Ships and Shipping in the Sixteenth and Seventeenth Centuries." In *Facts and Factors in Economic History: For Edwin Francis Gay.* Cambridge, Mass.: Harvard University Press, 1932. Reprinted New York: Russell and Russell, 1967.

Columbus and his Sailings, According to the 'Diary' of the First Voyage: Observations of a Geographer

Gaetano Ferro
Professore ordinario di Geografia e Preside della
Facoltà di Scienze Politiche dell'Università di Genova

ABSTRACT

The vicissitudes through which the manuscript of the Ship's Log of Columbus's first voyage passed are well known. A critical examination of the text shows that many problems still remain to be resolved regarding the route followed during the first crossing.

The author has examined the text from the geographic point of view, arriving at the following conclusions:

1 — The crossing was conducted depending primarily upon the naked eye, with approximate estimate of the distances which were reported on one or more nautical charts;

2 — Since all the distances traveled were over-estimated, through an error of Columbus and of the other pilots, the distances which the Admiral indicated to the crew — intentionally understated — turned out, in reality, to be fairly close to the true distances traveled;

3 — The use of instruments was very limited; the author rules out the possibility that Columbus used a certain table, the "taoleta de marteloio". His errors in latitude were intentional, determined by political reasons, in order to conceal from the Portuguese the true position of lands discovered;

4 — It is fairly certain, even notably reliable, that Columbus landed in the Bahamas and, in particular, at San Salvador;

5 — The use of nautical and geographic terms depends largely on the Portuguese and on the *lingua franca* in use in the ports of Europe, especially of Mediterranean Europe.

On the whole, Columbus's geographic and naturalistic knowledge doesn't turn out to be very deep or nearly complete.

For any consideration of Columbus's capacities as a sailor and for any reconstruction of the techniques of navigation which he applied, the *Ship's Diary* of the first voyage remains the essential — almost the sole — document. In fact, for his other oceanic crossings we have only fragments of reports and news received either indirectly or after having passed through many hands. And about the sailings undertaken before the transatlantic enterprises we know even less. For these we have only rough and sometimes questionable indications.

All these facts have provoked a renewed interest in a critical re-examination of this indispensable source, which has already been the subject of in-depth studies by Morison and Taviani.[1] For your speaker, as a geographer, such a re-examination is concerned with only certain geographical aspects regarding the ocean and the routes, with some reference to the maps and instruments employed.[2]

First of all, however, I want to recall some well-known circumstances: to wit, that which we have in our possession and upon which we are constrained to base ourselves is only a transcription — summary of the original itself by Columbus. This original was jealously kept in the archives of Ferdinand and Isabella. But, it can't even be ruled out that the original contained some intentionally falsified fact or even that it omitted news communicated only by word of mouth or at a later time.[3] Certainly, elaborations of that kind and, errors in part unintentional, in part intentional — existed in the copies that the various court scribes made of the original.[4]

We arrived, thus, at the summary-transcription of Father Bartolomé de las Casas, more summary than transcription, made in his own hand, as today I am inclined to believe, and as, it seems to me, is today generally accepted.[5]

To complete this work of selection, transcription and summary he added some glosses and notes which some unwary editor has mixed into the text of the *Diary*. The Dominican bishop was driven by the desire to prepare materials useful for his *Historia de las Indias*.[6] Besides, he had very precise ideas about the final purpose for which said work was intended: a substantial defense of the "Indians" against their Iberian conquistadors. To all this must be added, lastly, the fact that Las Casas, of Humanist formation, had not much familiarity with the natural sciences, geography, astronomy and nautical technique.

Therefore, our Author reports, copying long excerpts about the populations of the Antilles, their habits and their good natures, in their entirety, or nearly so, while, on the other hand, he summarizes in notations of a few dry and concise lines, the stages of the voyage during the return trip, except for the detailed account of the storm near the Azores. (Also, for the period from 11 October to 24 October the transcription is faithful and complete, at least as far as we can know, but with limited references to the navigation and with few geographical observations; while yet, at the same time, the period from the seventh to the eleventh of November [inclusive] is completely omitted.)

When the narration contained in the *Diary* coincides with that reported by Las Casas in his *Historia*, by their same facts and places, we have a further proof of the authenticity of the text, together with evidence that it appeared exhaustive and convincing enough for the Dominican bishop. On the other hand, in those places in the *Historia* where he adds greater detail or other particulars or his own digressions, with respect to the account of the *Diary*, one can only think (this isn't to say it must always or necessarily be so) that the text by Columbus did not turn out to be sufficiently exhaustive or satisfying to suit his purposes.

The above offers me an opportunity to wish for an expansion of the critical re-examination of the *Diary* even to the other sources, with synoptic (comparative) editions of the *Diary*, the *Historia* of Las Casas and of the *Historias* of King Ferdinand. My colleague, Professor Alessandro Martinengo, of the University of Pisa, has offered a sample — not yet complete — of this edition and it leads to very interesting results, above all from linguistic and literary points of view. But I don't want to venture, here, into an area which lies outside my own field of expertise.

In any case, it is by now certain (at least it seems certain to me) that what has come down to us of the *Diary* in its form as a text in part (the lesser part) transmitted intact and in part summarized by Las Casas, is authentic. The reservations put forward in the past, in this context, by polemical hypercritics have all, or almost all, fallen by the wayside. I believe that our colleague, Consuelo Varela, author of valuable studies on the Columbian sources and present here today, can confirm my opinion.[7] Even more certainly, it seems to me that if Las Casas could have been author of interventions and, on some occasions, of deformations with respect to the manuscript which he had before him, these ought not to have pertained to those passages concerning the nautical art, geography, astronomy and the natural sciences, disciplines with which he lacked sufficient knowledge, as has been seen. If anything, he couldn't understand these passages; for that reason in some cases he himself put forward reservations.

More than one error in the transcription of the cardinal points for the orientation followed on the various legs of the journey and confusion between "northwest" and "northeast," "southwest" and "southeast" can be found.[8] Thus even some errors are found in the transcription of the indications of distances, which the Admiral expresses almost always in leagues, after the Spanish manner; but, evidently because he has not entirely forgotten the custom of the Italians — used to expressing themselves in miles — sometimes those values are reported,[9] the case being rare, however, of an indication given only in miles.[10] However, when such a unit of measure is used it is always preceded by the indication of the average hourly velocity, this latter indication being always expressed in miles per hour,[11] as if Columbus's estimate of the distance traveled came more easily and more familiarly to him by making reference first to the mile and taking it as his point of departure for later calculating the number of leagues. Nor are errors lacking, evidently of transcription, even among these calculations.[12]

The proofs of the authenticity of this document and of its, albeit partial but substantial, adherence to the original text are diverse. Among them are the many ingenuous statements and the many repetitions of the enthusiastic description full of wonderment which Columbus gives of the new land-scapes, revealing, among other things, a limited imagination and a capacity for comparisons conditioned by a not very broad geographic culture.[13]

Even the fairly frequent contradictions into which the Admiral falls, such as, for example, praising Martín Alonso Pinzón at the start, then later frequently condemning his behavior and his person, or stating in the preamble that his (Columbus's) boats were "very apt" for the undertaking of discovery, only to lament, later, after the shipwreck of the Santa María, that she wasn't fit "for the task of discovery"[14] — these contradictions, I repeat, are well explained by considering the *Diary* as a collection of entries, written day by day, under the influence of the emotion of the moment, while the preamble must have been drawn up and added later, written as it is in a much more careful way in an almost courtly and elevated style.

Certainly the Columbian document is the first and the prototype of this genre, before the 1524 order of Philip II imposed upon the Spanish ships the keeping of regular journals of the more important sailings completed. In fact, even the *roteiros* of the Portuguese and those of the Arab ships' pilots which aided them in their voyages through the Indian Ocean are another thing, sometimes — as is the case with the Arab ones — written in verse, sometimes — the Portuguese ones — more similar to the medieval pilot-books of the Mediterranean. (The oldest *roteiros* that are known are in manuscripts of the sixteenth century, but it is known that some existed in the fifteenth century and perhaps even before, the texts probably being reproduced and brought up to date, from draft to draft and generation to generation.) One could say that, while for the "routine" sailing, on the internal seas or along stretches of coast already well-known, like those of Western Africa, sailors continued to use the nautical "guides," centuries old and limited to indications which could facilitate the practice of navigation, the new experiences of the transatlantic expeditions were entrusted to diaries and journals which could give an account — as much as possible —of the various and rich details of the discovered lands.

There has been cited as proof of the unreliability (or of the scant reliability) of the *Diary* the circumstance that, to a crew at least a little expert in matters of the sea or — at the least — to the ship's pilots and to the other officials of the expedition, the artifice invented by Columbus of the double calculation of the distances could not remain hidden. Now, it is the *Diary* itself which shows how that was possible by attesting to how the ship's pilots disagreed among themselves about the assessment of the distances: an example of this occurs on the date of the twentieth of September when, while the fleet was relatively near the Canary Islands, there is a discrepancy of 20 leagues between the estimate of the lead ship and that of the Pinta and of another 20 leagues between the Pinta's and that of the Niña — on the whole a difference of approximately 10 percent, with respect to the course traveled to that date. And during the return trip, on the tenth of February, Victor Yañez and another three pilots believed they were sailing "much

102

beyond the Azores to the east," while "the Admiral finds himself considerably off course, finding himself very much behind them . . ." (believing
himself to have scarcely arrived at the longitude of the island of Flores, in
the Western Azores).[15]

For the rest, the summation of the distances indicated as traveled from
day to day (such data isn't supplied for the Saltes-Canaries leg nor for the
Lisbon-Saltes leg, evidently because they were already known as it has
already been noted) doesn't always correspond to the total distances
traveled which Columbus sometimes indicated. Still, on September 19 the
total distance indicated by the Admiral is 400 leagues, but the one that one
arrives at by adding all the partial journal data is 436 leagues; similarly, on
the first of October, the *Diary* gives as a total figure 707 leagues; the sum of
the partial data is 675 leagues or slightly more, if one adds the fractions
(Don Fernando in the *Historie* says that instead, according to the pilot of
the Niña, 540 leagues had been traveled while, according to the pilot of the
Pinta, 634.) And other computational errors are found during the return
voyage, for example, on the twenty-first and twenty-second of January.[16]

Taken together, therefore, the estimated data of distances traveled
inferable from the *Diary* must be considered as approximate and must be
used with great prudence. In one of my papers at the Fourth International
Congress of Columbian Studies, in Genoa, October of last year, I repeated[17]
that Columbus's navigation was always carried out based on an estimate of
the longitude, and in turn was based on the estimate of the distances
covered, according to data that, as has been seen, were not agreed upon by
the various ship's pilots; the uncertainties of these data are reflected in the
fact that the verb which in the *Diary* conveys the indication of the leagues
traveled is very often in the conditional, the "hypothetical" form: "andaría"
or "andarían".

During the voyage out (and even during the return home) it seems that
no determination of latitude was made and that the pilots were limited to
controlling the heading through the use of the compass, the observation of
the North Star, and the map. It seems strange, without a doubt, that the
Diary does not even inform us of operations completed after the landfall on
San Salvador, when the quadrant and the astrolabe could have been used —
on land — with a certain good approximation, in order to attempt to
determine, through the latitude, the position of the island reached. It is
therefore reasonable to believe or suppose that such a determination was in
fact effected; but, once it was determined that Guanahani fell, according to
the Luso-Spanish accords of 1479-80 (the Treaty of Alcacoa and the Peace
of Toledo), in the zone of exclusive authority of the Portuguese, or simply
even after some well-founded suspicion in this regard had arisen, the result
must have been accurately hidden so that there is not even mention of it in
the *Diary*. In fact, the *Diary* on the thirteenth of October says only that San
Salvador is found at the latitude of the Canaries; this affirmation could have
been deduced from the total value, on the nautical charts, of the course

directions followed in the various legs of the journey; it is erroneous because the latitude of the Canaries is of about 28 degrees and that of San Salvador 22 degrees (but, a difference of 6 degrees can't be called relevant in those times, especially if derived from a determination of latitude effected through the measurement of the height of the stars); in any case it is confirmed by a note of Father Las Casas ("The islet . . . is at the height of that of the island of Fierro"). This supposition fits well in the question of the supposed errors that Columbus would have made in the successive determinations of the latitude of which the *Diary* speaks from the end of October to the thirteenth of December; in these cases, the notes of Las Casas warn that the datum is mistaken or unclear, that the position indicated could not correspond to the truth, but, the correct information isn't supplied or remains in blank on the manuscript. Comparing all that with meteorological observations about the temperature indicated as hot or cold and with the indications reported in the *Diary* concerning the duration of the day and night (these latter indications, three out of four times, are so grossly mistaken as to make one suspect an intentional error), I have come to the conclusion that Columbus did everything possible to hide the true position — in latitude — of the places at which he landed; the scribes that copied the *Diary* aided him in that effort and Las Casas, even though he was making his summary of such a source when new accords had already been reached between the Spain and Portugal, does nothing to supply exact data about the errors regarding the length of the day and night (and with relation to the meteorological and, above all, temperature conditions and other contradictory information he does not even take notice).

That precise data on latitude were absolutely lacking in the original of the *Diary* delivered, probably in Barcelona, by Columbus to Ferdinand and Isabella, is confirmed by the fact already noted that they — in view of the following expeditions — had to ask him to narrow down more precisely "the degrees" relative to the new lands. I must complete this scenario by saying that, as far as pertains to the alleged errors of latitude, my thesis follows the affirmations of Magnaghi and Taviani,[18] while the originality of my contribution consists of the observations about the meteorological and climatic conditions in general and the indications relative to the length of the day and night.

*　*　*　*　*

For other considerations, it is necessary for us to go back over the estimation of the distances traveled and therefore of the velocity of Columbus's ship. Las Casas already had expressed some doubt about the data reported in the *Diary* at the date of 8 October, in fact, he transcribes and summarizes in following way: at times, it appears they traveled fifteen miles per hour at night, if the letter does not deceive." Morison, in reconstructing Columbus's routes, has estimated that Columbus overestimated the distances covered on the average of 9 percent and, although more conservatively so, the same would be true even for the short crossings, like those of Crooked Island Strait and the Windward Canal.[19] For my part, I will limit myself to pointing out the evident exaggeration, speculating that the maximum speed one can hypothesize for ships like those of Columbus should vary from between 6 and 8 to 10 miles per hour.[20]

It turns out from this, at any rate, that the computation of the course traveled, believed true by the Admiral, in reality was not. If one accepts Morison's percentage, then, from the Canaries to Guanahani 982 leagues were covered, not the 1079 (or a little more, taking into account the fractions and approximations) which result from adding the journal data indicated in the *Diary*. If, instead, one keeps in mind the data of, what we might call the minor computation, that is, the one shown to the crews, one arrives at 900 leagues or a little more (for a few days, in fact, the Diary does not give news about the "discount" made to the crew).[21] So the false data was closer to reality than the true one.

I have already indicated, in other sessions[22] — and moreover it is known to all those who deal with nautical technique in the times prior to the discovery of methods and instruments for determining the longitude — what had to be the causes of such errors in the calculation of the distances traveled: the speed of the ship was estimated by observing how the vessel "slipped" (through the water), how the waves rippled and, above all, how the sails filled with the wind. In fact, Columbus wasn't able to use the depth gauge, which came into use in the first half of the sixteenth century; every leg traveled in a certain direction, during the sailing, which was exclusively and logically "by sight," was accounted by computing the elapsed time. In turn, this was measured by the sand-filled hour glass (the *ampolleta* recorded many times in the *Diary*), whose use could give rise to error, given the frequency with which the instrument had to be turned over, every half-hour; the Admiral himself attests to it, on the date of 13 December: ". . . there can be error, either because they don't turn it over quickly or something fails to occur."

At any rate, these errors in the measurement of the time mustn't have had great weight, given that a little bit of attention on the part of the sailor in charge was sufficient so that the operation was precise and the system worked. And, if there were a great "error," the total calculation of the distance traveled by Columbus would have been inferior to the one he himself held accurate (and not superior, as in reality his is). In my opinion, the major errors derive from the movements of drift which the marine currents imposed on the ships; it must have been a matter of errors all the greater, inasmuch as the system of currents in the open Atlantic were then unknown or little known, especially by one whose formation as a sailor took place in the Mediterranean.

There are signs, both direct and indirect, of such deviations many times in the *Diary*. For example, already on the ninth of September, "the sailors were steering badly, drifting over the compass point of Northwest, and even moving toward the next compass point"; and on the thirteenth "the currents were against him"; on the twenty-second "He sailed to the west northwest more or less, deviating to one side and then to the other." And, on the twenty-fifth of September, Columbus tells Martín Alonso that, if islands haven't been encountered, "the currents, which had always thrown the ship toward the northeast, must have caused it and they hadn't gone as far as the pilots were saying." During the return voyage, on the tenth of February, "the Admiral finds himself very much off his course," and, in the face of the contradictions and divergences between his computations and estimates and those of the other pilots, he says "by the grace of God, after they all see land it will be known who was traveling more true."

Having thus appraised the distances traveled and taken into consideration the headings followed, the estimate of the point reached was translated and registered on the chart. It is this operation that the pilots of the three ships make, for example, on September 19: "Here the pilots discovered their points," indicating after this the data of distances covered, divergent among the three vessels, as has been said.[23] It's evident that one can't think that these data revealed the height of the stars, the operation by which latitude is determined, in order to then calculate a distance traveled in longitude; rather, determining latitude meant different determinations and operations.

The experiences of the Portuguese, contemporary (or almost) to those of Columbus, demonstrate that it can't be strange that Columbus — during his voyage out — had crossed the Atlantic without completing one single determination of latitude. It isn't even certain, in fact, that the measurements effected in 1485 along the west coasts of Africa had been carried out at sea, but rather the opposite seems probable. Even if the astrolabe were already known to the Arabs and most assuredly to the astronomers of classical antiquity, and even if certain information about its use at sea was known to the Lusitanian navigators, not prior to 1485, it is not said anywhere, however, that satisfactory data were gathered from its use. This instrument, created for calculating, on *terra firma*, the passage of time, was complicated to use. Rather, its reduction to a relatively manageable apparatus — such that it could be used even on board ship — would be to the Portuguese's credit (or to those who worked for them). And, the Jews in the service of the Portuguese probably contributed to the dissemination of precise systems for determining the latitude by the measurement of the height of the sun and of the other stars, developing tables and guides that simplified the calculations for discovering the position of such stars in the course of the year.

True, the determinations of latitude made by Bartolomeo Díaz, in Southern Africa, in 1487, seem computed from solid ground or under the coast, with the resulting data in error by 10 degrees (at least this was the news Columbus possessed). It is true, also, that Vasco da Gama, in 1498, after having used the astrolabe on board ship, made control measurements from solid ground and with a larger apparatus.[24]

Finally, to return to Columbus, a reference to what must have been an attempt, during the return voyage, to determine latitude, with reference especially to the North Star, is contained in the *Diary* on the date of February 3: "The North Star seemed to him to be very high, as at the Cape of St. Vincent. He couldn't take the altitude with the astrolabe nor the quadrant, because the waves wouldn't allow it." But, the observation about the North Star is later contradicted on the Tenth of February — that is, a few days later — when the Admiral believes he finds himself on a route that would have carried him to Nafe (perhaps Safi, in Africa), to the north of Madeira, at a longitude very much lower.

In conclusion, therefore, there were astrolabes and quadrants on Columbus's ships; however, the data relating to the reckoning of latitude are omitted or altered and murky, almost certainly intentionally so, for political reasons; the results of the measurements carried out on board ship often lead to erroneous conclusions or conclusions which are very open to discussion, thus confirming, through the *Diary*, all that has been seen to be verified by the Portuguese.

The pages of the *Diary* relating to both the voyage out and, especially, to the return home, show how the results arrived at through such estimated navigation were approximate. On September 25, Columbus and Martín Alonso Pinzón discuss the position of the ships with respect to the Atlantic islands indicated on the map: on the seventh and the tenth of February, very divergent opinions are recorded about the position in which the Pinta and Niña find themselves; on February 15, when the Niña sights the island of Santa Maria, in the Azores, some believe that it is Madeira, and others believe they are seeing the Roca di Sintra, near Lisbon. Another erroneous reckoning of the distances, with respect to Madeira, is reported on February 27.

Probably, in order to explain such errors, it's necessary to recall the uncertainties and inexactness of the nautical charts then in use. Columbus, who was also, it seems, a map-maker, could not but know well the proto-types for the Mediterranean. But, in Lisbon and Seville he could not but compare them with the models in use in the Atlantic: all that he might have learned from his seamanship of the Ocean confirms his use in every other arena — a use which is constant in the *Diary* — of terms taken from the cardinal points in order to indicate the directions and the winds (and not of the corresponding terms *Tramontana, Scirocco*, etc., typically on the compass charts of the Mediterranean).

And on these charts, recopied from father to son, from teacher to pupil, from school to school, in which were mixed together ideas of various origins, the Atlantic islands were often or almost always in an incorrect position; some were even invented and placed there where tradition had it or where it pleased the map-maker. It is logical that the sailors, who traced the routes they had traveled, on such maps, would stumble into easy errors. Paradoxically, one can say that perhaps one of the less debatable facts of

Columbus's *Diary*, even if it has been more frequently discussed recently,[25] is the identification of Guanahani with the present-day Watling Island or San Salvador, thanks especially to the geographical fact of the existence of a lagoon at its center.

A last point which I believe worth treating, concerns the possibility that Columbus had used the "Taoletta de Martelogio" in order to avoid the course errors caused by the deviations and driftings of the ship. It was, in essence, as is known, a table (or set of tables) used in the Mediterranean to calculate the necessary route corrections. It probably had already been developed in the thirteenth century; a Genoese document of 1390 speaks of something similar to it; four editions of it are known to exist, of which the most important is the Atlas of Andrea Bianco of Venice, of the year 1436; all the copies known to us are in the Venetian dialect.

My colleague from the University of Rome, Osvaldo Baldacci, has recently and quite positively argued that Columbus made use of the *Martelogio* and asserts that a design attributable to Columbus, kept in the Columbian Library of Seville (it is an annotation to the *Imago Mundi* of Pierre d' Ailly) would be the first example known to date of a *Taoletta* simultaneously graphic and numeric.[26] I don't wish to discuss this second point, although in my opinion, this drawing simply refers to a quadrant.

I want only to dwell on the point of the use of the *Martelogio* by Columbus, which, in another place[27] I had judged possible, even if it is to be noted that the *Diary* never speaks about it. A rereading of the *Diary*, however, has convinced me that such a possibility doesn't exist or is very remote, so great are the errors in the reckoning of the distances covered and the headings followed, as has been seen. Furthermore, it was a question of a system in use, even later on, in the Mediterranean; but, about its use in the Atlantic we know nothing. And it seems strange to me that only Columbus, among the pilots and officials of the expedition, would use the *Martelogio*.

* * * * *

I wish to conclude by indicating that the *Diary* — as it seems to me and as these considerations show — if read and reread with attention, can still teach us much. Perhaps there will result from it an image of Columbus less hagiographic and charismatic, but more concrete and equally interesting. Also, unveiling him as a more realistic figure is a way of honoring him, which assumes particular significance in this land of San Salvador, which took its name from him and to which I have had the honor of being invited.

NOTES

1. Well known and classic is Samuel E. Morison's volume, *Journal and Other Documents on the Life and Voyage of Christopher Columbus* (New York, 1963); from the same author see also, *Admiral of the Ocean Sea* (Boston, 1942) and *Christopher Columbus Mariner* (Boston, 1955 and

London, 1956), *passim*. More recent are the works of Paolo E. Taviani, *Cristoforo Colombo. La genesi della grande scoperta [Christopher Columbus. The Origin of the Great Discovery]* (Novara, 1974), *passim*, and *I viaggi di Colombo. La grande scoperta [The Voyages of Columbus. The Great Discovery]* (Novara, 1984), vol. I, pp. 9-91; vol. II, pp. 10-179.

2. Cristoforo Colombo, *Diario di bordo*, ed. Gaetano Ferro (Milan, 1985), *passim*; I have also consulted Cristóbal Colón, *Textos y documentos completos*, ed. Consuelo Varela (Madrid, 1982), pp. 15-138.

3. It is not without reason that Ferdinand and Isabella, in light of the second voyage (and also of the others), request from Columbus, on September 15, 1493, clarifications regarding the position of the lands discovered and the route to follow to reach them: ". . . we have need to know the degrees within which the islands and land you discovered fall and the degrees of the path you traveled." The observation is derived from a manuscript of colleague Ilaria Luzzana Caraci, in the process of being published.

4. The scribes who made the copies were more than one; the examples of errors, due perhaps also in part to a misunderstanding of the original, are fairly numerous. Las Casas (*Historia de las indias*, p. 328) himself says he has before him not the original but a copy; he lets it be understood also in the *Diario*, on the date 30 October, where he speaks generally of "the writing from which I transcribed this."

5. In the "Introduction" to the *Diario*, translated and edited by me (p. 10), I supported the hypothesis that Las Casas in this task made use of some collaborator or scribe. Today, however, I believe the definitive word is that of Consuelo Varela, op. cit., p. xi and p. 15, which deems the text to be an "autograph copy" of the Dominican bishop.

6. Las Casas was often and for long periods in Seville after 1540 and was able to have direct access to the archive and to the books of the Columbus family; Don Fernando's large library passed, after his death (1539), to the Convent of San Pablo and there Las Casas was able to study, transcribe and summarize the *Diario*, for example between February and July of 1544 (so alleges Consuelo Varela, op. cit., p. x-xi). Naturally it is impossible to distinguish between the errors of transcription made by him and those already present in the copy of the *Diario* which he was using.

7. Besides the *op. cit.* note 2, see *Cartas de particulares a Colón y Relaciones coetáneas*, ed. Juan Gil and Consuelo Varela (Madrid, 1984), *passim*.

8. A representative example taken from the *Diario* on the date of October 16, concerning a stretch of the coast of Fernandina (Long Island): "it runs north-northwest and south-southwest," doesn't make sense and is obviously to be corrected to "from north-northwest to south-southeast"; and besides, on October 15, it is written that "all this part of the island runs northwest southeast" and that is reaffirmed on October 17. It is curious that Consuelo Varela, *op. cit.*, p. 36, rather than "north-northwest" transcribed

"northwest" which — from a geographical point of view — can be counter-posed neither to "south-southwest," nor to "south-southeast."

9. The first indication of distances in miles is on the eleventh of October, but it is preceded by the indication of the hourly average: "he probably traveled twelve miles each hour; and by two hours after midnight they probably traveled 90 miles, which are 22-and-a-half leagues."

10. The first indication of the hourly average is on the seventh of October: "they traveled 23 miles per hour for two hours, and afterward 8 miles per hour; and he probably traveled 23 leagues by one hour after sunrise." An example of a complete transfer from the appraisal of hourly velocity to the estimation, first in miles then in leagues, of the distance traveled, is had on the fifth of February: "he traveled 10 miles per hour, and thus in eleven hours they went 110 miles, which are 27 and-a-half leagues."

11. An example, among the many, occurs on October 27: "He traveled eight miles per hour."

12. Some examples, relative to the return voyage — excepting those days around the Azores — that perhaps Las Casas has summarized more hastily, judging them of minor interest: on the thirteenth of February there is a difference of a quarter of a league between the distance in miles and that in leagues, and on the fourteenth of the same month a half a league. Furthermore, the number of miles and of leagues is sometimes in ciphers and sometimes in Roman numerals.

13. Examples of naiveté and repetition are in Julio F. Guillen Tato, *La parla marinera en el Diario del primer viaje de Cristóbal Colón* (Madrid, 1951), p. 13-14. The comparative geographical references are, almost always, to localities and regions of the Iberian peninsula, which can be explained by the fact that the diary was directed to the Catholic Monarchs and to their court. For the importance which the marvellous and the hyperbolic have in the Diario see Joaquin Arce, *Significado lingüístico-cultural del Diario de Colón*, in *Diario de a bordo de Cristóbal Colón* (Alpignano, 1971), pp. 16-18.

14. See again Julio F. Guillen Tato, *op. cit.*, pp. 15-16.

15. In the reading of this passage of the *Diario* and of a preceding passage, dated February 7, a distinction must be made between that which was the estimate of the position actually reached and the one which was foreseen as the next route (see the edition already cited of the *Diario di bordo* notes 235 and 236).

16. See the details of such errors and others discernible in the text relative to February 27 in my previously cited edition of the *Diario di bordo*, notes 230, 231 and 247. At times, it's a matter of small difference but on the twenty-second of January there is written 72 miles and 18 leagues rather than 32 miles and 8 leagues; shortly after, it speaks of 6 leagues per hour, an impossible velocity, which must be corrected with 6 miles (always per hour). And the twenty-seventh of February the estimate of the presumed distance from Madeira is grossly in error.

17. See Gaetano Ferro, *Chiose e note al Diario di bordo di Colombo. Latitudine e longitudine, dì e notte, caldo e freddo*, in press. I have just presented a paper on *Terminologia geografica e voci marinaresche* to the "Third Hispano-Italian Colloquium: The Italian Presence in Andalusia in The Early Middle Ages and Sixteenth Century" (October, 1986).

18. See Alberto Magnaghi, *I presunti errori che vengono attribuiti a Colombo nella determinazione delle latitudini* (Roma, 1928), *passim*; Paolo E. Taviani, *op. cit., passim*. This thesis, as is known, contrasts with that of Samuel Morison who holds that Columbus had truly erred, sighting another star rather than the North Star.

19. Another question, which here — for reasons of time — it is not possible to address, concerns the possible and eventual use by Columbus here of another league, the dry land league (of obviously diverse measure from the maritime league) for the measurements near the coast; see Samuel E. Morison, *op. cit., passim*.

20. See in my previously cited edition of the *Diario di bordo*, note 34.

21. The computation, for the crew, on the first of October, registered 584 leagues, but perhaps this too was over-estimated; I have added to it the data, always those given to the crews, of the following days (but, instead, for the eighth and the eleventh the data held to be true, which are the only ones reported in the *Diario*); we thus have a total of approximately 900 leagues.

22. See, for example, Gaetano Ferro, *Ciose e note . . ., op. cit.*

23. In other passages of the *Diario* the use of nautical maps is attested to: September 25 and February 10.

24. See Gaetano Ferro, *Le navigazioni lusitane nell'Atlantico e Cristoforo Colombo in Portogallo* (Milano, 1984), *passim*.

25. For the question of Columbus's landfall, still the subject of discussion, see the contributions of diverse authors in *Terrae incognitae*, XV (1983).

26. See Osvaldo Baldacci, *Una "taoleta de marteloio" fatta da Cristoforo Colombo* (Roma, 1985), *passim*.

27. See Gaetano Ferro, *Chiose e note . . ., op. cit.*

BIBLIOGRAPHY

(limited to the works utilized for this paper)

Arce, Joaquin. "Significado lingüístico-cultural del *Diario* de Colón." *Diario de a bordo de Cristóbal Colón*. Alpignano: Impr. Tallone, 1971, 11-28.

Baldacci, Osvaldo. *Una "taoleta de marteloio" fatta da Cristoforo Colombo*. Roma: Università "La Sapienza". Facoltà di Lettere. Pubblicazioni Istituto Geografia, 1985.

Caraci, Ilaria L. "Colombo e le longitudini." *Boll. Soc. Geogr. Ita.*, 1980, 517-529.

Colombo, Cristoforo. *Diario di bordo. Libro della prima navigazione e scoperta delle Indie.* Ed. Gaetano Ferro. Milano: Mursia, 1985.

Colón, Cristóbal. *Textos y documentos completos.* Ed. Consuelo Varela. Madrid: Alianza Universidad, 1982 (2nd ed. 1984).

Dunn, Oliver. "Columbus's First Landing Place: The Evidence of the 'Journal'." *Terrae Incognitae,* 15 (1983), 35-50.

Ferro, Gaetano. "Chiose e note al *Diario* di bordo di Colombo. Latitudine e longitudine, dí e notte, caldo e freddo." *Atti IV Convegno Internazionale Studi Colombiani.* Genova, 1986, in press.

_____. *Le navigazioni lusitane nell' Atlantico e Cristoforo Colombo in Portogallo.* Milano: Mursia, 1984.

_____. "Terminologia geografica e voci marinaresche." *Atti III Coloquio Hispano-Italiano: la presencia italiana en Andalucia en la baja edad media y siglo XVI.* Seville, 1986, in press.

Gil, Juan and Consuelo Varela. *Cartas de particulares a Colón y relacines coetáneas.* Madrid: Alianza Universidad, 1984.

Guillen Tato, Julio F. *La parla marinera en el Diario del primer viaje de Cristóbal Colón.* Madrid: Instituto Historico Marina, 1951.

Kelley, James E. Jr. "In the Wake of Columbus on a Portolan Chart." *Terrae Incognitae,* 15 (1983), 77-111.

Las Casas, Bartolomeo de. *Historia de Las Indias.* Ed. J. Pérez de Tudela and E. López Oto. 2 vols. Madrid: Biblioteca de Autores Españoles, 1957-61.

Magnaghi, Alberto. "I presunti errori che vengono attribuiti a Colombo nella determinazione delle latitudini." *Boll. Soc. Geogr. It.,* 1928, 459-494, 553-558.

Molander, Arne B. "A New Approach to the Columbus Landfall." *Terrae Incognitae,* 15 (1983), 113-149.

Morison, Samuel E. *Journal and Other Documents on the Life and Voyage of Christopher Columbus.* New York: Heritage, 1963.

_____. *Admiral of the Ocean Sea. A Life of Christopher Columbus.* 2 vols. Boston: Little Brown and Company, 1942.

_____. *Christopher Columbus Mariner.* Boston, 1955 and London: Faber, 1956.

Parker, John. "The Columbus Landfall Problem: A Historical Perspective." *Terrae Incognitae,* 15 (1983), 1-28.

Power, Robert H. "The Discovery of Columbus' Island Passage to Cuba, October 12-27, 1492." *Terrae Incognitae,* 15 (1983), 151-172.

Taviani, Paolo E. *Cristoforo Colombo. L genesi della grande scoperta [Christopher Colombus. The Origin of the Great Discovery]*. 2 vols. Novara: Istituto Geografico De Agostini, 1974.

—————. *I viaggi di Colombo. La grande scoperta [The Voyages of Columbus. The Great Discovery]*. 2 vols. Novara: Istituto Geografico De Agostini, 1984.

Verhoog, Pieter. "Columbus Landed on Caicos." *Terrae Incognitae*, 15 (1983), 29-34.

Value of the Mile Used at Sea by Cristobal Colon During His First Voyage

Georges A. Charlier
Liège, Belgique

INTRODUCTION

A study of the route borrowed by Colon during his voyage of discovery of America has to refer to the indications given us in the extract made by Las Casas of the copy made by the royal copiers of the *Book of the First Navigation* that he gave to the Kings.

Because of the complex origins of this data, if a serious study is to be made, it will have to be verified as far as is possible in its authenticity, basis and logic.

As far as the value of the mile used at sea by Colon is concerned Europeans have, it seems, always taken for granted (perhaps too easily) that it was the Roman mile, or 1480 meters about, that was used. On the other hand, the American scholars are not unanimous on this point. I have here a book entitled *In the Wake of Columbus* in which a study is made concluding that the value of the mile does not correspond with the value usually admitted.

Since I have the solution to this question, I feel it my duty to share it with all scholars who might be troubled by this divergence of opinion.

The following will demonstrate quickly and unequivocally that the mile used at sea by Colon during his first voyage and, logically also during his other trips, was about 1480 meters as have accepted, without verification, many scholars.

STUDY

The determination of the length of this mile is so simple that one could compare this problem with the well known story of — Colon's egg!

In effect a simple, but careful, examination of a passage taken from a known and uncontested document gives us the answer. A document which everyone seems to have overlooked until now. What seems extraordinary isn't the fact that the real value of the mile has finally been determined but that someone else had not done it long ago!

115

Perhaps we should see in this the consequence of the fact that no true seaman seems to have closely examined the problems posed in Colon's navigation.

First Approach

Thanks to one clearly visible clue we can already safely presume that the mile used at sea by Colon was the Roman mile. In the *Extract of the Log* in the tenth and eleventh lines under the date Sunday, December 9, 1492 (at this date Colon was in the harbor he named Puerto de la Concepcion) Colon states: "This harbor measures at its mouth, one thousand paces which are one quarter of a league." And as far as known, only the Roman mile is said to measure one thousand paces.

Demonstration

If we still search for an irrefutable proof of the unit of measure used at sea by Colon, it is simply because we can find nowhere in the writing of Colon a clear definition of what he considered a mile to be. This would have satisfied scholars and thus ended the discussion. Unfortunately this is not possible.

In our day, when we speak of a length using a certain unit of measure, the unit of measure used is purely conventional and accepted by all. We would have great difficulty explaining its value, except by comparison. We could say for example: from here to here there are X units of measure; or, the unit of measure represents the length of this object. The definition of the meter is nothing more, nothing less!

From this it appears that the only possible method to determine the length of the mile of Colon, is that for a given distance, for example between two precisely located points, we can compare the value given in Colon's miles with that of the real distance.

But if, in principle, this seems simple, one has to find *where* to apply this ideal method! For, until now, no one has been able to find two points given by Colon for which he gave the distance separating them in miles. Either the measurements given by Colon didn't represent, or didn't form when added together, a complete distance between two points (not to speak of data clearly altered in successive copies which eliminates them automatically, and other distances clearly estimated and rounded off, which are automatically imprecise); or the two points of which Colon spoke are not clearly identifiable and therefore doubtful and subject to criticism. Should we then give up all hope of finding the true value of Colon's mile? No, we should not! For the necessary elements exist, and, even better, they exist in the *Extract of the Log*. The part of the Log that interests us in this demonstration is given at the end of this study. You may refer to it.

We will now go back to February 1493 . . .

After an agitated crossing from Hispaniola, during which a storm separated him from the Pinta, Colon found himself on the Isla de Santa Maria of the Azores. There, troubles with the local inhabitants cost him several days. Finally things were worked out. During the night of Saturday the 23rd — Sunday the 24th he lifted anchor and set sail to the east, toward Castille. That is, toward Palos, automatically passing by that remarkable landmark, the Cabo de San Vicente.

Notice that in doing this Colon navigates on the straight line joining his starting point, the Isla de Santa Maria, to his goal, the Cabo de San Vicente. This is easily seen on the map in Fig. 1. In this way we have two perfectly identifiable points given by Colon. Two points for which we know the real distance.

When Colon has completed about half of his trip, the weather changes and he sees that a storm is coming. Colon does what any seaman would do in these circumstances: he immediately makes the necessary calculation and estimations to find his position before the storm. In this way he possesses a precise point of reference before being thrown off course by bad weather. This will enable him to make a good dead reckoning after the storm in order to continue navigation toward his original goal.

Up until now Colon has been navigating unknown waters, waters for which there is no existing documentation. Now the situation is different. Maps exist, and evidently Colon has them in his possession.[1] Therefore, he will not be forced to chart his course on a map he draws himself as he progresses and says: "I estimate that I have traveled X miles (sometimes this is the sum of several shorter distances) on this course (this also may be the sum of several directions)", with this estimation originating from a point behind him.

Now he can put his finger on his map and simply say: "I am here in comparison to this and that point of reference on my map!"

This changes everything and this is our chance to find the answer to our problem. For Colon, by navigating practically in a straight line[2] joining two of his reference points, the Isla de Santa Maria and the Cabo de San Vicente, gives us, by the sum of the two distances separating himself from these two points, the distance between them, expressed in miles. The miles used by Colon! This number, compared to the real distance, will give us the value of the mile he used at sea.

Let us see what the *Extract of the Log* says for the date of February 27, 1493:

"... He was one hundred and twenty five leagues from the Cabo de San Vicente, eighty from the Isla de la Madera and one hundred and six from Santa Maria."

Therefore for Colon and in the miles used by him at sea, the distance between the Isla de Santa Maria and the Cabo de San Vicente would be: 125 leagues + 106 leagues = 231 leagues or 924 miles. And the distance between these two points is approximately 964 Roman miles of 1480 meters. The map in Fig. 2 helps us to visualize all of this.

But once we have established these figures are we going to make a ridiculous calculation telling us that Colon used a mile equal to 964/924 of a Roman mile or 1544 meters? Should we conclude that Colon used this unit of measure? A unit of measure with no historical basis which would be more than 68 meters longer than the well-known Roman mile! Of course not.

For what we measure in this way is simply the inaccuracy of the map with which he determines the distance separating the Isla de Santa Maria from the Cabo de San Vicente. For it is obvious that at this time the precision of sea charts was far from perfect and the approximately four percent of error we find here is already amazing!

CONCLUSION

From all of this, it is obvious that Colon really used the Roman mile of about 1480 meters. In fact this is what all the scholars, since they used this value in their work, had assumed intuitively without proving it.

NOTES

1. This new method of situating himself in relation to reference points he hadn't yet seen, and from which he says he is a given distance, is a particularity of navigation by map. It is also extremely logical that the seaman that Colon was would not leave without taking with him maps of regions he was susceptible of crossing. The precision of the map he used would lead us to believe that it was a map made by men who knew well this part of the ocean because of sailing there frequently. Therefore probably the Portuguese!

2. We say *"practically in a straight line"*, despite the fact that the text of Tuesday the 26th and Wednesday the 27th of February might lead us to think, after a first reading, that Colon was thrown off this course. We have several reasons to believe this: (1) the deviation from the straight line route resulting from the 8 leagues toward the east-northeast given Tuesday the 26th only represents an elevation to the north of 3. 2 leagues, which represent nearly nothing when compared to the total distance of 231 leagues. (2) while the deviation hinted at on the 27th is not given in figures, it shouldn't have been too large either. For the next day, when the deviation was large, he gave the necessary information. We should also note that, as we said in the study, it is more than probable that the point given by Las Casas is the point given before the storm. The point before being thrown off course. (3) All this is confirmed by the 80 leagues that Colon gives as his distance from the Isla de la Madera. For this is exactly the distance separating this island from the straight line joining the Isla de Santa Maria and the Cabo de San Vicente.

PARTS OF *EXTRACTS OF THE LOG* CITED

Sunday February 24th

. . . Seeing that the weather was favorable for traveling to Castille, he abandoned his idea of taking on wood and stones and steered to the east. Until sunrise, that is for about six and a half hours, he navigated at about 7 miles per hour, which made 45 1/2 miles. From sunrise to sunset, he navigated at 6 miles per hour for eleven hours. This made 66 miles, which with the forty-five and one half of the night gave 111 1/2 miles and in consequence 28 leagues.

Monday February 25th

Yesterday after sunset, he navigated on his course toward the east at five miles per hour. And during the thirteen hours of that night he traveled 65 miles which made 16 1/4 leagues. From sunrise to sunset he traveled another sixteen and one half miles and, thanks to God, on a flat sea. A very large bird that resembled an eagle came to the caravelle.

Tuesday February 26th

Yesterday, after sunset, he navigated on his course toward the east and, thanks to God, on a flat sea. He navigated 8 1/2 miles per hour the greater part of the night, thus traveling 100 miles which made 25 leagues. After sunrise, with a little wind and passing through some rain showers, he traveled about eight leagues to the east-northeast.

Wednesday February 27th

This night and today he navigated off his course because of contrary winds, great waves and the state of the sea. He was one hundred and twenty-five leagues from Cabo de San Vicente, eighty from the Isla de la Madera and one hundred and six from Santa Maria. He was quite dismayed at having to undergo a storm like this when he was at the doorstep of his house.

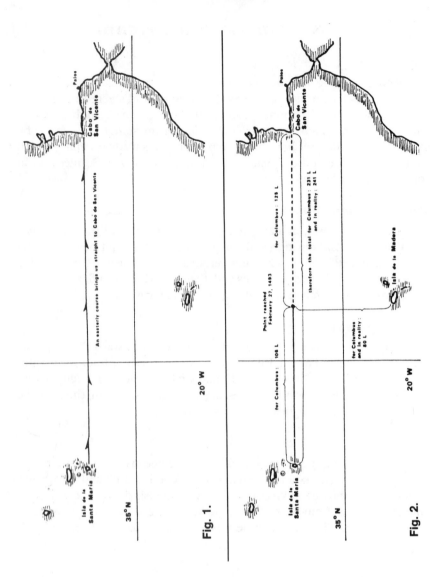

Fig. 1.

Fig. 2.

The Navigation of Columbus on His First Voyage to America

James E. Kelley, Jr.
Melrose Park, Pennsylvania

ABSTRACT

This paper summarizes results from a computer simulation of Columbus' navigation during his first voyage to America. It is based on course and distance data in his *Journal* and on information derived from other sources of 15th century cartography and navigation. Certain debated issues — the length of Columbus' mile unit, his "double accounting" of distances, his "land league", etc. — are discussed.

INTRODUCTION

Columbus' *Journal* of his first voyage to America is known only through an abstract made by Las Casas in the early 16th century.[1] Even so, this abstract contains an almost complete daily account of Columbus' ship movements during the whole voyage. Modeling the voyage with this data permits us to test hypotheses about the voyage, and to refine our knowledge of the navigation of southern Europeans in the 15th century.

Simulations have been done before, e.g. by Nunn (1924), McElroy (1941), Fuson and Treftz (1976), and Marden (1986) and Judge (1986), principally to locate Columbus' first landfall in the New World. Daily courses are converted to latitude and longitude positions and plotted on a Mercator chart to form a "Mercator course". Spherical trigonometry and considerations of magnetic declination, currents and leeway are involved.

Columbus had no concept of a "Mercator course". He simply laid off the ship's daily or half-day progress on a map as a line segment of appropriate length and bearing from the last reckoned position to form a "plane chart course" of the voyage. His is modeled by a course on a flat earth with meridians running vertically and lines of latitude running horizontally through every point. The Appendix gives details of his method.

The plane chart course of the *Journal* data shown in Figure 1 is Columbus' voyage as he saw it. The figure is the key to much of what follows. All relevant measurements used here are taken from it.[2]

HOW LONG IS COLUMBUS' MILE?

The simulation requires an estimate for the length of Columbus' mile or league. The *Journal* only tells us there were four miles to his league. Many writers believe Columbus used the Roman mile of about 4,850 English feet.[3] But a smaller mile of about 4,100 English feet is needed to keep the fleet from overshooting the Bahamas, and to return it to the Azores.[4] The question is, was there a short mile of this length in use by mariners in Columbus' time?

Evidence of the Charts

Measurements show that the western Mediterranean on many 14th and 15th century Italian and Catalan nautical charts is scaled to a mile of about 4,100 English feet. The first to study this subject in any detail were the geographer Hermann Wagner (1895), with his student Ernst Steger (1896), and the explorer Adolf Nordenskiold.[5] Wagner (1900, p. 280), whose analyses seem the most credible, concluded that the short mile was known to Columbus' contemporaries as the *millarium geometricum* of 1,000 *passus geometricus* of 5 *pes geometricus*, and that the Roman mile was 1,000 *passus vulgares* or 1,200 *passus geometricus*. Consequently, the geometric mile was 5/6ths the Roman mile, or about 4,045 English feet.

Evidence from Contemporary Commerce

Differences among contemporary commercial units of length indicate there may have been two Roman mile units in Columbus' day, one of about 4,823 English feet and another, the neo-Roman mile, of about 4,888 English feet. Machabey's (1962) extensive study of these commercial units provides a basis for defining the probable length of the geometric mile. Machabey defines ten groups of units, all built up from the Roman foot (= 29.4 cm.) of 16 Roman digits. For example, the neo-Roman foot of about 29.8 cm. is taken as 81/80ths (= 324/320) of the Roman foot, the ratio apparently deriving from the recalibration of a perch of 18 feet of 18 Roman digits to the foot (= 324 digits) to one of 20 feet of 16 (neo-Roman) digits to the foot (= 320 digits).[6]

The Machabey class of widest use is based on the foot of Bourgogne of 18 Roman digits (about 33 cm.) — close to the classical *pes Drusianus* of 33.3 cm. Two and one-half of these feet defined the *aune* of Provins, the standard measure of the Champagne fairs. One-third of the *aune* is the *palm* (*pan, empan*) of the Bourgogne foot (i.e. 3/4ths foot). The use of this *palm* at the fairs insured its use throughout the region from Venice to Catalonia — eight *palms* to the *canna* of the cloth trade. Columbus made explicit use of the *palm* (e.g. the entry for October 21), but not a "foot" unit.

The *palm* of the Bourgogne foot (= 24.75 cm., i.e. 3/4ths of 18 Roman digits or of 33 cm.) is undoubtedly the *pas geometricus* of the foot of the neo-Roman mile (= 24.83 cm., i.e. 5/6ths of 16 neo-Roman digits or of 29.8 cm.). A mile of 5,000 of these *palms* is about 4,060 English feet. This is the value taken here to represent the geometric mile of the portolan charts. Four of these miles, the "geometric league", is the length of Columbus' league used to scale the simulation.

WHO KNEW WHERE THE FLEET WAS?

The Pilots of the Fleet

Each ship in the fleet had an assigned pilot: Peralonso Niño of Moguer on the flagship, Christobal Garcia Sarmiento on *Pinta*, and Sancho Ruiz de Gama on *Niña*. When these "official" pilots were off duty others did their jobs. Bartolome Roldan, an able seaman on *Niña*, was probably apprenticed to Sancho Ruiz. The Captain or Master might also fill in for the pilot or perform independent checks of his work to insure against getting lost. Columbus was certainly keeping track of the fleet's progress independent of Peralonso. The *Journal* implies that Vincente Anes Pinzon, Captain of *Niña*, also was running a log of daily positions. Martin Alonso Pinzon, Captain of *Pinta* and Columbus had ship-to-ship discussions about the fleet's position. It is also probable that Francisco Martin Pinzon and Juan de La Cosa, respective Masters of *Pinta* and the flagship, could also pilot a ship.

Comparison of Position Estimates

A question of interest is how the pilots' navigational skills compare with Columbus', and with one another's. Since later writers disparage pilots' skills while putting Columbus on a pedestal, one wonders about the truth of the matter.

The first record of the pilots' estimates of western progress is on September 19: *Niña's* pilot, 440 leagues; *Pinta's*, 420; the flagship's, 400. Taking Hierro as the point of measurement, the distance to the computer plotted position (presumably Columbus' own estimate) is 420 leagues. At this point of the journey everyone was pretty well in agreement.

On September 25 the Admiral and Martin Alonso Pinzon discussed their current position relative to a map. But no comparative data is given. A relevant position check on October 1 is considered later on.

The most interesting records of the pilots' position estimates occur during the last two weeks before the fleet made landfall in the Azores. The dates: February 6-7, February 10, and February 15. The position estimates are given in terms of the nearest possible east-west (latitude) and north-south (longitude) landfalls, e.g. Madeira east, Flores north. This made it easy to plot them on a copy of Figure 1. Then their locations relative to the simulator-calculated fleet position for the day in question were read from the map and plotted in Figure 2.

In the days just before landfall Anes and Ruiz were estimating they were 55 to 65 leagues ahead of the simulation, but positioned in about the same latitude (the boxed points in Figure 2); Roldan and Peralonso were also estimating about the same latitude, but were running some 130 leagues ahead of the simulation. Columbus' stated east-west position estimate of February 7 is only 10 leagues ahead of the simulation (the first boxed point of his group of estimates) — reasonably consistent with his *Journal* data.[7] However, he thinks he is some 42 leagues north of the simulation. Perhaps he suspects the accuracy of his "chart pricking". On February 3, when the simulation puts him due west of Madeira, he notes that the height of Polaris suggests they are in the latitude of Cape St. Vincent, some 90 leagues further north. Perhaps the 42 league northerly displacement from the calculated latitude is a compromise based on that observation.[8]

The relative positions of the other groups of pilots do not change much for the period February 6-10. But on February 10 "the Admiral found himself much off his course," that is, off his plotted course as simulated in Figure 1. He set his east-west position back some 90 leagues from the simulation (his map plot) and 150 from the closest of the other pilots. He still believed the fleet to be some 18 leagues further north of the other pilots' estimates, but not as far north as he thought on February 7. Was visibility deteriorating in advance of the great storm about to hit the fleet, making him lose confidence in his earlier observation of Polaris?

Finally, they made landfall on February 15. Having set his estimated actual position so far back and a little north of his plotted position of February 10, Columbus logically concluded that he must be in the Azores (solid circle in Figure 2). Anes and Ruiz placed the fleet at Madeira since their plotted position on the 15th was under 30 leagues from that island. Roldan and Peralonso, plotting a position on the 15th far ahead and off the coast of Casablanca, reasoned that because of the cold, stormy weather they must be further north, near Lisbon.

Columbus' Use of Seamarks

Measurements of Figure 1 indicate that on February 10 the fleet's true position was about 140 leagues west of Santa Maria in the Azores. Columbus, setting himself 150 leagues behind the pilots, located the fleet 130 leagues west of Santa Maria (i.e. south and a little west of Flores), or 10 leagues east (ahead) of the fleet's true position; the simulator (i.e. Columbus' probable map plot) was 90 leagues further east; Anes and Ruiz were 145 (= 90 + 55) leagues east; and Roldan and Peralonso were probably still running 220 (= 90 + 130) leagues east. Columbus thought they were further north of their calculated latitude considering the height of Polaris and the colder weather. But why did he set himself some 90 leagues west of his plotted position? Though the reason is not indicated, a hint is given in the last sentence of the entry for February 10: "He also says here that he had made 263 leagues from the island of Hierro on the outbound voyage when he saw the first weed etc." Had Las Casas copied the full text of the original we might have the reason sought.

All during the voyage Columbus used and recorded seamarks — birds, vegetation, fish, etc. — as indicators of location, despite their mobility. In particular, he recorded sightings of seaweed as they crossed the Sargasso Sea. Marking Figure 1 for the days on which weed was seen shows that: From January 23 through 27 no sighting of weed is reported though the fleet's route parallels and crosses its course of the previous October 2 and 3 when weed was sighted. On September 29 and 30 they had also seen much weed. But from October 4 through 7 they reported no sightings. (At the time they were on the western limb of the Sargasso Sea.) Apparently Columbus reasoned on February 10 that they crossed their outbound route just ahead of their position on October 2 and 3, during which time they sailed some 86 leagues, enough to account for the 90 leagues in question.

This case illustrates well why Columbus was an outstanding navigator. His calculated positions are not significantly different from those of Anes and Ruiz. Though his map plot (the simulation) is some 60 leagues behind their's, and closer to the fleet's true position, the difference is under 3% of the 2,500 leagues or so they had travelled. What made his navigation superior was his willingness to use evidence other than his map plots to reckon his probable position at sea. Even so, he seems to have continued maintaining his original plane chart course just as the other pilots did. After all, if a seamark observed later on indicated an alternative interpretation, the basic course observations would be essential for an intelligent reappraisal.

WHY DID ALL THE PILOTS OVERESTIMATE THEIR EASTERLY PROGRESS?

The "Land League"

Knowing how Columbus may have detected his overestimate of progress on February 10 from the appearance of seaweed does not answer why the error was made in the first place. It so happens that Morison (1942, I, p. 248, 261) and others have observed that the fleet's progress along the coast of Cuba is much overestimated. To account for this, Morison suggests that the Admiral used a "land league" of about 1.6 nautical miles for distance measurement when sailing near land. It is numerically equivalent to two Roman miles or about 1.5 Arab miles.[9] However, if one reduces the simulator's east-west progress along Cuba and Española to the true distance in geometric leagues from Rio de Mares to Cabo del Enamorado, one can account for about 80 of the 90 leagues Columbus set back the fleet's position on February 10.

The postulated "land league" seems doubtful. The inconsistency of changing one's units of measure in the middle of a running calculation, and not labeling them differently in addition, is to invite problems. That pilots would knowingly operate as postulated seems illogical to some, including Verhoog (1954, p. 1105) and this writer.

Effect of Currents on the Fleet Near Cuba

There is an alternate explanation. The Pilot Charts for October through December show currents of 0.5 knots to 0.7-0.8 knots WNW along the northeast coast of Cuba. In 24 hours a 0.5 knot current can carry a ship 18 geometric miles. The Admiral complains of currents at several places near Cuba. On the night of November 20 he could not reach Puerto del Principe "because currents set him to the northwest."

Figure 3 (left) shows how the simulator plotted the fleet's progress south from Isabela and along Cuba. The fleet passed Puerto del Principe on November 13 and backtracked to anchor there on the 14th. On the 19th they set sail again, NNE, on a roundtrip of about 38 hours, not quite making Puerto del Principe because of the currents. So they went NE out to sea. It took them until the 24th to make land again, this time at the same point they passed on the 14th when they backtracked to Puerto del Principe.

The two plotted locations of Puerto del Principe and the more easterly landfall are separated by some 7 and 12 leagues, respectively. The differences are not identical because in the first instance the fleet was subject to the currents for 28 hours, in the second for 38 hours. A drift distance of seven geometric leagues in 28 hours, and 12 leagues in 38, imply currents of 0.67 and 0.84 knots, respectively — just in the range indicated on modern pilot charts.

Figure 3 (right) shows the course along Cuba replotted after subjecting the fleet to a conservative 0.5 knot northwesterly current. Now Puerto del Principe and the other landfall are brought into correct position.[10]

Table 1
True vs. Calculated Positions Corrected for Current

	BEARINGS			MODEL VS. TRUE DISTANCES				
FROM - TO	TRUE	MODEL	ERR	TRUE	GEO MI	%ERR	ROM MI	%ERR
Rio de Mares - Isabela	43	51	8	144	137	-4.9	164	13.7
Rio de Mares - C Lindo	115	120	5	119	125	5.0	150	25.5
P Principe - C Lindo	112	124	12	67	80	19.4	96	42.6
P Principe - R de Mares	298	293	-5	51	46	-9.8	55	7.7
P Principe - Isabela	23	32	9	139	122	-12.2	146	4.8
C Lindo - Isabela	358	359	1	153	148	-3.3	178	15.6
Average Error:			5 degrees E			-1.0%		18.3%

Implications of the Model Corrected for Currents

The plot of Figure 3 (right) has interesting implications. Three points of this traverse are generally considered to be positively identified: Rio de Mares (Gibara), Puerto del Principe (Bahia de Tanamo), and Cabo Lindo (Puente Fraile). Suppose the northern point of Isabela is actually Bird Rock, at the northwest point of Crooked Island, the fleet's still debated landfall of October 19. Table 1 compares the Mercator chart distance-bearing readings of these points with measurements from Figure 3 (right) which are converted to nautical miles. The assumption that the distances are in geometric miles fits the geography quite well with a - 1% average error. The Roman mile is a poor fit.

The bearings in Figure 3 (right) tend to be rotated east some five degrees, suggesting a westerly variation of the compass in the region just north of eastern Cuba in 1492-93. Columbus' statement about being subject to NW currents which actually bear about WNW also suggest a westerly variation. These observations are at variance with interpretations of Van Bemmelen's (1899) isogonic chart for 1500. That chart only estimates magnetic declination to 60 degrees west longitude, near which, at latitude 25 degrees, the westerly variation decreases slightly along Columbus track. McElroy (1941) and Morison (1942, I, p. 292) extrapolate the isogonic lines out to 70 degrees west longitude. If one extends the McElroy-Morison isogonic lines even further west, then an easterly variation is indicated for the region just north of eastern Cuba, with a value of 1 degree E at Watlings Island according to McElroy (1941, p. 225). Van Bemmelen's (1893) isogonic charts for the 16th century all show the Greater Antilles and Bahamas with a westerly variation. The effect of this local westerly variation, other things being equal, is to bring the fleet to a somewhat more southerly point in the Bahamas than McElroy's and Marden's calculations indicate. Clearly, Van Bemmelen's isogonic chart of 1500 should be revised if at all possible.

COLUMBUS' "DOUBLE ACCOUNTING" OF DISTANCES

On September 10, and elsewhere, Las Casas says that Columbus reported less progress than he reckoned "so that the men would not be frightened if the voyage were long." There are 23 such cases noted in the *Journal*. An interesting question is what kind of rule, if any, did Columbus use to refigure progress for the crew?

Columbus' 5/6ths Rule

Figure 4 shows Columbus' estimates of progress plotted against the figures he told the men. These data correlate well (correlation coefficient = 0.80) suggesting that the Admiral's personal estimates and those he reported to the crew are truely in the ratio of 5:6 — the slope of the line which runs through the datapoints. Many of the discrepancies seem to be due to roundoff or small arithmetic blunders. Although Columbus had a very slight statistical bias to quote an amount smaller than 5/6ths his personal estimate whenever it was large, the only datapoints one might suspect may have been deliberately underestimated are those of October 4 and 10.

The Portuguese Maritime League

The Portuguese maritime league of four neo-Roman miles and the geometric league of four geometric miles are in the ratio of 5:6. That is, $(4)(4,888) = 19,552$ English feet, and $(6/5)(4)(4,060) = 19,488$ English feet, respectively, a trivial difference of 64 feet.[11] Machabey (1962, p. 48) documents the existence in the early 16th century of a "league of Bourgogne" of 18,000 feet of Bourgogne of 33 cm. which is identical to the Portuguese maritime league.[12] Further, according to al-Farghani, the terrestrial degree is 56 and 2/3rds Arab miles, and the *parasang* is three Arab miles, making the *parasang* equivalent to the Portuguese maritime league.[13]

All these equivalents suggest that Iberians were familiar with an itinerary unit equivalent to the Portuguese maritime league. So one might presume Columbus was converting his own leagues in geometric miles into Portuguese maritime leagues for the crew were it not for the fact that Las Casas indicates that the Admiral meant to hide the truth. But the *Journal* suggests Las Casas may have been mistaken. On October 1 Columbus' pilot reported he reckoned they were 578 leagues west of Hierro. Here Las Casas also indicates that Columbus announced 584 leagues of progress to the crew, thus confirming Peralonso's estimate. But Las Casas also notes that the figure "he kept to himself" was 707 leagues. Note that 5/6ths of 707 is 589 Portuguese maritime leagues, close enough to 584 to blame the difference on an arithmetic blunder, or on a copyist's misreading of "9" for "4".

If Peralonso's 584 are geometric leagues then they made only 178 (= 578 - 400) leagues during the same 12 days the Admiral was estimating progress of 287 (= 707 - 420) leagues — an excessive relative error of some 38%. At the start of that period, September 19, Peralonso was only running 20 leagues behind the Admiral. How to explain these conflicting results?

Suppose the pilots reckoned their estimates in Portuguese maritime leagues, while Columbus reckoned his in geometric miles (and leagues). Whenever the Admiral wanted to make comparisons he would have to convert his figures to their units, or their's to his. Or if he wanted to communicate his estimates to them in their terms, he would be obliged to convert his units to their's. In this event the pilots' estimates of September 19 must have been converted by Columbus to units of geometric leagues for comparison purposes, since they correspond to the simulation results which are scaled in geometric leagues. Conversely, Peralonso's estimate of October 1 must be in Portuguese maritime leagues, considering that the Admiral's conversion of 707 leagues is close to Peralonso's estimate. These observations and the close correlation indicated in Figure 4 suggest that all the short estimates Columbus told the crew of daily progress are also in units of Portuguese maritime leagues.

One concludes, therefore, that Las Casas was mistaken. The Admiral seems never to have intended to keep the truth from the crew, but rather to relate progress in units they could most readily understand. Quoting his estimates in geòmetric leagues, which are numerically greater than the equivalent Portuguese maritime leagues, would both mislead and might unduly worry the crew on a long voyage. Eighty kilometers always seems further away than 50 miles though these distances are equal. Considering the close quarters aboard those ships and the large numbers of people who knew something of the pilot's craft if is hard to see how the Admiral could have sustained a conspiracy even had he intended to.

An Unexplained Difficulty

It is necessary to point out that the data for October 1 presents difficulties which may possibly weaken the foregoing argument. The simulation progress through October 1, measured on Figure 1 using dividers, is just about 648 geometric (542 Portuguese maritime) leagues, not the 707 (respectively, 584) estimated by Columbus. Since the sum of all the league distances up to this point is only 668.7, the "707" figure is probably a bad map reading. It is fairly easy to misread the scales of portolan charts by multiples of 50 leagues (the major scale division) since one must measure by counting unlabelled divisions. The simulation's estimate indicates that Peralonso's has either fallen back 70 (= 648 - 578) geometric leagues, or has jumped ahead 36 (= 578 - 542) Portuguese maritime leagues.

If Peralonso were using a geometric league then he lost 50 (= 70 - 20) leagues in 12 days, whereas he lost 20 leagues in the previous 10 days since they passed Hierro. If he were using the Portuguese maritime league then he gained 53 (= 17 + 36) leagues in the 12 days. Can we suspect that his estimate of September 19 was a bad map reading, some 50 leagues too short? Clearly there is a problem here, the solution to which is not evident. At present it takes too many questionable assumptions to resolve it.

CONCLUSIONS

The plane chart simulation of Columbus' first voyage to the New World is a useful contemporary view of the voyage that suggests alternate, mutually consistent, interpretations of some debated issues concerning the voyage. The value of such models is that one may explore the credibility of hypotheses to explain events (e.g. that the absence of seaweed on the homebound voyage caused Columbus to set his course back 90 leagues) and have some assurance that one is being consistent with other factors built into the model.

In addition, the model shows that Columbus' navigation is consistent with what is known of 15th century Italian practice.

It would probably be useful to fine-tune the simulation by reappraising the assumptions and data used in the light of what has been learned from this first version. Though difficult, and requiring the appraisal of several routes, the model revision should include a detailed analysis of the voyage leg from Guanahani to Cuba and the leg along the coast of Española, taking currents and leeway into account.

APPENDIX
THE ITALIAN METHOD OF OCEAN NAVIGATION

By Columbus' time Italian and Catalan seamen had had some 300 years of experience perfecting a graphical method for tracking their position at sea through the use of the magnetic compass, dividers, the sand glass, and the chart. There seems to be no single source which describes all the practical details of the method. The summary description that follows is derived from numerous primary and secondary sources, among the more important of which are Egerton MS.73 (British Library) and Cotrugli (1464), and printed compilations like Kamel (1926), Nordenskiold (1897), Kretschmer (1909), DaCosta (1939), and Cortesão and Albuquerque (1960), with hints of shipboard activity derived from the crusader (e.g. Roger of Howden), pilgrim (e.g. Friar Felix, von Harff), and seaman (e.g. Albizzi, in Mallet (1967)) literature. Perhaps the single most important source is Columbus' *Journal*.

The helmsman conned the ship under the supervision of the officer of the watch. He maintained the prescribed course by keeping the appropriate magnetic compass point aligned with the lubber line. Sail settings were adjusted to assist in maintaining the course. An observer might be assigned to verify the helmsman's constancy (two were required on important 16th century Spanish vessels). Columbus rebuked the helmsmen several times on September 9 for straying from the course.[14]

A ship's boy, positioned under the quarterdeck to keep the sand dry, maintained the ship's time during the watch by turning the half-hour sand glasses as the sand ran out and by hammering a gong or bell to announce the time. A second boy in the forecastle might operate a second sand glass as a check on the first.[15]

Periodically the pilot checked the ship's speed, especially upon a change in sailing conditions. Speed was estimated this way: At the start of the voyage a fixed distance (conjecturally 50 *palms*, about 40 English feet)[16] was marked along the rails. When a speed estimate was needed, the pilot (probably with an assistant) used a rhythmical ditty[17] to count the seconds it took for some flotsam or a wood chip to float the distance between the

130

rail marks. Using a conversion table (possibly carved in the ship's rail), or mental arithmetic, the pilot converted the time count to miles per hour. Fifty *palms* in 36 seconds is 1 mph, etc.[18]

The pilot recorded the relative change in the ship's position on his maneuvering board (*toleta del marteloio* = gridiron of the hammering), a vellum sheet with a large circle of radiating rhumbs and a mile scale or embedded square grid. Using dividers, he marked off the estimated distance travelled on the course bearing from the previously marked position.[19]

Every 12 or 24 hours (say at sunrise and sunset) the pilot measured the distance and bearing between the end points of the traverse marked on his maneuvering board to obtain the "course made good". The resultant bearing and distance was transferred to a nautical chart (called "pricking the chart" in later centuries). The course made good was also recorded in a journal or log book along with other pertinent data on the ship's progress, events and observations.[20] The marks on the maneuvering board were then erased in preparation for recording the next traverse.

At dawn and dusk (noon and midnight in later centuries) the pilots pooled their opinions about their actual position. The limitations of the maneuvering board method were understood, at least intuitively (viz effects of estimating errors, leeway, storms, etc.). Actual observations of natural phenomena (water conditions, sea life, star and sun positions, etc.) were compared to expectations for the apparent progress of the voyage. Columbus' *Journal* is particularly rich in examples of this sort.

The use of instruments for estimating latitude was lately growing in importance, especially for voyages down the coast of Africa. Without instruments the pole star or solar height of key coastal points might be memorized in personal units (e.g. "the height of a bent arm above the horizon"),[21] or in multiples of distances between well-known neighboring stars. Columbus records making such a non-instrumental latitude estimate on February 3, 1493. This method is quite old (Marcus, 1953). It indicated what a course due east or due west would lead to, but little else. See Kelley (1983, p. 107) for remarks on Columbus' use of the quadrant.

Observations of seamarks and latitude very much influenced daily changes of course. It is important to note, however, that these observations do not seem to have been incorporated into the pilot's formal navigation process involving the maneuvering board (*toleta*) and chart. That is, having concluded that he is, say, 50 leagues NW of his plotted position on his map, the pilot would not start tracking progress from that new position, but would continue from where he left off until land was sighted and identified. The *Journal* record of Columbus' route off Cuba (Figure 3 (left)) and his calculated positions (i.e. those of the simulation in Figure 1) versus his February 3 latitude estimate both suggest this conclusion. The pilot could easily use dividers to keep track of his assumed position relative to his dead reckoning (plane chart course) by laying off a previously noted distance and bearing from his current dead reckoning position.

The Italians taught all the western sea powers to use their method. With the 16th century it underwent various modifications as attempts were made to correct for the sphericity of the earth and for the magnetic declination of the compass.

NOTES

1. There are several Spanish transcriptions and English translations of the *Journal*, most recently by Dunn and Kelley (1987). Also see Morison (1963), and Jane (1960).

2. The technical data and procedures from which Figure 1 derives are described in Kelley (1983).

3. E. G. Markham (1893, p. 18, n2), Thatcher (1903, I, p. 516, n1), Nunn (1924, p. 18), DaCosta (1939, p. 180, n253), Jane (1960, p. 203, n3), Morison (1942, I, p. 247; 1963, p. 44).

4. d'Albertis' (1893) estimates Columbus' mile was 4,049. 3 English feet (1,234.24 m). McElroy (1941) calculates a Mercator course, modified to account for Van Bemmelen's (1899) estimates of magnetic declination in the Atlantic circa 1500, using a 4,393 English foot mile for the outbound leg, and 4,104 for the homebound leg. Had McElroy accounted for the prevailing westerly currents of about 0.4 knots his outbound mile would be 4,025 English feet, comparable to d'Albertis' estimate. Though Marden (1986, p. 577) theorizes Columbus used a league of 2.82 nautical miles (implies a 4,286 English foot mile), his calculations indicate it is too large by 9%. He must have computed the course with about a 3,900 English foot mile.

5. Nordenskiold (1897, p. 24) regarded the mile of the portolan chart as about one-fifth of a Spanish or Catalan league of 19,800 Toledo feet (of 19,426 Roman feet or of 18,844 English feet), or 3,769 English feet. This short mile seems much too short.

6. Kelley (1983, p. 103-4) summarizes Machabey's results. Dilke (1971, p. 82) also identifies these Roman foot units. He notes there was a normal Roman foot of 29.57 cm. (implies a 4,850.7 English foot mile), and an earlier foot of 29.73 cm. (essentially Machabey's neo-Roman foot). And from the third century AD there was a shorter foot of 29.42 cm.

7. True distances, converted to geometric miles, were substituted for missing data (documented in Kelley (1983)). Since *Journal* distances along Española tend to be overestimates, true distance substitutes would tend to shorten the track and explain why Columbus' stated position is 10 leagues ahead of the simulation.

8. On January 30 the fleet suddenly changed from a northeasterly trending course to S by E for 13. 5 leagues before reversing ground to a N by E course. If S by E is an error for N by E as McElroy thought, then subsequent simulation positions should be placed some 27 leagues further north and closer to the Admiral's supposed latitude positions of Feb. 7 and 10.

9. Probably a coincidence. However, Zupko (1968, p. 98) identifies two English agrarian leagues of 10,000 and 9,375 English feet which approximate Morison's "land league".

10. A northwesterly current conforms to Columbus' observation of its direction. The magnetic declination could have accounted for the two point difference in the current's bearing from the modern Pilot Charts.

11. DaCosta (1939, p. 216) takes the Portuguese maritime league to be 5,920 m, i.e. 19,422.6 English feet.

12. I.e. (18,000) (33 cm.) = 19,488 English feet.

13. I.e. (3 Arab mi.) (6080 ft./naut. mi.) (60 mi./degree)/(56.67 Arab mi./degree) = 19,312 English feet, close to other valuations of the Portuguese maritime league. See Mehren (1964, p. 8).

14. See Kreutz (1973) and Lane (1963).

15. For the sand glass see Balmer (1978). Morison (1942, I, pp. 220-239) gives a good description of the daily cycle of operations.

16. Decades later, log lines were knotted every 42 feet, the distance the ship would travel at 1 mph in 30 seconds. See Waters (1958, p. 139).

17. Just as the formula "one one-thousand, two one-thousand, ..." can be used to count off seconds, the repetitions of the then well-known ejaculations "*miserere*" or "*mea culpa*" could do the same job.

18. See Waters (1955). Alternatively, the "moment", an Italian unit of one-third second, may have been used to give more accurate results. See Egerton MS.73 (British Library, folio 43v), a collection of 15th century Italian charts and navigational works, inter alia, for the "moment".

19. A few maneuvering boards survive in 14th and 15th century atlases (see e.g. Kreutz (1973), DaCosta (1939), Taylor (1957, p. 116)). A small drawing of one and an essay on the trigonometry associated with it, the *raxon del marteloio*, is given in Egerton MS.73, folio 47v.

20. It is instructive to compare Columbus' *Journal* with Albizzi's (in Mallett (1967, p. 207-275)), a patron who was not also a working pilot.

21. See Taylor (1957, p. 129) for an example.

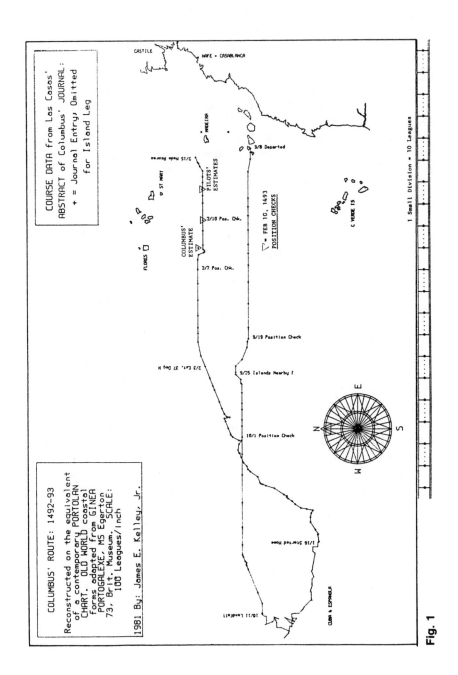

COURSE DATA from Las Casas'
ABSTRACT of Columbus' JOURNAL:
+ = Journal Entry; Omitted
for Island Leg

COLUMBUS' ROUTE: 1492-93

Reconstructed on the equivalent
of a contemporary PORTOLAN
CHART. OLD WORLD coastal
forms adapted from GINEA
PORTOGALEXE. MS Egerton
73, Brit. Museum. SCALE:
100 Leagues/inch

1981 By: James E. Kelley, Jr.

CASTILE

NAFE • CASABLANCA

MADEIRA

ST MRRT

2/15 Node Azores

PILOTS'
ESTIMATES

2/18 Pos. Chk.

2/7 Pos. Chk.

COLUMBUS'
ESTIMATE

FLORES

9/8 Departed

= FEB 10, 1493
POSITION CHECKS

C VERDE IS

2/3 Est, 37 Deg N

9/19 Position Check

9/25 Islands Nearby ?

10/1 Position Check

1/16 Steered Home

10/11 Landfall

CUBA & ESPAÑOLA

N
E
W
S

1 Small Division = 10 Leagues

Fig. 1

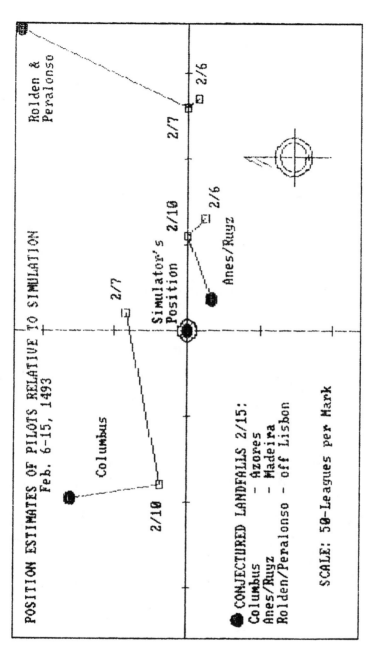

Fig. 2

135

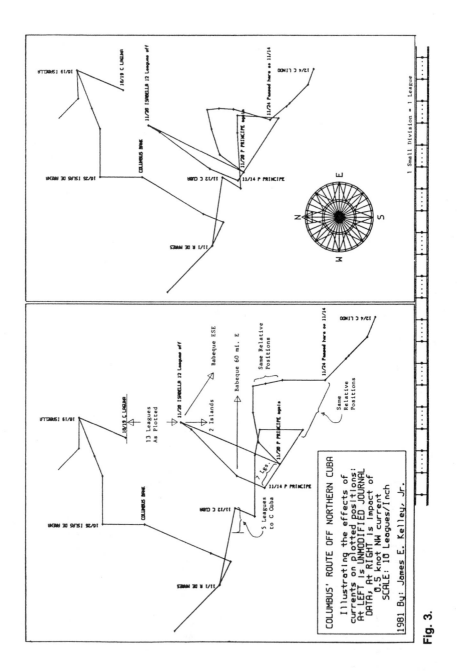

COLUMBUS' ROUTE OFF NORTHERN CUBA

Illustrating the effects of
currents on plotted positions;
At LEFT is UNMODIFIED JOURNAL
DATA, At RIGHT is Impact of
0.5 knot NW current
SCALE: 10 Leagues/Inch

1981 By: James E. Kelley, Jr.

Fig. 3.

1 Small Division = 1 League

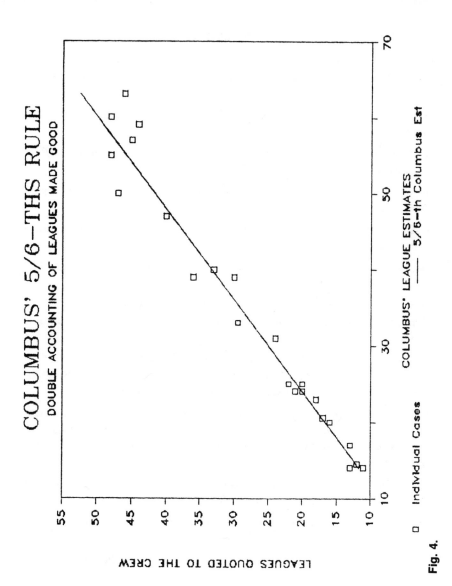

Fig. 4.

BIBLIOGRAPHY

Albertis, Eurico Alberto d'. "Le Construzioni navale e l'arte della Navigazione al tempo di Cristofero Colombo." in *Raccolta Colombiana*, Part IV, Vol. 1. Rome: 1893, 185-191.

Balmer, R. T. "The Operation of Sand Clocks and their Medieval Development." *Technology & Culture*, 19 (1978), 615-32.

Cortesão, Armando and Luis de Albuquerque. *Obras Completas de D. João de Castro*, 2 vols. Coimbra: 1968, 1971.

Cotrugli, Benedetto. *De navigatione liber*. Taylor MSS 557, pre-1600 series, Yale. Italy: 1464-5.

DaCosta, A. Fontoura. *A Marinharia dos Descobrimentos*. Lisboa: Agencia Geral das Colonias, 1939.

Dilke, O. A. W. *The Roman Land Surveyors*. Newton Abbot: David & Charles, 1971.

Dunn, Oliver C. and James E. Kelley, Jr. *The Diario of Christopher Columbus' First Voyage to America 1492-1493*. Norman, Oklahoma: Oklahoma University Press, 1987.

Fuson, Robert H. and Walter H. Treftz. "A Theoretical Reconstruction of the First Atlantic Crossing of Christopher Columbus." *Proceedings of the Association of American Geographers*, 8 (1976), 155-59.

Jane, Cecil. *The Journal of Christopher Columbus*. ed. L. A. Vigneras, New York: Potter, 1960. (Revised and corrected version of *The Voyages of Christopher Columbus, Being the Journals of his First and Last Voyages*. London: Argonaut, 1930.)

Judge, Joseph. "Where Columbus Found the New World." *National Geographic Magazine*, 170, 5 (1986), 566-599.

Kamal, Yusuf. *Monumenta cartographica Africa et Aegypti*, 16 vols. (1926-1951).

Kelley, James E., Jr. "In the Wake of Columbus on the Portolan Chart." *Terrae Incognitae*, XV (1983), 77-111.

Kretschmer, Konrad. *Die italienischen Portolane des Mittelalters*. Berlin: 1909. Reprinted Hildesheim: Georg Olms, 1962.

Kreutz, Barbara M. "Mediterranean Contributions to the Medieval Mariner's Compass." *Technology & Culture*, 14 (1973), 367-83.

Lane, Fredrick C. "The Economic Meaning of the Invention of the Compass." *American Historical Review*, 67 (1963), 60517.

Machabey, Armand. *La Metrologie dans les musees de province et sa contribution à l'histoire des poids et mesures en France depuis le treizième siècle*. Paris: C. N. R. S., 1962.

Mallett, Michael E. *The Florentine Galleys in the Fifteenth Century*. London: Oxford Univ Press, 1967.

Marcus, G. J. "The Navigation of the Norsemen." *The Mariner's Mirror*, 39 (1953), 112-31.

Marden, Luis. "Tracking Columbus Across the Atlantic." *National Geographic Magazine*, 170, 5 (1986), 572-577.

McElroy, John W. "The Ocean Navigation of Columbus on his First Voyage." *The American Neptune*, I (1941), 209-40.

Mehren, A. F. *Manuel de la Cosmographie du Moyen Age*. Amsterdam: Meridian, 1964.

Morison, S. E. "The Route of Columbus Along the North Coast of Haiti, and the Site of Navidad." *Transactions of the American Philosophical Society*. (Philadelphia, 1940), 239-285.

——————. *Admiral of the Ocean Sea*. 2 vols. Boston: Little, Brown and Company, 1942.

Morison, S. E. ed. and tr., *Journals and Other Documents on the Life and Voyages of Christopher Columbus*. New York: Heritage, 1963.

Nordenskiold, A. E. *Periplus, An Essay on the Early History of Charts and Sailing-Directions*. Stockholm, 1897.

Nunn, George E. *The Geographical Conceptions of Columbus*. New York: American Geographical Society, 1924.

Pilot Chart of the North Atlantic Ocean. Washington: Defense Mapping Agency Hydrographic Center, Sept. 1969 and Oct. 1975.

Steger, Ernst. *Untersuchen uber italienische Seekarten des Mittelalters auf Grund der cartometrischen Methode*. dissertation, Göttingen, 1896.

Taylor, E. G. R. *The Haven-Finding Art*. New York: Abelard-Schuman Ltd., 1957.

Thatcher, John B. *Christopher Columbus: His Life, his Work, his Remains*. 3 vols. New York: G. P. Putnam's Sons, 1903-04.

Van Bemmelen, W. *De Isogonen in de XVIde en XVIIIde Eeux*. (Dissertation: Leiden) Utrecht: Van Druten. 1893.

——————. "Die Abweichung der Magnetnadel." *Observations of the Royal Magnetical and Meteorological Observatory at Batavia*, 21. Batavia: 1899, Supplement.

Verhoog, P. "Columbus Landed on Caicos." *Proceedings of the U. S. Naval Institute* 80 (1954), 1101-11.

Wagner, Hermann. "The Origin of the Medieval Italian Nautical Charts."*Report of the Sixth International Geographical Congress* (London, 1895), 695-702.

——————. "Der Ursprung de 'kleinen Seemeile' auf den mittelalterlichen Seekarten der Italiener." *Kgl. Ges. d. Wiss. Nachrichten Philolog.-histor.* klasse 1900, heft 3, 271-85.

Waters, D. W. "Early Time and Distance Measurement at Sea." *J. Institute of Navigation*, 8 (1955), 153-173.

——————. *The Art of Navigation in England in Elizabethan and Early Stuart Times*. New Haven: Yale University Press, 1958.

Zupko, Ronald E. *A Dictionary of English Weights and Measures*. Madison, Milwaukee & London: The University of Wisconsin Press, 1968.

Egg Island is the
Landfall of Columbus —
A Literal Interpretation of His Journal

Arne B. Molander
Gaithersburg, Maryland

ABSTRACT

This paper will explain why there is a landfall "problem", where geographers have gone wrong in reconstructing the route of Columbus, how the overwhelming weight of evidence from multiple sources converges to a landfall in the northern Bahamas, and why most geographers seem reluctant to modify their positions.

There would not be a landfall problem today if 19th Century geographers had recognized the imperfections in the third-hand copy of the *Journal* found by Navarette. Otherwise, they would have developed their route reconstructions by synoptic consideration of all 98 clues in the *Journal*, and surely would have rediscovered the Egg Island landfall of the northern Bahamas route. As it was, when they backtracked the route from Cuba, an apparent mistranscription of 70 leagues as 7 locked them into the central Bahamas. With this erroneous start, geographers developed a variety of central routes having uniformly weak congruences with the other 97 clues in the *Journal*. Understandably, many of these succeeding misconstructions in the central Bahamas challenged others to find a "better way".

This paper shows that Columbus explored the Bahamas along a northern route and that the four islands he visited were probably Egg Island, New Providence, Andros (north end), and Long Island (southwest coast). Quantitative scoring of the northern route congruences with the 98 clues gives a 4-to-1 advantage over the currently accepted central route, with many of its features showing startling agreement with the *Journal*. The Egg Island landfall is confirmed by summation of his daily components of transatlantic travel. It is also strongly supported by three important quantitative descriptions of the discoveries from Independent contemporary sources. First, the Columbus letter to Santangel places his discoveries at 26 degrees latitude (rather than the 24 of the central routes). Second, in 1513 Ponce de Leon recorded the latitude of San Salvador as 25 degrees and 40 minutes (barely 10 miles north of Egg Island). Finally, the 1537 Chaves "rutter" (by the Spanish Pilot-Major) seems to place the landfall 6 miles to the southwest of Spanish Wells — on the south beach of Egg Island!

The 20th Century geographers seem to reject the Egg Island hypothesis because they insist on a perfect match with an imperfect source document. If they would accept the overwhelming weight of evidence for the northern route, the landfall "problem" would disappear overnight.

141

INTRODUCTION

Despite the official recognition of Watlings Island by the Bahamas Parliament in 1926, reinforced by the imprimatur of S. E. Morison in 1942, this identification of San Salvador is still very much in doubt.[1] The continuing debate climaxed in 1985 with publication of "In the Wake of Columbus — Islands and Controversy", which presented arguments for northern (Egg Island), central (Watlings), and southern (Grand Turk) landfalls.[2] This paper summarizes my 37-page contribution, arguing for a northern route with its landfall on Egg Island at the entrance to Northeast Providence Channel.[3] (See Figure 1.)

My methodology has been to compare all the clues in the *Journal* of Columbus with the earliest available descriptions of known locations along the northern route, aware that changing conditions since 1492 might have altered some of the congruences, for better or for worse. Because of its widespread availability, I selected the Cecil Jane translation of the *Journal* as the primary data source. Nevertheless, in several important and revealing instances I have pointed out how his translation was transparently adjusted to better accommodate the official route.[4] From this primary data source I have synthesized an alternative to the official route which has a much better congruence with the *Journal* clues.

My analysis is presented in three parts: the transatlantic navigation of Columbus; his route through the Bahama Islands; and other contemporary data sources. All three of these analyses converge to a landfall at Egg Island!

PART I
TRANSATLANTIC NAVIGATION

Columbus departed from Gomera in the Canary Islands on September 6, sailing due west along his departure latitude of 28 degrees until October 7, or so he recorded in his *Journal*. Although he never revealed his method of navigation, it was clearly his intent to sail due west from Gomera to his Oriental objective, Cipangu (Japan). For when his daily components of travel are summed through October 7, they describe his perceived location as about 900 leagues west of Gomera and only six leagues north!

On October 7, Columbus altered his course to WSW to follow the route of the migrating birds until the afternoon of October 11, when he resumed his westward course to his landfall. Again, if we assume his *Journal* entries are accurate, then summation of his daily travel components through October 12 places his landfall along the southern shore of Northeast Providence Channel!

The actual latitude of his landfall is strongly dependent on whether Columbus navigated by latitude sailing or dead reckoning. Latitude sailing to a strange shore is far safer than dead reckoning, since one of the ships's coordinates is always known, independent of errors in ship's speed and heading. With this technique, the navigator sails a fixed latitude by maintaining a constant elevation angle to the solar and stellar meridians. Each morning and evening, weather permitting, he would check the heights of the circumpolar stars above the northern horizon. If he found himself drifting away from the latitude, he would adjust his compass as necessary, thereby correcting for changes in compass variation as he crossed the ocean. With the aid of this accurate celestial navigation, he knows he (or any subsequent rescue party!) will eventually reach the far shore at the desired latitudè, although speed errors may alter his time of arrival. The major limitation of latitude sailing is that it can only be used efficiently when the objective lies at the same latitude as the point of departure, as was apparently the case with Columbus.[5]

In contrast, dead reckoning combines compass headings with speed estimates to obtain the increments of ship's position. One advantage of this form of navigation is that it is applicable to any direction of sail, not just those along a fixed latitude, an attribute of no apparent use to Columbus in his quest for Cipangu. A second advantage is that it can be conducted in cloudy weather as it requires absolutely no reference to the stars. However, Las Casas recorded two instances when Columbus noted variations between his compass and Polaris, an indication that he performed this ritual daily at twilight and was, in fact, utilizing latitude sailing. The disadvantage of dead reckoning is that it is dangerously inaccurate for transatlantic navigation, being subject to speed estimate errors, compass variation, unknown currents, and leeway. It was this inaccuracy which led Columbus's contemporaries to rely on latitude sailing when venturing out on their first Atlantic crossings. Morison himself cites the 1497 performance of John Cabot, who employed latitude sailing to reach Newfoundland from Ireland with only four miles of error.[6] Again, in 1534, Jaques Cartier used the same method of navigation to reach Newfoundland from Saint-Malo, France, with only three miles of error.[7]

In light of these exceptional performances, it is not surprising that the independent navigation experts all seem to believe that Columbus must have used latitude sailing on his first voyage to the New World. This list includes modern-day explorers such as Thor Heyerdahl[8] and Tim Severin,[9] as well as the theoreticians G. J. Marcus[10] and The Oxford History of Technology.[11] Morison, on the other hand, publicly argued that dead reckoning was the navigation method of Columbus, in order to explain how compass errors might have caused him to drift 90 miles south of the course described in his *Journal*. But, in 1972, Morison answered my query responding "Of course Columbus was attempting latitude sailing."[12]

If Columbus used latitude sailing, it still remains to determine whether its accuracy could have permitted him to unknowingly drift 90 miles south to Watlings Island. Note that during his ocean crossing Columbus would have seen the bright star Duhbe trace its diurnal circle around the north celestial pole, tangent to a line about 2.5 degrees above the northern horizon. Thus, the heavens provided him with an accurate and simple reference for maintaining a 28 degree latitude by watching the Big Dipper take its nightly scoop from the North Atlantic.[13] If he had drifted 90 miles south, then Duhbe would have been a full "isba" (finger width at arms length) closer to the northern horizon! Columbus's Arabian contemporary, Ahmad lbn Majid, wrote that it would be *disgraceful* for a latitude sailor to be off by as much as a quarter isba (22 miles), "especially when making landfalls on routes which are almost due east and west."[14]

In summary, I (and the independent experts) believe that Columbus used latitude sailing because this method of navigation was many times more accurate than dead reckoning for reaching an objective due west of Gomera. Summation of his daily travel components in the *Journal* brings him into the Bahamas off the north coast of Eleuthera at the edge of the reefs lining Northeast Providence Channel. The first anchorage accessible to his fleet was where the reef ends at Egg Island, the aptly-named birthplace of Western Civilization in the New World! (See Figure 2.)

PART II
THE BAHAMA ODYSSEY

This part of the paper compares the four islands of my northern route with some of the 98 clues I extracted from the Columbus *Journal* and have italicized in this text. I have tried to include enough examples of Morison's weak congruences to convince the reader that the overwhelming evidence favors the northern route.

San Salvador (Egg Island)

Rodrigo de Triano sang out "Tierra!" from the rigging of the Pinta on that fateful morning of discovery when he spotted the surf of low-lying Man Island *two leagues* (6 miles) off the port quarter. Figure 2 shows that Columbus jogged at the mouth of NEP Channel until daybreak before following the reef to its first break where he came to an *islet* now called Egg Island. He found a comfortable *anchorage* on the Bahama Bank just off the south beach of Egg Island. Watlings Island has problems with both these clues because its limestone cliffs would have been clearly visible at twice that range,[15] and the Morison reconstruction necessarily has him casually pass up an adequate anchorage at French Bay for a very rough one in Fernandez Bay after 36 days at sea.[16]

When Columbus went ashore to claim this 200-acre *isleta* for Spain, he correctly noted that it had a large *lagoon* in its center (See Figure 3), and had *no beast of any kind...except parrots*. In stark contrast Watlings Island fails to match any of these clues. At 60 square miles it is far too large to be described as an isleta,[17] has at least half a dozen *lakes* rather than a single lagoon,[18] and has eight reptile species including the Giant Iguana,[19] a reportedly delicious morsel which the Tainos certainly would have offered to these "Gods".

144

On Saturday, the first full day in the New World, the Indians came by *dugout canoe* from Royal Island, Spanish Wells and Eleuthera. Using ships chalkboard or outlines in the sand they managed to sketch their island shapes for Columbus, although they must have had some difficulty in conveying size and the distinction between islands and banks. Of primary importance were their route instructions for Cuba which could be reached by *going to the south or going around the island to the south*. This clue makes immediate sense at Egg Island because of the Indians possible concern about whether his large ships could have passed over the Bahama Bank on a direct route to Cuba. It is senseless at Watlings which has a deep-water route directly south to Cuba. Of secondary importance, his emphatic declaration that San Salvador lay *in one line from east to west from Hierro* fits Egg Island far better than Watlings.

But the biggest support for Egg Island comes from Sunday's exploration of Royal Island, *la otra parte, que era de la otra del Leste que habia.*[20] It probably took his men two or three hours to row the 3 miles *NNE along the island* to reach Royal Harbour, one of the best natural *harbors* in the Bahamas *large enough for all the ships of Christendom, the entrance to which is very narrow.*[21] There they literally found *the sea no more disturbed than the water in a well, a piece of land . . . that could be converted into an island in two days*, and the source of *freshwater* clearly marked on British Admiralty Charts. Returning to the Egg Island anchorage, he saw a lovely *group of trees* at the south end of Royal Island and *so many islands*. Even ignoring the impossible 20-mile rowing circuit imposed by Morison, not a single one of Sunday's eight important clues is as well-matched on Watlings Island!

Space doesn't permit the review of all 26 San Salvador clues. Suffice it to say that Egg Island received a 10-fold scoring advantage over Watlings in my detailed analysis. The only significant clue won by Watlings is when Columbus describes it as being *fairly large*, which I have generously balanced against the *isleta* clue, although this discrepancy is better explained on the banks of northern Eleuthera than it is at Watlings Island. Thus the Egg Island landfall from Part I is strongly reinforced by the Admiral's detailed description of San Salvador's latitude, harbor, flora, fauna, and geography.

Santa Maria de la Concepción (New Providence)

Columbus departed his Egg Island anchorage *Sunday afternoon* in order to take advantage of the strong tide flowing off the Bank from Current Cut that would have opposed him if he had waited for Monday morning.[22] As yet unsure of his Indian guides, he chose to awkwardly stand off the Bank until sunrise. That same *tide* flowing out NEP Channel kept him from making the exactly *seven leagues* in a *southwest* direction (as shown on Figure 4) until midday. Returning to the Bahama Bank near Rose Island, his lookouts spotted the blue hills behind Nassau on *the larger island to the west*, and he

145

resolved to *sail all day* along the *east-west side* past Paradise Island to reach the *westerly cape*, even though his Indian guides probably had warned him that there were no safe anchorages on the way.[23] Apparently combining New Providence with its eastern islets, he overestimated its size as *five by ten leagues* before safely anchoring south of Lyford Cay. On Tuesday morning a canoe came from Clifton Point (*de otro cabo*) as he was departing his anchorage.

The only clues matched as accurately by the central route are the distance and direction from Watlings Island to Rum Cay. Otherwise, this candidate offers no reason for his early San Salvador departure, no tide to impede his progress to Rum Cay, which is far too small in area and has no larger island visible to the west, and has him sail both (!) sides of the island past a good anchorage at Port Nelson in mid-afternoon to barely reach a non-existent one at its western end, which also lacks the dual cape. My detailed scoring for this second island of discovery also gave a 10-fold advantage to New Providence over the weak congruences of Rum Cay.

Fernandina (Andros)

Tuesday morning, Columbus departed the *islands* of New Providence for Andros Island, lying almost *8 leagues* across the Tongue of the Ocean. In the middle of this *Gulf*[24] he picked up an Indian in a canoe before continuing on to this *very flat* island exactly *28 leagues* in length. On Wednesday he *anchored* on the reef in front of Mastic Point which he precisely described as *this cape where I came, and all this coast, runs NNW and SSE* as shown in Figure 5. After rowing in from the reef he enthused about the many varieties of *reef fish* and for the first time mentioned *lizards*,[25] which are found in great abundance on Andros. At Mastic Point he quaintly described the groves of *mastic* trees[26] with their many varieties of epiphytic vegetation.

Returning to his anchorage. he was informed that the Indians thought it would be easier *to round Andros in a NNW direction* than trying the direct route to Cuba across the shoal water south of the Tongue of The Ocean. *Two leagues from the head of the island* he anchored outside Conch Sound, *more than wide enough for 100 ships*, which would have been a *wonderful harbor*, except that it was too *shallow*, and it looked like *the mouth of a river*. After filling his *water casks*, Columbus sailed to the north end of Andros where the *coast runs east and west*.

Up to this point, *all* of the first 20 clues describing Fernandina have had a closer congruence with Andros than with Long Island. In fact, most of the clues don't fit Long Island in the slightest while having a near-perfect congruence with Andros. Long Island is too close to Rum Cay; not separated by a gulf; too short; too dry; too rugged; without anchorages; without the described cape; without the mastic trees; without the reef fish; and without the wide but shallow harbor that looks like the mouth of a river. On top of all that, there is no sensible reason for his ships to sail counter-clockwise

146

around Long Island — in fact, Morison himself admits that it would have been impossible![27]

That Wednesday afternoon, one of the most important wind changes in history forced Columbus to discontinue his counter-clockwise circuit of Andros which almost certainly would have brought him to the shores of Florida and re-written the history of the Western Hemisphere. A strong norther, so typical of the northern Bahamas after the hurricane season, swept across Northwest Providence Channel and drove him down the Tongue of The Ocean on a direct route to Cuba.

Since my long route down the Tongue of The Ocean differs markedly from Morison's, it is important to justify my interpretation of the *Journal* in some detail. My first point is to demonstrate how certain we are that Columbus faced a very large storm by comparing his *Journal* with a modern description of winter northers which "typically start with the wind veering to the South and Southwest (*Wednesday midday*). When the cold-front arrives the wind shifts suddenly to Northwest (*Wednesday afternoon*), then works through North (*Friday*) and blows itself out from Northeast (*Saturday*). In mid-winter this cycle takes several days...and varies ...from brisk sailing breezes, through 20-25 knot winds, to anchor-rattlers."[28] Since the easterly tradewinds were not re-established until Wednesday, we can be sure that this was indeed a massive storm that drove Columbus to Long Island.

My second point is that the Cecil Jane translation may have distorted the translation of "el era poco y..." by assuming "viento" for the missing noun. However, this noun occurs 62 words earlier in a text which has subsequent masculine nouns. In fact, "tiempo" occurs only 5 words earlier and may make more sense in the face of a norther. Whatever the correct translation, we know that Columbus did *not* anchor that night, and that a huge high-pressure system was relentlessly pushing into the Bahamas. Therefore, we can be certain that he had access to high-velocity winds through most of the night.

Isabela (Long Island)

By now Columbus must have developed considerable confidence in his Indian guides, for he ran all night before the storm with unfurled sails at speeds that must have approached seven or eight knots.[29] By morning he was *at the end of the island to the south-east*, about 100 miles SSE of Mastic Point. That morning he *sailed before the wind* and extended his exploration well into the shoal water south of The Tongue of The Ocean. This day has by far the shortest entry in his *Journal*, reinforcing his implicit difficulties in sailing 60 miles across this shoal water. In contrast, the central route has Columbus averaging only three or four knots that windy night, and has no explanation of why he only sailed 10 or 15 miles the next day without any mention of shore explorations.

147

Dawn Friday, Columbus fanned out his fleet between ESE and SSE as he ventured from the Bahama Bank into the deep waters west of Long Island, far from the Egg Island home of his Indian guides. Before sailing three hours, they saw *an island to the east. . .and all three vessels reached it by midday*. (See Figure 6) They saw an *"isleo" pointing back towards Andros Island with a reef of rocks at the northern end and another between it and Long Island*. From there *the coast ran for twelve leagues to a cape (Cape Verde) which was round and in deep water with no shoals off it*. Columbus noted that this island was *higher than the others, had much water in the center, and had a sharply curving coast on its north-east side*. All of these clues fit the northern route. Few of them are congruent with the central route.

By Sunday morning the storm had blown itself out to the northeast. It was not until Wednesday when the tradewinds began to reassert themselves that Columbus was able to start his journey for Cuba. Here occurs the single clue which cannot be explained along the northern route, for Columbus recorded . . .*Cape Verde, in the island of Fernandina. . .lay to my northwest and was seven leagues distant from me*. This clue fits the central route pretty well, except that the south end of Long Island was really only five leagues distant, no such cape had been previously hinted at on the central route, and there was no valid reason for identifying this xerophytic limestone cape as "verde". My northern route fits this clue not at all without my assumption that 70 leagues was miscopied as 7 leagues in this third-hand account. But after this assumption is made, the northern route provides an excellent fit because Mastic Point lies 70 leagues (exactly 4 degrees, each of 17.5 leagues) to the northwest, as shown in Figure 1, and fits the name "verde" perfectly.

Considering all the clues for Isabela, the central route comes out surprisingly well with a score that is essentially equivalent to that of the northern route. However, taking the scores for all four Bahama islands together, the northern route scored an impressive four-to-one advantage over the central route! Thus, Part II of the analysis remarkably converges to the same Egg Island landfall specified by the analysis in Part I.

PART III
INDEPENDENT DATA SOURCES

Both contemporary latitude measurements strongly support the northern route. In his letter announcing the discoveries to Santangel,[30] Columbus describes them as being at 26 degrees, while 20 years later Ponce de Leon[31] suggests greater precision in placing San Salvador at 25 degrees and 40 minutes. Consider that Egg Island is only 10 miles south of this latitude, while Watlings is 100 miles away, and the other candidates even further removed.

Another source is Ferndinand's biography[32] of his father which describes San Salvador as 15 leagues in length with a peninsula which would have required "at least three days of hard rowing to round." This description does not come close to any of the candidates, most especially little Egg Island. However, it does correspond well with Eleuthera, which may have been accepted as the landfall location at the time of the biography. Such an extension in concept could also explain why Las Casas described San Salvador as having the shape of a large bean. For while Egg Island and some of the other candidates can be considered as vaguely bean-shaped by their advocates, only Eleuthera appears to have been so described by independent assessment.[33]

Subsequent *Journal* entries along the coast of Cuba are as supportive of the northern route as they are of any of the central routes. In particular, on November 20 the 12-league distance from Isabela while sailing 25 leagues from Puerto del Principe[34] is as good a congruence with the southern end of Long Island (northern route) as with the Crooked-Acklins group (central route).

However, there is one very important document from 1537 which strongly supports the northern route while completely rejecting all others. The "Espejo de Navegantes" was compiled by Alonso de Chaves while he was pilot-major of Spain and certainly would have had complete access to the journals and maps of the explorers. While his description of Guanahani fits none of the candidates, it could be construed as the northern part of Eleuthera. However, Chaves describes "Samana" as being 8 leagues WSW of the landfall.[35] The physical description of "Samana" fits New Providence so perfectly as to rule out every other island in the Bahamas. Residents of Nassau know that they are very close to 8 leagues (25 miles) WSW of Egg Island, giving new and substantial support to the northern route. But the strongest support from Chaves is his description of "Triangulo" as an "isla de los Lucayos, son unos tres isletas puestas en trianulo al nordeste de Guanahani, y distaran de ella 2 leguas."[36] While this clue makes absolutely no sense at any of the other suggested landfalls, it fits Egg Island *perfectly*. For 6 miles to the NE of Egg Island's south beach are located the 3 islets named Russell, St. Georges, and Charles arranged along the legs of a triangle at Spanish Wells. (See Figure 7.) Not only do these islets fit geographically, but they fit functionally because Spanish Wells was so-named for the importance of its sweet water to Spanish seamen. This earned them a mention in the Espejo while scores of larger islands were ignored. This fortuitous mention provides strong independent confirmation of the Egg Island landfall from Parts I and II, while having an extremely negative affect on all of the other candidates.

SUMMARY

Columbus employed accurate latitude sailing to arrive at the mouth of Northeast Providence Channel according to his *Journal* entries. It follows that Egg Island is a logical choice for San Salvador because it would have been the first land accessible to his fleet along the southern reefs of NEP. The extreme weight of evidence from the *Journal* also supports a route through the Bahamas from Egg Island to Cuba, and rescues Columbus's reputation as a precise navigator. Finally this route also fits the quantitative independent data sources far better than any other candidate route.

The single *Journal* entry that is totally at variance with the northern route is the description of a cape 7 leagues to the NW when it probably read 70 leagues to the NW in the original *Journal*. Geographers should not abandon the northern route because of this single mistranscription in the third-hand copy of the *Journal*. They should consider the weight of evidence rather than expecting a perfect match with an imperfect source document. If they did this, they would certainly conclude that there really was a landfall problem because of the overwhelming weight of evidence from all sources points to Egg Island.

Once this identification of the landfall is established, it is possible to clear up several mysteries that have previously clouded the history of the Bahamas. Knowing that Ponce de Leon's latitude measurements are accurate, we now realize that he must have returned to the Little Bahama Bank rather than entering the Gulf of Mexico. This means that his fight with the Indians took place not at Charlotte Harbor, Florida, but 400 miles to the east at Cherokee Point on Abaco! Finally, from the Chaves "Espejo", we can now confidently identify the early names of Bahama Islands such as New Providence, Abaco, Andros and Cat Islands. Thus correct identification of the landfall is not just a stimulating puzzle, but the keystone to Bahama's early history.

NOTES

1. Samuel Eliot Morison, *Admiral of the Ocean Seas*, vol. 1. (Boston, 1942).

2. Louis De Vorsey, Jr. and John Parker, eds., *In the Wake of Columbus — Islands and Controversy* (Detroit, 1985).

3. *Ibid.*, pp. 113-149.

4. Cecil Jane, trans., *The Journal of Christopher Columbus*, ed. L. A. Vigneras. appendix by R. A. Skelton (New York, 1960). Some of the simple words mishandled by Jane include *isleta, laguna, cabo*, and *golfo*, all which are vital to an exact reconstruction of the route followed by Columbus. Jane also occasionally mistranslates literal phrases as idioms when necessary to better fit the *Journal* to the officially accepted reconstruction of Morison.

5. Samuel Eliot Morison, *The European Discovery of America: The Southern Voyages* (New York, 1974). The Martin Behaim globe, reproduced on pp. 32-33, shows the twenty-eighth parallel slicing through the Canary Islands and northern Cipangu.

6. Samuel Eliot Morison, *The European Discovery of America: The Northern Voyages* (New York, 1971), p. 174.

7. *Ibid.*, p. 346.

8. Letter from Thor Heyerdahl to A. B. Molander, 8 June 1981.

9. Letter from Tim Severin to A. B. Molander, 17 May 1983.

10. G. J. Marcus, *The Conquest of the North Atlantic* (New York, 1981), p. 118.

11. C. Singer, et al., *A History of Technology, Vol. III, from the Renaissance to the Industrial Revolution, circa 1500-1750* (London, 1969), p. 544.

12. Letter from Samuel Eliot Morison to A. B. Molander, 17 November 1972.

13. Latitude sailing requires no knowledge of absolute latitude, only detection of latitude differences. Thus, the 30 minute horizon refraction errors reported by Bowditch, *The American Practical Navigator* (Washington, D.C., 1977) are of no concern in latitude sailing. However, small latitude sailing errors are introduced by random fluctuations in this refraction angle. Bowditch estimates the magnitude of these random variations at from two to three minutes of arc, tantalizingly close to the navigation accuracies achieved by Cabot and Cartier.

14. G. R. Tibbetts, *Arab Navigation in the Indian Ocean Before the Coming of the Portuguese*, a translation of the works of Ahmad b. Majid al-Najdi (London, 1971), p. 93.

15. The horizons can be calculated as 13 miles for the barren limestone hills and 8 miles for Rodrigo in the rigging of the Pinta, giving a detection range of about 20 miles in the clear daylight atmosphere of the Bahamas.

16. In May 1983 we made a comfortable overnight anchorage at French Bay. The next day we were dissuaded from attempting an anchorage in Fernandez Bay by the large swells that forced us to take refuge in the nearby man-made harbor.

17. Columbus later used the term *isleta* to describe 15 identifiable islets along the north shores of Cuba and Hispaniola. He never applied this term to islets having more than a couple square miles of area.

18. The biased translation of Cecil Jane renders this term as "lake", which is still a poor fit with the multitude of separate lakes shown on DMA Chart 26281.

19. William P. Mclean, Richard Kellner and Howard Dennis, *Island Lists of West Indian Amphibians and Reptiles*, Smithsonian Herpetological Information Service, No. 40 (1977). This reference indicates that no reptiles are now found on Egg Island.

20. While Columbus seems to have added the final two words for emphasis, Cecil Jane mysteriously renders this as "and its character", while Eugene Lyon, in his recent contribution to the *National Geographic* position (*A Columbus Casebook*, a supplement to "Where Columbus Found the New World") simply ignores these two words of emphasis. As every island

has an eastern side, it seems unlikely that the efficient text of Columbus would have wasted a dozen words to thus describe the landfall unless it truly did have a separate part which lay to the east.

21. There is no question that Royal Harbour fits the mold of the flask-shaped harbors that Columbus identified along the north coasts of Cuba and Hispaniola, while Graham's Harbour would have barely fit his criteria for anchorages. I have recently satisfied myself as to the suitability of Royal Harbour for a match to the large size described by Columbus. For, on December 21 he measures the harbour at Santo Tomas at 5 leagues, which corresponds closely with the length of protected anchorage in front of the harbor mouth, while the harbor proper is less than one league in length. I believe that Columbus was telling his sovereigns that all the ships of Christendom could have safely anchored on the Bank while waiting their turn for Royal Harbor.

22. Harry Kline, ed., *The Yachtsman's Guide to the Bahamas*, 22nd ed. (Miami, 1972). A map on page 181 shows a strong easterly set adjacent to the Egg Island anchorage which well could have impeded his headway through most of the morning.

23. Hurricane Hole on Paradise Island would have been a difficult anchorage to reach that afternoon with headwinds and a strong current now flowing against him in the Nassau Channel.

24. Cecil Jane incorrectly translates *golfo* as *channel* aware that the open ocean between Rum Cay and Long Island could in no sense be described as a gulf. Along the coasts of Cuba and Hispaniola, Jane is not constrained by Morison's reconstruction. He thus feels free to correctly render *golfo* in almost every subsequent use.

25. Maclean et al. list 20 species for Andros on page 13.

26. George Burbank Shattuck, *The Bahama Islands* (New York, 1905) restricts the Mastic tree to the northern islands of Eleuthera, New Providence and Andros on page 205 of their comprehensive description of Bahama flora. On the other hand, it describes the xerophytic growth of Long Island on page 239 and mentions on page 594 the once-thriving salt industry on Rum Cay and Long Island, hardly compatible with the growth conditions required for the forests that Columbus strolled through.

27. Morison, *Admiral of the Ocean Sea*, p. 243.

28. *Guide*, p. 18.

29. While Columbus only averaged about 4 knots on his trans-atlantic run, 8 of those days included periods of "calm". On those days in which he did not mention any "calm", he averaged almost 5 knots, assuming Morison's length for the league. On his best three days he averaged 2.5 leagues per hour (8 knots) *around the clock*, exceeding even this speed during the last 8 hours prior to the landfall. Surely, the massive high-pressure system then flowing into the Bahamas could have propelled him at average speeds of 6 or 7 knots through Thursday afternoon.

30. Cecil Jane, pp. 191-202.

31. Antonio de Herrera y Tordesillas, *Historia General de los hechos de los Castellanos en las islas i terra firma del mar oceano*, trans. Thomas Frederick Davis (Jacksonville, 1935), p. 16.

32. Fernando Colombo, *Historie del S. D. Colombo*, (Venice, 1571).

33. *Skindiving Magazine*, (September, 1981), describes Eleuthera as having the shape of "a snap bean pod". On 1 November 1986, Ms. Consuelo Varela assured me that Las Casas was not describing an individual bean but, rather, "a green bean pod."

34. Cecil Jane, p. 66.

35. P. Castaneda, M. Cuesta and P. Hernandez, *Alonso de Chaves y el Libro IV de su "Espejo de Navegantes*, Madrid, 1977, p. 87.

36. *Ibid.*, p. 88.

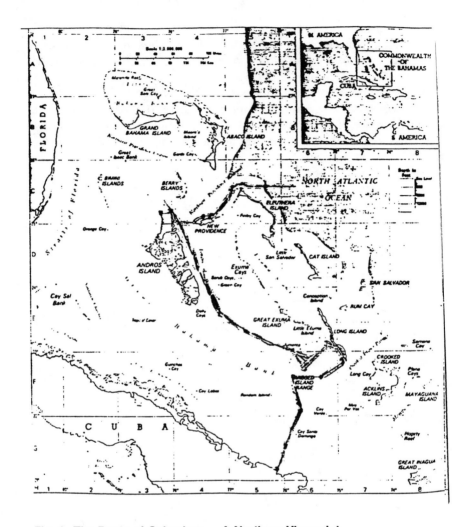

Fig. 1. The Route of Columbus — A Northern Viewpoint

154

Fig. 2. Northern Eleuthera

155

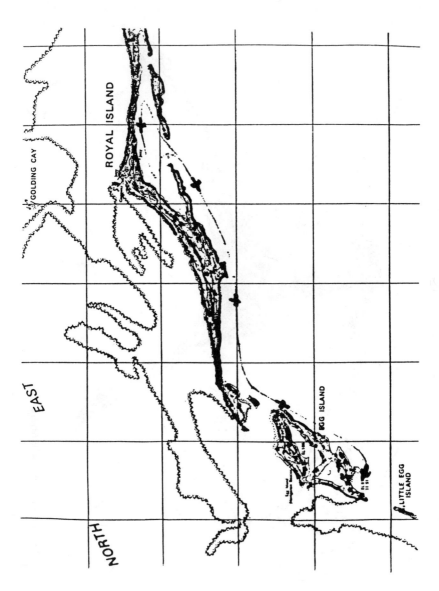

Fig. 3. Egg and Royal Islands (San Salvador)

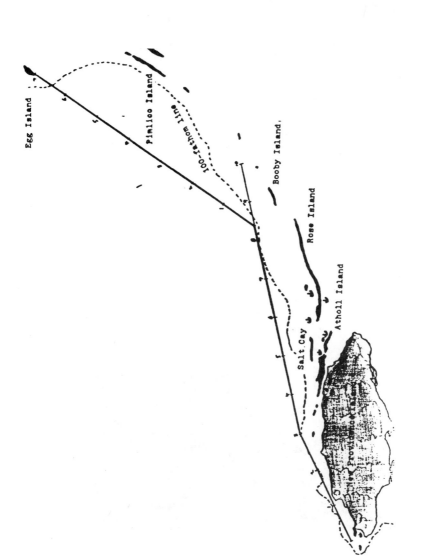

Fig. 4. New Providence (Santa Maria de la Concepcion)

Egg Island

Pimlico Island

100-fathom line

Booby Island,

Rose Island

Salt Cay

Atholl Island

New Providence

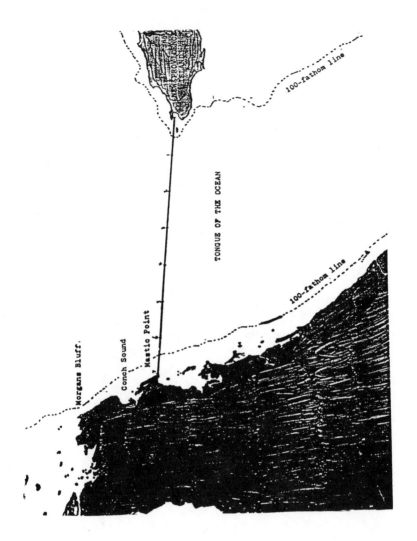

Fig. 5. Northern Andros (Fernandina)

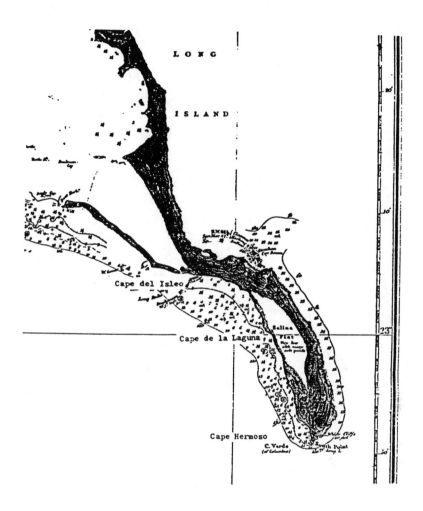

Fig. 6. Southern Long Island (Isabela)

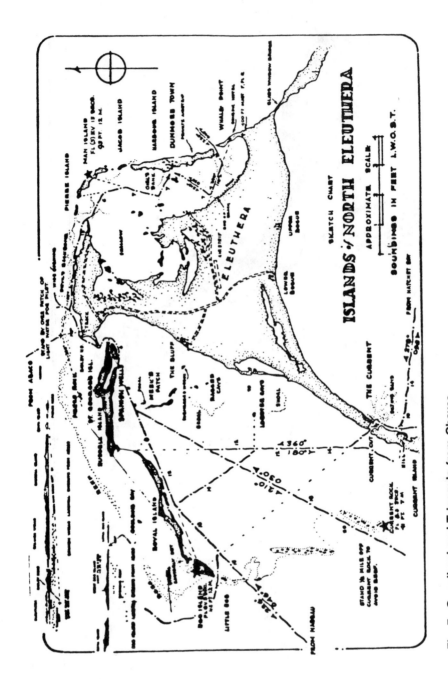

Fig. 7. Guanihani and Triangulo from Chaves

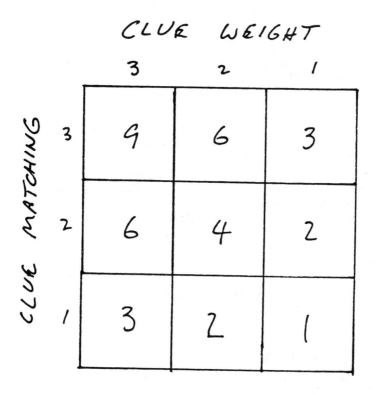

Fig. 8. Scoring Method used in Evaluating Alternative Route Reconstructions

Clue No.	Clue Description	Candidate Scoring		
		Northern Route	?	Central Route
S-1	Disputed Columbus sighting of light 36 nm before landfall sighting		2	
S-2	"...land appeared, at a distance of about two leagues from them."		3	
S-3	"...they reached a small island (isleta) of the Lucayos,"	4		
S-4	"which is called in the language of the Indians 'Guanahani'."		2	
S-5	"Immediately they saw naked people..."	1		
S-6	"...they saw very green trees and much water and fruit of various kinds."	1		
S-7	"...come here from the mainland (tierra firme) to take them for slaves."	1		
S-8	"I saw no beast of any kind in this island, except parrots."	4		
S-9	"...in one line from east to west from the island of Hierro in the Canaries."	6		
S-10	"...in boats which are made of a treetrunk like a long boat and all in one piece."	1		
S-11	"...going to south or going around the island to the south..."	4		
S-12	"...there was land to the south and to the southwest and to the northwest,"		3	
S-13	"So I resolved to go to the southwest (the following afternoon)...		3	
S-14	"This island is fairly large and very flat."			4
S-15	"...in the center of it, there is a very large lake (laguna)..."		2	
S-16	"...(cotton) grows here on this island..."			2
S-17	"...went along the island in a NNE direction to see la otra parte, que era de la otra del Leste que habia..."	9		
S-18	"...I soon saw two or three villages..."		2	
S-19	"...some brought us water..."	4		

Fig. 9. Columbus Route Evaluation Summary

162

Clue No.	Clue Description	Candidate Scoring		
		Northern Route	?	Central Route
S-20	"...a great reef of rocks which encircled the whole of that island,"		2	
S-21	"while within there is deep water (entre medias queda hondo) and a harbour large enough for all the ships of Christendom, the entrance to which is very narrow."	3		
S-22	"...inside the reef there are some shoals, but the sea is no more disturbed than the water in a well.	6		
S-23	"...a piece of land, which is formed like an island although it is not one, on which there were six houses; it could be converted into an island in two days..."	6		
S-24	"Near the said islet, moreover, there are the lovliest group of trees that I have ever seen; all green and with leaves like those of Castile in the months of April and May..."	2		
	SAN SALVADOR SCORING SUMMARY	53		6
M-1	"I saw so many islands that I could not decide to which I would go first...they mentioned by name more than a hundred."	6		
M-2	"I sought for the largest (island)...it is 5 leagues away from this island of San Salvador, and of the others, some are more and some are less distant."	4		
M-3	"All are very flat, without mountains, and are very fertile; all are inhabited..."		1	
M-4	"I stood off that night, fearing to come to anchor before daylight, as I did not know whether the coast was free from shoals."		2	
M-5	"...and as the island was more than 5 leagues, being rather about 7,"		3	
M-6	"...and the tide was againstme, it was mid-day when I arrived at the island."	6		
M-7	"...the side which lies toward the island of San Salvador runs N-S for a distance of 5 leagues, and the other side, which I followed, runs E-W for more than 10 leagues."	6		
M-8	"...from this island I saw another and larger to the west..."	6		

Fig. 9. (continued)

Clue No.	Clue Description	Candidate Scoring Northern Route	?	Central Route
M-9	"I set sail to go all day until night, since otherwise I should not have been able to reach the westerly point (cabo del Oueste)."	6		
M-10	"...about sunset, I anchored off the said point (cabo)...My wish not to pass any island without taking possession of it...and I anchored there..."	9		
M-11	"...there now came from another direction (de otro cabo) another small canoe"	6		
M-12	"with a man who wished to barter a ball of cotton..."			1
M-13	"...all the coasts are free from rocks, except that they all have some reefs near the land under water..."		2	
M-14	"...the waters are always very clear and the depth can be seen."		2	
M-15	"At a distance of two lombard shots from land, the water off all these islands is so deep that it cannot be sounded."		3	
M-15	"I departed from the islands of Santa Maria de Concepcion when it was already midday..."	4		
	SANTA MARIA DE CONCEPCION SCORING SUMMARY	56		4
F-1	"This island is distant from that of Santa Maria about 8 leagues, almost from east to west..."		3	
F-2	"...and this point (cabo) where I came, and all this coast runs NNW and SSE;"	6		
F-3	"It seems that on this side the coast may extend for some 28 leagues or more;"	4		
F-4	The island is very flat, without any mountains..."		2	
F-5	"Being in the middle of the channel (golfo) between these two islands..."	6		
F-6	"...I stood off and on all that night until day when I came to a village and anchored.."	6		
F-7	"...they brought us water...I sent the ships boat ashore for water, and they...showed my people where the water was and themselves carried the full casks to the boat..."	4		

Fig. 9. (continued)

Clue No.	Clue Description	Northern Route	?	Central Route
F-8	"These people...seem to me to be somewhat more domesticated and tractable..."		1	
F-9	"I saw quite 20 leagues of it, but it did not end there..."	3		
F-10	"This island is very green and flat and fertile..."	2		
F-11	"I saw many trees...one branch has leaves like those of a cane and another leaves like those of a mastic tree, and thus, on a single tree, there are 5 or 6 different kinds.."	6		
F-12	"...there are some (fish) shaped like dories of the finest colors in the world, blue, yellow, red and of all colors...there are also whales."	4		
F-13	"I saw no land animals of any kind except parrots and lizards."	2		
F-14	"(Pinzon) told me that one of them had very definitely given him to understand that the island could be rounded more quickly in a north-northwesterly direction."	6		
F-15	"I saw that the wind would not help me for the course which I wished to steer and that it was favorable for the other course, and I sailed NNW."		3	
F-16	"...two leagues from the head of the island, I found a very wonderful harbor...with two mouths, since there is an islet (isleo) in the middle, and both mouths are very narrow, and within it is more than wide enough for a hundred ships, if it be deep and clear and there be depth at the entrance."	6		
F-17	"...I anchored outside it, and went into in with all the ship's boats, and we saw that it was shallow. And as I thought...that it was the mouth of a river..."	9		
F-18	"...showed us a village near there, where I sent the people for water...and as it was some distance away, I was kept there for the space of two hours."	4		
F-19	"There are here mastiffs and small dogs..."		1	

Fig. 9. (continued)

165

Clue No.	Clue Description	Candidate Scoring Northern Route	?	Central Route
F-20	"Navigating so far to the NW that I discovered all that part of the island until the coast runs east and west."	6		
F-21	"...Indians repeated that this island was smaller than the island of Samoet and that it would be well to turn back in order to arrive at it sooner."			4
F-22	"I therefore turned back and navigated all that night in an ESE direction, sometimes due east and sometimes south-east...to keep clear from the land, because there were very thick clouds and the weather was heavy. There was little wind and this prevented me from coming to land to anchor."(el era poco)			3
F-23	"...it has rained, more or less, every day since I have been in these Indies..."	1		
F-24	"We are at the end of the island to the SE, where I hope to anchor until the weather clears..."	2		
	FERNANDINA SCORING SUMMARY	82		7
I-1	"When the weather had cleared, I sailed before the wind and continued the circuit of the island when I could do so, and anchored when it was not well to navigate. But I did not land, and at dawn I set sail."			6
I-2	"...sent the caravel Pinta to the ESE, and the caravel Nina to the SSE, while I in the ship went to the SE...before we had sailed for 3 hours, we saw an island to the east... and all 3 vessels reached it before midday,"		3	
I-3	"at its northern point, where there is an islet (isleo) and a reef of rocks on its seaward side to the north (fuera de él al Norte) and another between it and the main island...and said islet (isleo) lay on the course from the island of Fernandina, from which I had navigated from east to west."		3	
I-4	"Afterwards the coast ran from that islet (isleo) to the west and extends for twelve leagues to a cape, which I named Cape Hermoso.	9		

Fig. 9. (continued)

Clue No.	Clue Description	Northern Route	?	Central Route
I-5	"It is on the west coast...round and in deep water, with no shoals off it. At first the shore is stony and low, and further on there is a sandy beach...there I anchored this night, Friday, until morning."	4		
I-6	"All this coast, and the part of the island which I saw, is mainly a beach;"		2	
I-7	"the island is the loveliest thing that I have seen...It has many trees, very green and tall,			1
I-8	"and this land is higher than the other islands which have been discovered. There is in it one elevation, which cannot be called a mountain, but which serves to beautify the rest of the island,"		2	
I-9	"and it seems that there is much water there in the center of the island."			4
I-10	"On this north-eastern side, the coast curves sharply (de esta parte al Nordeste hace una grande angla)..."	6		
I-11	"I wished to anchor there...but the water was of little depth and I could only anchor at a distance from the shore,	2		
I-12	"and the wind was very favorable for reaching this point (cabo) where I am now lying at anchor..."		2	
I-13	"...many herbs and many trees which will be of great value in Spain for dyes and as medicinal spices..."		1	
I-14	"There is no village except further inland."		1	
I-15	"I believe that it is an island separated from that of Samoet, and even there is another small island between them."	4		
I-16	"Today, at sunrise, I weighed anchor from... the south-west point (cabo) of this island of Samoet, to which I gave the name Cape de la Laguna..."		3	
I-17	"...in order to steer to the northeast and east from the southeast and south (para navegar al Nordeste y al Leste de la parte del Sueste y Sur)."			3

Fig. 9. (continued)

167

Clue No.	Clue Description	Northern Route	?	Central Route
I-18	"I found the water everywhere so shallow that I could not enter or navigate to that point, and saw that, following the route to the southwest (del Sudueste), it would be a very great detour."		3	
I-19	"Therefore I determined to return by the way which I had come, to the NNE from the west (del Nornordeste de la parte del Oueste) and to round this island in that direction."			3
I-20	"At ten o'clock I arrived here at this <u>Cape del Isleo</u> and anchored..."		3	
I-21	"...only a single house...There are very extensive lagoons, and by them and around them there are wonderful woods..."	2		
I-22	"...flocks of parrots darken the sun, and there are large and small birds of so many different kinds and so unlike ours..."		2	
I-23	"As I was going round one of these lagoons, I saw a snake, which we killed...it is seven palms in length (56 inches)..."		2	
I-24	"Here I recognized the aloe, and tomorrow I am resolved to have ten quintals brought to the ship..."		2	
I-25	"...in search of very good water, we arrived at a village near here, half a league from where I am anchored...I asked him for water; and after I had returned to the ship, they came presently to the beach with their gourds full...I was anxious to fill all the ships casks with water here..."		2	
I-26	"I shall presently set out to go round the island...after that I wish to leave for another very large island, which I believe must be Cipangu...They call it 'Colba'..."			2
I-27	"Beyond this island, there is another which they call 'Bofio'(Hispaniola)...The others, which lie between them (son entremedio), we shall see in passing..."	2		
I-28	"But I am still determined to proceed to the mainland and to the city of Quisay."		2	
I-29	"They brought...some skeins of cotton..."		2	

Fig. 9. (continued)

Clue No.	Clue Description	Candidate Scoring		
		Northern Route	?	Central Route
I-30	"We took water for the ships in (en) a lagoon which is here near Cape del Isleo..."		2	
I-31	"I see that here there is no goldmine..."		1	
I-32	"I weighed anchor from...Cape del Isleo, which is on the north side (de la parte del Norte) where I had stayed..."			3
I-33	"...they indicated to me that I should steer WSW to go there. This I am doing..."		3	
I-34	"...little wind until after midday, and then it began to blow very gently...until night-fall, when Cape Verde, in the island of Fernandina, which is on the south side in the western part (de la parte de Sur a la parte de Oueste) lay to my northwest and was seven leagues distant from me..."			9
I-35	"...that night we made less than two leagues ...After sunrise...made five leagues. Afterwards he changed the course to west...and went (11 leagues). They then sighted...7 or 8 islands in a row, all lying north and south. They were five leagues distant from them, etc."			6
	ISABELA SCORING SUMMARY	35		37

SCORING TOTALS	Northern	Central
San Salvador	53	6
Santa Maria	56	4
Fernandina	82	7
Isabela	35	37
	226	54

Fig. 9. (continued)

BIBLIOGRAPHY

Agassiz, A. *A Reconnaissance of the Bahamas and of the Elevated Reefs of Cuba in the Steam Yacht "Wild Duck" January to April, 1893.* Cambridge: University Press, 1894.

Bahamas Lands and Surveys Department. *Eleuthera Map, Sheet 1.* Nassau, 1972.

Bahamas Ministry of Education. *Atlas of the Commonwealth of the Bahamas.* Kingston: Kingston Publishers Inc., 1976.

Barrow, J. *A Chronological History of Voyages into the Arctic Regions.* London: John Murray, 1818.

Boorstin. D. J. *The Discoverers.* New York: Random House, 1983.

Bowditch, N. *American Practical Navigator.* Washington: United States GPO, 1962.

Castenada, P. et al. *Alonso de Chaves y el Libro IV de su "Espejo de Navagantes".* Madrid, 1977.

Catesby, M. *The Natural History of Carolina, Florida and the Bahama Islands.* London, 1731-1743.

Collinder, P. *A History of Marine Navigation.* London: B. T. Batsford Ltd.

Colombo, Fernando. *Historie del S. D. Colombo.* Venice, 1571.

Davis, F. D. trans. Antonio de Herrera y Tordesilloa. *Historia general de los heschos de los Castellanos en las islas i tierra firme del mar oceano.* Jacksonville, 1935.

De Vorsey, L. and Parker, J., eds. *In the Wake of Columbus — Islands and Controversy.* Detroit: Wayne State University Press, 1985.

Didiez Burgos, R. J. *Guanahani y Mayaguain.* Santo Domingo: Edidtora Cultural Dominicana, 1974.

Dodd, E. *Polynesian Seafaring.* New York: Dodd, Mead & Company, 1972.

Fonfrias, E. J. *De La Lingua De Isabel La Catolica a la Taina Del Cacique Agueybana.* San Juan: Club de la Prensa, 1969.

Jane, Cecil. *The Journal of Christopher Columbus.* New York: Bramhall House, 1960.

Kline, H., ed. *The Yachtsman's Guide to the Bahamas.* 22nd ed. Miami: Tropic Isle Publishers, 1972.

Landstrom, B. *Columbus.* New York: Macmillan, 1967.

Leatherwood, S. M. and Balcomb, K. C. *The World's Whales — The Complete Illustrated Guide.* Smithsonian Books, 1984.

Lewis, D. *The Voyaging Stars.* New York: W. W. Norton and Company, 1978.

McLean, W. P. et al. *Island Lists of West Indian Amphibians and Reptiles.* Smithsonian Herpetological Information Service, No. 40 (1977).

Marcus, G. J. *The Conquest of the North Atlantic.* New York: Oxford University Press, 1981.

Morison, S. P. *Admiral of the Ocean Sea.* Boston: Little, Brown, 1942.

Morison, S. P. *The European Discovery of America.* 2 vols. New York: Oxford University Press, 1971-1974.

Olson, S. L. *Fossil Vertebrates from the Bahamas.* Smithsonian Institution Press, 1982.

Sanz, Carlos, *Diario de Colon: Libro de la primera navegacion y descubrimiento de las Indias.* 2 vols. Madrid: Graficas Yagues, 1962.

Shattuck, G. B. *The Bahama Islands.* New York: Macmillan, 1905.

Singer, C. et al. *A History of Technology, Vol III: from the Renaissance to the Industrial Revolution, circa 1500-1750.* London: Oxford University Press, 1969.

Tibbetts, G. R. trans. Ahman b. Majid al-Najdi. *Arab Navigation in the Indian Ocean before the Coming of the Portuguese.* London: Luzac and Company Ltd., 1971.

Villiers, Capt. A. *Men, Ships and the Sea.* Washington: National Geographic Society, 1962.

United States Defense Mapping Agency. *Charts 26258, 26281, 26300 and 26305.* Washington, 1979.

United States Naval Hydrographic Office. *Sailing Directions for the West Indies, vol. 1: Bermuda, Bahamas and Greater Antilles.* H. O. Pub 21, 3rd ed., 1958.

Wingate, D. B. *A Checklist and Guide to the Birds of Bermuda.* Bermuda, 1973.

The Turks and Caicos Islands as Possible Landfall Sites for Columbus

Robert H. Fuson
Professor Emeritus of Geography
University of South Florida
Tampa, Florida

ABSTRACT

Between 1625 and 1986, nine different islands in the region of the Bahamas have been identified as the *San Salvador* of Christopher Columbus. More than thirty different people have been associated with the quest and have published their findings. Those islands nominated as *the* first landfall are: Cat, Watlings, Grand Turk, Mayaguana, Samana, Conception, Caicos (considered to be one island), Plana Cays, and Egg/Royal. Grand Turk Island has been advocated by six investigators: Caicos, by three. Since the search for *San Salvador* began, there have been new and accurate transcriptions/translations of the Las Casas abstract of Columbus' *Journal*, the route across the Atlantic has been re-plotted, and the *Journal* has been subjected to computer analysis. Intensive investigation of the problem, largely initiated by *The Society for the History of Discoveries*, and recently completed by the *National Geographic Society*, has solved the five-century riddle. Caicos no longer has any supporters: Grand Turk, only two. It is the opinion of the author that Grand Turk can no longer be considered as a viable candidate for the first landfall and, along with Caicos, must be rejected.

INTRODUCTION

Between 1625 and 1986, nine different islands in the region of the Bahamas have been identified as the *San Salvador* of Christopher Columbus.[1] More than thirty different people have been associated with the quest and have published their findings. In historical sequence the islands nominated for the landfall honor are: Cat, Watlings, Grand Turk, Mayaguana, Samana, Conception, Caicos (with South/East/Middle/North Caicos considered to be one island), Plana Cays, and Egg/Royal.[2]

The Turks and Caicos Islands, geographically a part of the Bahamas but politically a separate British possession, have been identified as the general area of landfall by nine people, six having selected Grand Turk and three, Caicos.[3]

This number, however, has not remained constant. One early advocate of Grand Turk abandoned the region entirely, shifting over to Watlings. Another moved first from Caicos to Grand Turk, and then to Samana. If all nine Turks and/or Caicos supporters were living today, the score would be Grand Turk: 5, Caicos: 2.

THE GRAND TURK ADVOCATES (1825-1847)

The first person to suggest a landfall at Grand Turk was Martín Fernández de Navarrete (1825), a man who certainly needs no introduction to those of us who study Columbus.[4] Almost in passing, and as a footnote in his transcription of the Las Casas abstract of the *Journal*, Fernández de Navarrete suggested Grand Turk.[5] His basis for this identification derived almost entirely from an impression that Columbus was passing through an archipelago of many islands. In his haste to move Columbus on to Cuba, Fernández de Navarrete ignored the very document that lay in front of him, and the sailing directions *eastward* from Island III to Island IV were side-stepped. In all fairness, Fernández de Navarrete did not place a very high priority on nailing down the route. It was as though it were an after-thought, but apparently more reasonable to him than either Cat or Watlings, the two leading contenders at that time.

Two years later, in 1827, Samuel Kettell published the first English-language translation of Fernández de Navarrete's transcription. In this he supported the Grand Turk hypothesis, without offering any new evidence for it.[6] In essence, Kettell merely re-stated the notion that the voyage was a direct one to Cuba (Grand Turk-Caicos, Little Inagua-Great Inagua) and did not concern himself with the fact that the *Journal* contained contrary information for the period between 11 October and 27 October. Further, his translation was abominable.

In 1846, George Gibbs entered the arena, making a much better case *against* Cat Island than for Grand Turk.[7] For all practical purposes, Gibbs added little to the casual and fleeting remarks made by Fernández de Navarrete and Kettell, though he did remind his audience that the *Journal* places Islands I and IV too close together to allow a landfall as far north as either Cat or Watlings. Also, it must be noted that Gibbs was a resident of Grand Turk; an excellent example of the parochial, partisan advocate, defending the home turf.

The last of the 19th-century Grand Turk sponsors was R. H. Major, who, in 1847, joined the Fernández de Navarrete school, largely because of the influence exerted by Gibbs.[8] Later, in 1871, Major formally withdrew his advocacy of Grand Turk and allied himself with the Watlings group.[9] At the time when Major was actively supporting a Grand Turk landfall, he added nothing new to the distorted, direct route to Cuba. Further, when he lined up with A. B. Becher, sometime after the latter's 1856 pronouncement that Watlings was the rediscovered *San Salvador* he contributed little to that scheme, either.[10]

THE CAICOS ADVOCATES (1947-1984)

There have only been three students of the landfall to attempt to equate *San Salvador* and Caicos: two of these are deceased and one has fled northwestward to Samana.

Pieter H. G. Verhoog, in 1947, reopened the landfall campaign with a salvo directed primarily at Samuel E. Morison, but also at all of the earlier Watlings forces.[11] He constructed what may have been the first plotting chart of the voyage, starting with X-marks-the-spot, when the light was possibly seen on the night of 11 October, and continuing until landfall of The Spanish Island (*La Isla Española*).[12] For each Columbian mile recorded in the *Journal* Verhoog used one millimeter on his chart. By following the bearings given in the *Journal*, to the best of his ability, Verhoog "reconstructed" a chart of the islands involved. The resulting plotting chart is so nearly identical to the actual islands he matched that one can only believe that it was "made to fit." He may have begun with no preconception, but as his scheme evolved there is every reason to suspect that real islands replaced hypothetical ones.[13]

Verhoog's total acceptance of the light episode forced him to produce an island many miles *east* of San Salvador, namely Grand Turk. His acceptance of 60 Columbian miles for the length of *San Salvador* (derived from Las Casas' *Historia* and Ferdinand's *Historie*, but not found in the abstracted *Journal*) led him next to Caicos (viewed as one large island). Assuming that these things were correct, and that the Caicos Bank was the harbor large enough for all the ships of Christendom, how did Verhoog sail *southwest* for 20 nautical miles to find an island that Columbus said was almost as long as Caicos? The answer is simple: do what everyone else had done; ignore any parts of the *Journal* that are unappealing and write new ones! Verhoog then sailed for Mayaguana, going in the wrong direction for the wrong distance to an island of the wrong size!

Island III (*Acklins-Crooked*) must have been a welcome discovery for Verhoog (if not for Columbus), because it at least has a coast that trends NNW-SSE in part, and is of sufficient length to meet the *Journal* requirements. There is even a place for *Cabo Verde* at the southern end and a shallow harbor with two entrances (although blocked by a reef). But now the Commodore runs into very heavy seas.

Columbus sailed from Island III to Island IV in six hours or less, and had Island IV in sight for the last three hours of that run. At a steady speed of 8 knots (better than *double* the average trans-Atlantic speed of the *Santa Maria*), it takes *nine* hours' sail from Acklins (Verhoog's III) *to even see* Little Inagua (Verhoog's *isleo* off IV), and 11 hours to get there. Verhoog would have Columbus make this run of 87 nautical miles in less than six hours and then have him go as far as *Cabo Hermoso*, another 36 nautical miles, before dark. Everything else being equal, this alone disqualifies Verhoog and eliminates him from the game.

If the above facts can be overlooked or somehow explained, then the run from Little Inagua to the Ragged Islands (*Islas de Arena*) may not be. It is much too far in the time allotted and in the wrong direction. But Verhoog found a method for correcting the direction; he invented a compass variation of 15° E, which was as handy to him as the invention of the "land league" was to Morison.[14]

Looking at all of this from the perspective of a Monday morning quarterback, and knowing full-well that hindsight always affords 20/20 vision, it is absolutely astounding that other reasonably intelligent people would stumble ashore on Caicos, thinking they had discovered *San Salvador*. Columbus, even without a chart, never made this mistake!

But in 1955, Edwin A. Link, accompanied by Mrs. Link, P. V. H. Weems, and Mendel. L. Peterson, landed on Caicos.[15] Their purpose was not to find *San Salvador* per se, but to compare the Verhoog and Morison tracks. This they did, in a most unique, compromising, and astounding way.

The Link expedition accented Verhoog's Island I (Caicos), then sailed 80 nautical miles to Mayaguana (Verhoog's II) *without stopping* believing (as some others have) that Columbus by-passed an unnamed, second island. The Links then continued northwest for *another* 125 nautical miles to Samana, their choice for *Santa María de la Concepción*. Despite this impossibly long distance, and forgetting that Columbus said that he intended to sail southwest, and did eventually reach an island 30 nautical miles in length only 20 nautical miles away, the Links said of nine-mile-long Samana, "It looked like a large island."[16]

When Link left Mayaguana (Verhoog's II and the island Link thought Columbus skipped), he also left Verhoog. From Samana, Link had to get to the Ragged Islands, one of the few locations everyone accepts. Well, if you can pass one island, you can pass another, so Link by-passed Acklins-Crooked to the north and sailed 60 nautical miles to Long Island. Here he joined Murdock and Fox at the southern part of Long, then went to Bird Rock with Becher-Murdock-Thacher-Morison.[17]

I was the third and last Caicos advocate, coming to its shores in 1961.[18] I knew enough of the *Journal* twenty-five years ago to know that Watlings was not *San Salvador*. I also knew enough about sailing, navigation, and geography to realize that the Link track was a mathematical impossibility. That left me with Verhoog, since everybody before his time (such as Fernández de Navarrete, von Humboldt, Irving, Fox, et al) had been eliminated by others wiser than I. Verhoog had a new idea, and we all know that newer is better.

I constructed my own plotting chart, using the recipe found in the *Journal*, plus the 45 nautical miles for *San Salvador* from the *Historia* and the *Historie*. It looked almost exactly like the one prepared by Verhoog. I did not realize it then, but I am fully cognizant now, that I made my chart fit the real one. This is why I said earlier that Verhoog may have begun with no preconception, but hypothetical islands evolved into real ones. I knew every island between Florida and the Greater Antilles; there was no way I could push this aside as I created islands from the descriptions of Columbus. I would like to say that it was subconscious, which I believe it was, but only a person with zero knowledge of the islands could construct an unbiased chart from the *Journal*.

When I placed my reconstruction over a modern map the fit was rather good. Verhoog appeared to be vindicated and I published my findings, something I still regret.

The publication brought my first letter from Verhoog, and we maintained a lively correspondence until shortly before his death in 1984. During these years, when the letters were flying back and forth between Tampa and Noordwijk-Zee, I found a re-kindled interest in the first voyage, especially in the *Journal* itself, and I began to find flaws in the transcriptions and translations. These were of no interest to Verhoog, who would not budge a millimeter from his original 1946 position.

I went to Spain in 1972 and examined the critical documents in Madrid and Sevilla. I made my own transcription and translation of the relevant parts and journeyed to Mexico City in 1979 to present my findings.[19] I became convinced that, if everything else would fall into place, it was still impossible to follow the *Journal* from Acklins to Little/Great Inagua and thence to the Ragged Islands. But nothing I said to Verhoog moved him. More than a dozen times he wrote, "I have never found a single serious objection against Caicos as the landfall of Columbus in 1492." He even put this identical sentence into print in 1983.[20]

I asked him, if a navigationally impossible course was not a "serious objection," what would he call it? His answer was that I should re-read my 1961 paper, for it was based on the same hard facts that he had used, and facts are facts. Period.

I questioned Verhoog on the point that if the north coast of Island IV ran east-west for 36 nautical miles, (1) why did not Columbus see it before he reached the *isleo*, and (2) why did he not run aground when he sailed southwest from the northeast point of Island IV? He answered, "You have let yourself be overwhelmed by a hopeless Marion Link."[21]

Verhoog's course remained unaltered in 1980, when his Caicos argument was placed before the annual meeting of *The Society for the History of Discoveries*. Although it shed no new light on the old controversy, it did ignite the fires of research in a few.

THE GRAND TURK ADVOCATES (1981-1986)

As a direct result of Verhoog's 1980 paper, restating his 1947 position, a special Columbus session was organized for the 1981 meeting of *The Society for the History of Discoveries*. With renewed vigor, the landfall issue was attacked. Portions of the *Journal* were freshly transcribed and translated. A history of the transcriptions, translations, and interpretations was offered. For the first time, high technology was brought into play, with a computer analysis of portions of the route and, among other things, a detailed examination of the length of Columbus' units of measurement. These papers, after revision, were twice published.[22]

It was this surge of activity that caused Joseph Judge, Senior Associate Editor of the *National Geographic Magazine*, and a member of the *Society for the History of Discoveries*, to recall the words of Sherlock Holmes. "When you have eliminated the impossible, whatever remains, however improbable, must be the truth." Judge knew that the game was afoot and the hunt was on.[23]

Among these papers was one by Robert H. Power, reviving the Grand Turk theory for the first time in over a century. Loaded with cartographic and pictorial evidence, and fresh from field work in the Turks and Caicos Islands, Power made an impassioned plea for a reconsideration of a Grand Turk landfall.

Power brought to the Columbus fray the objectivity that had served him so well in a long-waged battle to correctly identify the movements of Sir Francis Drake in the San Francisco area. He entered the arena with no pre-determined islands nor foregone conclusions. His logic and evidence were sufficient to cause me to backtrack 20 miles to the east, escaping the quicksand of the Caicos shores and forever leaving Verhoog and Link stranded, with no hope of rescue.

I returned to the islands, finding everything necessary to convince me that Grand Turk was *San Salvador*. I also encountered local historian H. E. Sadler, whose arguments were basically those of Fernández de Navarrete and Gibbs. I also found a man as rigid as Verhoog, who refused to take the *Journal* requirements seriously.[24] Though Sadler published his findings the same year that Power delivered his paper (1981), there is little there to support a Grand Turk landfall if the complete route is considered. He takes the direct Grand Turk-to-Cuba track, pioneered by Fernández de Navarrete over 150 years ago.

My stay on Grand Turk caused me to write a piece for a local magazine (1982), another grievous error on my part. While supporting Power in general, I did disagree with all of the other Grand Turk routes.[25]

In 1983 Power published a formal revision of his 1981 paper.[26] In this he accepted my position that the *Journal* laid down an impossible condition for sailing from Acklins-Crooked to Little Inagua. This had been my earlier source of discontent with Verhoog. By placing Columbus at Hogsty Reef on the night of 18 October, the distance and direction became palatable. Of course, I sacrificed *Cabo Verde* and had a difficult time matching the *Journal* description of *Fernandina* to Mayaguana (my Island III). And I still could not explain the actions at Great Inagua or why Columbus would go 200 miles out of his way to Cuba (mostly in the wrong direction) when Cuba can be seen from Great Inagua. Also, where was I going to find another island for the frequently mentioned *Babeque*?

178

My proposed track from Grand Turk to South/East/Middle/North Caicos, accounting for Islands I and II, seemed reasonable. At first I was willing to go to Mayaguana for III, but beyond that the *Journal* requirements would not justify a longer route westward. I prepared a chart based solely on time sailed and found that even Mayaguana was too far, and that unless Providenciales were Island III, the route did not jibe with the *Journal* up to that point in space and time. And, if Providenciales were III, nothing afterwards would fit.

Power, as I, needed a *Cabo Verde* and a NNW-SSE coast, about 21 to 24 nautical miles from Providenciales. He fell back on a trick used by Becher: he invented a new island by combining several. Power's "Large Island of Fernandina begins with a cape located 20 nautical miles from the nearest land, and includes Mayaguana, the Plana Cays, Acklins-Crooked, and over 2,000 square miles of the Atlantic Ocean![27] At this point, like Martín Alonso Pinzón, I departed the fleet.

I undertook a thorough re-study of the issue and, fortuitously, I had the opportunity of seeing two new, and very accurate, transcriptions/translations of the *Journal*.[28] There is now no doubt in my mind that the *Journal* was, in its original form, a remarkably precise account of the voyage, and that the Las Casas abstract preserves all of the major aspects and is virtually the *entire* Journal of Columbus.

CONCLUSION

No landfall island may be determined unless it articulates with the *entire* voyage to Cuba. Simply being a "good fit" for the *Journal* description of *San Salvador* means absolutely nothing. Grand Turk is an excellent choice if we are looking for one island only. Half a dozen islands, for that matter, meet the *Journal* requirements for *San Salvador*, even Watlings. But there must be linkage to all the other islands.

Grand Turk articulates only with Island II, and only if Columbus did not sail southwest on the afternoon of 14 October. Caicos fits nothing, for there is no Island II of the right size within reach, and certainly none to the southwest. The route starting at Grand Turk and the one starting at Caicos require impossible sailing directions and distances at the end of the Bahamian odyssey.

In the past I have made a plea for objectivity in this quest, and would be the first to admit that I have not always possessed this quality. I have also said that this is a question of science, not of religion.[29] The former is tentative and always subject to revision. Most students of the landfall puzzle, however, have not approached it as scientists would, but as religious zealots. This is why only three of the more than thirty published investigators have altered their positions in over 300 years of debate. And this is why many here, at this *First San Salvador Conference* will depart with the same landfall baggage they brought with them to this island.

In 1961 I felt that there were more facts to support a Caicos landfall than any other. Additional information came to me after that, mainly from colleagues whom I often did not agree with but to whom I listened. By 1979 I knew I had been wrong. By 1981, after additional field work in the islands, I became a strong advocate for Grand Turk.

The last five years has been a period of intense study of the problem. As with any other significant change, many elements had to come together. And at the right time and in the right place.

Unlike some of my colleagues, I have no regrets that the problem has now been solved. I do owe an apology to untold numbers of students and peers who have been mis-led by my ideas that have now been proven erroneous. But I find great pleasure in the fact that Gustavus V. Fox has been restored to his rightful place in history by the recent work of the *National Geographic Society*.[30] I fully support the Samana-Acklins/Crooked-Long-Fortune route as the one sailed by Columbus during that fortnight so many years ago.

NOTES

1. The primary sources for the first voyage of Columbus are Martín Fernández de Navarrete, *Viajes de Cristóbal Colón* (Madrid, 1934); Bartolomé de Las Casas, *Historia de las indias*, 3 vols., ed. Agustín Millares Carlo (Mexico City, 1951); and, Ferdinand Columbus, *Historie del S. D. Fernando Colombo*, trans. by Benjamin Keen as *The Life of the Admiral Christopher Columbus* (New Brunswick, 1959).

2. The best summary of the several landfall theories appears in, John Parker, "The Columbus Landfall Problem: A Historical Perspective," *Terrae Incognitae*, XV (1983), 1-28.

3. Though some of the islands advocated involved more than one person, such as the Link expedition of four, the assumption here is that each theory had one main proponent.

4. In addition to being the man that discovered the lost abstract of the Columbus *Journal* and gave us the first transcription in 1825, Fernández de Navarrete was an authority on the Spanish language, recognized as such after his publication of *Ortografía de la lengua castellana* (Madrid, 1815). He also created the definitive work on Cervantes, *Vida de Miguel de Cervantes Saavedra* (Madrid, 1819). More than fifty major works were written by Fernández de Navarrete, including many on maritime history and discoveries.

5. Fernández de Navarrete, *Viajes*, op. cit., p. 24. "Examinado detenidamente este diario, sus derrotas, recaladas, señales de las tierras, islas, costas y puertos, parece que esta primera isla que Colón descubrió y pisó, poniéndole por nombre *San Salvador*, debe ser la que está situada mas al Norte de las Turcas, llamada *del Gran Turco*. Sus circunstancias conforman con la descripción que Colón hace de ella."

6. Samuel Kettell, *Personal Narration of the First Voyage of Columbus* (Boston, 1827).

7. George Gibbs, "Observations to Show That the Grand Turk Island, and Not San Salvador, Was the First Spot on Which Columbus Landed in the New World," *Proceedings of the New York Historical Society*, 1846, 137-148. The library of the NYHS contains several interesting letters from Gibbs. One, dated 20 October 1857 is a copy of a letter to Capt. A. B. Becher of the Royal Navy, in which Gibbs states, "He who is convinced against his will, is of the same opinion still." He also denies the charge of parochalism.

8. R. H. Major, *Select Letters of Christopher Columbus, With Other Original Documents, Relating to His First Four Voyages to the New World,* (London, 1847).

9. Ibid., 2nd ed., 1870.

10. A. B. Becher, *The Landfall of Columbus on his First Voyage to America* (London, 1856).

11. Pieter H. G. Verhoog *Guanahaní Again* (Amsterdam, 1947). Essentially the same article, accompanied by Verhoog's plotting chart, appears as, "Columbus Landed on Caicos," *United States Naval Institute Proceedings*, LXXX (October, 1954), 1101-1111.

12. Throughout the literature, beginning with Las Casas, the name Columbus bestowed upon the large island east of Cuba, called *Bohío* by the Indians, is corrupted to *Española* (and expressed even more vulgarly in English as Hispañola). Columbus named this land *La Isla Española*, The Spanish Island. By the time Las Casas began his abstract the name had been shortened, but it is incorrect to refer to this island as *the island of Spanish!* *Española* is an adjective, and was never used otherwise by Columbus. Its appearance on the sketch of the island that is alleged to have been made by Columbus during the first voyage is clear proof that Christopher never drew it.

13. Verhoog, op. cit., pp. 1102 and 1103.

14. The U. S. Coast and Geodetic Survey, Analysis Branch, Geomagnetism Division, states that there is no way to derive isogonic lines in the past, unless there is an independent method of dating magnetic alignments, such as matching tree rings with disturbed magnetic particles in the American southwest. Personal correspondence from K. L. Svendsen, chief, May 19, 1967. All reference to past compass variation is guesswork, otherwise.

15. Edwin A. Link and Marion C. Link, "A New Theory on Columbus's Voyage Through the Bahamas," *Smithsonian Miscellaneous Collections*, CXXXV (January, 1958).

16. Ibid., p. 13.

17. See Parker, op. cit., for a summary of these. Other supporters of this general route have been C. R. Markham, R. T. Gould, J. W. McElroy, Edzar Roukema, and Ruth G. D. Wolper.

18. R. H. Fuson, "Caicos, Site of Columbus' Landfall," *The Professional Geographer*, XIII (March, 1961), 6-9.

19. National Council for Geographic Education, Annual Meeting, Hotel El Presidente Chapultepec, Mexico City, Mexico, October 31-November 2, 1979.

20. Pieter Verhoog, "Columbus Landed on Caicos," *Terrae Incognitae*, XV (1983), p. 34.

21. Personal correspondence, May 29, 1982.

22. Louis De Vorsey and John Parker, editors, *Terrae Incognitae*, XV (1983). This issue of the *Journal of The Society for the History of Discoveries* was also issued as a trade book under the title of *In the Wake of Columbus* (Detroit, 1985).

23. Joseph Judge, "Where Columbus Found the New World," *National Geographic Magazine*, CLXX (November, 1986), p. 572.

24. H. E. Sadler, *Turks Island Landfall*, vol. 1 (Grand Turk, 1981).

25. R. H. Fuson, "Grand Turk *Was* Guanahani and *Is* San Salvador," *Turks and Caicos Current* (July/August, 1982), 21-30.

26. Robert H. Power, "The Discovery of Columbus's Island Passage to Cuba, October 12-27, 1492," *Terrae Incognitae*, XV (1983), 151-172.

27. Ibid., p. 162.

28. Eugene Lyon, "The Diario of Christopher Columbus: October 10-October 27, 1492," in *A Columbus Casebook*, supplement to "Where Columbus Found the New World," *National Geographic Magazine*, CLXX (November, 1986), supplement pp. 5-45; Oliver C. Dunn and James E. Kelley, Jr., *The Diario of Christopher Columbus' First Voyage to America 1492-1493* (Norman, in press). Both of these are line-by-line transcriptions and translations, but Lyon only covers a two-week portion of the voyage, whereas Dunn and Kelley transcribe and translate the entire journal. In addition, the latter work includes detailed notes, an index, and a computerized concordance. The concordance alone may be the single most important contribution to the study of the first voyage since Fernández de Navarrete transcribed the Las Casas abstract.

29. R. H. Fuson, "The *Diario de Colón*: A Legacy of Poor Transcription, Translation, and Interpretation, *Terrae Incognitae*, XV (1983), p. 75.

30. Judge, op. cit., 566-599.

BIBLIOGRAPHY

Becher, A. B. *The Landfall of Columbus on His First Voyage to America*. London: J. D. Potter, 1856.

Columbus, Ferdinand. *Historie del S. D. Fernando Colombo*, translated by Benjamin Keen as *The Life of the Admiral Christopher Columbus by His Son Ferdinand*. New Brunswick: Rutgers University Press, 1959.

De Vorsey, Louis and Parker, John, editors. *Terrae Incognitae*, The Journal of the Society for the History of Discoveries, XV (1983).

_____. *In the Wake of Columbus*. Detroit: Wayne State University Press, 1985.

Dunn, Oliver. "The Diario, or Journal, of Columbus's First Voyage: A New Transcription of the Las Casas Manuscript for the Period October 10 through December 6, 1492," *Terrae Incognitae*, XV (1983), 173-231.

Dunn, Oliver and Kelley, James E. *The Diario of Christopher Columbus' First Voyage to America 1492-1493*. Norman: University of Oklahoma Press, in press.

Fernández de Navarrete, Martín. *Viajes de Cristóbal Colón*. Madrid: Espasa-Calpe, S. A., 1934.

Fox, Gustavus V. "An Attempt to Solve the Problem of the First Landing Place of Columbus in the New World," *Report of the Superintendent of the U. S. Coast and Geodetic Survey for 1880*, Appendix 18. Washington: Government Printing Office, 1882.

Fuson, Robert H. "Caicos: Site of Columbus' Landfall," *The Professional Geographer*, XIII (March, 1961), 6-9.

_____. "Grand Turk *Was* Guanahani and *Is* San Salvador," *Turks and Caicos Current*, (July/August, 1982), 21-30.

_____. "The *Diario de Colón:* A legacy of Poor Transcription, Translation, and Interpretation," *Terrae Incognitae*, XV (1983), 51-75.

Gibbs, George. "Observations to Show That the Grand Turk Island, and Not San Salvador, Was the First Spot on Which Columbus Landed in the New World," *Proceedings of the New York Historical Society*, 1846, 137-148.

Judge, Joseph. "Where Columbus Found the New World," *National Geographic Magazine*, CLXX (November, 1986), 566-599, and Supplement titled *A Columubs Casebook* (70 pp.).

Kelley, James E. "In the Wake of Columbus on a Portolan Chart," *Terrae Incognitae*, XV (1983), 77-111.

Kettell, Samuel. *Personal Narration of the First Voyage of Columbus*. Boston: T. B. Wait, 1827.

Las Casas, Bartolomé. *Historia de las indias*, 3 vols., ed. Agustín Millares Carlo. México: Fondo de Cultura Económica, 1951.

Link, Edwin A. and Marion C. "A New Theory on Columbus's Voyage Through the Bahamas," *Smithsonian Miscellaneous Collections*, CXXXV (January, 1958).

Lyon, Eugene. "The Diario of Christopher Columbus," *National Geographic Magazine*, CLXX (November, 1986), supplement, 5-45.

Major, R. H. *Select Letters of Christopher Columbus, With Other Original Documents, Relating to His First Four Voyages to the New World.* London: Hakluyt Society, 1847.

_____. *Select Letters of Christopher Columbus, With Other Original Documents, Relating to His First Four Voyages to the New World.* Second Edition. London: Hakluyt Society, 1870.

Morison, Samuel E. *Journals and Other Documents on the Life and Voyages of Christopher Columbus.* New York: The Heritage Press, 1963.

Murdook, J. B. "The Cruise of Columbus in the Bahamas, 1492," *United States Naval Institute Proceedings* X (April, 1884), 449-486.

Parker, John. "The Columbus Landfall Problem: A Historical Perspective," *Terrae Incognitae*, XV (1983), 1-28.

Power, Robert H. "The Discovery of Columbus's Island Passage to Cuba, October 12-27, 1492," *Terrae Incognitae*, XV (1983), 151-172.

Sadler, H. E. *Turks Island Landfall.* Vol. 1. Grand Turk, 1981.

Thacher, John B. *Christopher Columbus: His Life, His Work, His Remains*, 3 vols. New York, 1903-04.

Verhoog, Pieter H. G. *Guanahaní Again.* Amsterdam, 1947.

_____. "Columbus Landed on Caicos," *United States Naval Institute Proceedings*, LXXX (October, 1954), 1101-1111.

_____. "Columbus Landed on Caicos," *Terrae Incognitae*, XV (1983), 29-34.

Columbus' First Landfall: San Salvador

Mauricio Obregón
Columbian Ambassador at Large in the Caribbean
Bogotá, Columbia

INTRODUCTION

In order to try to understand any event in history, it is necessary not only to examine the event itself, but also to study what went before it, and after it. Consequently it is not enough, when looking into the matter of Columbus' landfall, to read for a few weeks an English translation of Las Casas' transcription of Columbus' Journal. Let us go a little further:

WHO WAS COLUMBUS?

When he accepted the "Capitulaciones", at a time when people were relatively short and seldom reached sixty, Columbus was tall, imposing and just over forty years old. He had blue eyes, and his reddish hair was prematurely greying. Always courteous, even to the lowliest sailor, he pointed out right from the start that the gentle "indians" would better be gained "for our holy faith" by kindness than by force. But his salient trait was his single minded vocation. We have all met individuals with one overriding vocation; they are either irresistible or unbearable. Columbus was both, in turns.

Like Taviani, I have little doubt that the Discoverer was born Genoese; but the Discovery was neither Italian nor hardly even Spanish. It was Castillian and Aragonese, for Italy had not yet emerged as a nation-state and a unified Spain was just about to see the light.

Like every genius, Columbus had complexes, at least three. He was a snob who wanted to prove his noble birth, though his parents and grandparents were modest textile workers (he never married Beatriz Enriquez de Arana, the mother of his most talented son, Fernando, because she was a commoner). He insisted on proving that he was a scientific navigator, when in fact he was the greatest instinctive navigator of all time (as Peter Martyr put it, "Nada me gustan a mi las razones de este Almirante"). Finally, he had a persecution complex, and when one shows what one fears, one often achieves it. On the other hand, his principal values were these: loyalty to the crown, ambition for gold (for the reconquest of Jerusalem, he insisted),

185

and faith in God, who had chosen him to carry Christ to another world ("Otro Mundo"). Cristo Ferens, he called himself. Why then is he not a Saint?

When I first visited the Monastery of La Rábida, the brother-porter who opened the door said he would be glad to show me in, but only if I first listened to his reasons for believing that Columbus did in fact marry Beatriz. I listened, but, like the Church, I was not convinced. This was at least one reason why Columbus was never canonized. Sainthood is a full time job.

Saint he was not, but poet he was. "Era grande el gusto de las mañanas", "el viento tornó a soplar amoroso"; his writings are full of such beautiful phrases. America bears that name because Americo Vepucci was a journalist whose boisterous letters were immediate bestsellers which soon reached some 40 editions, while Columbus' first letter, one of the most important in History, only achieved a dozen. History, like Universities, often favors those who publish over those who discover.

We are dealing, then, with a visionary, a complex genius, and an instinctive, not scientific, sailor. Precise information could not be his forte, and his Journal shows it.

IN WHAT MOMENT OF HISTORY DID COLUMBUS SAIL?

The Discoverer had one foot in the Middle Ages and the other in the Renaissance. He found it difficult to deal with true Renaissance princes like Joao II of Portugal, who refused to have his devils exorcised "lest his angels leave with them". With Queen Isabella of Castille he did better, but she also belonged more to the Renaissance than Columbus (her library included Boccacio).

For the new Spain the opportunity was perfect: her champions had for centuries been pushing frontiers against the Moors, and now the war was over. "Yo vide poner los estandartes de vuestras majestades sobre las torres del Alfambra", said Columbus, and his project was approved at Santa Fé precisely when Spain was ready to start pushing frontiers again, this time across the Ocean. But the incipient unification of Spain had a high price: Moors and Jews who would not join her unified Christendom were exiled, and the very day that Columbus weighed anchors from Palos, a shipload of weeping exiles crossed, as he did, la Barra del Saltes, out to sea. So Spain lost some of her best scientists and cartographers. But make no mistake: this was not a racial persecution. It was religious; and a converted Jew, Luis de Santangel, was confirmed as King Fernando's treasurer, and put up the money to equip for Columbus the ships which Palos owed the crown; and it was to Santangel that Columbus sent his first letter. (I am sorry, but the Queen did not have to pawn her jewels). On the other hand, despite Madariaga, there is no hard evidence that Columbus himself may have been a Jew.

186

Nor is there any real evidence that some old sailor had already crossed the Ocean and showed Columbus the way. I have followed the route of the Vikings and I am convinced they did reach Newfoundland. But they did not inform the rest of the world, and to discover is to rend the veil and to pass on what one has discovered, not to run into something and forget it. And Columbus did not seek "Skrelings" in the North; he sought the Grand Khan in the Tropics. In any case, the first to bump into America was probably not a Viking but an African, for winds and currents flow irresistibly from Guinea to the Caribbean.

Also, let us not forget that the first modern grammar, that of Nebrija, was published the very year Columbus sailed. So we are dealing with memoirs born on the frontier between the Middle Ages and the Renaissance, and also on the frontier between Spain's war of independence and a new, unified Spain. A moment of transition, not of standardized words and measures. So Columbus' Journal must be honestly interpreted as well as read.

HOW DID COLUMBUS SEE HIS WORLD?

It seems likely that Toscanelli, the Great Florentine doctor and cosmographer, passed on to Columbus the world-view of Henricus Martellus and of Martin Behaim, who in 1492 produced the first known globe. National Geographic Magazine has recently published the best rendering I have seen of this globe, which is in Nuremberg.

It has been said that Columbus thought that the circumference of the globe was smaller than Eratosthenes had calculated three centuries before Christ, an estimate which Islam had since confirmed; more important, he obviously calculated that Asia reached much further around the globe than it does, leaving only some three thousand nautical miles of ocean between Asia and Europe. Not a surprising mistake, for Asia had been described by Muslims, and by Marco Polo, whom Columbus avidly read, and the fact is that, seen from a camel or from a small lateener, Asia must have seemed almost endless. But the three commissions which examined Columbus' project, one Portuguese and two Spanish, knew better: they calculated that the distance to Asia was three times greater than Columbus estimated, and their negative reports were only overruled by Santangel's good judgment when he told the Queen, "What have we to lose?".

Great decisions often require as much good judgment as they do science, and so does the study of Columbus' route.

WHAT MEANS DID COLUMBUS HAVE AT HIS DISPOSAL?

The Discoverer's three ships ranged between 60 and 100 tons, and the Caravel, Niña, was re-rigged by Columbus with a square mainsail, the better to run with the wind (tacking up-wind was a Portuguese specialty which cost Portugal the discovery, for to sail West from the Azores is still almost impossible). We have no complete description of a caravel, but Gene Lyons' document, also published by National Geographic, does add a great deal of above-decks information about Niña's later voyages, and Roger Smith of INA tells me that we are at last finding remains of a Caravel near Turks and Caicos. (He and I both searched unsuccessfully for Columbus' last Caravels in St. Ann's Bay, Jamaica; and perhaps one can be found at Isabella, Santo Domingo or at Porto Bello, Panamá.)

I propose that caravels were faster than naos not only because they were sleeker, but also because they were doubled-ended, at least below the water-line, which made them hydrodynamically more efficient. But, except in the most favorable following wind, the relatively clumsy nao Santa Marìa must have set the limit to the fleet's speed.

Life on board the nao and the two caravels was at best spartan. The Captain did have a cabin to himself in the sterncastle, while most of the others slept wherever they could. But even the Captain's cabin was not a comfortable place to sleep; into it protruded the great tiller, probably held in place with block and tackle, which must have creaked hideously all night. Food on board was rudimentary, and as far as I know, Sebastian Cabot, that scoundrel, was the first to bring along a cook. Before that, salted meat, fish, flour, and chickpeas were prepared by the crew over coals in an iron box under the fo'castle, then eaten in any relatively cozy corner, washed down with watered wine while it lasted, and then with rotting water until rain could be caught in a sail. Mealtime conversation surely concentrated on things most missed: women, citrus fruit and green vegetables. And let us not avoid speaking of the body's necessities; they were done from a swing hanging over the gun'l and certainly not to the windward. Spanish sailors called the swing "El Jardin"; a splendid euphemism.

All this discomfort was not much greater than that suffered by any peasant of the time, and it was continually relieved by the beautiful traditions of the sea, especially by songs such as the one sung out each half hour when the hour-glass was turned (hence our ship's bells): "Bendito sea el dìa en que Dios naciò, San Juan que lo bautizò, y Santa Maria que lo pariò"; and the Salve Regina, sung at sundown to much the same tune as we use today. Not everything has been changed by the Vatican Council, and Columbus was so devout that he did not need a chaplain.

Nevertheless, we can hardly expect navigators living and working under such conditions to be precise in modern terms, and we must read the chroniclers accordingly.

HOW DID COLUMBUS NAVIGATE?

The basic system was dead reckoning (direction, speed, and elapsed time) and it was obviously approximate. Time was measured with the hour glass, which a sea-sick cabin boy might delay turning; and it could only be corrected at high noon, and only for local time, so that longitude could not be figured. Direction was measured with a compass which was divided into 32 points instead of our 360 degrees, so that one must allow a tolerance of up to 11 1/2 degrees each way when translating points to degrees. Variation and deviation were only then beginning to be studied, but the compass could be corrected at midday with a gnomon. Speed was estimated by the time it took a bow-wave or a floating object to travel the length of the ship. Three fifths of the waterline in feet divided by the number of seconds gives the speed in knots; I have tried it with a champagne cork and it works, even after champagne. The Journal of Oct. 25 gives us the average speed of Columbus' fleet with a favorable wind; 2 leagues, or some 6 knots, a reasonable speed which agrees with many other instances in which the Journal gives distance and elapsed time.

But there is evidence that dead reckoning was carefully checked by latitude sailing, a method used centuries before by Greeks and by Polynesians. For example, in the Journal of his third voyage, on July 7, Columbus says that he plans to sail Southwest down to a parallel with the lands of Sierra Leone. Even with the naked eye one can easily follow known overhead stars along a given latitude (again, I have tried it with success); and when Columbus sailed in 1492, the Pleiades, or Seven Sisters, and Castor and Pollux, the twins, sailed with him near the latitude of Ferro in the Canaries, which Columbus said was the same as that of the Island of San Salvador.

This might support Arne Molander's Northern Bahamas landfall hypothesis, which he has presented here; but the fact is that the difference between San Salvador's latitude of 24 degrees and Ferro's of 27.5 is equivalent only to a sighting over two knuckles held at arms length. If you look straight up tonight near midnight, you will see the Pleiades. Hold up your fist and check if you can tell whether the Seven Sisters are a couple of knuckles off.

Columbus did try to use a quadrant, but it gave him very poor results (before you criticize the Discoverer, please try it on a pitching ship).

Morison and McElroy interpreted Columbus' league to be equivalent to 3.18 nautical miles. Marden of National Geographic prefers a league of 2.82 nautical miles, and to keep the transatlantic course from running into the Continent (or Cuba), a correction of 9-10% has to be applied. Once again, historical perspective has something to teach us. The smallest estimate for the length of a medieval league is to be found, in my opinion, in the "Siete Partidas" of Alfonso X el Sabio (late XIII Century), and it works out at a little more than 2 nautical miles per league. The greatest estimate for a Renaissance league is that of Hernando Colón, the Discover's son, whose testimony at the Junta de Badajoz (April 13, 1524) works out at some 4 nautical miles per league. But the estimates of several of his colleagues at Badajoz work out at less than 3 1/2. So I submit that the best we can do is to figure somewhere around 3 nautical miles to the league. And there is practical evidence for this approximation: in his first letter from America, Columbus states that the distance from Cuba to Hispaniola was 18 leagues, which makes the league equivalent to some three nautical miles; and one generation later, Juan Sebastian de Elcano, Magellan's successor (whose Diary I was lucky enough to find) says that Magellan's Strait is one hundred leagues long, and its length is in fact some three hundred nautical miles.

So we are dealing with eye-ball estimates by Columbus expressed in approximate units, and to crank Columbus' data into a computer to two decimal points is obviously foolhardy.

All this and much more must be taken into account when trying to deduce Columbus' landfall from Las Casas' transcription of Columbus' Journal. The original Journal is lost, and Las Casas' transcription itself must be taken with a grain of salt since it was written by a Bishop, not a navigator, who corrected headings or distances more than 50 times in his text on the first voyage, by crossing out, inserting, etc.

THE ATLANTIC CROSSING

As always, the National Geographic Magazine has made a splendid presentation which will reach several million people and will be accepted by many of them as final. Therein lies the danger; for on the subject of Columbus' route, and especially on the subject of his landfall, it is unlikely that anyone will soon say the last word, unless Varela finds the original Journal for us.

The first assumption that National Geographic's Luis Marden makes in plotting Columbus' course across the Atlantic, is that in his Journal Columbus simply noted his heading and his estimate of distance made good over the water. To this Marden applies a correction for wind and current based on average modern conditions. But is it conceivable that such a navigator would altogether omit correcting for drift? The fact is that Columbus often *did* correct for wind and current. There are several instances throughout his Journals, but two should suffice: on September 13, 1492, he notes his estimate and then says that he will write down less because the current is against him. And on September 25, 1498, he says that the current must have set the ships to the Northeast.

The point is that by applying an average correction to a course which Columbus had in many cases already corrected, Marden is surely compounding some corrections. So, Geographic's conclusion that the entire course leads to Samanà Cay carries no weight: over such a long distance, any minor daily error in Columbus' corrections, or in Marden's, can easily add up to a much greater difference than the one degree of latitude which separates San Salvador from Samanà. In fact, Marden himself points out that half a knot difference in leeway can make a sideways difference of 12 nautical miles in 24 hours, which adds up to 396 nautical miles in the 33 days of Columbus' Atlantic crossing. This could place Columbus' landfall anywhere from Walker's Key, the Northernmost point in the Bahamas, to Great Inagua, the Southernmost.

So to try to approximate leeway any more than Columbus himself did, proves nothing as to his landfall, and we must fall back on a much shorter leg of the voyage: Columbus' course from his first landfall to a well established point on the north coast of Cuba, via the islands which the Journal describes.

COLUMBUS' COURSE THROUGH THE BAHAMAS

We have seen why no hypothesis can fit the geography perfectly, so until new evidence turns up, we must interpret leagues, compass points and average speeds with the tolerances already described, and be satisfied with the proposal which presents the least difficulties. Two pieces of information are basic: The Journal (Oct. 26) makes it clear that the indians led Columbus along their traditional canoe route, the only route they knew (they had no sail); second, the indians kept insisting that the island from which their gold came was a large one, and lay to the Southwest (Journal, Oct. 16 and 17).

For me the least problematic route goes as follows:

Sun. Oct. 14: The fleet left Guanahaní (San Salvador) at about 1600 hours. At night, lay to. Wind probably E, and contrary current. At dawn, sailed SW 7 leagues (23 Nautical Miles on a modern map) to Santa Maria de la Concepción (Rum Cay), arriving Mon. 1200.

Mon. Oct. 15: 1200 — 1800. Sailed down E coast and along S coast of Rum Cay (map, 12 NM).

Tues. Oct. 16: 1000 (1200?) — 1800. SE wind, then calm. Sailed 8 Lgs. W (map 19 NM) to Northern Fernandina (Long Island). Spent the night becalmed off the island til early morning, then sent longboat ashore for water.

Wed. Oct. 17: 1200 — 1800. Wind SW and S. Sailed NNW to port with two mouths. Stayed two hours, then sailed NW to end of island. Wind veered to WNW. Sailed all night ESE outside the reefs, probably at 3 kts., half average speed.

Thurs. Oct. 18: 0060 — 1800. Sailed on with same wind and heading, to the S end of the island. Total length of island 20 Lgs. (map 57 NM). Spent the night on board.

Fri. Oct. 19: 0600 — 1200. N wind. In six hours sailed 25 NM (map) E to Cabo del Ysleo, Ysabela-Saometo (Bird Rock, Crooked Island). Then sailed 12 Lgs. (map 18 NM) along E (N?) coast to Cabo Fermoso, on a separate island, arriving in the evening, and staying til the morning. Shallow bight to the NE. Sailed to Cabo de la Laguna, on the SW end of Saometo.

Sat. Oct. 20: 0600. Tried to sail NE and E from C. Laguna. Too shallow. Very light wind. At night, lay too.

Sun. Oct. 21: 0600 — 1000. Sailed back to C. Ysleo. Explored the island until late at night.

Wed. Oct. 24: 0000 — 0600. Sailed WSW, probably about 18 NM at maximum 3 kts. because of proximity of Cape Verde at night. Then becalmed to 1200. 1200 — 1800 sailed same heading with the wind, to "Cape Verde Fix" (36 NM at 6 kts). At night, shortened sail and lay to.

Thurs. Oct. 25: 0600 — about 1730. Sailed 21 Lgs. WSW and W to Islas de Arena (Ragged Islands). Total on map 85 NM.

Fri. Oct. 26: Staid South of Ragged Islands.

Sat. Oct. 27: 0600 — 1800. Sailed 17 Lgs. to Cay Santo Domingo (map, 28 NM). Staid the night on board.

Sun. Oct. 28: Sailed 42 NM to Rio San Salvador, Isla Juana (Puerto Gibara-Bariay, Cuba). Diary says it used to take the indians 1 1/2 days in their canoes to sail from Ragged Island to Puerto Gibara-Bariay, 70 NM on the map, which works out quite acceptably at under 2 knots.

Wolper has given a good explanation of the light Columbus saw before the sighting of San Salvador, and the island corresponds almost exactly to the Journal's description of Guanahani, with its many bodies of water and a lagoon in the center (Journal, Oct. 13). Columbus must have landed on the Western side of the Island for two reasons at least: the reefs along the Eastern side make it almost impossible to approach (it is studded with modern wrecks), and the "beach-rock" which Columbus describes as natural building blocks (Journal, Jan. 5, 1493) occurs only on the Western side. To row some 20 NM from Fernandez Bay to Graham's Harbor with its "Peninsula", and back, between dawn and mid or late afternoon (Journal, Oct. 14) is no problem; and in any case Columbus does not say that his men rowed; in fact he makes a clear distinction between the Caravels' "barcas" and the Naos "batel", so the Nao probably carried a "Yole" with a lateen sail. As to the many islands Columbus saw as he sailed away from Guanahani (Journal, Oct. 14), all reasonable hypotheses have to use hills appearing over the horizon as islands, so this is no argument against San Salvador.

The route does present one problem: Rum Cay is less than half as big as the Journal's "Concepción", 5 x 10 leagues (Oct. 15). I find it hard to accept two kinds of leagues, and Kelley has demonstrated that Columbus' overestimation of the coasts of Cuba and Hispaniola can be explained by his having underestimated the current out of the East. The same explanation might apply to Rum Cay, for Columbus does say he encountered a contrary current; but it seems more likely that Las Casas once more confused leagues with miles, and forgot to correct his error. In miles, his figures would be quite close.

On the East coast of Northern Long Island, at Fish Pond Cape, there is a break in the reef, and nearby, the remains of old indian villages have been found. To the Northeast there is a good but shallow "port with two mouths", Newton Key Harbor or Seymour's, with what looks like a river mouth inside it. All this fits the Journal's descriptions (Journal, Oct. 16-17), and even though trade moves artifacts around, so that archaeology cannot give us a final answer, it can certainly help, as Charles Hoffman, Kathy Deagan, Steven Mitchell, and William Keegan have shown. Continuing Northwest along the coast, one reaches a point where it turns sharply Southwest and then South. This is not exactly East-West (Journal, Oct. 17), but it does not necessarily contradict Columbus' description. And once Columbus turned back to sail Southeast along the same coast, he could easily have sailed the 20 leagues (60 NM) he claims to have seen of Fernandina in 24 hours (Journal, Oct. 16), probably shortening sail at night, and certainly staying away from the reefs which line the shore, as he says he did. The all-important objection that the wind was too light is quite unwarranted by the Journal.

Crooked-Fortune Islands correspond well to the Journal's description of Ysabela-Saomete (Journal, Oct. 19-24), except for the coast which the Journal says runs West from "Cabo del Ysleo" (Bird Rock) to Cabo Hermoso (Journal, Oct. 19). Columbus says that the North wind was good for sailing from Ysleo to Hermoso, and Las Casas crossed out West and then wrote it in again. The coast could not run West, or it would have stood in Columbus' way as his voyage continued. So it must have run South, and, to the South as Columbus points out, there is a break in the coast (Journal, Oct. 19). From C. Hermoso Columbus tries to enter a large bay but it is too shallow (The Bight of Acklins). Then he goes to Cabo de la Laguna for water (Frenchwells), and finally back to C. Ysleo whence he will sail WSW.

The Ragged Islands (Islas de Arena) and Puerto Gibara-Bariay, Cuba (Rio San Salvador) are not disputed, and in between there is no land but Cay Santo Domingo (Journal, Oct. 27).

So, you see, the San Salvador route works well within the limits we have set, and the principal objections which have been raised by National Geographic's Joe Judge are not valid; nor for that matter are his remarks about Morison having had to change his mind: wise men do change their minds. And Morison's work needs no defense: it stands alone.

The route from Samanà, on the other hand, does not fit our criteria; and Samanà Cay itself does not correspond to the Journal's description of Guanahanì. It runs East-West instead of roughly North-South (Journal, Oct 14), and it has no big central lagoon (Journal, Oct. 13).

Judge's proposal for Concepción presents much worse problems than does Rum Cay. He proposes a Concepción composed of the North coasts of Acklins and Crooked Islands, unaccountably joined together. To get there from Samanà, Columbus must sail South instead of South-West (Journal, Oct. 13); and the eastern coast of this composite Concepción does not face Samanà as it should (Journal, Oct. 15).

Judge then sends Columbus on a short voyage up and down the South-eastern extreme of Long Island (Fernandina), much less than the Journal's 20-28 leagues (Journal, Oct. 15 and 16); and this exploration ends where the coast, far from finally turning East-West, turns briefly Northwest in full view of the rest of the island. Then he brings Columbus back to tiny Fortune Island, better known as Long Cay, and identifies it with Columbus' Ysabela, the indians great Saometo, the island of gold (Journal, Oct. 16 and 17). Fortune is almost attached to the Crooked Island which Judge has already used for Concepción. Columbus would hardly have named it for Queen Ysabela, and there is no break in its short coast. According to Judge, Columbus has sailed two continuous legs to the West, and another back East: is this a logical canoe route to the Southwest whither the Journal states repeatedly that Columbus' objective lies (Journal Oct. 13, 17, 24)? Other proposed landfalls, such as Turks-Caicos, present the same problem.

Judge makes much of moving "The Cape Verde Fix" some 10 nautical miles to the Southeast from Morison's location, but, as I read the Journal, it must lie considerably further to the West; and, more important, one can sail to Cuba, or back to San Salvador, from any of these fixes, so their exact location is not that important.

The 40-hour "Gap" which Judge suggests exists as the fleet approaches Cuba is not really a gap; the Journal does omit some pieces of information, but it always gives enough to permit the estimates which are necessary all along, such as "a distance of a day and a half in a canoe . . . without sail" (Journal, Oct. 16), and "17 leagues to the SSW" (Journal, Oct. 27).

Finally Samanà presents a worse problem. Juan de la Cosa was with Columbus at the landfall, as Master of the Santa Marìa, and in 1500 he drew the first map of America, which hangs in the Naval Museum of Madrid. (See Taviani Landfall peper Figure 1, this volume.) In this map he places two islands in approximately correct relationship and labels one "Guanahanì" to the North, and the other "Samanà" to the South. He is thus giving eye-witness testimony while Columbus is still very much alive, that the landfall is different from Samanà. Moreover, in 1526, Alonso Chàvez, in his "Espejo de Navegantes" which Geographic quotes in its supplement, describes Island number 15 as Samanà, and Island number 16 as Guanahanì which Chàvez specifically identifies as the landfall. So again, they are not the same island.

There is some discussion as to whether there was one Juan de la Cosa or two, and as to the exact date of the map. Personally I always prefer the simpler solution, and the invention of a second Juan de la Cosa seems to me unnecessary and unfounded. But even if there were two Juan de la Cosas, and even if the date marked on the map is inexact, it is still the first map of America, and it shows quite clearly that Samanà is not Guanahanì, a fact which Chàvez confirms one generation later. Historical place-names can be nomads, but it is hardly likely that less than a decade after the Discovery one island should become two, and that it should repeat the trick one

194

generation later. So Columbus' contemporaries and immediate successors appear to have been sure that the first landfall did not occur on Samanà.

These are the principal reasons why I continue to favor San Salvador over Samanà. But the important thing is not so much to try to reach a definitive conclusion; it is to avoid being dazzled by Geographic's splendid presentation, and to keep the subject open, accepting in the meantime the least problematic hypothesis, for me San Salvador.

Tonight on San Salvador I want to conclude our talk by reminding you that though, as far as we know, Columbus loved three women (Felipa de Perestrello, Beatriz de Arana and Inés Bobadilla de Peraza), his greatest love was surely the Caribbean Sea. I agree with him: it is a sea made by God to the scale of man for his enjoyment, like the Mediterranean and like the South China Sea. So I have little doubt that when in his testament he asked to be buried in Santo Domingo, he remembered the star-studded nights of the Caribbean, as you and I will long remember the firmament which tonight crowns San Salvador.

Why We Are Favorable for the Watling-San Salvador Landfall

Paulo Emilio Taviani
Senato della Repubblica
Roma, Italia

PART I
INTRODUCTION

During numerous surveys made in the Bahamas we have visited Eleuthera, Cat Island, San Salvador (Watling), Rum Cay, Conception Island, Samana, Great Exuma, Long Island, Crooked Island, Long Cay (Fortune), Acklins Island, Mayaguana, Great Inagua, Little Inagua, Caicos and Grand Turk.

We have also paid attention to the waters between islands, keeping in mind the route indicated by Morison and those indicated by Navarrete, Varnhagen, Fox and, above all, by those who came after Morison: Verhoog, Link, Didiez Burgos and Robert H. Fuson.

The latter's scientific essays are particularly worthy of respect and consideration. The hypotheses expounded by Robert H. Power corresponds almost exactly to that of Verhoog. And the very accurate arguments of Oliver Dunn constitutes a strengthening of support for Verhoog's and the Link's hypotheses and against Morison's theory.

We are convinced that in the great debate involving many choices and many arguments, some contrasting and come converging, four hypotheses are scientifically strong, many times verified on the site, and therefore worthy to be taken into consideration: the Watling's (today's San Salvador) hypothesis, expounded for the first time by Munoz and later supported and verified on site by Becher, Murdock, Morison, McElroy, Wolper, Taviani and Kelly; the Grand Turk-Caicos' hypothesis, expounded the first time by Navarrete and then supported and verified on site by Gibbs, Link, Fuson and Power; the Cat Island hypothesis, suggested to Washington Irving by his naval counsellor, which was accepted by that greatest geographer Humboldt and recently reaffirmed by the Portorican Columbist Aurelio Tio; and the Samana hypothesis, suggested by Harrisse and Fox and lately supported, after long research, by Joseph Judge, Luis and Ethe Marden and Eugene Lyon.

197

We will examine in due time in proper notes the Caicos hypothesis (in particular that of the Links), the Cat Island hypothesis (particularly Aurelio Tio's), and the Samana hypothesis.

We intend now to explain the reasons why the author of these notes and his assistant, Dr. Paolo Masetti, lean toward the Watling-San Salvador hypothesis.

The first important argument against the hypothesis of the Links, and of all those who want to place the Landfall on Caicos or on Grand Turk, concerns the route of Columbus's Atlantic crossing from the beginning to its end.

It is quite impossible to agree on the exactness of the route indicated by Morison and McElroy: there are arguments concerning the measures of the mile and the league adopted by Columbus and the figures he gives are entirely approximate, being very rudimentary computations of the ship's speed and of the longitudes.

We want also to take into consideration the test made by Luis and Ethe Marden with the scientific support of Lyon. The hypotheses of the Altantic routes — the one of Morison and McElroy and that of the Marden and Lyon — are both approximate, but they have a common ground: neither places the arrival point south of 23°. Grand Turk and East Caicos are at 21°30′N. and at 21°40′N of latitude.

However one interprets the daily figures for the route (the true ones and those altered for the sailors) written by the Genoese in his *Journal*, it is very difficult to suppose that his ships were displaced 6 degrees SW in reference to the starting point. Indeed the displacement from 27°42′N. (Iron Island's latitude) to 23°56′N. (according to Morison-McElroy) or at 23°5′N. (according to the Mardens) — notwithstanding the deviation toward NW from September 19 to 24 — can be justified only thanks to the remarkable change of route in the last days following the birds' flight. To suppose instead that the ships were displaced south of the 6° seems to us difficult indeed, if not impossible.

This is already an argument that we might consider decisive to exclude, not the hypothese regarding Cat Island and Samana, which are on latitudes near enough to those of San Salvador, but the Caicos and Grand Turk hypothesis, which seems to be the one highly favored in relation to the hypothesis of Morison-Wolper-Taviani-Kelley.

But we do not intend to close our address with this argument, although it is important. The scruples and passion of contemporary scholars who support the original hypothesis of Navarrete regarding Grand Turk-Caicos (Link, Verhoog, Power, Fuson, Dunn) are such that they deserve thorough analysis in all their aspects. That of the Atlantic crossing route is only one of them; the other three aspects are the characteristics of the Landfall island, the course along the coast of this island, and the course and its halting-places in the Bahamas archipelago.

Regarding this last subject, a first fact is evident; opponents of Morison's hypothesis do not agree on the indication of the course between islands and do not agree either on the exact identification of the first island.

While it is evident that for the Links the landfall would have been in the present East Caicos, for Fuson and Power it would have occurred in Grand Turk, since to this island Fuson attributes the name of Guanahani-San Salvador.

But more important are the divergencies about the route. Let us leave aside Navarrete and Kettel, who did not conduct verification on the spot, and analyse the hypotheses proposed by those who traced the routes after having confirmed them in person.

Route according to Gibbs

Grand Turk → Caicos → Little Inagua → Great Inagua → Cuba.

Route according to Verhoog

Grand Turk → Caicos → Providenciales → Mayaguana → Plana Cays → Crooked Island → Fortune (Long Cay) → Acklins Islands → Little Inagua → Ragged Islands → Cuba.

Route according to Link

Grand Turk (only the light) → Caicos (Landfall) → Providenciales → Caicos → Mayaguana → Plana Cays → Samana → Long Island → Crooked Island → Fortune (Long Cay) → Ragged Islands → Cuba.

Route according to Power

Grand Turk (Landfall) → Providenciales → Caicos → Mayaguana → Plana Cays → Acklins Islands → Great Inagua → Little Inagua → Ragged Islands → Cuba.

There are therefore four different hypotheses that oppose that of Morison-Wolper-Taviani-Kelley.

There is also another variation, the first assumption of Becher regarding a stop in Great Exuma, an assumption correctly criticized by Fox. If Exuma is eliminated, what is constant in all the authors is: Watling (San Salvador) → Rum Cay → Long Island → Crooked Island → Fortune (Long Cay) → Ragged Islands → Cuba.

Already this has persuaded me to be skeptical about the method used to solve the Landfall problem by focusing on the route really taken by the three vessels of the discovery, all extraordinarily undamaged between the treacherous waters and beaches of the isles and of the coral cayos.

There are some parts of the *Columbus's Journal*, between the 14th and 24th October, which give information and measures that do not fit any of the hypotheses proposed, neither those which offer a single solution (Murdock-Morison, McElroy, Taviani, Kelly) nor those which propose various solutions (Gibbs, Verhoog, Link, Power, Fuson).

Our impression is also strengthened by the results of the expedition of the Links, accompanied by Capt. Weems and by Commodore Mendel L. Peterson of the Smithsonian Institution.

In a boat and in an airplane (at a height of 65 feet) they explored all the possible routes of Columbus. These were their conclusions: for 11 reasons Watling should not be the Landfall island; for 13 reasons the route indicated by Verhoog should not be valid, except for its indication that the Landfall should be in the Caicos islands. Such results should agree with Link's theory: Caicos → Samana → Long Island → Crooked Island. But we'll see in another paper (Part II, this presentation) how this theory is instead unacceptable, according to my opinion.

What is interesting next is to establish whether the method can be used to obtain, if not with certainty at least with probability, the exact Landfall island, and to leave aside the interpretation of the route of Columbus' cruise in the Bahamas, starting on October 15, and focus attention on the characteristics of the island, as the Genoese navigator describes it.

In favor of this method there is another argument, at least in our point of view, conclusive.

The information that Columbus gives us on the first island discovered may be affected by his excited state, by his need to find everything attractive, by his desire to report strong and astonishing reactions. On the whole, however, substantially the information is valid.

However, the accuracy of the substance of the information Columbus gives on the route is doubtful. First of all, the Genoese is never precise — and he couldn't be — in his sight measurements, especially the terrestrial ones. It is not to be forgotten with how much confidence he will assure us that Hispaniola is larger than England (when in fact it is less than a third) and that the mountains around Baie de l'Acul are higher than the Peak of Tenerife (when they don't reach even half of its height). It is, on the other hand, recognized by everybody that more than once in the *Journal* miles are confused with the leagues and vice versa, and sometimes a confusion on the cardinal points occurs.

But there is more. We shall see further on that the latitude grades of Cuba were wrong, as there is no doubt that the mistakes were made either by Columbus or by the copyist, so that later, competing explorers could not take advantage of it. We can't therefore even be certain that also for the route through the Bahamas the hand of some copyist has not intervened to alter some number. This is not the case with the geographical, hydrographical, orographical, botanical, and maritime particulars, which Columbus speaks of in detail in presenting to us the island of his first landfall.

Decided upon the priority of the method, we now proceed examining, one by one, the characteristics of Guanahani, of the local inhabitants of Columbus's San Salvador, as they are described in the *Journal*.

On the 11th of October the *Journal* says "illegaron a una isleta de los Lucayos"; on the 13th of October: "esta isla es bien grande".

The apparent contradiction is easily explained. On the 11th of October the one who writes is Las Casas, a copyist and summarizer of the diary: on the 13th of October, as it seems from the context, the one who writes is Christopher Columbus.

To Las Casas, and to all of us from the Mediterranean, all of the Bahamas islands — except one — are "isletas". Only Andros, the surface of which (about 6 thousand square kilometers) is three quarters of Corsica and nearly the double of Maiorca, would be called an island.

Columbus instead calls it "bien grande", meaning that it is not a small island, but not a rock either. It is to be remembered that on the 13th of October the Genoese had already seen many rocks, small islands, and cayos after arriving at and sailing around San Salvador. Comparing them with San Salvador — with its 155 km^2 — it fits the definition of "bien grande", while to Las Casas — with the European islands and the major Caribbean ones, to him now already known, in mind — it fits to the definition of "isleta".

Let us now examine the other islands that compete for the title of the Landfall island.

To the double definition of Las Casas correspond also Mayaguana (285 km^2), Cat Island (388 km^2) and Caicos. This last one — and we'll talk about it again when speaking about Link's theory — was an island only at the end of the 15th century; today it is divided by marine canals into four islands (North Caicos, South Caicos, Middle Caicos, East Caicos) that in area add up to about 300 km^2. Therefore Caicos has the conditions of being an "isleta" for Las Casas and "bien grande" for Columbus.

But Grand Turk doesn't at all match these conditions: it is a very modest island, 10 km long from north to south, less than 4 km wide at its widest point from east to west. And also Samana Cay doesn't fit: it is a simple cay 14 km long from east to west and less than a kilometre wide south to north. We now examine again the features mentioned in the *Journal*.

"Muy llana"
Each of the islands examined is flat. It is enough to remember that the highest point of all the Bahamas Islands is 69 meters.

"Sin ninguna montaña"
None of the islands in question has mountains.

"Una grande restinga de piedras, que cerca toda aquella isla alrededor"
The coral reef which surrounds the entire island is a peculiar characteristic of San Salvador, of the Caicos Islands, of Grand Turk and, even if less, of Mayaguana, but it is not found either in Cat Island or in Eleuthera.

"Una laguna en medio muy grande"
This is a characteristic only found in San Salvador. Here there was, and today is as well, a large lagoon (Great Lake) about 16 km long from north to south, and at the largest point, more than 3 km wide. Caicos as well has many lagoons, but of modest proportions. There is not a "en medio", a "muy grande" lagoon.

201

"Muchas aguas," "y much agua"
San Salvador has a lot of fresh water, especially during the rainy season, and October is its end. There is plenty of fresh water on Mayaguana, Cat Island and Samana. Not Caicos and neither Grand Turk, which suffer from lack of fresh water.

"De arboles muy verde"
This characteristic is to be connected with abundance of water and automatically eliminates Caicos, which was dry and deserted. It has none of the full bloom that Columbus attributes to San Salvador.

In October, San Salvador was — and is — covered with a blooming vegetation. Flora is basically changed from Columbus's time. Of the big mahogany trees, today in San Salvador there are only the trunks. The transformation occurred during the North American War of Independence, when colonists loyal to the English Monarchy — and therefore known in history as Monarchists — moved from the continent to the islands with their black slaves, and cut down forests, changing them into cotton plantations. When the cotton cultivation became unprofitable, the plantations were abandoned: one can still see here and there some plants with white flooks. Besides mahogany, which is now only a memory, there were and still are in San Salvador many trees, which make it in every month of the year very green and pleasant to view. Woods and brush are very thick and tangled, covering it completely, and between the various plants there are the Sabal dwarf palm and the *Lignum vitae*.

To conclude: Grand Turk and Samana are to be excluded because they are small islands — neither "isleta", nor "bien grande".

Cat Island is to be excluded because it lacks abundant water and vigorous vegetation; but also has only a small lake in the southern part and certainly not in the middle; and it doesn't have "la grande restinga de piedras" which "la cerca toda alrededor".

Mayaguana is to be excluded because, although it has a lot of fresh water, it hasn't any lagoon in the middle, nor in any other place.

Eleuthera is to be excluded, as well, even though it has a lot of water and vegetation, because there is no lagoon and it isn't completely surrounded by a coral reef.

Caicos is finally also to be excluded because its lagoons are of modest proportions; it hasn't much water and vegetation and it is, on the contrary, dry and desolated.

Up to now we have followed the more certain text, the *Journal*. Let us now examine Las Casas' and Don Fernando's texts.

Las Casas in the *Historia* repeats "sin montaña alguna", "como una huerta llena de arboleda verde y fresquisima toda baja", features already mentioned in his copy of the *Journal*. He also adds new information, "isla de quince leguas de luengo, poco mas o menos", and he specifies that the lagoon which "estaba en medio" was "de buena agua dulce de que bebian".

Las Casas in the *Apologética Historia* always says that in the "cartas del marear" it is called "Triango, como ignorantes los pintores de la antiguedad" (that is to say: the map-makers do not know the Indian name). And he adds that "tiene la diche isla forma de una haba".

Don Fernando is more moderate. He only says that "era una isla de XV leghe di lunghezza, piana e senza montagne, piena di alberi verdi e di bellissime acque, con una gran laguna in mezzo, popolata di molte genti".

It is important that Don Fernando, and also Las Casas, does not say that the lagoon was fresh water. Because — as is well known — the big lagoon in San Salvador is sea-water. The abundance of fresh water is however real, especially in October, at the end of the rainy season. As Las Casas had never been to the Lucayan Islands nor to San Salvador, it is obvious that the sentence "de buena agua dulce de que bebían" is an arbitrary addition.

The particulars of the form of the island, "triango" and "forma de una haba", refer to the maps of the time, particularly during the ensuing period of Spanish explorations (the greatest which included them all, that of Ponce de Leon's in 1513). Two are the particulars which suit perfectly to Watling-San Salvador Isle; and which do not suit any other island, let us say, in competition.

The only new information which disturbs our thesis is the length of 15 leagues. Great importance does not attach to this number because more than once in the *Journal* there is some confusion between miles and leagues. If instead of 15 leagues we substitute 15 miles, the measurement corresponds nearly perfectly to the length of San Salvador from south to north: 13 miles, which means 21 km, corresponds almost exactly to the 15 Mediterranean miles of Columbus: a little more than 22 km.

The reason why Columbists haven't given a great importance to the above mentioned detail is that the number of 15 leagues is completely out of proportion not only for San Salvador-Watling but also for Caicos and even more so for Grand Turk and Samana. Since our opponents all lined up for the Caicos-Grand Turk solution, they are obviously in accord with us in accepting the hypothesis of a confusion between leagues and mi. `s. There is only one hypothesis which takes the 15 leagues into serious cons. eration and it is the one which identifies Cat Island as the Landfall. This hypothesis is discussed in the paper we have already circulated.

So far, from this initial discussion, San Salvador would seem to be the Landfall site. But there is more to it.

On the 14th of October, Columbus sails along the coast of the island in the direction of North/North-East. The natives invite him to land, but he "wanted", he writes on the *Journal*, "to see a great reef of rocks which encircled the whole of that island, while within there is deep water and a harbour large enough for all the ships of Christendom, the entrance to which is very narrow. It is true that inside the reef there are some shoals, but the sea is no more disturbed than the water in a well. And in order to see all this, I went this morning, that I might be able to give an account of all

203

to Your Highness and also say where a fort could be built. I saw a piece of land, which is formed like an island although it is not one, on which there were six houses; it could be converted into an island in two days".

This harbor, protected by the coral reef — the waters being as still as in a well, that can receive all the vessels of Christianity — is to be found only in San Salvador. It is Graham's Harbor: it was identified by Morison, by Wolper and by the author of this essay.

We have also discovered the peninsula which "with a couple day's work can become an island". The slow, inexorable action of the sea has made it into an island, wearing away the thin isthmus made of rocks and digging a real canal in which one can walk on foot during the low tide. Either some natural phenomenon caused this or the corsairs (who frequented and inhabited Watling) or the English, sometime during their history there employed the small island as a fortress. An old iron gun was found there at the end of last century.

As to the six houses on the peninsula, today an island, which the *Journal* refers to, Wolper was able to trace them as a sure ancient sign of Indian habitation.

Objectively, we must say that this port, which Wolper, Morison and we have identified as being Graham's Harbor, is, to an extent, a source of contradiction.

Among the supporters of the Grand Turk hypothesis there is one (Power) who denies that Graham's Harbor might be the port of which Columbus speaks on the date of October 14th; and there is one (Fuson) who denies that Columbus had gone with long boats toward it in the morning of that October 14th.

Let us face the first objection. The *Yachtsman's Guide to the Bahamas* — says Power — demolishes Morison's theory of the port. *The Guide* says: "There are no real sure ports in San Salvador but the anchoring is quite comfortable in Cockburn Town (the capital). There is then the open anchoring of Graham's Harbor, which is situated in the north-east side of the island where a boat with a draught of 7 feet can enter. The legend says it is the one Columbus described which "could contain all the vessels of Christainity".

This reference to the *Guide* doesn't seem at all pertinent to us. It is obvious that today's *Guide* must advise the tourists on the risks of shallow waters of the Graham's Harbor, risks Columbus never hid or left out.

He in fact wrote: "Es verdad que dentro d'esta cintha ay algunas baxas". Today's *Guide* has and must have a different vision about the sea than the one Columbus had, as he was used to 100 tons ships. And on the other side Columbus — during all his first journey — was generally elated and this many times induced in him fantastic exaggerations about ports, bays and river estuaries.

We know that Wolper's interpretation which is very important is completely different. But as from now we can affirm owing to much personal experience, that it concerns a pond of over 30 km², that there are many shallows and that in some points the seabottom is more than 10 meters deep. It is clear even today that the island (peninsula) could serve as a fortress.

While Power denies that Graham's Harbor might have been the port which Columbus talks about in the *Journal* on the 14th of October, his colleague Fuson says it might be and — to oppose our theory and Morison's — he troubles himself to demonstrate that Columbus didn't go to that port on that important morning of October 14th.

To argue this, Fuson interprets the Spanish language in his own way and particularly the phrase "en el camino de": a conception which would allow him to affirm that Columbus — in the morning of the 14th — would have sailed not towards the North-East — toward where Graham's Harbor is situated — but towards the South-West.

One of Fuson's supporters, Oliver Dunn, thinks he can demolish Morison's hypothesis and ours on the Landfall by utilizing alleged transcription mistakes in the *Journal*, so we go back to the text of October 14th, in its absolute literal transcription: "fue al luégo dla ysla en el camino del nornordeste *pa* ver la otra *pte* que era de la pte del leste q avia". We think that this passage should be interpreted to mean: "fue al luego de la ila en el camino *del* Nord-nordeste para ver la otra parte, que era de la parte del Leste, que avia".

Up to here there should be no controversy. The controversy starts here, regarding the translation of the few words we have italicized. Fuson translates *del* as meaning from. "He went along the island on the route *from* the north-northeast in order to see the other part which was the eastern part, that was there". Through such a device one would understand that Columbus went South instead of North-East, and wasn't able to find Graham's Harbor. In this way an important proof in favor of Watling (today San Salvador) collapses.

We can't understand for what reason one would translate *en el camino de* as *from*. We have compared the three Italian translations. Ferro, Caddeo and Braibanti translate the passage in question: "I led myself along the island, on the North-North-East route to see the other side" (Ferro); "I went out to sail along the coast of the island in direction North-North-East to examine the opposite coast" (Caddeo); "I sailed along the coast of the island in direction North-North-East, to see its oriental part" (Braibanti).

But first of all, Las Casas himself, copyist of the *Journal*, in writing the *Historia General de las Indias*, refers this way to the passage in question: "comenzo a caminar por el luengo de la costa de la isla, por el Nornordeste, para ver la otra parte de ella".

The elaborate disquisition made by Fuson is therefore without grounding.

We have stopped on this point for a time because the argument against the hypothesis of Watling-San Salvador constitutes one of the most exploited arguments. The question finds credit because, while it is easy to translate from Castilian into Italian, it isn't easy to translate from Castilian into English.

Another issue often raised by the opponents of Watling-San Salvador is the reading of the *Journal* on the date of October 15th. It concerns some rather confused periods in which an island of 5 leagues from North to South and of 10 leagues from East to West is mentioned. Then another island which should be larger on the West side is also mentioned. The interpretation which we give — in accord with Morison — is that the first island is Rum Cay, called by Columbus Santa Maria de la Concepción, and that the second island is Long Island, called by Columbus Fernandina.

Fuson, Power and the sustainers of the Grand Turk hypothesis object that they do not match at all the measurements indicated by the *Journal*. And here they are right; but we do not worry about the question, as many other times Columbus gives wrong or inexact measurements, and sometimes even fantastic ones.

They also add that from the text it seems that the islands mentioned by Columbus are three: the first, which has no name (unnamed); the second, named Santa Maria de la Concepción; the third, Fernandina. And as there are not three islands, but only two in the part of sea considered on the Western side of Watling-San Salvador, the hypothesis that the latter is really the Landfall island would fall down.

We suggest the reader very carefully go through the sentences of the *Diary* that are object of conflict. They are very confused but the claim that they refer to three islands and not two is absolutely unfounded. The Spanish text and the Italian translations of Ferro, Braibanti and Caddeo (who have no preconceived ideas regarding the Landfall) leave no doubts at all. It concerns two islands. But the most decisive argument, which demolishes the objection, is that Las Casas (in chapters XLI and XLII of the *Historie*) interprets this part of the Journal without leaving any space for doubts: the islands are two: Santa Maria de la Concepción and Fernandina. The third island not named doesn't exist in their texts; its existence rises only from a biased reading of the *Journal*.

One more question. At the end of October 14th, the Admiral writes: "I looked at all the port and then went back to the ship and raised the sails, and I saw many islands and I couldn't decide to which to go to first. And then the men I had taken were telling me, by gestures, that there were so many that they could not enumerate them, and they named more than a hundred. Therefore at the end I chose the largest one and towards that I decided to go, and so I did; it must be away from San Salvador 5 leagues and so the other".

This passage of the *Board Journal* contains the most serious evidence against the hypothesis of the Landfall in San Salvador-Watling. The ship of Columbus was anchored in the sea, while raising the sails in that place no island can been seen, unless one wants to consider as islands — and it would be absurd — the rocks and the coral reef of San Salvador.

However, it is to be stressed that Columbus doesn't say he saw the islands at the moment he raised the sails. He writes: "yo miré todo aquel puerto y después me bolví a la nao y dí la vela y vide tantas islas..." In the same sentence Columbus lists four successive actions — four events, which, obviously, were subsequent in time. Some hours have certainly passed between the event "me bolví a la nao" and the "dí la vela" one. More hours might also have passed between the "dí la vela" and "vide tantas islas". In those hours a good part of the sea might have been crossed. Coming from San Salvador towards the South-West, one must cover between 20 to 25 miles to arrive to a point where Rum Cay and Conception might be seen with all their surrounding cayos. We have crossed this part of sea many times and therefore we make this hypothesis out of direct experience. This explanation is supported by the *Historia* of Las Casas (cap. XLI).

Another explanation is Morison's. To whomever comes from San Salvador, Rum Cay seems to have six points on the sea, which at first sight seem to be six different islands. Only as one gets near does one realize that the six promontories belong to but one island, which is Rum Cay. Morison's explanation is neither wandering or arbirtrary. We have repeated as well — myself and Dr. Masetti — the experiment and the first impression of being in front of six islands was verified in a very clear way. It is as Morison says.

In the end it must be remembered that the Indians said to the Admiral that the islands were "many many so it was impossible to count them and they nominated more than one hundred".

The question is explained with a geography text underhand: the Bahamas comprise 30 major islands, 660 small islands, and 2400 rocks; Turks are 6 islands and various rocks; Caicos 6 as well, 16 small islands and numerous rocks. The Indians, who usually exaggerated, didn't exaggerate at all in this occasion.

There could be many more disquisitions on the route subsequent to the Landfall, but the doubts, arguments, and discrepancies related to this route concern the distances and they are of no great importance.

Our method — it should be clear by now — is not to rely on Columbus's measurement of the distances, but, for the Landfall indications, to focus on the comparison of the characteristics of each island. From this point of view Eleuthera appears remote from any correspondence to the characteristics mentioned in the *Board Journal*. Therefore, we cannot accept the conclusions of Molander's study (not lacking in sharp and interesting remarks) in reference to an eventual northern route in the Bahamas' archipelago.

In regard to the Mayaguana hypothesis, I have no knowledge that it has ever been verified on site by Varnhagen or even by Didiez Burgos.

Worthy of particular attention are instead the elaborate theory of the Links and any hypotheses of Cat Island and Samana: to these we will turn in separate lectures.

In conclusion, we repeat what we emphasized earlier: these problems cannot be solved within mathematics. There is no certainty, only a high percentage of probability. In this context, we lean to the Landfall in Watling, which, very opportunely, the Bahamian government renamed San Salvador.

GENERAL BIBLIOGRAPHY

F. Colombo, *Historie di Cristoforo Colombo*, capp. XXI, XXII, XXIII.

B. de Las Casas, *Historia General de Las Indias*, lib. I, cap. XXXIX.

B. de Las Casas, *Apologética Historia*, cap. I.

G. Fernandez de Oviedo, *Historia general y natural de Las Indias*, lib. II, capp. V, VI.

P. Martire D'Anghiera, *De Orbe Novo*, decade I, lib. 1.

AA. VV., "La prima isola scoperta da Colombo nel 1492," *Riv. Geogr. Ital.* (Firenze, 1952), 138.

J. M. Asensio, *Cristóbal Colón, su vida, sus viajes, sus descubrimientos*, Vol. I, lib. II (Barcelona: Espasa y Compania, 1893), pp. 301-307.

A. Balesteros Beretta, *Cristóbal Colón y el describrimiento de América*, t. II, vol. I (Barcelona-Buenos Aires: Salvat, 1945), pp. 68-70.

A. B. Becher, *The Landfall of Columbus on his First Voyage to America* (London: J. D. Potter, 1856), p. 11.

R. Caddeo, *Nota 1 a F. Colombo, Historie de Cristoforo Colombo*, vol. II (Milano: Alpes, 1930), pp. 163-164.

E. A. D'Albertis, "Sulla traccia del primo viaggio di Cristoforo Colombo ver so l'America," *Boll. Soc. Geogr. Utal.* (Roma, 1893), 741-751.

R. J. Didiez, *Guanahaní y Mayaguain* (Santo Domingo: Editora Cultural Dominicana, 1974), pp. 148-167, 400-413.

O. Dunn, "The Diario, or Journal of Columbus's First Voyage: A New Transcription of the Las Casas Manuscript for the Period October 10 through December 6, 1492," *Terrae Incognitae*, vol. 15 (Detroit, 1983), 173-231.

M. Fernandez de Navarrete, *Colección de los viajes y descrubrimientos que hicieron por mar los españoles desde fines del siglo XV*, vol. I (Madrid: Atlas, 1954), p. 95.

C. Fernandez Duro, "La isla Guanahaní," *Ilustracion española y americana* (Madrid, 1891), 221.

G. V. Fox, "An Attempt to Solve the Problem of the First Landing Place of Columbus in the New World," *Report of the Superintendent of the U. S. Coast and Geodetic Survey*, Appendix 18 (Washington, 1880), 346-417.

R. H. Fuson, "Caicos: Site of Columbus's Landfall," *The Professional Geographer*, n. 2 (Washington, 1961), 65-97.

R. H. Fuson, "Caicos, Confusion, Conclusion," *The Professional Geographer*, n. 5 (Washington, 1961), 35-37.

R. H. Fuson and W. H. Treftz, "A Theoretical Reconstruction of the First Atlantic Crossing of Christopher Columbus," *Proceedings of the Association of American Geographers*, n. 8 (New York, 1976), 155-159.

R. H. Fuson, "The Diario de Colon: A Legacy of Poor Transcription, Translation and Interpretation," *Terrae Incognitae*, vol. 15 (Detroit, 1983), 51-75.

G. Gibbs, "Observations to Show That the Grand Turk Island, and Not San Salvador, was the First Spot on which Columbus Landed in the New World." *Proceedings of the New York Historical Society* (New York, 1846), 137-148.

R. D. Gould, "The Landfall of Columbus: an Old Problem Restated," *The Geographical Journal*, I (London, 1927), 403-429.

R. D. Gould and G. H. T. Kimble, "The Four Voyages of Columbus," *The Geograhical Journal*, I (London, 1943), 260-265.

K. Hellweg Larsen, *Columbus Never Came* (London: 1963).

A. von Humboldt, *Examen critique de l'histoire de la géographie du Nouveau Continent*, vol. III. (Paris, la ed., 1836-37).

W. Irving, *A History of the Life and Voyages of Christopher Columbus* (Paris: A. and W. Galicani, 1828), vol. I, p. 247; vol. IV, pp. 245-278.

J. Judge, "Where Columbus Found the New World," *National Geographic*, vol. 170, n. 5 (November, 1986), 566-599.

J. Judge, E. Lyon, and L. Marden, *A Columbus Casebook*, a supplement to "Where Columbus found the New World," *National Georgraphic* (November, 1986).

J. E. Kelley, Jr., "In the Wake of Columbus on a Portolan Chart," *Terrae Incognitae*, vol. 15 (Detroit, 1983), 77-111.

S. Kettel, *Personal Narrative of the First Voyage of Columbus to America* (Boston: Thomas B. Wait & Son, 1827), p. 34.

J. Knox, *A New Collection of Voyages*, vol. II (London: J. Knox, 1767), p. 77.

E. A. Link and M. C. Link, "A New Theory on Columbus's Voyage Through the Bahamas," *Smithsonian Miscellaneous Collection*, vol. 135, n. 4 (Washington, 1958), 6-45.

R. H. Mayor, *Select Letters of Christopher Columbus, with other Original Documents, Relating to his Four Voyages to the New World* (London: Hakluyt Soc., 1870, I ed. 1847).

J. W. McElroy, "The Ocean Navigation of Columbus on his First Voyage," *American Neptune* (Salem, 1941), 208-240.

A. M. Manrique, *Guanahaní. Investigaciones historico-geograficas sobre el Derrotero de Cristóbal Colón por las Bahamas y Costa de Cuba, que comprenden la situación exacta de la Primera Tierra descubierta del Nuevo Mundo* (Arrecife: Imprenta de Lanzarote, 1890), pp. 97-110 e passim.

L. Marden, "The First Landfall of Columbus," *National Geographic*, vol. 170, n. 5 (November, 1986), 572-577.

C. R. Markham, "Sul punto di approdo di Chistoforo Colombo," *Boll. Soc. Geogr. Ital.* (Roma,1889), 101-124.

A. B. Molander, "A New Approach to the Columbus Landfall," *Terrae Incognitae*, vol. XV (Detroit, 1983), 113-149.

B. de Montlezun, "Revue nautique du premier voyage de Christophe Colomb," *Nouvelles annales des voyages et sciences géographiques*, vol. X (Paris, 1828-29), 299-350.

S. E. Morison, "Text and translations of the 'Journal of Columbus', First Voyage," *Hispanic American Historical Review* (Durham, 1939), 235-261.

S. E. Morison, *Admiral of the Ocean Sea. A Life of Christopher Columbus* (Boston: Little Brown, 1951, ed. 1983).

S. E. Morison, *Journal and Other Documents of the Life and Voyages of C. Columbus* (New York: Heritage, 1963).

S. E. Morison and M. Obregon, *The Caribbean as Columbus Saw It* (Boston: Little Brown, 1964), p. 25.

S. E. Morison, *The European Discovery of America*. 2nd. vol.; *The Southern Voyages: A. D. 1492-1616* (New York: Oxford Univ. Press, 1974), pp. 61-65.

J. B. Muñoz, *Historia del Nuevo Mundo* (Madrid, 1793).

J. B. Murdock, "The Cruise of Columbus in the Bahamas, 1492." *The Proceedings of the U. S. Naval Institute* (Annapolis: 1884), 449-486.

L. S. Olschki, "What Columbus Saw on Landing in the West Indies," *Proceedings of the American Philosophical Society* (Philadelphia, 1941), 633-659.

J. Parker. "The Columbus Landfall Problem: A Historical Perspective," *Terrae Incognitae*, vol. 15 (Detroit, 1983), 1-28.

R. H. Power, "The Discovery of Columbus's Island Passage to Cuba, October 12-27, 1492," *Terrae Incognitae*, vol. 15 (Detroit, 1983), 151-172.

P. Revelli, *Cristoforo Colombo e la scuola cartograficia genovese*, vol. II (Genova, 1937), pp. 178, 189-190.

J. B. de la Roquette, *Relations des quatre voyages entrepris par Christophe Colomb*, vol. II (Paris: Treuttel & Wurts), pp. 37-88, 339-345.

S. Ruge, *Columbus* (Dresden: Ehlermann, 1892).

A. Suarez Chiglioni, "Primera isla de las Américas que descubrio Colon," *El Archivo Ibero-Americano* (Madrid, 1892).

P. E. Taviani, *I viaggi di Colombo, la grande scoperta* (Novara: Istituto Geografico De Agostini, 1984), vol. I, pp. 30-38; vol. II, pp. 54-61.

J. B. Thacher, *Christopher Columbus, His Life, His Works, His Remains*, vol. II (New York: Putnam's son, 1903), pp. 23-26;

F. A. de Varnhagen, "La verdadera Guanahaní de Colón," *Anales de la Universidade de Chile*, vol. 24 (Santiago, 1864), pp. 1-20.

P. Verhoog, "Columbus landde op Caicos 12 Oct. 1492," *Tijdschr. V. H. Kon. nederlandsch. Aardijksk Genoots* (Amsterdam, 1952), pp. 96-109.

P. Verhoog, "Columbus Landed on Caicos," *Proceedings of the U. S. Naval Institute*, vol. 80 (Annapolis, 1954), pp. 1101-1111.

P. Verhoog, "Columbus Landed on Caicos," *Terrae Incognitae*, vol. 15 (Detroit, 1983), pp. 29-50.

R. Durlacher Wolper, "A New Theory Identifying the Locale of Columbus' Light, Landfall and Landing," *Smithsonian Miscellaneous Collections*, vol. 148, n. 1 (Washington, 1964), pp. 1-39.

SPECIFIC BIBLIOGRAPHY

On the question of Graham's Harbor see:

A. Braibanti, *Il giornale de bordo di Cristoforo Colombo*, p. 73.

R. Caddeo, *Il Giornale de bordo (1492-1493)*, p. 49.

O. Dunn, *Columbus's First Landing Place: The Evidence of the Journal*, cit., pp. 40-42.

G. Ferro, *Note* a C. Colombo, *Diario di Bordo, Libro della prima navigazione e scoperta delle Indie*, trad it., Mursia, (Milano, 1985), pp. 48-50.

211

R. H. Fuson, *The Diario de Colón: A Legacy of Poor Transcription, Translation and Interpretation.*, cit., p. 63.

R. H. Power, *The Discovery of Columbus's Island Passage to Cuba, October 12-27, 1492*, cit., pp. 156-160.

Yachtsman's Guide to the Bahamas, The Ministry of Tourism, (Nassau, Bahamas, 1974), pp. 9, 262-263.

R. G. Durlacher, *A New Theory Identifying the local of Columbus's Light, Landfall and Landing*, cit., pp. 27-29.

For the ambiguous Board Diary passages on the date of October 15th see:

F. Colombo, *Historie di Cristoforo Colombo*, cap. XXXIV.

B. de Las Casas, *Historia general de las Indias*, lib. 1, capp. XLI and XLII.

R. H. Fuson, *The Diario de Colón: A Legacy of Poor Transcription, Translation and Interpretation*, cit., pp. 64-65.

R. H. Fuson, "Grand Turk was Guanahaní," *Turks & Caicos Current*, (July-August, 1982), 21-30.

L. A. Leicester, "Columbus First Landfall," *Sea Frontiers*, XXVI (1980), 27-78.

S. E. Morison, *Admiral of the Ocean Sea*, cit., pp. 239-240.

R. H. Power, *The Discovery of Columbus's Island Passage to Cuba, October 12-27. 1492*, cit., 161-163.

P. E. Taviani, *I viaggi di Colombo, la grande scoperta*, cit., vol. II, pp. 56-58.

PART II
LINK'S THEORY ON THE LANDFALL

We have already said that only three hypotheses among the ones which contrast with what we have argued about the identity of San Salvador, deserve special mention, not only because of the seriousness of their elaboration, but also for their notes on the places from which something real is tried to be found.

Let us examine the hypothesis of Grand Turk-Caicos. It must immediately be said that while the Links — like Verhoog — incline to the Landfall in Caicos, Power and Fuson prefer Grand Turk.

We have already said in the previous notes that Grand Turk is a small island, the characteristics of which do not correspond to what Columbus writes on the 11th, 12th, 13th and 14th October.

Following Edwin and Marion Link, only the light seen by Columbus the night previous to the Landfall should be situated in the extreme northern point of Grand Turk; the island of the Landfall should therefore be identified in Caicos, and more precisely in the present East Caicos.

The Links have done careful research in all of the archipelago of Turks and Caicos and Bahamas. On the basis of measurements reported by Columbus and the actual ones, they arrive at the conclusion that the itinerary of the Admiral in the Bahamas is the one we have already mentioned and which we repeat here: Grand Turk (light seen), East Caicos (island of the *Landfall*), *Mayaguana (only seen)*, *Samaná* (baptized Santa Maria de la Concepción) and then Long Island and Crooked Island and for the rest of the roiute the reconstruction made by Morison and validated by our on-site researches.

Following the Link's idea, the light seen by Columbus and by Pedro Gutierres — "the light of a candle which rose and went dimmer" — would have been in a Taino camp situated at the extreme north point of Grand Turk, where today is the lighthouse. After catching sight of it, the small fleet seems to have proceeded in a straight line towards the west and at 2 o'clock of October 12 Juan Rodriguez Bermejo, alias Rodrigo de Triana, seems to have seen the first American land in the whitish cliffs of East Caicos and more precisely in one called Grassy Creek, in the actual Columbus Cay, two miles down Cape Comete (today Drum Point) where there is still a beach with very white sand.

Here Columbus dropped anchor, disembarked and stayed for three days, exploring the island and making the first contact with the inhabitants. He seems to have then proceeded North-North-East and — still following the Links — he doubled Cape Comete. Changing the route to West-North-West, he went towards the north coast of East Caicos, where, protected by the continuous coral reef line, he found the famous port described in his *Journal*, so large "that it could receive all the vessels of Christendom and the entrance of which is very narrow".

213

It is the port which we have identified instead, in accordance with Morison and Wolper, as Graham's Harbor at San Salvador Island.

From this port Columbus saw "many islands", among which he did not seem to be able to choose the one to go to.

The Links's attention focuses for a long time on the study of the numbers adopted by various authors concerning the measurements attributed to Columbus, by Las Casas and Don Fernando, about the dimension and locations of the various islands seen or visited before arriving at Cuba.

Following Links's notion, the second island (Santa Maria de la Concepción) is not Rum Cay, because it is too small compared with the one described in the *Journal* and because it·is situated further than the 5 leagues indicated by Columbus in respect to San Salvador. The second island should be identified as Mayaguana, which, however, could have only been seen by the Genoese, who did not disembark there. The real Santa Maria de la Concepción should be instead Samaná, where, following the notes of the *Journal*, the ships anchored on the western coast for one night.

Columbus should have passed Long Island (Fernandina) and from here the route, following the Links, starts to correspond to Murdock's and Morison's (and my) hypothesis. Only one difference: the North American husband and wife team identifies as the "maravelloso puerto" not the one situated a few miles north of Burnt Ground but the one in Clarencetown port, which is much farther south although on the eastern coast of Long Island.

In spite of the respect due to the seriousness of the inquiry made by the Links, we are still of the opinion that the real San Salvador is Guanahani, and for the following reasons:

(1) It is not understandable why the Genoese, instead of making the landfall in Grand Turk, where he seems to have seen the light, has continued. Towards what? Columbus knew that after Grand Turk there was the Caicos group. Why would he have dared to proceed towards the unknown when he had found a sure indication of land and life?

(2) The reconstruction of the Links does not explain why Columbus, supposing he really made landfall in Caicos — therefore the first land of the New World — did not circumnavigate it and didn't arrive at the Providenciales and didn't go back to recognize the Turks where, in the extreme north of Grand Turk, the famous light has been seen.

The Admiral would have described in a detailed way this island or such a group of islands, but instead, plainly for four days, he describes the natural characteristics and the population of only one island, Guanahani.

The characteristics of Guanahani described by the *Journal* correspond to those of San Salvador-Watling. Caicos — which at Columbus's time was an island — doesn't correspond at all to the description made by the Genoese.

It is true that lagoons are found in Caicos as well: one in East Caicos, one in North Caicos, one in Grand Caicos. These lagoons are of modest proportions. It might also be that these lagoons once were of larger proportions, that they became basins of sea water that today have opened a route towards the sea and now are gulfs. In such a case, the lagoon of East Caicos could be "muy grande" in respect to East Caicos. But at Columbus's time it didn't exist. Only one Caicos island existed, which later broke into South Caicos, East Caicos, Grand Caicos and North Caicos. In respect to Caicos, not even a larger lagoon than the one existing presently in East Caicos would be in "en medio" or "muy grande". Caicos has sea-water lagoons, low and full of coral, so that the island is absolutely without the abundance of water which Columbus mentions.

The nature of Caicos today — dry and desolated — doesn't allow in any way the supposition that, at the time of the discovery, it was blooming and luxuriant like the first island he described. San Salvador instead has, now as well, good vegetation, with forest remains which allow us to suppose that at that time before the ruin was effected to obtain space for the cotton plantations — the island was, like the other Bahamas, covered with an even richer and luxuriant flora. The climate then is much more pleasant than that of Caicos.

It is true that traces of inhabitants were found in Caicos, but it seems that their numbers were few or limited. While Columbus speaks, from his arrival, of many people and many different populations met during the circumnavigation of the island, it is Wolper's carefully researched conclusion that towards the end of the fifteenth century the inhabitants of San Salvador were at least four times the supposed number.

(3) Let us now face the interesting point, that of the place of the Landfall indicated by the Links as being two miles under Cape Comete, on the east coast of East Caicos. It is absolutely unthinkable that Columbus, expert and careful seaman that he was, could have even tried to anchor and effect a landfall on the east coast of East Caicos. This coast — as we were able to observe during our explorations — is totally exposed to the trade-winds coming from the East-North-East, which are always blowing and which, when they are strong, make it impossible even for a boat to go near or land.

On this side of the island the beaches are rare. The navigation — on this side of the coral reef — is very dangerous because of the banks of coral of every form and dimension which occur everywhere. Even a small boat with a small draught risks serious difficulties. Often, the one on which we made our inspection had to raise the propeller and proceed very slowly, rowing after being anchored, even when the keel was flat.

Only in the northern part of East Caicos, within Drum Point and Jacksonville, does the sea become calmer and the coral reef, which proceeds without continuity, creates a vast and rather tranquil area, but wide and characterized by shallow waters. This however, absolutely cannot be the bay in which Columbus wanted all the vessels of Christianity to anchor and where, as he says, there are shallow waters but also parts of the sea which are deep.

215

Such a site can't be found anywhere in the Caicos today, while — as we said — we have clearly identified it in San Salvador.

(4) A grave contradiction is also noted, due to the exploration Columbus made on October 14th, between the itinerary indicated by the Links and the route which results from the *Journal*. The Links state that Columbus, after having doubled Drum Point, arrived, sailing towards the west, in the large tranquil bay in the north-western part of East Caicos. This interpretation is the result of a wrong translation of Columbus' text we have talked about in criticising the argumentations of Fuson.

(5) The question brought out by the Links — the "large number of islands" mentioned by the Admiral in the *Journal* of the 14th of October — has already been debated. We have admitted that from San Salvador neither Rum Cay nor the other islands which were explored afterward by the Genoese can be seen, but this negative information is also valid for Caicos, which, and it must be again underlined, was then one whole island. Neither from South Caicos nor from East Caicos is it possible to see the Turks Group (about 20 miles away). It is true that, leaving the coast, Columbus might have seen Providenciales and many other cayos in the Caicos Bank. But it is also true that in such a case the distance indicated by Columbus (5 leagues, perhaps 20 miles) would certainly be inadequate.

Different would be the question of the landfall — and the Links don't say this, while Fuson and Power do — if it had been in Grand Turk. We must honestly admit that the terminal parts of the Diary of the 14th October adapt perfectly to the hypothesis of the Landfall in Grand Turk. But it concerns only this argument. It seems to us not too scientific to stick to a hypothesis just because it has one element in its favor, forgetting all the others which are definitely contrary.

(6) Concerning the distance between the various islands and their extension the Links insist on the discrepancies between the measurements of Columbus and the real ones.

It must first of all be noted that today the islands of the Bahamas seem much smaller than they seemed to the eyes of the Genoese and to his crew. A land, an island, or even a small island or a rock, if it is covered by thick vegetation, seems — in the absence of instrumental relevations — larger, and even an expert observer might make mistakes about relative size.

But an even better explanation must be found in the inexactitudes, inaccuracies and contradictions noticeable in the numbers, the measurements and the type of miles and leagues Columbus adopted in the same *Journal* as well as in the texts of Las Casas and Don Fernando. We have already said so and we have also advanced the suggestion that the *Journal* has been altered on purpose in the numbers even in this part, because of the secret nature of news about the newly discovered lands.

(7) Let us come back again to our first question. The reconstruction of the route of the Atlantic crossing of Columbus allows us to suppose that the Santa Maria and the other two caravels might have previously been sailing

towards the West — not without a variation to NW — and declined to SW for 4 grades, arriving at the Bahamas on a latitude of about 24°. It doesn't seem possible to us to demonstrate how they could have declined SW of 6° and more, arriving under the latitude of 22° at Grand Turk and Caicos.

BIBLIOGRAPHY

A. A. Link and M. C. Link. "A New Theory on Columbus's Voyage Through the Bahamas." *Smithsonian Miscellaneous Collection*, n. 4 (Washington, 1958), 6-45.

PART III
THE CAT ISLAND HYPOTHESIS

The route of the Atlantic crossing which places the landfall in Grand Turk and Caicos is not valid — as we have already noted — for the people that place it on Cat Island.

Among these people there are some famous names, such as Washington Irving and Humboldt. We, however, in dealing about it in these notes, prefer to recall the studies made by Aurelio Tió, not only because they are more recent, but also because they have depended on local inspections of the lands and seas they treat.

Aurelio Tió bases his theory on the analysis of the *Board Journal* of Columbus compared with the *Diario de Navegación* of Ponce de León as transcribed by Herrera. This *Diary* concerns the voyage of the discovery in Florida made by Ponce de León in 1513. During this trip Ponce de León touched some islands in the Bahamas in March of that year and in August during his journey back.

Tió does a careful study of the map which Herrera obtained from the *Diary* of Ponce de León and shows how it is rather insufficient; from it — and this is Tió's idea — came the error of R. H. Mayor who, as we know, was one of the first and more important supporters of a landfall in Watling. The *Diary* of Ponce de León is — for Tió — a more authentic source than the *Carta* which Herrera obtained. Better evidence of Ponce de León's voyage would be found — as suggested by Justing Winsor — in the map of Count Ottomano Freducci, copied from the map of Ponce de León, which contained details of the map of Christopher Columbus.

This interesting and complex study induces Tió to state that Ponce de León identified Guahananí of the landfall as Cat Island. From this comes Tió's hypothesis: Columbus saw the light at ten o'clock on the evening of 11th October on the northern coast of San Salvador-Watling while Bermejo, Rodrigo de Triana, would have seen the Columbus Point at the south-east extremity of Cat Island at 2 o'clock. The landfall would have been in Port Howe, a bay on the southern coast.

We think that the thesis that Ponce de León identified Guanahaní as Cat Island is acceptable. This explains also how Makenzie might have suggested to Washington Irving the hypothesis of the landfall in Cat Island and how it seemed right to the important historian Humboldt to believe it.

This, however, doesn't cancel the fact that we today may correct Ponce de León's interpretation, because we can today verify the details which were in the *Journal*, in the *Historia*, in the *Apologética Historia* of Las Casas, in the *Historia* of Don Fernando, and in Herrera's text.

We find ourselves, with the hypothesis revived by Tió, confronted with not a complete change of the Morison-Wolper-Taviani thesis but a variation of the same.

218

We have already said that San Salvador-Watling and Cat Island are on a terminal latitude of the ocean crossing of the three ships of Columbus's first voyage. We now add that the hypothesis of Tió, Irving, and Humboldt does not change anything in our view of the following route: Tió takes for granted the fact that the stops of the following route are Rum Cay (Santa Maria de la Concepción). Long Island (Fernandina), Crooked Island (Isabela), Ragged Islands (Islas de Arena) and Cuba.

It is therefore a change that exclusively concerns the landfall. We find ourselves in a different position in regard to the Grand Turk-Caicos' hypothesis: this one has proved to be unacceptable for the reasons explained in previous notes. We can't, however, deny Tió's hypothesis — which once was Irving's and Humboldt's — for it has charming arguments.

It is in fact also supported by another argument which we can't forget: the length of Cat Island from South to North is a little less than 15 leagues, by Columbus's measurements. There, a mistake between miles and leagues should not be considered a mistake by Columbus and repeated by Las Casas and Don Fernando as we, and with all Watling-San Salvador supporters were obliged to hypothesize.

However, together with other attractive aspects of Cat Island there are other points which induce us to incline to a landfall in San Salvador-Watling.

The most doubtful point of the Cat Island hypothesis seems to be raised by what Columbus writes in the *Journal* for the 12, 13 and 14th October. From such evidence it is clear that Columbus had a very precise idea of the whole island at which he made landfall: he talks about "a great reef of rocks which encircled the whole of that island"; he says that in the middle of it there is "a very big lagoon"; he explores the northern coast to see the east side (and on this last question we have dwelt for a long time, in polemic with Fuson and Dunn).

In order to accept the fact that the landfall island is Cat Island it should be understood that the visit and the explorations of Columbus were limited to a small part of the whole island, at its southern part, which is the largest from east to west, but which is 45 miles from the northern point of the island. It is really unthinkable that — on the morning of October 14th — Columbus rowed more than 40 miles by boat.

In fact, the interpretations Tió gives regarding the movements of Columbus are not persuasive.

Hawksnest Creek doesn't correspond to what Columbus says on October 14th about the peninsula which "with a couple days' work can become an island". We (the writer of these notes and Dr. Masetti) have visited Hawksnest Creek and we had a different impression from the one we had after visiting Graham's Harbor.

In Graham's Harbor everything corresponds to Columbus's considerations. In Hawksnest Creek there isn't the part of the peninsula which could, according to Columbus, be cut in a couple of days' work and there also isn't the large port "which may receive all the vessels of Christianity". Tió says that the Old Bight is "una grande ensenada muy bien resguardada de los vientos prevalecientes del nordeste, tan perfectamente que allò el mar "no se mueva màs que dentro un pozo", as Columbus wrote in his "*Diario de Navegación*". There is nothing to object to in this. However, Columbus says that the large port is between the peninsula, which can be island, and the coral reef which surrounds Guanahaní, while the "grande ensenada" of the Old Bight is only a large bay which has in front, on the western side, the open sea.

Moreover, where is the large lagoon mentioned by Columbus? Tió replies that the Great Lake of the southern part of Cat Island was probably connected — 500 years ago — with some small lakes around it and was therefore larger than the present one. But, however large it might have been, it was never in the middle of the island — as is the lagoon of San Salvador-Watling — but in the middle of the southern part of an island which extends farther toward north for another 40 miles.

Tió insists on two characteristics which do not favor the lagoon of San Salvador-Watling. One is that this lagoon is salt water and not fresh water. But we have already pointed out how the qualification "de buena agua dulce" is only found in the *Historia* of Las Casas: it is not found in the *Journal* or in the *Historia* of Don Fernando. It is an arbitrary insertion of Las Casas.

The other characteristic on which Tió insists is that the lagoon of San Salvador-Watling is not a lagoon, but a complex of eight or nine lagoons. There are really in San Salvador-Watling eight minor lagoons, but the Great Lake is by far the largest and covers on the whole the extension of the part which is "en medio" of the island. Indeed, the large lagoon "en medio" exists on San Salvador-Watling and not on Cat Island.

There is also another fundamental condition which can't be forgotten: the coral reef, the "grande restinga de piedras, che cerca toda la isla al rededor".

For all these reasons, although we appreciate the investigations of Tió, we can't accept his hypothesis which remains only a possiblity for those who would want to reject at all costs the hypothesis of Watling-San Salvador, which is more than 90% probable.

BIBLIOGRAPHY

A. Tió, *Dr. Diego Alvarez Chanca (Estudio Biográfico)*, Publicaciones de la Asociación Medica de Puerto Rico, Instituto de Cultura Puertorriqueña, Universidad interamericana de Puerto Rico, 1966, pp. 307, 310, 313, 316-18, 321-26.

J. Winsor, *Christopher Columbus and How he Received and Imported the Spirit of Discovery*, Houghton, Mifflin & Company (New York 1891), p. 560.

On the theme, developed by Tió, of the identifications (or confusions) of the islands corresponding to the names of Guanahaní, Guanina and Triango, from the discoveries (or rediscoveries) of Ponce de León till the whole seventeenth century, see also:

R. Durlacher Wolper, *New Theory Identifying the Locale of Columbus's Light, Landfall, and Landing*, cit., p. 3.

PART IV
THE SAMANÁ HYPOTHESIS

The hypothesis of a landfall in Samaná, put forward for the first time by Captain Gustavus Fox, was taken up again by Harrisse, who nevertheless never had the opportunity to make on-site visits in the archipelago of the Bahamas.

The author of this paper, with his assistant Dr. Masetti, visited the island of Samaná in 1974, and again in 1986 accompanied by Dr. Donald T. Gerace, director of the CCFL Bahamian Field Station. None of us noticed in this island the characteristics of San Salvador described by Christopher Columbus, Don Fernando, and Las Casas.

In 1986 the *National Geographic* launched with much fanfare an article in its November issue with the ambitious title *Our Search for the True Columbus Landfall* signed by its senior associate editor Joseph Judge.

An essay by Joseph Judge himself criticizes the arguments favoring Watling-San Salvador. He believes he found in Samaná the characteristics described in the *Board Diary* of Christopher Columbus. In another essay, concerning the routes of the Atlantic crossing of Columbus, Luis Marden intends to prove by using computer calculations of the *Board Diary* data that the Genoese Navigator on the night of the thirty-third day should have been at 23°09′ N latitude and 73°29′13″ longitude W, rather than at 23°56′ N latitude and 74°20′ longitude, which we endorse.

The work done by Marden is of great diligence and the scholarly construction which he elaborated commands respect; the trouble lies in the foundations.

During the San Salvador conference, the geographer Gaetano Ferro demonstrated that it is not possible to consider as reliable data the numbers offered by the Genoese in his *Board Diary* during the thirty-three days of the crossing. They are, due to the instruments of the time, approximations, often off-the-cuff calculations. Columbus himself often uses the conditional tense when reporting them: "saremmo andati. . ." "avremmo percorso. . .". It is also certain that in some cases the numbers have been altered either by the Admiral or by the copyists of the court of Spain to deceive likely competitors, above all, the Portuguese. Hence, the impossibility of knowing with mathematical precision the route of the Atlantic crossing.

Morison never expected to indicate the route which Columbus certainly followed. As he repeatedly told his assistant Obregon, who so confirmed it in the San Salvador conference and to the author of this paper personally, he wanted to present a probable route hypothesis. Marden's hypothesis is not very different and many other similar ones could be formulated.

Marden also claims that the league of Columbus cannot correspond to the 3.18 nautical mile of today, because, were it to be so, the sum of the numbers indicated in the Board Diary would produce an itinerary ending "west of present-day Miami". This realization is not at all a novelty. Earlier,

Morison, Ferro and myself, and other Columbian scholars had pointed out that the sum of the leagues actually covered by Columbus is closer to the sum of the leagues falsely passed on to the crew than to the sum of the leagues reported as truthful in the diary. McElroy calculated the sum of the false numbers to be less than 9% of the sum of the leagues actually covered. Marden is of the opinion that the sum should be less than 10.5%, and to explain this discrepancy he holds the league of Christopher Columbus to have been of 2.82 modern-day nautical miles rather than 3.18 nautical miles. As a matter of fact, the 2.82 value corresponds to the 16th-century Spanish league, as evidenced by two English navigational manuals published in 1574 and 1594.

Columbus nonetheless was still a 15th century navigator. And the majority of the Columbus scholars agree with Morison, Gaetano Ferro and Charlier: Columbus took his measurements in Italian miles and figured out the league by multiplying the mile by 4. As I have shown elsewhere, this procedure is proven to be above debate, given the many examples of it in the *Board Diary*.

We are then faced with superfluous disquisitions, because — as we stated it repeatedly earlier — the data under discussion are in any case approximations and are derived independently from the adopted method.

Luis Marden wanted to take into account also the incidence of the wind and sea currents for the different points touched by the Atlantic route of Columbus. It is then possible to hold that, by rough calculation, the winds and currents have not substantially changed from 1492 to today. In the case of large approximations we are dealing with high numbers. However, when small numbers are involved, the exact incidence could have been altered from his time to today; in fact, it does change from season to season, day to day, and occasionally from hour to hour.

Pretending to define the arrival point of the Atlantic route of Columbus by means of computer-managed data as contained in the *Board Diary* and to define such landing point by taking into consideration with mathematical precision the winds and currents in the various points of high sea amounts to a welter of incredible ingenuousness.

The study by Luis Marden deserves respect for the diligence and extreme care with which it was conducted. As we already stated, the scientific conception is well thought out; however, its foundation is fragile — in fact it is built on quicksand and the hypotheses that condition it are equally fragile and exposed to the volatile nature of the situation.

No rigorous and precise conclusion can be ever arrived at on the question of the route: only possible and more or less probable hypotheses can be reached. Not even the main figure of the great discovery crossing could succeed in giving us the exact high sea route followed were he alive today.

The other essay by Judge deals with the characteristics surrounding the Landfall and of the interpretation of the *Board Diary* dates of October 11 and the days following.

In regard to the latter Judge repeats the arguments already presented by Fuson and others who have criticized the Watling-San Salvador hypothesis: the "many islands", and the distance from Rum Cay and its dimensions. He adds a new argument of some importance concerning the amount of time needed to traverse the stretch of coastline between Long Bay and Graham's Harbor by rowboat.

We have elsewhere answered this new argument as well as the older ones. We will thus limit our remarks to listing the reasons for which Samaná should be excluded from the possible candidates for the coveted Landfall title.

We have no reservation in recognizing that some of the characteristics of Samaná correspond to the *Board Diary* indications.

Samaná is "muy llana". It is "sin ninguna montaña". It has "mucha agua"; "muchas aguas". It has "arboles muy verde". There is also the "grande restinga de piedras, que cerca toda la isla abrededor".

Samaná — today a deserted island — was then populated. It has always been known that the archipelago of the Bahamas in the 15th century had an ethnographic density four or five times the population of today. However that may be, recent archeological excavations by Dr. Charles Hoffman and by Judge himself leave no doubt about the presence of human settlements in Samaná.

On the other hand, other features remain that do not in any way fit Samaná. Having visited and revisited it we realize that:

(1) Samaná is a very small island of 14 kilometers². Columbus could not have called it (as he did) "isla bien grande".

(2) In the island of Samaná there is not "una laguna in medio muy grande"; there are only some very modest ponds.

(3) The harbor believed by Judge to be identifiable with a bay on the southern coast could contain one or two dozen XVth-century ships at the most — quite a divergence from the Admiral's precise indication that "It can accommodate all the ships of Christendom".

Besides these considerations, there are two arguments that exclude Samaná from the number of possible Landfall candidates: the early geographic maps of America and the very name of Samaná.

In the first known map of America, by Juan de la Cosa, dated 1500, "Guanahani" and "Samana"[1] appear as two quite distinct islands. The latter is south-east of the former just as we see San Salvador and Samaná today. (See Figure 1.)

In regard to the map of Juan de la Cosa, it must be specified that the year-long debate on whether there were one or two Juan de la Cosas has no bearing on the topic under our consideration. Even those who consider Juan de la Cosa, the author of the famous map, to be a different person from the Juan de la Cosa who took part in the first Columbus voyage, are of the opinion that he, too, had been in America during the successive discovery voyages and that thus he had direct knowledge of the Caribbean Sea.

In the map of the Portuguese Pedro Reinal (1519), preserved in Lisbon, "Guanaha" (sic) and "Amana" (sic) are depicted quite distinctly.

In the map of the Portuguese Diogo Ribeiro of 1529, "Guanahan" (sic) appears in the form of a swollen cross surrounded by cays. Samaná does not appear.

In the manuscript of the Catalan Alonso de Chaves, *Quatri Partitu en cosmografia practica, y por otro nombre espejo de navegantes* (1526), "Samana" and "Guanahani" are listed respectively under numbers 15 and 16 in Chapter VII, which deals with the Lucayan islands. The indications regarding the relationship and size of the two islands are extravagant: 25°; 8 leagues from northwest to southeast and 4 leagues from northeast to southwest for either one of them and thus "Guanahani se parece con Samana" making them one and the same. However, it is worth pointing out that the two islands are drawn as two distinct islands and that only of "Guanahani" (and not of "Samana") it is said: "Esta es la isla que primero fue hellanda cuando se descubrieron estas Indias".

In the map of Sebastian Cabot of 1544, the island "Samana" is reproduced as an island distinct from "Triangula": we know from Las Casas (*Apologética Historia*) that the name "Triangulo" was attributed by cartographers to Guanahaní.

In Pierre Desceliers' map (1546) the name "Samana" appears to the west of the name "Guanahani" and to the south east of an island surrounded by cays indicated as "Guanima".

In the map of Gillermo Le Testu of 1555 the island of "Samana" is clearly represented south-east of a larger island named "Guanima".

In the map of the Greek Georgio Sideri (known as Callapoda) (1563) appear the names "Guanaha" (sic) and "Amana" (sic). The latter is placed in a position such as to make it considered related to the gulf of Samaná on the island of Hispaniola.

Battista Agnese (of the 16th century) in his map puts the island "Guanaani" (sic) on the 24° parallel with various islands southeast of it and "Maniga", "Cayas", and "Cuaba". Samaná is not represented.

In the Portuguese map of the Biblioteca Riccardiana of Florence (still of the 16th century) appears only "Ganahani" (sic).

Among the Lucayos islands represented in the map of Bartolomé Olives (1563) one finds the island "Guanahani", while any indication of Samaná is missing.

Finally, in the map of Antonio de Herrera, who wrote at the end of the 16th and the beginning of the 17th century on the basis of manuscripts and news of the time of the first discovery, "Guanihana" (sic) appears to be northwest of "Samana".

The testimony of the first map of Juan de la Cosa would certainly have been sufficient; however, we have preferred to furnish a list of many early maps in which Guanahaní and Samaná appear, together or alone, so that no doubt would remain in regard to this question.

Finally, a simpler argument but a most important one, which is in our view decisive.

The terms Guanahaní and Samaná are Taino names. They are not English names like Watling, Crooked Island, and Long Island. They are not Anglo-Spanish like Cat Island, formerly Isla del Gato. How could the island that was then called with a name given to it by the Taino population — and Samaná is certainly a Taino word — have two names and also be called Guanahaní? Samaná did indeed maintain its original Taino name throughout the XVIth-century maps. It did not change its name and the Taino term has come down to us today. On the other hand, Guanahaní was named time after time San Salvador, Trianglo, then again Guanahaní, and then later Watling.

Notwithstanding all these name changes, one sure thing remains about which no doubt could be nourished, and that is that Columbus' Landfall was on an island called by the Indians Guanahaní, and not on the one the Indians called Samaná.

NOTE

1. We have copied without accent the names as they appear in the old maps. We will use the accent when we are not directly citing names on the maps.

BIBLIOGRAPHY

R. Almagiá. *Monumenta Cartographica Vaticana*, vol. I, Carte nautiche, planisferi e affini, Biblioteca Apostolica Vaticana, Città del Vaticano 1940, tav XLIII b.

M. Cappon. "Ma dov'é l'America di Colombo? dove sbarcò il Genovese il 12 ottobre 1492: a San Salvador o a Samaná Cay?" *Epoca*, XXXVII, n. 1885 (Milano, 21 novembre 1986).

G. Charlier. *Valeur du mille utilisé en mer par Cristóbal Colón durant son voyage*, 244. Liège: Boulevard d'Avroy, 1986.

Alonso de Chaves. *Quatri partitu en cosmografía práctica, y por otro nombre espejo de navegantes*, manoscritto del 1526 edito e trascritto da P. Castañeda Delgado, M. Cuesta Domingo y P. Hernández Aparicio. Madrid: Instituto de Historia y Cultura Naval, 1983, pp. 316-318.

S. Conti. "San Salvador rimane San Salvador, Demolita la sensazionale notizia del National Geographic." *Columbus 92* (Genova, nov. 1986).

G. Ferro. "Colombo e le sue navigazioni secondo il diario del primo viaggio. Osservazioni di un geografo." *Atti del Convegno in San Salvador 30 ott. — 2 nov. 1986*, in corso di stampa.

J. Judge. "Where Columbus Found the New World." *National Geographic* (November, 1986), pp. 566-599.

K. Kretschmer. *Die Entdeckung Amerika's in ihrez Bedentung für die Geschichte des Weltbildes.* Berlin: W. H. Kühl, 1892, vol. II, Atlas, tavv.: VII, XV, XVI, XVII, XXII, XXXV.

L. Marden. "The First Landfall of Columbus." *National Geographic* (November, 1986), pp. 572-577.

R. Montojo. *Las primeras tierras descubiertas por Colón,* Madrid: Sucesores de Rivadeneira, 1892, lam. III.

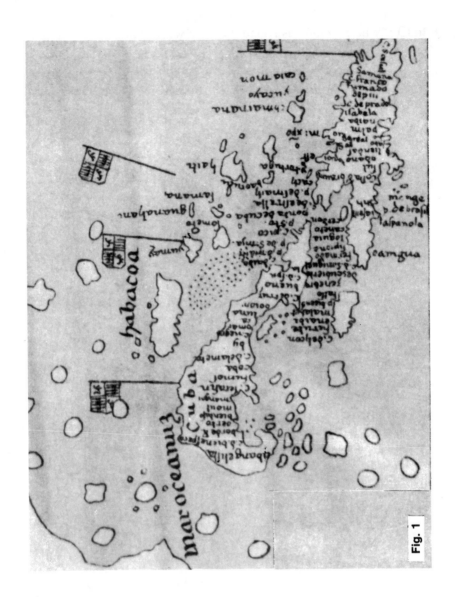

Fig. 1

228

Additional Comments Relating Watlings Island to Columbus' San Salvador

Donald T. Gerace
CCFL Bahamian Field Station
San Salvador, Bahamas

Having resided on San Salvador, formerly Watlings Island, for the past sixteen years, I have learned certain facts from the local residents and observed certain features of the island which relate to the Columbus landfall issue. The following discussion will reveal that some of the criticisms of the Watlings Island as Columbus' San Salvador theory are based on imprecise knowledge and not on known facts and experiences of people who live on San Salvador and sail it's waters.

Watlings Island generally fits the features of Guanahani as described by Columbus in his Journal, except for a few discrepancies. One of these, believed by some, is that Columbus could not have made the exploration expedition with the ships' small boats on October 14, starting at dawn and rowing to a harbor or port that would hold all the ships of Christendom and returning in time for the fleets departure in mid-afternoon.

The problem begins with defining the location of where Columbus first began this rowing expedition. Unfortunately Columbus did not describe in his Journal exactly where his first anchorage was located. Nor did he describe how he got to this anchorage on the morning of October 12th.

If the present San Salvador is Guanahani the general location of this first anchorage can be found, since there is a fringing reef that surrounds the island and there are only a few anchorages available.

Captain Bernie Storr, a second generation seaman and pilot for all large vessels approaching anchorages off San Salvador, states there are only four suitable anchorages off the island: Grahams Harbor at the north can accommodate seven foot draft vessels; Pigeon Creek at the southeast is adequate for vessels of four foot draft or less; French Bay at the south is a coral anchorage used only during a northwest storm; and the anchorage in the area from Bamboo Point to Riding Rock Point off the northwest coast of the island.[1]

Anthony Leichester very adequately describes why the landing could not be on the east side of San Salvador in these words, ". . . no seaman in his senses would have anchored off a lee-shore with a sea running, nor could the ship's boats have got over the reef."[2]

The entrance to French Bay would have been very difficult for a mariner to locate without prior knowledge that a passage is there. Also, a coral anchorage would not be preferable, especially in a bay that would be untenable in a strong east or southeast wind.

The only anchorage possible is where present day deep draft vessels anchor, that area from just south of Bamboo Point north to Riding Rock Point. It would have been impossible for a vessel of over four foot draft to moor further south along the west coast of San Salvador because of the massive back reef area. While students at the CCFL Bahamian Field Station and divers at the Riding Rock Inn have enjoyed these spectacular back reefs for the past sixteen years, I have never seen a vessel of any size (with a draft of four feet or more) anchored in this area. The limits of the Bamboo Point to Riding Rock Point anchorage can be clearly seen in the areal photograph of Figure 1.

Paul Tappan saw the treacherous reefs south of Bamboo Point when he arrived with his yacht *Heloise*. The anchorage at Bamboo Point, where Mr. Tappan erected a monument in 1951 to indicate Columbus' first landing place, would have had merits for the first island explorer.[3] Located on the lee shore, it has good holding ground and adequate depth close to shore. This would allow the vessels to protect any landing party with their bombardas and be readily accessible if the natives proved unfriendly.

To be as thorough as possible with this report, I must mention that there are two locations south of Bamboo Point where sisal was loaded aboard shallow draft sailing vessels during the early part of this century, Hall's Landing and Strachan's Landing. Because of the poor roads at that time, sisal was loaded at the closest landing available to the fields. A very shallow draft sailing vessel was used with expert native mariners to pick their way through the corals.[4]

One may question at this point, did the corals of 500 years ago have the same general location as they do today? We know that they were there 200 years ago, during the Loyalist period, and from scientific evidence we know that the water level has only risen about 2 or 3 cm and there has been no great change in the wind and wave patterns. We can therefore state that the present corals would be similar to those seen 500 years ago.[5]

From this information it seems likely that Columbus would have had his first anchorage somewhere near Bamboo Point, and it would have been somewhere near this point that the ships' small boats set out for their expedition of exploration of the island on October 14th. To quote Eugene Lyon's translation:

"At dawn, I ordered the ship's boats and the caravels' small boats readied and went along the island on a north-northeast course in order to see the other part, which was the eastern part, and also in order to see the settlements. And I saw then two or three, and the people who all came to the beach calling us and giving thanks to God. Some brought us water, others other things to eat. Others, when they saw that I did not bother to go ashore, threw themselves into the sea and came swimming, . . ."[6]

From this it is obvious that Columbus must have rowed his boats very close to shore, since the Indians swam out to meet him.

To continue Lyon's translation:

". . . I was alarmed at seeing a large reef of rocks which surrounded that entire island. And in between, it remained deep and a port for as many ships as there are in all Christendom, and the entrance of it very narrow. It is true that within this belt there are some shallows, but the sea does not move more than within a well. And, in order to see all this, I moved forward this morning so that I might know how to give a report of everything to Your Highnesses, and also where one could build a fort. And I saw one piece of land that is made like an island even though it is not, on which there were six houses, which one could cut into an island in two days, . . ."[7]

If the present San Salvador is Guanahani, then it is Grahams Harbor, at the north of San Salvador, which is the port Columbus describes, and it is Cut Cay, an island at the end of North Point, which is the island he felt would be suitable for a fort (see Fig. 1).

Although there have been many critics of the possibility of rowing this distance along the shore of San Salvador, the local San Salvadorians have never doubted that it could be done. Max Ferguson mentioned that before outboard motors were available he used to scull from Sue Point to Green Cay or Gaulin Cay, fish all day, and return home.[8] Finally, after many requests, Max Ferguson agreed to row from Grahams Harbor to Bamboo Point. This was done in a wooden row boat owned by the CCFL Bahamian Field Station. He departed from the dock located at the foot of North Point on the Eastern end of Grahams Harbor, rowed northward until he could see the channel between North Point and Cut Cay, and then rowed westward and southwestward to Bamboo Point. The trip was monitored and timed by the Commissioner of San Salvador, G. Hasting Strachen, and other members of the Kiwanis Club of San Salvador.

I established this trial rowing trip to determine the average speed of one person rowing this distance in a wooden boat, and to learn how fatiguing a trip of this nature would be. Mr. Ferguson started out at 10:51 AM and arrived at Bamboo Point at 2:11 PM, a distance of approximately 9 miles covered in 3 hours and 20 minutes (see Fig. 2). The important fact here is that Mr. Ferguson rowed at an average speed of 2.70 miles per hour, and looked and felt that he had enough energy to make a return trip. If the total round trip distance had been 20 miles, it would have taken him 7.4 hours. If the distance was as much as 25 miles, as expressed by Dunn,[9] it would have taken 9.26 hours. Using the greatest distance of 25 miles, Columbus could have started out at dawn as described in the log (6:00 AM), made the round - trip, and returned to the ships in the mid-afternoon (3:30 PM).

Personally, I think a man with the intellect of Columbus would certainly not plan on retracing his exploration trip, and therefore, I suggest what has been previously expressed by other scholars, and although it is conjecture, Columbus had his fleet follow him northward, staying seaward off the fringing reef. Reading Lyons' translation further convinces me that this was indeed the case in this statement, "I was alarmed at seeing a large reef of rocks which surrounded the entire island." [10] Was he alarmed because after finding his way blocked from going to the East by North Point, he would not be able to return to the ships because of the reefs without rowing back to Bamboo Point the way he came? Further, I feel he would not have been able to find the narrow channel he mentions, which lies just south of Green Cay, if he did not leave the harbor through that channel with his small boats. For what other reason did he go to Green Cay, 3 miles from Cut Cay and at least one mile from the nearest shore in Grahams Harbor? A good reason he would have gone in this direction was to look for an opening in the reef in order to meet the fleet which was waiting for him. This possibility, and we will probably never know if this really happened, would have given Columbus even more time for his exploration trip.

In summary, if the present San Salvador was Guanahani, the first landing of Columbus was probably along a two mile anchorage from just south of Bamboo Point to Riding Rock Point. This anchorage shortens the rowing distance to 18 or 19 miles, round trip, which a boat going at the speed of Mr. Ferguson would cover in about seven hours. If the distance covered by Columbus' rowing expedition was a maximum of 25 miles (from the Wolper monument at Long Bay), and based on our determined rate of speed of one man rowing, he could have made the journey in time to meet the fleets departure from San Salvador in the mid-afternoon. However, if one man can make an average speed of 2.70 miles per hour, three men would be able to make much better time, and we are aware that the launches of the day had more then one man rowing.

This exercise proves, without a shadow of a doubt, that the rowing ordeal from his anchorage to Grahams Harbor and back could have been made within the time period Columbus indicated.

NOTES

1. Bernie Storr, personal communication.

2. L. Anthony Leichester, "Columbus's First Landfall," *Sea Frontiers*, 26, 5 (September-October, 1980), pp. 276-278.

3. W. R. (Dick) Tappan, *Cooking with the Tappans* (New York, 1986), pp. 47-48.

4. Samuel Edgecomb, personal communication.

5. Dr. Philip Dustan, Department of Biology, College of Charleston, Charleston, SC, personal communication.

6. Eugene Lyon, "The Diario of Christopher Columbus," *A Columbus Casebook*, A Supplement to "Where Columbus Found the New World", *National Geographic Magazine* (November, 1986), p. 17.

7. *Ibid.*

8. Maxwell Ferguson, personal communication.

9. Oliver Dunn, "Columbus's First Landing Place: The Evidence of the *Journal*," *In the Wake of Columbus* (Detroit, 1985), p. 42.

10. Lyons, op. cit.

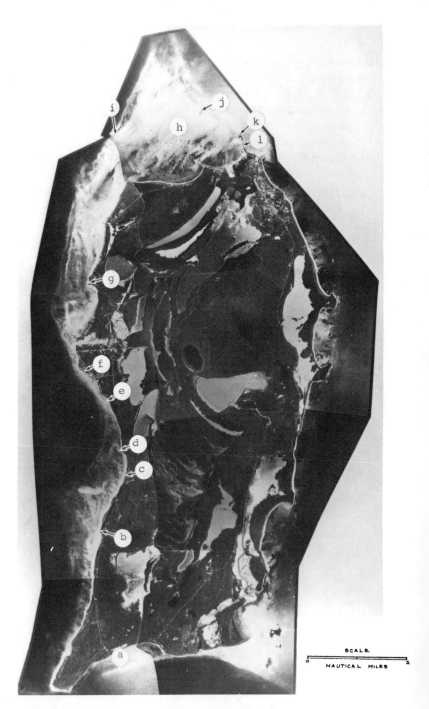

Fig. 1. Aerial photograph of San Salvador Island. *a.* French Bay; *b.* Strachan's Landing; *c.* Wolper Monument; *d.* Hall's Landing; *e.* Bamboo Point; *f.* Riding Rock point; *g.* Sue Point; *h.* Grahams Harbor; *i.* Green Cay; *j.* Gaulin Cay; *k.* Cut Cay; *l.* North Point.

234

MEMORANDUM

DEPARTMENT OF LOCAL GOVERNMENT

COMMISSIONER'S OFFICE,

COCKBURN TOWN,

San Salvador, Bahamas.

Your Reference ....

Our Reference ....

To: ....

Date: ....

This Certificate dated this 28th day of October in the year of Our Lord One Thousand Nine Hundred and Eighty-Six witnesseth that I, the undersigned, G. Hasting Strachan Commissioner of the District of San Salvador and Rum Cay, in the Commonwealth of The Bahamas, was present and witnessed:

1. That on the 28th day of October, 1986 A.D., Mr. Maxwell Stephen Ferguson, a resident of North Victoria Hill, in the Island of San Salvador, one of the Islands of the Commonwealth of the Bahamas, left Graham's Harbour in San Salvador, by Row Boat.

2. That the name of the said Row Boat was the Columbus I.

3. That the time of departure from Graham's Harbour was 10.51 a.m. on October 28th, 1986.

4. That the said Maxwell Stephen Ferguson rowed the said Boat, from Graham's Harbour to Bamboo Point in San Salvador where Yawl Heloise Monument is located.

5. That the time of arrival of Mr. Maxwell Stephen Ferguson at the said Monument was 2.11 p.m. on the 28th day of October, 1986 A.D.

6. That to the best of my knowledge and belief the foregoing is correct and true.

7. In witness whereof I, the said G. Hasting Strachan place my Hand and Seal of Office

This 28th day of October,
1986 A.D.

G. Hasting Strachan
Commissioner
District of San Salvador and Rum Cay.

Fig. 2.

Archaeological Investigations at the Long Bay Site, San Salvador, Bahamas

Charles A. Hoffman
Northern Arizona University
Flagstaff, Arizona

ABSTRACT

The first place in the New World where Christopher Columbus went ashore on 12 October 1492 was the Island of San Salvador in the Bahamian archipelago, in the northern part of the Caribbean. There has been much debate over the years as to just which island is the real San Salvador. We have come to assume, especially after the works of Samuel Morison and Ruth Wolper, that it is the island presently bearing that name. But Joseph Judge has built a strong case for it being another, farther south. Historic records reveal that Columbus saw people on the island, and that he exchanged many trinkets with them — glass beads, fragments of crockery, coins, and other things. Archaeological research presented in this paper covers four seasons of excavations at a site of aboriginal occupation situated close to the presumed San Salvador landing place, and the finding of prehistoric pottery in direct association with objects similar to those Columbus reported trading to the Indians. This evidence, in turn, supports a strong case for the present-day San Salvador being the site of that momentous first landing.

INTRODUCTION

Certainly one of the great Columbus scholars was Samuel Eliot Morison.[1] Working from his own translations of Bartolome de las Casas, who, in turn, was supposedly quoting directly from Christopher Columbus' journal, Morison traced the route of Columbus' little flotilla from Spain to the West Indies, paying especial attention to where the landfall might have taken place in the Bahamas. Working closely with Ruth Wolper, he concluded[2] that the island which we call San Salvador today was the scene of that momentous occasion. Much of the eastern side of San Salvador is bordered by reefs. According to Morison, Columbus sailed along the south end of the island and then turned northward along the west coast. While there are reefs along the western side, there are occasional openings, and inside, between the reefs and the beach, is sufficient water for anchoring any of Columbus' ships. Actually, many sailing ships today anchor just outside the west coast reefs between the so-called "wall," where the ocean bottom drops off quite steeply and the reefs themselves. Columbus could have anchored his three ships in 30 meters of water, away from the reefs, yet only a few hundred meters from the beach, if he did so in the vicinity of Bamboo Point near present-day Cockburn Town. The first opportunity to pass through the reefs, if approaching from the south, is at Long Bay, or Fernandez Bay. I believe that Morison and Wolper postulate that Columbus did enter Long Bay and anchored approximately in the center, in quiet water, only meters from the beach. There are at least three places where the Long Bay reef may be threaded by small boats; I have done so myself while spearfishing there. However, I suspect, if he did land on San Salvador, he did so at the north end of that Bay, off what is today called Bamboo Point. There, as I said, deep water comes very close to the shore, and until it was removed a few years ago, there was a sand bar about 200 meters from the beach, an easy swim for the native islanders.

When Columbus did land, he records that many of the natives came out to his ships by boat and by swimming. The following is translated by Morison from Las Casas.[3]

> I . . . gave to some of them red caps and to others glass beads, which they hung on their necks, and many other things of slight value, in which they took much pleasure. They remained so much our [friends] that it was a marvel, later they came swimming to the ship's boats in which we were, and brought us parrots and cotton thread in skeins and darts and many other things, and we swopped them for other things that we gave them, such as little glass beads and hawk's bells.
>
> This island is very big and very level; and the trees are very green, and many bodies of water, and a very big lake in the middle; but no mountain, and the whole of it so green that it is a pleasure to gaze upon, and this people are very docile, and from their longing to have some of our things, and thinking they will get nothing unless they give something, and not having it, they take what they can and swim off. But all that they have, they give for whatever is given to them, even bartering for pieces of broken crockery and glass. I even saw 16 skeins of cotton given for three *ceitis* of Portugal, which is [equivalent to] a *blanca* of Castile. (Brackets Morison's.)

Morison footnotes[4] that Columbus shipped quantities of hawk's bells, as well as glass beads, brass rings, red caps, and such trifles because he had found them to be in great demand in his travels along the Guinea coast of Africa. From Columbus' journal of the 22nd of October, after landing at the island of Isabela he said the Indians "brought darts and some skeins of cotton to barter, and which they swopped with some seamen for pieces of glass, broken drinking vessels, and pieces of earthenware."[5] Later, during his landings on the north coast of Cuba, after leaving the Bahamas, the

238

Admiral records on 3 December that the Indians were "given hawk's bells and brass rings and green and yellow glass beads."[6]

Thus we learn that the following European objects were traded to the Indians: crockery, glass, glass beads, brass rings, coins, and hawk's bells. Reflecting upon this it seemed to me that if we are able to find glass beads and coins dating from Spanish times in the rather acidic soils of Florida, then I should be able to find them in the soils of the islands of the Bahamas. And, the best place to look would have to be the island upon which the best evidence suggests that Columbus first landed. Further, the aboriginal village closest to the actual landing beach would probably have been the recipient of the greatest quantity of these items. At the time there were three major contenders for the title of being the island of the first landing. Egg Island in the northern Bahamas, San Salvador, and Grand Turk in the southern end of the archipelago.

In 1971 I had visited the Turks and Caicos, and surveyed much of Grand Turk, but found no sites there.[7] I did locate sites on Providenciales, however,[8] but did not believe Columbus would have landed in the Caicos without at least mentioning having seen Grand Turk. And, because I knew little of the argument for it, I discarded Molander's Egg Island entirely. Thus, I resolved to return to San Salvador.[9]

When, at the Caribbean archaeology meetings in Dominican Republic in 1981, I was invited by Donald T. Gerace, Director of the CCFL Bahamas Field Station on San Salvador, to return to the Bahamas to carry out archaeological research, I welcomed the opportunity. I had decided that I would want to excavate a site of prehistoric activity somewhere along Long Bay, preferably toward the north end, close to Bamboo Point. In 1960 John Goggin found a site at the southern end of the Bay and in 1965 I had found one at the northern. In 1981 John Winter located several sherds of Palmetto Ware, fish bones, and fragments of old shell on the surface of the ground just below the Long Bay settlement in almost the direct center of the Bay, not far from a cross Mrs. Wolper had erected in honor of Columbus having landed there.

THE LONG BAY SITE

The Long Bay site lies between 100 and 200 meters from the beach of Long Bay. It is on the back (east-facing) gentle slope of the beach ridge. It is bordered on the west by the ridge, and on the east by a low ground which parallels the shore along the southern half of Long Bay. All the area behind the beach is fair to good farming land. However, Don Gerace made arrangements with the owner, Mr. Vernon Knowles, who graciously gave us permission to excavate. We were working side by side with people actually farming, using a slash and burn technique, planting with the aid of a digging stick and/or machete. Dense brush makes it difficult to determine the true area of the site, but it appears to cover quite a few hectares. Because of the surface finds at the north and south ends of the Bay, and at occasional gardens between those two places, a tentative conclusion is that there may have been a series of occupation or activity areas of varying intensities on the eastward-facing gradual slope behind the beach ridge; a series of huts, probably in clusters here and there, along the entire length of the Bay. This involves a linear distance of some 7 km.

Immediately east of and paralleling this ridge, at least along the southern half of the Bay, is the low-ground area mentioned above, which may be the remains of a late Pleistocene or Recent inlet or embayment, of which there are several on San Salvador. Natives on the Island say that the low ground will, in rainy weather, fill with fresh water. We found the remains of an old well about 100 meters northeast of the site in the lowest part of this low ground. This low area parallels the beach until it "comes out" in a small cove about 3.2 km. south of the site. At places along the low ground I observed standing sweet water in 1983, 1984, 1985, and 1986. Whether the result of surface run-off, a spring, or an aquifer recharge, I do not know, but standing fresh water is not a common occurrence anywhere in the Bahamas, including San Salvador. There may have been an obvious connection between the proximity of the site and the availability of fresh water, yet close to the sea.

Test excavations were begun at Long Bay in the summer of 1983 with students from Northern Arizona University and representatives of the Bahamas Archaeology Team from Nassau. An innovation in our excavation procedure was the use of a fine-mesh screen. I made this decision primarily because I wanted to recover any tiny glass beads (I was afraid they might fall through the quarter-inch-mesh hardware cloth) and partly as the result of discussions with Elizabeth S. Wing, zooarchaeologist at the Florida State Museum. Wing felt that the quantity (and representativeness) of faunal remains increases significantly with the use of the fine-mesh screen[10] (a conclusion to which she no longer subscribes). We set up a kind of double-deck system. Most of the soil excavated was first passed through standard quarter-inch mesh hardware cloth, and then through a 1/16-inch mesh screen. Our progress was slowed considerably, but I felt that it would be worth it.

During the summers of 1983, 1984, and 1985, we excavated 19 two-meter squares to a maximum depth of 60 cm. in some, to 40 cm. in others. In general the sub-surface profile was uniform. Below a thin to absent layer of root mat was approximately 40 cm. of grey soil. Below that, in most instances, the soil color changed abruptly to a sterile whitish yellow. Under some squares we found limited distributions of loosely cemented rock, similar to that found on the sand beaches around the Island. There seemed to be no connection between the rock and cultural activity; it was probably decaying "beach rock," perhaps from the late Pleistocene or Recent when that part of the Island was itself a beach.

RESULTS OF EXCAVATIONS

The first indication that all our efforts might be worthwhile came on 13 June 1983 when we recovered a tiny fragment of plain white, grey paste majolica at 18 cm. below the ground surface. A few centimeters away we found a metal D-ring, apparently hammered out of bronze. Then, small fragments of metal began showing up on the fine screen from the 20-30 cm. level. On 17 June we found a large metal fragment, perhaps a bent bolt or end of a large nail in the 10-20 cm. level, and on the 19th a large flake of metal alongside sherds of Palmetto Ware and fish bones. The hints were tantalizing, but the tiny fragment of majolica really told us we were on the trail of Columbus. Then came a week of exceedingly hot days, a minor insurrection of no-seeums, and little else. The crew begged for the 4th of July off. We worked. Fortunately. In the 20-30 cm. level we recovered a metal "planking nail" or spike at 26 cm., an apparent metal blade or knife at 29 cm., and a yellow or amber-colored glass seed bead in the fine screen.

The next day we found a similar bead, green in color, fragments of honey-colored melado ware, and a bronze buckle, similar in shape to several illustrated by Bernardo Vega as part of the early Spanish times in Dominican Republic.[11] On the 6th we found a green glass bead *in situ* at 28.5 cm. below the ground surface. Still other objects of apparent Spanish origin were found — beads and bead fragments, planking nails, a bent nail or hook. A few days before we were to close up the 1983 season student James McGuinness and BAT member Aline McLaughlin found a copper coin at about 19 cm. down. We also noted the presence of tiny, pin-head size fragments of what appear to be sulfur. The coin has since been identified as a *blanca*,[12] minted probably in Sevilla, in honor of Henry IV, between 1471 and 1474.

A tiny sliver of a broken glass bead, the coin, the two buckles, and some of the pottery were sent to Robert Brill at the Corning Museum of Glass in New York. Brill arranged for lead isotope analysis of the specimens, the results of which indicated that the leads used in their manufacture were almost certainly mined in Spain.[13]

In addition to plain and decorated Palmetto Ware pottery, shell "heishi" beads, fragments of shell, and fish bones, over the 1983, 1984, and 1985 seasons we recovered:

1 amber glass seed bead,[14]
6 whole and 3 fragments of green glass seed beads,[15]
38 sherds of melado pottery,[16]
2 sherds of majolica (too small to classify, grey paste, white enamel, no marks or decoration),
10 planking nails or spikes (the metal has apparently been almost entirely replaced),
2 metal hooks (or bent planking nails),
4 metal knife (blade?) fragments,

1 bronze D-ring,
1 bronze buckle,[17]
1 copper coin,
1 copper grommet,
1 metal button, plain,
Many fragments of flat metal,
Many fragments of green glass,

All of these materials were found in direct association with sherds of Palmetto Ware, previously believed to have been made by pre-Columbian occupants of the Bahama Islands. During the summer of 1984 we found several pieces of melado lying flat, right next to pieces of Palmetto Ware on a flat rock. The rock measured about 10 by 20 cm. and was 29 cm. below the ground surface, a few centimeters from a polished petaloid celt from the same level. Several of these flat rocks were found throughout the excavations, generally at the same level, all lying in a flat position. I believe they were shelves such as people living in sandy areas might use for placing items upon. It appeared that the fragments of Palmetto Ware pottery and melado ware had been placed next to each other on that shelf.

CONCLUDING THOUGHTS AND SPECULATIONS

It would seem that the Long Bay site is an early historic/ prehistoric site. A site of Spanish contact with American Indians. The beginning date for the contact period of the site would have to be 12 October 1492. Las Casas reports that by 1513 no Indians could be found in the Bahamas when Spanish ships went there looking for slaves to carry off to Hispaniola to mine gold or to the pearl beds of Nueva Cadiz.[18] Inasmuch as San Salvador was one of the islands already known to the Spaniards, it seems likely that they would have included that Island in their slave-raiding itinerary. We might, then, consider the possibility that the end date for appearance of Spanish trade goods on the Island was 1513. The type of glass beads traded by Columbus was manufactured until about 1516.[19] It was then replaced by a larger, more ornate bead. To be more conservative I might estimate that the historic artifacts appeared at the Long Bay site between 1492 and 1560.

Because of the few Columbus' documents we have, I assume that the people found on his San Salvador spoke the Arawakan language. I further assume that they were related to, perhaps even descended from, other Arawak speakers on the mainland of Hispaniola to the south. There were either Taino Indians from Hispaniola, or people who were related to the Taino of Hispaniola. Indeed, I would venture to say that Hispaniola was the Saomete that Columbus reported the Indians pointing to, rather than another island in the Bahamian archipelago.

As you can see, the description of the island by Columbus matches San Salvador today: green, inland lakes, rocks along the shore suitable for erecting public buildings, a north-northeast boat trip from the original docking place to the north end of the island, a harbor that could hold all the ships in Christendom, and even an island that is not quite an island. And, there is a site of aboriginal activity near where it is presumed Columbus went ashore. And, in that site we found the kinds of artifacts Columbus reported trading to the Indians in direct association with what we would have otherwise considered to be prehistoric Indian pottery. So. Is San Salvador the real first landing place of Columbus?

In the past few weeks Joseph Judge has postulated Columbus landed on Samana Cay some 65-70 miles to the southeast. He is basing this on several lines of reasoning.[20] I believe his strength lies in his reconstruction of the route Columbus took through the Bahamas after he left San Salvador. Columbus reported seeing several islands, and stopping at three more of them. By taking into consideration the distance he traveled each day, the directions, and island descriptions, it would seem that Judge's proposed landing on Samana Cay has a lot of merit. Far more merit, say, than Morison's second island, Rum Cay. Morison has it half the size Columbus reports. I agree with Judge that it is not sufficient to say that Columbus was using a different form of measurement when the island doesn't fit. Accepting that, however, Morison would have Columbus leave Rum Cay and head for the east-west coastline at the north end of Long Island. There doesn't seem to be an east-west coastline at the north end of Long Island. Then Morison has Columbus traveling from the north end of Long Island to the south end in a matter of a few hours. In a calm sea. Again, there is something wrong. If Long Island is Columbus' third island, I have to agree with Judge that Columbus landed further south, probably in the vicinity of Adam's Hole harbor at the south end; the east-west coast line would be that near Clarence Town. There are other areas where I find I have to agree with Judge. I shall report on them in detail in the future.

Meanwhile, Luis Marden collaborated with Judge on the project to determine the real San Salvador. Marden used a computer to track Columbus' fleet as it progressed across the Atlantic. By adjusting the tract to take into consideration set and current along the way, he concluded that Columbus had to land some 60 miles farther south than San Salvador, right where Samana Cay happens to be. The real problem I have with this is the obvious possibility of error, in a seaman dozing off at the tiller, the compass not being accurate, an accumulated error in reading direction and/or distance traveled.

Judge's argument, with or without Marden's trans-Atlantic track is a good one. Samana Cay could have been the first landing place. However, there are other problems. Columbus describes his Fernandina (supposedly Long Island) as being all beach and lower than his San Salvador. No matter which San Salvador you choose, neither one is higher than the east coast of Long

Island. Long Island has a very hilly eastern coastline, a high rocky shoreline, and only occasionally are there beaches between the rocks. Further Columbus reports that he could not sail around the south end of Fernandina and up the west coast. While on Long Island this summer I saw several ships, easily drawing as much water as Columbus' ships, traveling at least a third of the way up the west coast.

What other island could be Fernandina? To me the only other one that fits his description is Andros. Arne Molander has already suggested Andros is Fernandina. Is he correct? If so, we are faced with the same problem, of even greater magnitude, of Columbus traveling from the north end to the south end in a matter of a few hours. Moreover, what happens to his fourth island, Isabela? There is no island where Isabela would be if Columbus sailed southeast from the south end of Andros. Columbus said he could see the southern tip of Fernandina and Isabela from one place. The only islands southeast of Andros are the Ragged Islands, over a hundred miles away. It is doubtful Columbus could have seen both Andros and the Ragged Islands at the same time.

We are left, I fear, with the conclusion that if San Salvador were where Samana Cay is, we would have no problem. But if Samana Cay is the real San Salvador, then the problem is, how did all those historic artifacts get on present-day San Salvador.

NOTES

1. But see also Cubitt, George. *Columbus: on the Discovery of America.* Boston: D. Lothrop & Co, 1881; Durlacher-Wolper, Ruth C. *A New Theory Clarifying the Identity of Christophorous Columbus.* The New World Museum, 1982; Floyd, Troy S. *The Columbus Dynasty in the Caribbean.* Albuquerque: University of New Mexico press, 1973; Fox, Gustavus Vasa. *An Attempt to Solve the Problem of the First Landing Place of Columbus in the New World.* Washington, 1882; Irving, Washington. *The Life and Voyages of Christopher Columbus.* New York: A. L. Burt, Publ., n.d.; Wolper, Ruth G. Durlacher. *A New Theory Identifying the Locale of Columbus's Light, Landfall, and Landing.* Washington: Smithsonian Institution, Smithsonian Miscellaneous Collections, Vol. 148, No. 1, 1964, among others.

2. Morison, Samuel Eliot. *Admiral of the Ocean Sea.* Boston: Little, Brown and Co., 1942; Morison, Samuel Eliot. *Christopher Columbus.* New York: The Heritage Press, 1963.

3. *Ibid.,* p. 67.

4. *Ibid.,* p. 66.

5. *Ibid.,* p. 78.

6. *Ibid.,* p. 108.

7. Hoffman, Charles A. "Caribbean Research," in *American Antiquity.* Society for American Archaeology, 1972.

8. *Ibid.*

9. I had carried out excavations at the Palmetto Grove site at the northern end of the Island in 1965, but found no historic objects during the course of that work. See Hoffman, Charles A. "Bahama Prehistory: Cultural Adaptation to an Island Environment," Ph.D. dissertation, University of Arizona, 1967; and *The Palmetto Grove Site on San Salvador, Bahamas*, Contributions of the Florida State Museum, Social Sciences, No. 16., University of Florida. Gainesville: University of Florida, 1970.

10. The fine-mesh screen was not used in the excavations at Palmetto Grove. I found it quite helpful at Long Bay as far as the beads are concerned, but there were artifacts recovered there which would have been caught in the quarter-inch-mesh hardware cloth. We did not, however, improve our recovery of tiny fish bones with this system.

11. Vega, Bernardo.

12. The coin was identified by two independent coin specialists in Madrid, Spain. See also unpublished manuscript *Glass Beads and Other Artifacts Recovered from the Long Bay Site, San Salvador, Bahamas.* by Brill, Robert and Charles A. Hoffman.

13. *Ibid.*

14. Smith, Marvin T. and Mary Elizabeth Good. *Early Sixteenth Century Glass beads in the Spanish Colonial Trade.* Greenwood: Cottonlandia Museum Publications, 1982. See Number 106 illustrated in Figure 7, Page 43.

15. *Ibid.*, Bead Number 105, Figure 7, Page 43.

16. See Goggin, John M. *Spanish Majolica in the New World*, Yale University Publications in Anthropology, Nr 72. New Haven. Department of Anthropology, Yale University, 1968.

17. Vega, Bernardo

18. Las Casas, Bartolome de. *Historia de las Indias*, 11, Edited by Jose M. Virgil, Biblioteca Mexicana. Imprenta y litografia de Ireneo Paz, Mexico, 1877, pp 347-348; also *Ibid.*, pg. 100.

19. Smith, Marvin T. personal communication, 1983.

20. Judge, Joseph. "Where Columbus Found the New World," in *National Geographic*. Washington: The National Geographic Society, 1986.

Laboratory Studies of
Some European Artifacts
Excavated on San Salvador Island

Robert H. Brill
The Corning Museum of Glass
Corning, New York

I. Lynus Barnes
National Bureau of Standards
Gaithersburg, Maryland

Stephen S. C. Tong
Corning Glass Works
Corning, New York

Emile C. Joel
Smithsonian Institution
Washington, D. C.

Martin J. Murtaugh
Smithsonian Institution *Corning Glass Works*
Washington, D. C.

ABSTRACT

Recent excavations at The Long Bay Site uncovered artifacts of European manufacture intermingled with native Indian artifacts. These include seven very small
glass beads (and fragments of three others), a coin, a small metal buckle, a
"D-ring", 32 sherds of *melado* ware, and two small sherds of white-glazed ware.
Laboratory studies have been conducted to help determine the origins and dates
of these artifacts.

The glass beads are wire-wound and have an extremely unusual high-lead chemical composition. The coin is a billon *blanca* of Henry IV minted between 1471
and 1474. Both buckles were found to be lightly-leaded bronzes. The melado
ware has a lead glaze, as do the white wares, although the latter also contain tin.

All of the artifacts contain intentionally-added lead. Their isotope ratios spread
over a range, but all are consistent with Spanish origins. The data indicate that
the San Salvador artifacts were made in three locations within Spain.

INTRODUCTION

At the outset of this conference, debate still continues as to the identity
of Guanahani, Columbus's San Salvador. The debate has, indeed, recently
intensified with the announcement of a claim by a team working under the
auspices of the National Geographic Society,[1] disputing the widely-held
opinion that Columbus's San Salvador is the present day Bahamian island

247

bearing that same name. Although the present authors have certain reservations regarding the case as so far stated for Samana Cay, we will leave the navigational, historical, and observational aspects of that subject to be argued out by those better qualified than we. Instead, this paper deals with the archaeological finds recently made on San Salvador. Until now, these finds appear to be the only archaeological evidence yet uncovered which might plausibly relate to Columbus's first landing in The New World. Whether or not these finds remain unique will depend upon future excavations both there and at other sites, including Samana Cay. But one thing is readily apparent. An entirely new dimension — archaeological studies — has now been added to the investigation of Columbus's voyages of discovery. This new dimension comprises not only the newly uncovered artifacts dealt with here, but also the application of archaeology in general which will contribute to a clearer understanding of the people whom Columbus encountered during his voyages into their homelands.

Whichever translation one uses of the Bartoleme de Las Casas abstract of Columbus's journal of his first voyage, there seems to be no disagreement as to his description of certain events of October 12th recorded in his entry for October 13th. As worded in Morison's version,[2] along with Las Casas' remarks that these particular passages quote the Admiral's own words, Columbus wrote: "I, in order that they might develop a very friendly disposition towards us. . .gave to some of them red caps, and to others glass beads, which they hung on their necks, and many other things of slight value, in which they took much pleasure. . . .later they came swimming to the ship's boats in which we were, and brought us parrots and cotton thread in skeins and darts [spears?] and many other things, and we swopped them for other things that we gave them, such as little glass beads and hawk's bells." On October 13th he also noted ". . .they readily bartered for any article we saw fit to give them in return, even such as broken platters and fragments of glass. I saw. . .sixteen balls of cotton thread. . .given for three Portuguese *ceutis* (sic)." In the days which follow, Columbus made several more entries referring to glass beads and other trifles traded to the Indians. For October 15th he stated that the Indian he met traveling over open water possessed a basket containing some glass beads and two Spanish *blancas*. From this Columbus surmised the man had come from San Salvador. On December 3rd, having by then become involved in an exploration of Cuba, Columbus set out up river from the coast with an armed party, and trekked through heavily wooded country until they came upon a large village, whose inhabitants the Admiral gave ". . .hawk's bells and brass rings and green and yellow glass beads, with which they were well pleased." Later in the day, during a decidedly less friendly encounter, he pacified a group of Indians and ". . .demanded their darts, for which I gave to some a hawk's bell, to others a brass ring, to others some beads, so that all were pleased. . .".[3]

248

From the foregoing, it is evident that among the small items Columbus and his crew traded or used as gifts on his first voyage, were hawk's bells, metal rings (described as "brass"), low-denomination copper-based coins, (*ceutis* at Guanahani and *blancas*, by implication, at Guanahani), fragments of broken glass and pottery, and glass beads — specifically green and yellow glass beads. Another reference, without citing a primary source, adds to this list "fragments of shoe-latchets."[4] That the Indian recipients were delighted is to be expected, because the same results had been obtained with the same items (augmented by more substantial goods when serious trading began) by Portuguese merchants and explorers working down the West Coast of Africa. Indeed, Columbus was probably involved in that trade himself, and would naturally have taken an ample supply of the same such trinkets on his voyage to "The Indies."[5]

In another paper at this conference, Charles Hoffman has described his excavations at The Long Bay Site.[6] The coastal area around the bay had been surveyed previously by John Winter.[7] These excavations produced a number of European-made artifacts intermingled with Lucayan Indian artifacts which normally would be considered prehistoric. The objective of the present study was to learn as much as possible about the European-made artifacts through laboratory examinations and analyses in the hope that the results might lead to conclusions regarding their dates and places of manufacture.[8]

THE OBJECTS STUDIED

The European-made finds consist of the following: Seven tiny glass beads with fragments of three others, one coin, one small buckle, one somewhat larger metal D-ring, a sherd of *melado* (or honey-glazed) ware, and two sherds of plain white-glazed ware, (possibly "majolica" in The New World usage), three planking nails, one copper grommet, one metal hook, and fragments of metal which might have come from knives or swords.

The objects discussed in this paper, along with some parallels, are described in the catalogue of samples and illustrated in Figures 1 through 9. Table 1 summarizes the analyses and tests carried out on each object.

Only minute samples of the objects were sacrificed for study. Approximately one-half of each of the two smallest glass bead fragments was removed. The original fragments consisted of only about one-quarter of a bead and measured no more than 1.5 mm in greatest dimension. A tiny snippet of the perimeter of the coin was removed from an edge which was already bent and about to become dislodged. The buckle and D-ring, being larger and less fragile, were sampled by drilling thin shallow holes into the metal. The holes were then filled and painted over to minimize the slight disfigurement which otherwise would have been visible. Minute portions of glazes and bodies were removed from the edges of two of the pottery sherds and petrographic thin sections were prepared. The nails, hook, grommet, and knives or sword fragments have not yet been analyzed.

The Glass Beads

The seven glass beads and three fragments are all of the same type. (Figures 2 and 3.) This is a rather distinctive type; once seen and handled, other examples should be easily recognized. On the other hand, without having examined them, a casual observer could easily be misled into thinking these beads are the same as other far more familiar and ubiquitous types of seed beads.

The San Salvador beads are varieties VIDle and VIDlf in the typology defined by Marvin Smith and Mary Elizabeth Good in their publication on early Spanish beads found in The New World.[9] The beads correspond to nos. 105 and 106 in Figure 7 of that publication.[10] The San Salvador beads have a distinct shape and are best described as tiny "ringlets," although they are not always perfectly round. They are small, measuring only 2.5-3.5 mm in "maximum diameter" and have relatively large, roughly circular perforations[11] ranging from 1.5 to 2.3 mm. Most are somewhat thicker on one side than the other.

These beads were unquestionably made by winding, as is evidenced by the internal cords (striations) which spiral through the bead and around the axis of the perforation. They contain quite a few seed (small bubbles) which are generally sphericalized. The seed occasionally occur in bubble chains which follow the cord patterns. In all examples there are protrusions on the thicker portion corresponding to "winding-thread pull-offs," that is, places where the thread of glass was separated from the main body of the bead during its manufacture. Most of these once had sharp, cracked-off edges which have since been worn down by erosion, but some were originally rounded, having become fire-polished during manufacture.

The perforations are straight-sided and have surfaces which, weathering effects aside, are what one expects to see on beads wound around a wire. No traces of scale or other metallic corrosion products are preserved on the surfaces, although one bead (5714) does contain a few black flakes (which look metallic) trapped inside the glass itself. In places, elliptically-shaped half bubbles are seen on the walls of the perforations. These resulted from air trapped between the softened glass and wire when the beads were wound. The half bubbles are elongated in the direction of winding.

The ringlet form of these beads is distinctly different from the shape of most tiny seed beads — which, by the way, are often even smaller than the San Salvador beads in outside diameter. The vast majority of seed beads were made by drawing out hollow tubes of glass, giving them a shape which is usually distinctly drumlike and more cylindrical than the ringlet shape of the wirewound San Salvador beads. It is fortunate in terms of this investigation that the excavated beads have such a distinctive and recognizable form, for that separates them sharply from the far more abundant drawn beads, thereby offering greater promise for locating their places and dates of manufacture. Moreover, one of the colors is also quite unusual. Of the ten

250

beads and fragments, nine are a bright green transparent color, and one a rather pale yellowish amber. The green transparent is not a true emerald green; nevertheless it is distinctly brighter than, and distinguishable from, the iron green of most early glasses. This distinctive, sparkling color should also be of help in identifying the place and date of manufacture.

The glasses are heavily weathered although few traces of weathering products still adhere, having been eroded away by the action of the soil in which they were buried. Nevertheless, all show the heavy tell-tale pitting characterizing glasses which have been weathered over the course of two or three centuries or more.

Marvin Smith, then of the University of Florida, and the late Charles Fairbanks, have provided four additional samples of beads which are virtually identical to the San Salvador specimens. The differences between them and the San Salvador beads (except that one is yellow opaque) are visible only under magnification. They have the same ringlet form, approximately the same dimensions and proportions, a very similar sparkling green color, and were also made by winding. They differ only by being somewhat less weathered, and slightly less seedy. Unfortunately, only one, 5700, comes with a provenance. It is from Nueva Cadiz, and should date between 1515 and 1545. The others were obtained from dealers and are said to come from the Sinu region of Colombia and from Peru. As was borne out by the analyses discussed below, these four beads are clearly very closely related to the San Salvador specimens in a chemical sense as well as in their physical appearance.

Quantitative chemical analyses were made of all six of the beads described above: two fragments from San Salvador and the four comparative specimens. Quantitative determinations of the major and minor elements of the four latter glasses were carried out by atomic absorption, and semi-quantitative analyses of the trace elements by emission spectrography. For these glasses, the silica was estimated by difference from 100%. Because the samples of the San Salvador beads were so small, they were analyzed by the electron microprobe. The results are reported in Table 2.

Two important observations can be made immediately. First, all six of the glasses are very similar in composition; similar enough that we are willing to attribute them to the same general region and traditions of manufacture — possibly, even, to the same factory. Second, the composition is extremely unusual. It is really a two-component lead-silica glass ($PbO:SiO_2$). The presence of lead, even in rather sizeable concentrations, is not unusual throughout the history of glassmaking, however, these 65-75% lead oxide contents are much higher than those seen in virtually any other category of early lead glasses from the Western World.[12] The very high lead contents result in the very high specific gravities and indices of refraction measured for some of the beads and reported in Table 2. This is useful to know because it affords a means of estimating the lead contents of suspected parallels to the San Salvador beads without subjecting them to chemical analysis.

251

The high lead content of the San Salvador beads produced a glass with a low softening point which would have allowed it to have been drawn out in threads and wound around a wire at relatively low temperatures. From the viscosity-temperature curve for a very similar glass, we estimate that glasses with the composition of the San Salvador beads would have been soft enough to have been worked in this manner at a temperature of 750-800°C. This would be some 250-300° lower than required for a soda-lime glass. It is probable that such beads could have been made with an alcohol lamp equipped with a small blowpipe. One could visualize a kind of cottage industry in which cullet, or perhaps glass already drawn into thin rods or threads, was softened and formed into the beads in small workshops. Indeed, it is difficult to visualize how such tiny beads could have been made at all in large numbers if the glass would have had to have been worked at the glory hole of a furnace.

Although copper produces a blue transparent color in soda-limes and other common glasses, the sparkling, bright green of these beads is typical of the color produced by copper in a high-lead matrix. The yellowish amber glass is probably a so-called "carbon amber."[13] The yellow opaque bead (5721) from Colombia is obviously colored with the $PbSnO_3$ yellow colorant-opacifier. (Microscopic flakes of the pigment can be seen in the glass.) This pigment is related to the better-known $Pb_2Sb_2O_7$ antimony compound used in ancient glasses. The tin pigment gradually replaced the antimony pigment starting sometime around the 1st-2nd cent. A.D.[14] Although both were used from time-to-time after that, the tin-containing pigment, judging from analyses of mosaic tesserae, appears to have seen somewhat wider use from Medieval times onward.[15]

The analyzed chemical compositions of the six glasses were used to back-calculate batch formulas which could have been used to prepare the glasses. The mean of the $PbO:SiO_2$ ratio is 2.94, indicating that the basic recipe, on a weight basis, was probably 3.0 parts of litharge to 1.0 part of sand. The deviation of the calculated ratio from this ideal 3:1 ratio is only about 2 relative percent. This deviation is readily accounted for by the alumina, iron, and other impurity oxides which affect the calculation. Transformed to a volume basis, the basic recipe is very close to a 1:1 ratio of sand to litharge[16] with a deviation amounting to only 6%. Both of these recipes conform to common sense, and the choice of one over the other depends only upon whether one chooses to believe that glassmakers of the period worked with weight batches or with volume batches.[17] In either case, a small quantity of copper-containing colorant was also added to form the green color. We believe this was in the form of an oxide scale from a piece of scrap brass. Calculations show that the colorant could have been an alloy with a composition 78Cu:19Zn:3Sn. This is reasonable for a brass of the period.[18]

One further point deserves consideration. The composition of these glasses is actually closer to the composition of enamels than it is to glasses ordinarily used for vessel manufacture. It would not be surprising to find that these beads originated in some location where glass or metal enameling was practiced.

In summary, the San Salvador beads are all very closely related to one another, and to the four comparative beads from early Spanish Colonial sites in The New World. They are a distinctive and recognizable type visually, were made by the relatively rare wire-wound technique, and share an unusual chemical composition which can be explained on a reasonable technological basis. The next question arising is where these beads might have been made. The possibilities which come to mind are Spain, Portugal, and Venice. The authors have not yet had opportunities to investigate this question as thoroughly as required, and glass specialists consulted so far have been helpful but have not provided definitive answers. Venice is always first among the usual suspects rounded up as the source of any glass bead. Although records exist which document the export of Venetian beads through commercial trading centers (including Lisbon) it would do an injustice to Spanish glass industries of the time to settle too hastily upon Venice in this instance. There were fluorishing glass industries in Spain at the time of Columbus's departure, and they should be considered prime candidates for the place of manufacture. Elena Ramirez-Montesinos has told us she believes that green glass beads with very high lead contents might have been made at Maria or Puebla de Don Fadrique.

The Metal Buckles

The two excavated buckles, (4691 and 4692) are illustrated in Figures 3 and 4. No. 4692 is quite small, measuring 2.4 cm across the straight shank. It might have been a shoe buckle. No tongue was found to accompany this buckle but perhaps it never had one. It is said that imitation buckles, never intended to be worn, were sometimes made for use as trade trinkets. Such buckles would not show any wear along the straight side where the tongue would have been mounted. Indeed, this buckle does not show such wear, but one wonders if a real buckle would show wear either if it were this heavily corroded. For the moment then, this point remains unresolved.

Jaime Barrachina has recently published the archaeological finds excavated at *El Castell de Llinars del Valles*, a castle near old Barcelona.[19] Among the finds were assorted types and sizes of bronze and/or brass buckles, some of which resemble the San Salvador buckle in form and in size. In a personal communication Dr. Barrachina has stated that the example he sees as being the closest parallel for the San Salvador find[20] was common in the early 15th century at his site, and that that type was made until at least as late as 1485.

There are two differences between the buckles from Llinars and the San Salvador object. The groove for the tongue in the San Salvador buckle is triangular in section, as if it (or the prototype for the mold in which it was cast) had been cut with the edge of a file. The grooves on the buckles from Llinars seem instead to be square in section. There is also a more subtle conceptual difference between the designs. The rounded portion of the San Salvador buckle looks like a semi-oval, with a straight bar placed across the ends of it and extending beyond the ends. All the buckles from Llinars look instead like semi-ovals with rounded ends extending beyond a straight bar joining them inside the ends.

Professor Barrachina's information is encouraging, in that it establishes that small buckles, possibly shoe buckles, similar (although not identical) to the San Salvador specimen were in use in Cataluña towards the end of the 15th century. Much further research must be done to see what small buckles from other places were like at that time. For all we know at present, similar buckles might have been used in many other parts of Europe.

Barrachina also shows examples of D-rings from Llinars.[21] However, his finds were made of iron, whereas that from San Salvador (4691) is made of bronze.

Bernardo Vega[22] illustrates two buckles similar to those found at Long Bay. Vega, then director of the *Museo del Hombre Dominicano in Santo Domingo*, Dominican Republic, reported finding 29 metal artifacts of European origin, together with stone and amber objects of Taino origin. Twelve croissant-shaped metal pieces were analyzed and turned out to be brasses containing about 85% copper and 13% zinc. We have not examined the buckles Vega illustrates. However, the two illustrated closely resemble Barrachina's in that the rounded ends project beyond the straight bar joining them inside the ends. The composition of the metal of the buckles is not given.

Chemical analyses of the San Salvador buckles are shown in Table 4. The analysis of the small buckle (4692) yielded only a surface composition because it was done by x-ray fluorescence.[23] Nevertheless, the results are sufficient to establish that the alloy is a lightly-leaded bronze. The D-ring (4691) was analyzed by a combination of atomic absorption and emission spectrography, because it was possible to obtain a sample without disfiguring the object. This alloy is also a lightly leaded bronze. The D-ring could have served any number of purposes, although the fact that it is bronze might suggest it also had a partially decorative function, or had been used for maritime purposes, where resistance to corrosion was required.

The Pottery and Pottery Glazes

Small samples of the glazes of two of the pottery sherds from San Salvador (Figure 9) were analyzed qualitatively with the electron microprobe by one of the authors (SSCT).[24] The analyses established that both are lead glazes. The *melado* ware (4697) contains only lead in substantial proportions, but the white-glazed ware (4698) contains tin in addition. The fragment of white-glazed ware, which is too small to tell whether its parent object was decorated or undecorated, could be from a piece of Columbia plain ware. This type of pottery, thought to have been made in Triana (a suburb of Seville), is common on 15th- and 16th-century Spanish Colonial sites in The New World.[25] The one example of Columbia plain we have analyzed so far is a broken plate similar in color and fabric to the tiny white-glazed sherd from San Salvador. This plate, now in the collection of The Hispanic Society of America, was excavated at the Convent of San Nicolas near Santo Domingo. It is our sample 4699. The plate is identical, or nearly so, to one excavated at La Vega Vieja and illustrated by Goggin.[26]

X-ray diffraction by one of the authors (MJM) established that Quartz, Calcite, Augite and the clay mineral Chlorite are the major mineral constituents in the *melado* sherd (4697) and the white-glazed sherd from San Salvador (4698), and also in the Columbia plain sherd from Santo Domingo (4699). Thin-section analysis (by MJM and John F. Wosinski of Corning Glass Works) established that the non-matrix constituents consist of well-sorted quartz silts, larger fragments of quartz sand, randomly dispersed books of Biotite, some amphiboles and pyroxene (Augite) in a fine-grained matrix of Calcite and clay. The only difference among the three sherds is a slight color difference between samples 4697 and 4699. This is due simply to the sherds having been fired under somewhat different redox conditions. In light of present knowledge it seems unlikely that the sampled wares could have been made in the New World. These findings are consistent with the literature of Spanish Colonial majolica ceramics.[27]

The above analysis indicates that all three sherds were made from very similar clay sediments, and suggests that they could have been made in the same general region. Because the Columbia plain ware is thought to have been made near Seville, the evidence further suggests — but does not prove — that the San Salvador sherds might have come from some place not far from Seville. In support of this, one can look at those geological environments where the principle clay mineral, Chlorite, can occur. Chlorite will form as a secondary mineral phase in low-grade metamorphism, often associated with the formation of talc via a retrograde metamorphic sequence. With these particular samples such is not the case; the presence of amphiboles, pyroxene (Augite) and mica (Biotite) indicates a plutonic origin for the clay sediments, an origin in which Chlorite is the weathered by-product of amphiboles and mica. Large clay deposits of Chloritic clays will occur via detrital processes, i.e., alluvial processes. Based on our present knowledge, the mineral assemblage of the three sherds is compatible with the geo-environment of southern Spain.

A *Blanca* of Henry IV

The most useful find of the excavation, as far as dating is concerned, is a billon coin (Figures 5 and 6). The coin is in very poor condition, being heavily corroded, fragmentary, and possibly partially defaced. It is so thin that it must have been badly worn before having been buried. The corrosion has produced an overall green patina with microscopic bead-like protrusions containing cores of cuprite. A segment of the coin had been broken away in the distant past as evidenced by the presence of corrosion products on the broken edges. Dr. Doty (see below) is of the opinion that it was probably broken accidentally because billon, a copper-based alloy containing varying amounts of silver, is often very brittle. On the other hand, part of the coin also appears to have been scratched before burial with a pointed tool, perhaps an iron nail, and possibly had been hammered before burial. If this had been in an attempt to puncture it, with the intention of stringing it as a bead, then the breakage also might have been deliberate.

In order to identify the coin, the authors examined it with Richard G. Doty (then of the American Numismatic Society) and three experts in Madrid who are specialists in Spanish coins of the period in question. They are: Antonio Orol Pernas, Juan J. Rodriguez Lorente, and Carlos Castan.

The corrosion is so heavy that at first it was thought an identification would be impossible. Under the microscope, however, several features can be discerned which match features on *blancas* of Henry IV of Castile (1454-74). For comparison, uncorroded specimens of the same coin are illustrated in Figures 7 through 8. Fortunately, certain of the preserved features are unique to *blancas* of Henry's reign, thereby making the identification conclusive. Among these features are squared-off corners of the castle in the upper left quadrant of the coin; a floret near the perimeter at 5 o'clock; the ground line of the castle running horizontally near the bottom; and on the reverse, parts of the lion. In addition, parts of the beaded circular outline on the obverse and straight lines of the lozenge enclosing the lion on the reverse are preserved. Most definitively, traces of some of the lettering on each side are visible, although in some cases only faintly so. Mr. Orol Pernas was able to decipher parts of the legend, which would have read *"ENRICUS DEI GRACIA REX"*, when complete.

The part of the coin where the mint mark should appear (just below the center of the castle) is badly corroded. There is a faint suggestion, however, of the corner of a feature below the ground line. This might be part of a stylized aqueduct, the mint mark for Segovia.

When excavated, a small piece of the coin preserving no diagnostic elements was almost ready to separate from the coin itself. This piece was removed for chemical analysis and lead-isotope determinations. Where it was snipped away, the exposed uncorroded metal has a bright, somewhat brassy, color. The sample was so small that after a portion had been removed for lead isotope analysis, the remaining portion could only be analyzed by the electron microprobe.

An electron microprobe analysis of the coin was carried out by one of the authors (SSCT). Small samples removed from four known billon coins of Henry IV were used as reference standards (4676-79). These had been purchased from the trade for this purpose. Although all came from Henry's reign and all bear known mint marks, none are dated. They were analyzed by a combination of atomic absorption and emission spectrography. The microprobe analysis of the San Salvador coin (4693) is reported in Table 4. For comparison, analyses of ten other *blancas*, and three Henry IV billon coins of higher denominations, all from known mints, were carried out by atomic absorption and emission spectrography (Table 4). It was hoped that the chemical analyses of the additional specimens could be used for identifying the mint in which the San Salvador coin had been struck, but there is only partial correlation between the alloy compositions and mint locations. Nos. 4643 and 4647 both struck in Toledo, have significantly lower silver than the others; 4644 and 4650 (Cuenca) have higher lead; 4646 and 4649 (Segovia and Avila) have higher gold; 4642 and 4648 (Segovia and Burgos) have lower lead; 4645 (Seville) has higher silver. Unfortunately, the gold content of the San Salvador coin is below the limit of detection for the microprobe, so no gold content was available for comparison. Although the data are sparse, the analysis of the San Salvador coin seems to resemble those of the two coins from Segovia and Burgos more closely than the others, mainly on the basis of its rather low lead value.

The analysis confirmed that the San Salvador coin is made of billon and contains 3.97% silver. The silver contents of the comparative *blancas* range from 2.51 to 4.71%. Henry's reign was plagued by severe economic difficulties, but the variability in silver contents does not seem great enough to have come from deliberate debasement. It is more likely to have come from random sources.

The reign of Henry IV extended from 1454 to 1474. He was succeeded by his half sister, Isabella, who married Ferdinand. Because Henry's reign ended eighteen years before Columbus's first landing in 1492, the finding of one of his coins on San Salvador — or anywhere in The New World, for that matter — is at first quite surprising. The coin seems almost too early. However, the *blanca* was a coin of low value and circulated widely for many years, as small change of the times. This particular *blanca* is known to have been issued only between 1471 and 1474. Following Isabella's succession in 1474, no other copper-based coins were issued until the coinage reform of 1497. (Those are much larger in size and cannot be confused with Henry's *blanca*.) Mr. Orol Pernas remarked, "The copper-based coins in the pockets of Christopher Columbus and his crew would be expected to have been *blancas* of Henry IV, just like this one, or else Portuguese *ceities*".

LEAD-ISOTOPE ANALYSES

Isotope analyses of lead extracted from archaeological objects can be used to identify the mining regions from which the lead could or could not have come. The determinations are made by high-accuracy, high-precision mass spectrometry. The resulting ratios can be compared with those for other objects, or galena (lead sulfide) ores from known mining regions.

This, in turn, allows one to learn more about where the objects themselves might have been made.

The method has found widespread and growing application.[28] Its advantages are that only very minute samples need be sacrificed and that the isotope ratios measured for a sample today, regardless of its chemical form or physical condition, are exactly the same as they were when the object was made. The two disadvantages are that while the ratios determined are characteristic of a given mine or mining region, they are not necessarily unique to that region, and also, when leads from different sources are mixed together, the resulting ratios will be somewhere intermediate between those of the starting leads. These two difficulties are called, respectively, overlapping and mixing.

As shown by our preceding chemical analyses, the glass beads from San Salvador, the buckle, the D-ring, the two pottery glazes, and the *blanca* all contain lead. In some cases, for example the glass beads and glazes, the lead was a deliberate addition. In the case of the alloys from which the two buckles were made, we are not sure whether the lead is present as a deliberate addition or as an accidental impurity. The lead in the *blanca*, however, because it is at such a low level (0.09%), must be from an impurity in either the silver (produced by cupellation of lead) or, less likely, the copper, from which the billon was made.

Lead-isotope analyses for all seven San Salvador objects, and for several related objects, were carried out at the National Bureau of Standards by two of the authors (ILB and ECJ). The three specific objectives were:

1. To identify artifacts which were made nearby one another,

2. To verify (based on preceding chemical analyses and examinations) the suspected Spanish origins of the artifacts, and

3. Depending upon the above, to locate, eventually, the regions within Spain where the artifacts are most likely to have been made.

An *a priori* decision was made that if the results for the artifacts turned out to be consistent with the results for the Spanish coins (which certainly contain Iberian lead), then overlapping with other countries on The Continent should not be considered a serious complication.

The data are reported in Table 4. Previous research at the Bureau of Standards, done largely in collaboration with The Corning Museum of Glass, has yielded data on approximately a thousand samples of lead from ancient objects and ores.[29] Figure 10 summarizes the results on several hundred early objects and illustrates that isotope ratios vary widely among objects of different dates and places of manufacture. All the samples analyzed in this study lie close to Group S which contains Spanish lead.[30] That part of the graph is expanded in Figures 11-14. The isotope ratios of the San Salvador and related specimens spread out somewhat, but are clustered together in small groups. These are the kinds of results expected for samples of different materials, made over some period of time, in one general area, but drawing on leads from various mines within that area.

The interpretation of the data is not only complicated in itself, but also very difficult to explain. One of the most salient points, however, can be simply stated: The data are consistent with the hypothesis that all seven of the objects from The Long Bay Site were made in Spain.

In all, 38 samples are involved: 8 from San Salvador, 6 from other New World sites, one from West Africa, 12 Spanish coins, and 11 ores or miscellaneous samples from the Iberian Peninsula. Figure 11 contains the data for the artifacts; Figure 12 the billon coins; Figure 13 the ores and miscellaneous materials. In Figure 14, the data have been divided, somewhat arbitrarily, into groups of samples containing similar leads. These are enclosed in loops labeled I-V. For convenience, the samples are also listed in Table 6 grouped according to their isotope ratios. Proximity in the table corresponds to proximity on the graphs, so that objects close to one another in the listing might very well contain lead from the same mining regions.

Unfortunately, we have at present only a few analyses of Spanish ores for comparison, so it is not yet possible to identify the sources of the lead in the objects very specifically or unambiguously. Nonetheless, it is entirely possible that in some instances those mining regions represented by the few ores already at hand could have provided the lead in certain of the objects.

Some Artifacts: Group II (Figures 11 and 14)

Considering first the artifacts, one group of six forms a rather tight cluster near the lower left of the graph (Group II). All were probably made with lead from a single source. The group includes the two green glass beads from San Salvador (Pb-1485 and 1486), the D-ring (Pb-1493), the excavated *blanca* (Pb-1494), and two of the beads from other sites — a green one from Nueva Cadiz (Pb-1487) and a yellow opaque from Sinu (Pb-1489). Mixed in are three *blancas* and a silver from Almeria (NBS-691). It seems reasonable to infer that in all likelihood these objects were also all manufactured in the same region as one another. Considering that the *blancas* must almost certainly have been made from metals mined in the Iberian Peninsula, we conclude that all of the artifacts were made in Spain. These isotope ratios do not match any of the few Spanish ores we have so far analyzed. They are a very close match, however, for a galena ore from Albergaria-a-Velha, near Aveiro in Portugal (NBS-707). Similar ores must also occur somewhere in Spain, but only future analyses will reveal where.

Some Artifacts: Groups III and IV A (Figures 11 and 14)

Near the center of the graph is another cluster of four artifacts, including the San Salvador bronze buckle (Pb-1492), the green glass bead said to have been found in Peru (Pb-1490). and two *blancas*. These samples resemble two lead ores (one from the Los Belgas Mine) from the Sierra de Gador, just west of the city of Almeria (NBS-681 and 676, Figure 13). It may be significant that the Sierra de Gador is not far from the location of 15th-century glass factories lying somewhat to the north. Close to these samples on the graph is Pb-1491, from a lead pistol ball. This was excavated by Mary Jane Berman at the Three-Dog Site, about 2.7 km south of where the other San Salvador objects were excavated. We conclude that all these excavated objects are of Spanish origin, and could have come from a region making use of lead from the Sierra de Gador. Two other galenas, from Posadas and Granada (NBS-708 and 677, Figure 13) are also quite similar to these objects, but are not quite as close a match as those from the Sierra de Gador. (In particular, it should be added that the isotope analysis proves that the lead in the pistol ball definitely is not an English lead.)

Some Artifacts: Group IV B (Figures 11 and 14)

The leads in the two pottery glazes from San Salvador (Pb-1495 and 1496) are virtually identical to one another, but differ from those in the other San Salvador artifacts. They are quite similar to a galena ore, a metallic lead, and two earthy mineral samples (possibly litharge or jarosite) from the Rio Tinto mining area, and also to a galena ore from the Centenillo Mine, near Linares in the Sierra Morena. Consequently, lacking any further evidence, the sherds might tentatively be attributed to either of these regions. (There may be complications, however, as explained below.) Even though the ratios of these two samples are at the upper range of the ratios for the artifacts in Fig. 11, it can be seen in Fig. 14 that there are three coins having still greater ratios, thus the two San Salvador glazes are bracketed by leads known to have been mined in Spain.

The most significant point concerning the glazes is that these two sherds, which are so different in their outward appearances (one being a honey-glazed terra cotta and the other a lead-tin glazed whitish ware) contain exactly the same kind of lead. This amounts to near-proof that they came from workshops nearby one another, as would be expected for wares taken on board an outgoing vessel just before embarkation. If the lead actually came from the Rio Tinto, located only 70 km from Palos de la Frontera, Columbus's port of embarkation, it is precisely what one would expect to find in the glazed pottery wares with which his ships would have been fitted out. Because this lead is different from that in the glass beads, the beads were possibly not made close to Seville, but came from elsewhere in Spain.

A third pottery sherd, Pb-1499, the Columbia plain ware from Santo Domingo, differs markedly from the two Long Bay sherds, in its lead-isotope composition and, hence, was glazed with lead from some other mine. At present, however, we have no way of telling how close or how far away that other mine might have been. The difference is somewhat surprising. Because the fabric of the Columbia plain ware is so similar to that of the San

Salvador white-glaze ware it had been surmised that they had been made nearby one another. Remarkably, the Columbia plain lead glaze is a near-perfect isotopic match for the two beads, the D-ring, and the *blanca* from Long Bay, all of which lie in Group II. It seems probable that this sherd was glazed with lead from the same source as the leads in those four artifacts. Clearly, it is important that more pieces of Columbia plain ware be analyzed, a project we hope to continue soon.

Another truly intriguing isotopic match is found in the upper right of the graphs. We have begun, but not yet completed, a search for archaeological parallels to the San Salvador beads. To date, aside from the four New World specimens, the only near parallel uncovered is a bead from Igbo-Ukwu in Nigeria.[31] This is a single, very small, wire-wound specimen found among several hundred drawn beads (and much larger wound beads) submitted by Thurstan Shaw for analysis. The date of this bead is uncertain, but it could be from the 15th century. It is yellow opaque and virtually identical in size and appearance to the San Salvador beads. However, it does not have the same unusual high-lead chemical composition. (The bead was not chemically analyzed, but its specific gravity is only 2.6, too low for a PbO content in the 70% range.)[32] Nevertheless, it does contain lead in its yellow opacifier. That lead (Pb-1062) is a very close match for the two San Salvador pottery glaze samples. It is thus reasonable to infer, at least as a working hypothesis, that this yellow opaque bead, traded down the coast of Africa, was probably made in Spain or Portugal, possibly near Seville or the coastal regions to the south, or possibly near the Sierra Morena mountains.

Some Artifacts: Group I (Figures 11 and 14)

The one bead which is out of line with the others, Pb-1488, the green bead said to be from Sinu, falls well to the left of the graph. We had not previously seen leads with these lower ratios in objects or ores from Spain. However, the leads in three *blancas* are close matches to that in the bead. Calling again upon the argument that Spanish coins should be made of metals occurring in the Iberian Peninsula, we should anticipate that future studies will turn up ores with these same isotope ratios somewhere in Spain.

Pb-2220, a small fragment of *"latticinio"* glass excavated at En Bas Saline, also falls in *Group I.* The fragment measures only 1.6 cm in greatest dimension. There is reason to believe that the site is the location of El Navidad, the settlement founded by Columbus after the *Santa Maria* was wrecked on Christmas Eve, 1492. It is extremely difficult to distinguish between complete *latticinio* glasses made in Venice, the Tyrol, the Lowlands, and Spain — and all but impossible (within the framework of our present knowledge) to make a confident attribution for as small a fragment of glass as this, on a stylistic basis. Therefore, the sample was analyzed chemically and for lead-isotope ratios at the request of Kathleen Deagan, the excavator, who will publish a final interpretation.

261

The lead in the glass matches those in three *blancas*. Thus, the lead-isotope data are consistent with a Spanish attribution for the glass. That, along with the general similarity of its lead-isotope ratios to those of four of the samples from Long Bay (Group II), tends to strengthen the case for the identification of En Bas Saline as the location of El Navidad. Also, the chemical analysis of the glass gives some reason to believe that it differs from the few Venetian *latticinio* glasses we have so far analyzed.

The Coins (Figures 12, 14, and Group V)

In order to understand better the lead-isotope results for the *blanca* excavated at Long Bay (Pb-1494), lead-isotope analyses were also made for twelve of the other billon coins of Henry IV which had been analyzed chemically. Of these, nine are *blancas* struck at known mints and three are of higher-denominations. The results verify again that Spanish leads spread out over a considerable isotopic range. Unfortunately, the ratios do not seem to correlate well with the locations of the six different mints represented, although it is noteworthy that the three higher-denomination coins form a group of their own in the upper right of Figures 12 and 14 (Group V).

The spread in the coin data may have a ready explanation. To begin with, the isotope ratios really serve more as an indicator of the sources of the bullion from which the coins were struck, rather than the mints. Also, as was pointed out above, the lead in the billon coins probably came in as an impurity of the silver component of that alloy. Because it is a precious metal, silver was rarely discarded, as base metals sometimes were, but has always been saved and melted down for reuse. Thus it is to be expected that the interpretation of isotope ratios of lead extracted from silver objects may be subject to mixing complications. Probably the leads at the higher and lower limits of the range are relatively free of mixing and represent ores from specific mining regions, but some of the intermediate ratios could be the results of mixing. Nonetheless, some of the intermediate ratios probably do represent specific mining regions, particularly where they are found to match the lead in other artifacts. The lead in the glasses and bronzes should have been less susceptible to mixing complications because lead would not have been hoarded as scrupulously, and is less likely than silver to have been transported over long distances for reuse.

Concerning Pb-1494, the *blanca* from San Salvador, the lead-isotope data for the other *blancas* do not seem to be very helpful. Its lead is a close match for individual coins struck in Cuenca, Seville, and Segovia (Pb-1450, 1445, and 1442), which are widely separated geographically. However, all could have been struck from alloys prepared with silver bullion from a common source. (As noted above, the chemical analyses suggested a common source with coins struck in Segovia and Burgos.)

What is most significant is that the San Salvador *blanca* is a very close match for the two beads and the D-rings from San Salvador. Find the source for the lead in any one of these, and you might well have found the source for all of them.

Ores (Figures 13 and 14)

As shown in Figure 13, the few Spanish ores and other minerals analyzed so far vary in their isotopic compositions. While sufficient to establish that the San Salvador artifacts were made in Spain, they fall far short of enabling one to pin down reliably locations of the mines which might have supplied the leads in the artifacts. Many more data are needed. Even so, there are some promising prospects. For example, the Sierra de Gador ores resemble the buckle and a bead from Peru, and the Centenillo Mine ore resembles the glazes and the bead from Igbo-Ukwu. However, the latter ore also illustrates the complications of overlapping within Spain, because its ratios are very similar to those of samples from the Rio Tinto, lying, more-or-less, at the other end of the Sierra Morena.

The situation in the Rio Tinto is particularly confusing.[33] There is said not to be much native galena there. It is believed that in Roman times lead used for cupellation had to be brought into the region. For the present, therefore, we have used the term *Rio Tinto* loosely, with the understanding that it refers to the type of lead *in use* at Rio Tinto. If brought in from elsewhere, however, that source was probably not very far away, possibly even as close as Nerva, only a few km away from the main mining, smelting, and cupellation remains at Rio Tinto.

Relationships with Other Leads from the Continent (Table 5)

Up to this point, the interpretation of the data, although complicated, does lead to some very useful results. We are well satisfied that all the San Salvador objects and the other glass beads must have been made in Spain. However, there are other interesting aspects of overlapping which should not be overlooked. Objects from other European contexts are already known which contain leads isotopically similar to those in the San Salvador objects, and still others will undoubtedly come to light. These include some white lead pigments from Italian, Dutch, and Flemish paintings of the 15th century and a few Benin bronzes reported in the literature.[34] At first, these might seem rather startling companions for the San Salvador artifacts, but a moment's reflection suggests plausible explanations.

In the opinion of one of the authors (RHB), many of the Benin bronzes — perhaps more than usually recognized — were made from metals imported into West Africa by Portuguese traders. Hence, the isotope ratios of the lead in those bronzes (and brasses) should match those in ores from Portugal or neighboring Spain. Concerning the Dutch and Flemish white lead pigments, realizing that there are no lead deposits in the Low Countries, it is apparent that either the pigments themselves or the lead to make

263

them must have been imported. Since there were well-established trade and political connections between the Low Countries and Spain at this time, some of that lead could well have come from Spain even though there is evidence that some also came from England.[35] English leads, however, are easily distinguished by their isotope ratios which are different from those discussed here. Interestingly, the two leads in the present study which overlap Group E (the bead from Sinu and the *blanca* minted in Seville) are almost identical to the white lead pigments from six paintings[36] (one Flemish, one Dutch and four Italian.) The Italian paintings date from 1450, 1482, and 1492, while the others are from 1587 and 1651. Taken together, the eight objects constitute a tight cluster lying isolated among a few dozen unrelated ancient objects. We fully expect to locate someday an Iberian lead matching those ratios.

We know there are some ores occurring in Italy which have ratios similar to some of those occurring in Spain. For example, there are ores from Bottino much like those from the Sierra de Gador (Table 5) and we suspect that region might be the source of the white leads in the Italian paintings. As far as the San Salvador artifacts are concerned, the overlapping effect can be disregarded because of a obvious fact stressed previously. The lead in the Spanish coins — whatever the mechanism by which it found its way into the alloys of the coins — is virtually certain to have been mined in Spain. Hence, the close proximity on the graph of the *blanca* Pb-1494 to the other San Salvador objects — the glass beads and the D-ring — points to Spain with equal certainly as being the source of the lead in those San Salvador objects.

Concerning the possibility of mixing, we are inclined to believe it is not a major problem here, because matches with ores have been found for the intermediate groups of three samples; furthermore the group of six samples including the four San Salvador objects are too diverse in character for their isotopic matches to be explained by fortuitous mixing.

CONCLUSIONS

Stylistically, all the artifact evidence seems consistent with Spanish origins and consistent with late-15th or very early 16th-century dates. It is surely significant, too, that the artifacts were found in rather high concentration, archaeologically. The main outcome of the lead-isotope determinations is that the isotopic types of lead found in all seven of the San Salvador artifacts, and in the four beads from Spanish Colonial sites in The New World, are consistent with the hypothesis that these objects were all made in Spain, although possibly in two or three different regions.

Archaeologically, stylistically, and archaeometrically, the San Salvador artifacts form a coherent group — coherent in the sense that there is nothing among them which does not plausibly belong there. This, particularly when coupled with the similarities of the isotope data among such diverse types of objects, suggests that they all found their way to San Salvador on a single voyage. Moreover, the resemblance of the leads in the pottery glazes to Rio Tinto lead suggests the likelihood of that voyage having embarked from southern Spain. Further research on the lead-isotope ratios of Spanish ores and artifacts in the future is likely to allow the wording above to be strengthened into more definitive statements and to specify particular regions of manufacture.

The glass beads are of an unusual type, being wire-wound, in contrast to the more ubiquitous drawn beads of the time. They have a distinctive appearance and an extremely unusual chemical composition, employed for an easily-explained technological reason. Consequently, there is a good chance that further research will reveal just where in the Iberian Peninsula they were made.

The identification of the excavated coin as a *blanca* of Henry IV seems definite. Struck between 1471 and 1474, preceding a hiatus lasting until 1497 during which no other small, low-denomination copper-based coins were minted in Spain, it appears to be precisely one of the types of small change which would have been "carried in the pockets of Columbus or his crew."

The artifacts clearly represent a very early Spanish contact with The New World. Turning to the question of a possible association between the artifacts excavated at The Long Bay Site and the verification of the contention that Columbus's first landing was at San Salvador, it will not have escaped the reader's attention that the objects uncovered correspond very closely to what Columbus is said to have recorded in his journal. The little green and yellow beads fit his descriptions, as do the D-ring and the buckle — at least if a shoe buckle without a tongue is regarded as having been made to serve as a trinket and not to fasten a shoe. (It would be interesting to know if the translation of the rings as being "brass" is strictly accurate — or whether brass and bronze might not then sometimes have been confused for one another in everyday speech — just as they frequently are today by the general public.) The coin, too, is not only of an interesting date, but fits in very well with the *ceitis* and *blancas* mentioned in the journal. Even the small pottery sherds were mentioned — "broken platters and glass." In fact, if an archaeologist started out with a shopping list of what they would hope to find to confirm evidence of Columbus's landing, it would pretty much match what was found at Long Bay. Only the hawk's bell and the red cloth cap are missing.

Until now, the San Salvador artifacts appear to be the only objects excavated anywhere which seem to have a chance of being associated with Columbus's first landing on his first voyage.

It is also worth noting that no records have yet been uncovered of other early visitors to the present San Salvador, except possibly for Ponce de Leon who, in 1513, reported the island to be uninhabited. However, other visitors there must have been — the slavers responsible for the depopulation.[37] Whether or not their visits would have left behind artifact evidence of the sort excavated is open to speculation.

It can be argued that Columbus left similar trinkets on other islands he visited; in fact, he *says* he did. The present day San Salvador could then have been one of his later stops although that would raise objections from other quarters.

Archaeological evidence of the sort discussed here cannot, in itself, be taken as proof that this site was visited by Columbus, because there are other means by which such artifacts as these could have reached Long Bay. Suffice it to mention only one, namely, that even if they had been given by Columbus or his crew to Indians elsewhere, the Indians themselves could have brought the artifacts to Long Bay. Afterall, only three days after his landfall Columbus encountered on open water, an Indian carrying some of the beads and *blancas* he had traded them on Guanahani. The Indians probably moved around a lot more often and more widely than is ordinarily appreciated.

The argument is far stronger, however, in the other direction. To whatever extent one believes, for whatever *independent* reasons, that Columbus made his first landfall on San Salvador, then, to that same extent, one should be entitled to believe that these artifacts probably were actually given or traded to the Indians on that occasion. The archaeological evidence is extremely persuasive as corroborative evidence.

Presumably debate as to where the landfall occurred will continue for some time. For the present, some will choose to base their opinion upon computations of extraordinary precision applied to data of dubious accuracy, some on observational aspects, and others upon archaeological evidence, the interpretation of which is subject to vagaries of its own. Future excavations throughout the Bahamas, whether the results be positive or negative, will surely cast further light on the subject. In any event, no one should lose sight of the fact that after all is said and done, it is *Columbus* who made a great discovery — not those who merely seek to identify where it occurred.

ACKNOWLEDGMENTS

The authors gratefully acknowledge the assistance of many people from diverse disciplines who have contributed to this work and hope they will continue to collaborate as the project progresses.

Special thanks are extended to Charles A. Hoffman, who excavated the site, to Nancy Watford Hoffman, Assistant Archaeologist, to Gail Saunders of the Ministry of Education and Culture of the Bahamas, to Donald T. Gerace, Director of the CCFL Bahamian Field Station, and to Kathy Gerace, Assistant to the Director, for their unfailing support and cooperation. John Winter, who originally located the site, made numerous valuable suggestions. We especially thank Richard G. Doty, Antonio Orol Pernas, Juan J. Rodriguez Lorente, and Carlos Castan for their identification of the coin. We also thank James Blackman and Steven W. Mitchell for their helpful suggestions regarding the pottery analyses. For various help we thank Marvin Smith, Vivian Hibbs, Kathleen Deagan, Thurstan Shaw, George Reilly, Janice Carlson, the late Charles B. Wray, the late Charles Fairbanks, Jaime Barrachina, Elena Ramirez-Montesinos, Mary Jane Berman, Astone Gasparetto, Marie Manuela Marques Mota, Susan Hanley, Jorge Alarcao, Beno Rothenberg, Daniel Wood, and Elizabeth R. Brill. The photographs were taken by Nicholas Williams and Raymond Errett.

SAMPLE DESCRIPTIONS

*   indicates chemical analysis completed
+   indicates lead isotope analysis completed
p   indicates some physical properties measured

Glass Beads (San Salvador)

* + p   5710   San Salvador, fragment of glass bead. Bright green transparent glass, heavily pitted, cordy with some spherical seed. Wire-wound, perforation straight-sided. Contains single flake of yellow colorant opacifier. Fragment represents approx. 30% of complete bead, apparently from thinner part. Excavated 6/84. (Same as Pb-1485.)

* + p   5711   San Salvador, fragment of glass bead. Bright green transparent glass, heavily pitted, cordy with some spherical seed. Wire-wound, perforation straight-sided, cords following winding pattern. Fragment represents approx. 40% complete bead. Distorted ring shape; apparent maximum original o.d. 3.5 mm, i.d. 2.5 mm, thickness 1.8 mm. N10 E6, 20-30 cm (27 cm). Excavated 7/83. (Same as Pb-1486.)

5712   San Salvador, glass bead. Bright green transparent glass, heavily pitted, cordy with some spherical seed. Wire-wound, two sharp winding-thread pull-offs, perforation straight-sided, cords following winding pattern. Distorted ring shape; o.d. 2.7-3.3 mm, i.d. 1.5-2.1 mm, thickness 1.2-1.5 mm, N4 E6, 20-30 cm, 7/5/83; SS9, no. 884.

5713   San Salvador, glass bead. Bright green transparent glass, heavily pitted, very cordy with many spherical seed and flake-shaped stone. Wire-wound, one sharp winding-thread pull-off and one firepolished, perforation straight-sided, cords following winding pattern. One large elliptical bubble trapped at original interface with wire and oriented in direction of winding. Nearly circular ring shape; o.d. 2.9-3.1 mm, i.d. 1.6-1.8 mm, thickness 1.0-1.5 mm. N10 E10 10-20 cm, SS-9, no. 318.

5714   San Salvador, glass bead. Bright green transparent glass (stronger but slightly more yellowish than 5712 and 5713), heavily pitted, cordy with some spherical seed, a batch or refractory stone, and three black inclusions, possibly from a metal tool or wire. Wire-wound, two sharp winding-thread pull-offs, perforation straight-sided, cords following winding pattern. Nearly circular ring shape; o.d. 2.4-2.5 mm, i.d. 1.5-1.6 mm, thickness 0.8-1.5 mm, N8 E8 10-20 cm, 6/22/84. Found with shell bead.

5715 San Salvador, glass bead. Bright green transparent glass (more nearly emerald green than others), heavily pitted with some weathering products remaining, cordy with some spherical seeds. Wire-wound, no winding-thread pull-offs evident, perforation straight-sided, cords following winding pattern. One large elliptical bubble trapped at original interface with wire and oriented in direction of winding. Distorted ring shape; o.d. 3.3-3.6 mm, i.d. 2.1-2.3 mm, thickness 1.1-1.3 mm. Ring was broken in distant past, possibly just after manufacture. (Fractured surfaces are weathered.) N6 W12 0-1- cm, 6/20/84; SS-9, no. 292.)

5716 San Salvador, glass bead. Pale yellowish amber transparent glass, heavily pitted, cordy. Wire-wound, cords following winding pattern. Nearly circular ring shape; o.d. 3.2-3.5 mm, i.d. 2.7, thickness 1.0 mm. N8 E6, 20-30 cm, south end, 7/4/83.

Glass Beads (Other)

+ p 5550 Igbo-Ukwu, Nigeria, very small glass bead. Yellow opaque glass, moderately weathered, cordy with many spherical seeds. Wire-wound. o.d. 3.2 mm, i.d. 1.7 mm, thickness 1.5 mm, sp. gr. 2.55. Excavated by Thurstan Shaw; location I-362-R. His type L-3; See: Thurstan Shaw, *Igbo-Ukwu*, vol. 1, Northwestern University Press, Evanston, 1970, plate 5. (Same as Pb-1062.)

* + p 5700 Nueva Cadiz, glass bead, 1515-45. Emerald green glass, little or no weathering, some spherical seed. Wire-wound, one sharp winding-thread pull-off and one firepolished, perforation straight-sided. Somewhat distorted ring shape, o.d. 4.0 mm, i.d. 1.7-2.1, thickness 2.0 mm. Excavated by John Goggin and Jose M. Cruxent in 1954; submitted for analysis by Charles Fairbanks of the University of Florida on Oct. 10, 1972. From Trench 9, section 4-6 m, 0-15 cm depth. (Same as Pb-1487.)

* + 5720 Sinu area, Colombia, fragment of glass bead. Bright green transparent glass, little or no weathering, some spherical seed. Wire-wound, perforation straight-sided. Fragment represents 40% of complete bead, from a thickened part. Ring-shaped, approximately same size as 5700. Purchased from a dealer, submitted for analysis by Marvin T. Smith (then of the University of Florida) on Dec. 30, 1983. His no. 187. (Same as Pb-1488.)

* + p 5721 Sinu area, Colombia, glass bead. Yellow opaque glass, little or no weathering, large flakes of yellow opacifier. Wire-wound, one winding-thread pull-off lightly ground down,

269

5721 (cont.)   and one firepolished, perforation straight-sided. Nearly circular ring shape; o.d. 4.0 mm, i.d. 2.0 mm, thickness 1.5-2.0 mm; weight 0.0774 g. Purchased from a dealer, submitted for analysis by Marvin T. Smith (then of the University of Florida) on December 30, 1983. His no. 187. (Same as Pb-1489.)

* + p   5730   Peru, glass bead. Emerald green glass, little or no weathering. Wire-wound, two sharp winding-thread pull-offs, perforation straight-sided. Nearly circular ring shape; o.d. 4.0-4.2 mm, i.d. 2.0 mm, thickness 2.0-3.0 mm; weight 0.1064 g. Purchased from a dealer, submitted for analysis by Marvin T. Smith (then of the University of Florida) on Dec. 30, 1983. His no. 197-3. (Same as Pb-1490.)

Metals, Glass, Ceramics (San Salvador and Elsewhere)

* +   4092   En Bas Saline, near Cap Hatien, Haiti, fragment of "*latticinio*" glass. Colorless glass vessel wall with colorless glass rib containing white opaque (SnO_2) threads, moderately weathered. Excavated by Kathleen Deagan at what might have been the location of Navidad. EBS 1984/Unit 7. 7162/FS #3771. Wall glass is non-lead, but rib glass contains 20.4% PbO. (Same as Pb-2220.)

* + p   4691   San Salvador, bronze "D-ring". Bronze, with greenish gray corrosion patina. Rounded with straight shank. Beveled corners formed by mold seams create diamond-shape cross-sections in most parts; possibly finished by filing. Maximum diameter across rounded portion 3.9 cm, length of straight shank 2.7 cm, thickness varies from 2.5-4.0 mm. (Same as Pb-1493.)

* + p   4692   San Salvador, bronze shoe (?) buckle. Bronze with dark greenish gray corrosion patina. Rounded with single straight overlapping shank and triangular slot. No keep attached, and no wear where it would have been attached at shank. Appears to have been molded and possibly finished by filing. Length across shank 2.0 cm. (Same as Pb-1492.)

* +   4693   San Salvador, coin. Billon *blanca* of Henry IV of Castile (1454-74). Heavily corroded on all surfaces, original struck impressions barely legible in places, possibly deliberately defaced. Segment broken or snipped out before burial. (Same as Pb-1494.)

*   4694   San Salvador, Indian pottery sherd. Rim fragment, reddish-brown, friable, coarse-textured ware with many white inclusions. N4 E6, 20-30 cm.

    4695   San Salvador, Indian pottery sherd. Similar to 4694.

	4696	San Salvador, Indian pottery sherd. Similar to 4694.
* +	4697	San Salvador, European pottery sherd. Example of *melado* ware. Wall fragment, salmon-colored with honey-colored glaze on one side. Found in same context as Indian wares. N4 E6, 10-20 cm, 6/6/83. (Same as Pb-1495.)
* +	4698	San Salvador, European pottery sherd. White-glazed ware ("majolica"). Small sherd, grayish with thick dull white glaze. Found in same context as Indian wares. N6 E6, 10-20 cm, 6/13/83.(Same as Pb-1496.)
* +	4699	Convent of San Nicolas, Santo Domingo, Dominican Republic, European pottery sherd. Example of Columbia Plain ware. Large fragment of a plate, cream-colored with white enamel glaze. Similar in appearance to 4698. From The Hispanic Society of America, no. LE 1036; Cruxent Donation, 1974. Submitted by Dr. Isadora Rose-de Viejo. An identical plate is illustrated by Goggin, *loc. cit.*, pp. 117-126 and Plate 3. (Same as Pb-1499.)

Castilian Coins

* +	4676	*Cuartillo* (= 4 *dineros*), Enrique IV (1454-74) Castilla y Leon, Toledo mint. Castle in sexfoil; lion in sexfoil. Billon. Purchased from Henry Christensen, Inc., who identified the coin. (Same as Pb-1476.)
* +	4677	Half *cuartillo* (= 2 *dineros*), Enrique IV (1454-74) Castilla y Leon, Toledo mint. Castle in sexfoil; lion in sexfoil. Billon. Purchased as above. (Same as Pb-1477.)
* +	4678	Half *cuartillo* (= 2 *dineros*). Enrique IV (1454-74) Castilla y Leon, Cuenca mint. Castle in sexfoil; lion in sexfoil. Billon. Purchased as above. (Same as Pb-1478.)
* +	4679	*Blanca*, Enrique IV, 1471-74, Castilla y Leon, Seville. Castle in lozenge; lion in lozenge. Billon. Purchased as above. (Same as Pb-1479.)
* +	4742	Same, Segovia. Donated by Antonio Orol Pernas. (Same as Pb-1442.)
* +	4743	Same, Toledo. Donated as above. (Same as Pb-1443.)
* +	4744	Same, Cuenca (?). Donated as above. (Same as Pb-1444.)
* +	4745	Same, Seville. Donated by Carlos Castan. (Same as Pb-1445.)
* +	4746	Same, Segovia. Donated as above. (Same as Pb-1446.)
* +	4747	Same, Toledo. Donated as above. (Same as Pb-1447.)
* +	4748	Same, Burgos. Donated as above. (Same as Pb-1448.)
* +	4749	Same, Avila. Donated as above. (Same as Pb-1449.)
* +	4750	Same, Cuenca. Donated as above. (Same as Pb-1450.)

LEAD ISOTOPE SAMPLES

From San Salvador: 8
Other New World Sites: 6
Spanish Coins: 12
West Africa: 1
Spanish Ores and Slags: 12
S: denotes San Salvador

	Lead No.	Analytical Sample No.	Brief Description
	Pb-1442	4742	Billon *blanca*, Segovia mint
	Pb-1443	4743	Billon *blanca*, Toledo mint
	Pb-1444	4744	Billon *blanca*, Cuenca mint
	Pb-1445	4745	Billon *blanca*, Seville mint
	Pb-1447	4747	Billon *blanca*, Toledo mint
	Pb-1448	4748	Billon *blanca*, Burgos mint
	Pb-1449	4749	Billon *blanca*, Avila mint
	Pb-1450	4750	Billon *blanca*, Cuenca mint
	Pb-1476	4676	Billon *cuartillo*, Toledo mint
	Pb-1477	4677	Billon half-*cuartillo*, Toledo mint
	Pb-1478	4678	Billon half-*cuartillo*, Cuenca mint
	Pb-1479	4679	Billon *blanca*, Seville mint
S	Pb-1485	5710	Green bead, San Salvador
S	Pb-1486	5711	Green bead, San Salvador
	Pb-1487	5700	Green bead, Nueva Cadiz
	Pb-1488	5720	Green bead, Sinu
	Pb-1489	5721	Yellow bead, Sinu
	Pb-1490	5730	Green bead, Peru
S	Pb-1491	—	Lead pistol ball, San Salvador From Three Dog Site, not Long Bay. Excavated by Mary Jane Berman
S	Pb-1492	4692	Bronze shoe (?) buckle, San Salvador
S	Pb-1493	4691	Bronze D-ring, San Salvador
S	Pb-1494	4693	Billon *blanca*, San Salvador
S	Pb-1495	4697	Honey-glazed ware, San Salvador
S	Pb-1496	4698	White-glazed ware, San Salvador
	Pb-1499	4699	Columbia Plain ware, Santo Domingo
	Pb-1062	5550	Yellow bead, Igbo-Ukwu
	Pb-2220	4092	*Latticinio* glass, En Bas Saline
	Pb-89	—	Rio Tinto, galena
	Pb-847	—	Rio Tinto, metallic lead
	Pb-848	—	Rio Tinto, earthy material
	Pb-849	—	Rio Tinto, earthy material

Lead No.	Analytical Sample No.	Brief Description
NBS-676	—	Almeria, Sierra de Gador, galena
NBS-681	—	Almeria, Los Belgas Mine. Laujar (?). Sierra de Gador, galena
NBS-691	—	Almeria, Frederick Julian Mine, Sierra de Gador, silver
NBS-677	—	Granada, galena
NBS-679	—	Centenillo Mine, Sierra Morena, north of Linares, galena
NBS-708	—	Posadas, Santa Barbara Mine, Cordova, galena
NBS-707	—	Albergaria-a-Velha, nr. Averio, Portugal, galena

NOTES

1. Joseph Judge and James L. Stanfield, "The Island of Landfall," *National Geographic*, 170, 5 (November, 1986), 566-97.

2. Bartolome de Las Casas, *El Libro de la Primera Navegacion*. The manuscript is in the collection of the Biblioteca Nacional, Madrid. Throughout we have quoted English passages as they appear in Samuel Eliot Morison, *Journals and Other Documents on the Life and Voyages of Christopher Columbus*, The Heritage Press, New York, 1963. Morison worked from a photographic copy of the Las Casa manuscript (his p. 47, note 3).

3. There are further entries describing the articles. On October 16th, having proceeded to *Fernandina* he presented each man who visited him with strings of ten or a dozen glass beads, plates of brass, and thongs of leather. On October 21st he mentions trading hawk's bells and glass beads for water, and again on October 22nd hawk's bells and glass beads — this time for gold. On December 12th the Spaniards captured a young woman. He presented her with glass beads, hawk's bells and rings of brass. Again, on December 16th, they met an Indian crossing the open water alone in a canoe. They presented him with glass beads, hawk's bells and brass rings. On December 17th, in Hispaniola, they bought pieces of gold beaten into thin plates, for strings of beads, and on December 21st, gave presents of the same three items, glass beads, hawk's bells, and brass rings, in appreciation of a gift of parrots and other things. On December 22nd, Columbus criticized the greed of his Spanish crew and praised the generosity of the Indians. He mentions the barter of a piece of gold for half a dozen strings of beads. On January 14th, shortly before departing for home, they still had some trinkets left, for he recorded presenting an Indian with a red cap, some beads, and red cloth. References in Columbus's later voyages indicate that the hawk's bells were much more highly prized by the Indians than glass beads. On his fourth voyage, while stranded in Jamaica (July 1503), it is remarked "...if they brought rounds of the bread which they call *cassava*, made with the grated roots of a plant, we gave them two or three green or yellow rosary beads; if they brought a large quantity of anything, they got a hawk's bell;..."

4. Van Wyck Brooks, *Christopher Columbus, Journal of First Voyage to America*. New York: Albert and Charles Boni, 1924, p. vi.

5. Apparently Columbus was on one or two Portuguese voyages to Sao Jorge da Mina between 1482 and 1484. Samuel Eliot Morison, *Admiral of the Ocean Sea, A Life of Christopher Columbus*. Boston: Little, Brown and Co., 1942, pp. 40-42. Portuguese trade, including reference to glass beads, is described in A. F. C. Ryder, *Benin and the Europeans 1848-1897*, New York: Humanities Press, 1969, pp. 37, 40, *passim*.

6. See also: Charles A. Hoffman, "Bahama Prehistory: Cultural Adaptation to an Island Environment," (Ph.D. dissertation, University of Arizona, 1967); also, Charles A. Hoffman, "The Palmetto Grove Site on San Salvador,

Bahamas," *Contributions of the Florida State Museum, Social Sciences,* no. 19, Gainesville: Florida State Museum, 1970. The site bears the designation SS-9 and has sometimes also been called The John Winter Site. The excavation was conducted under the auspices of the College Center of the Finger Lakes Bahamian Field Station in cooperation with the Ministry of Education and Culture of the Bahamas.

7. John Winter, *Archaeological Site Reconnaissance on San Salvador, 1980. Bahamas Archaeology Project Report,* San Salvador, Bahamas: College Center of the Finger Lakes' Bahamian Field Station, 1980. See also similar reports for 1981 and 1982 surveys.

8. A preliminary account of some of the laboratory investigations was presented at the Tenth Congress of The International Association for the History of Glass, in Madrid, September 24, 1985.

9. Marvin T. Smith and Mary Elizabeth Good, *Early Sixteenth Century Glass Beads in the Spanish Colonial Trade,* Greenwood, Mississippi: Cottonlandia Museum Publications, 1982.

10. There is a typographical error in Chapter III, on page 3, where these varieties are discussed in connection with Columbus's journal. Variety VI is clearly intended where the text says variety IV.

11. We dislike using *perforation,* which seems to imply a drilling operation, but that term appears to have become standard useage among many bead people.

12. There are exceptions, a group of Islamic cameo glasses and some deep-cut glasses from Serce Liman. All date probably from the 11th and 12th centuries. This group of glasses, numbering fewer than a dozen at present, are probably not related to the beads under study here. However, there might have been an indirect technological relationship. See: I. Lynus Barnes, Robert H. Brill, Emile C. Deal, and G. Venetia Piercy, "Lead Isotope Studies of Some of the Finds from the Serce Liman Shipwreck." (In press). Justine Bailey, by personal communication, has told us she has found a similarly high lead content in a Viking bead excavated at York. In his *L'Arte Vetraria,* published in Florence in 1612, Antonio Neri gives batches for several emerald green glasses for use as artificial gems. They are lead-silicas with high lead contents colored with calcined brass.

13. J. W. H. Schreurs and R. H. Brill, "Iron and sulfur related colors in ancient glasses," *Archaeometry,* 26, 2 (1984), pp. 199-209. The high-lead copper green has been duplicated in the laboratory of The Corning Museum of Glass.

14. Robert H. Brill, "The Scientific Investigation of Ancient Glasses," *Proceedings of the VIIIth International Congress on Glass, London,* Sheffield, England: The Society of Glass Technology, 1968, pp. 47-68.

15. Unpublished analyses by The Corning Museum of Glass.

16. For a similar calculation see: Robert H. Brill, "Scientific Investigations of the Jalame Glass and Related Finds," in G. D. Weinberg's forthcoming book on the Jalame excavations.

17. In Roman times, we believe volume measurements were often used. See preceding note.

18. For example, see the following, which report compositions for brasses from elsewhere in Europe: H. K. Cameron, "Technical Aspects of Medieaval Monumental Brasses," *The Archaeological Journal*, 131, 1974, pp. 215-237 and O. Werner, "Analysen Mittelalterlicher Bronzen und Messinge, II and III," *Archaologie und Naturwissenschaften*, 2, 1981.

19. Luis Monreal and Jaume Barrachina, *El Castell De Llinars Del Valles*, Publicacions de l'Abadia de Montserrat, 1983.

20. *Ibid.*, p. 259, no. 4, and object 1058 in Plate 115.

21. *D-ring* might not be a legitimate historical term, but it conveys the shape of the object very well.

22. Bernardo Vega, "Metals and the Aborigenes (sic) of Hispaniola." *Proceedings of the Eighth International Congress for the Study of The Pre-Columbian Cultures of the Lesser Antilles*, Anthropological Research Papers No. 22, Arizona State University, Tempe, 1980, pp. 488-497.

23. George Reilly and Janice Carlson of the Winterthur Museum Laboratory carried out this completely nondestructive, nonsampling analysis.

24. A sample of the local Indian palmetto ware (4694) was analyzed by atomic absorption and emission spectrography. The analysis showed that the fabric contains an extraordinarily high lime content (43.2% as $CaCO_3$) owing to the presence of shell temper. Thermoluminescence dating was attempted for four sherds of this pottery, and one of the *melado* ware, but the results were erratic and must be checked.

25. John M. Goggin, *Spanish Majolica in The New World*, Yale University Publications in Anthropology, No. 72, New Haven, 1968, pp. 117-126.

26. Goggin, *op. cit.*, plate 3 a & b.

27. J. S. Olin, G. Harbottle, and E. V. Sayre, "Elemental Compositions of Spanish and Spanish-Colonial Majolica Ceramics in the Identification of Provenience" in *Archaeological Chemistry II*, Advances in Chemistry Series 171. Edited by Giles F. Carter. Washington: American Chemical Society, 1978, pp. 200-229; M. Maggetti, H. Westly, and J. S. Olin, "Provenance and Technical Studies of Mexican Majolica Using Elemental and Phase Analysis" in *Achaeological Chemistry III*, Advances in Chemistry Series 205. Edited by J. B. Lambert. Washington: American Chemical Society, 1984, pp. 151-191.

28. For example, see: Robert H. Brill and J. M. Wampler, "Isotope Ratios in Archaeological Objects of Lead," *Application of Science in Examination of Works of Art*, Boston: Museum of Fine Arts, 1965, pp. 155-166. Robert H. Brill, "Lead Isotopes in Ancient Glass," *Proceedings of the IVth International Congress on Glass, Ravenne-Venise,* Liege: International Congress on Glass, 1969, pp. 255-261. Robert H. Brill, "Lead and Oxygen Isotopes in Ancient Objects," *The Impact of the Natural Sciences on Archaeology*, London: The British Academy, 1970, pp. 143-164, and Robert H. Brill and William R. Shields, "Lead Isotopes in Ancient Coins," *Special Publication No. 8*, Royal Numismatic Society, Oxford: University Press, 1972, pp. 279-303.

29. The program is currently funded in part by the Conservation Analytical Laboratory of the Smithsonian Institution.

30. For convenience lead-isotope data were summarized in our earlier publications as Groups L, X, E, and S. Group S contained leads from Spain, Wales, and Sardinia; Group E from England, Italy, and Turkey; Group L from Laurion in Greece.

31. Thurstan Shaw, *Igbo-Ukwu*, vol. 1, Evanston: Northwestern University Press, 1970.

32. Note added in proof: An electron microprobe analysis shows that the bead is made of a soda-lime glass, made with plant ash, colored with lead antimonate, and contains 4.05% PbO.

33. Beno Rothenberg, personal communication.

34. Candice L. Goucher, Jehanne H. Teilhet, Kent R. Wilson, Tsaihwa J. Chow, "Lead isotope studies of metal sources for ancient Nigerian 'bronzes'," *Nature*, 262, no. 5564, 1976, pp. 130-131.

35. Unpublished analyses of the National Bureau of Standards and The Corning Museum of Glass. Isabella herself was a patron of Dutch and Flemish painters, who might have either painted in Spain or used white lead pigments prepared from Spanish lead.

36. Unpublished analyses from the National Bureau of Standards and The Corning Museum of Glass.

37. The heaviest slaving raids took place in 1509-1512 throughout the Lucayas in general. See C. O. Sauer, *The Early Spanish Main*, Berkeley: University of California Press, 1966, pp. 159-60. Ponce de Leon must have been one of the last of the earlier explorers to visit San Salvador itself. He was there in 1513, at which time the island is generally thought to have been uninhabited.

Fig. 1. Four bright green transparent glass beads from San Salvador. From top left to lower right: nos. 5712, 5714, 5713, and 5715. Diameter (horizontal) of 5715 is 3.6 mm.

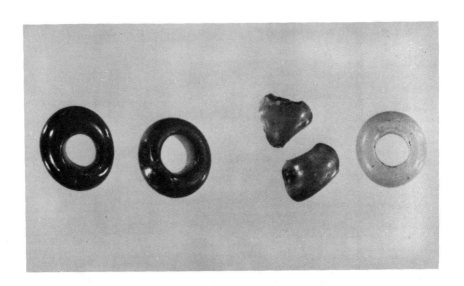

Fig. 2. Glass beads from various sources. From left to right: no. 5700 (Nueva Cadiz, emerald green), 5730 (Peru, emerald green), 5720 (Sinu, bright green transparent, two fragments), and 5721 (Sinu, yellow opaque). Diameter of 5700 is 4.0 mm.

Fig. 3. Bronze buckle from San Salvador. No. 4692 (Pb-1492). Length of shank 2.0 cm.

Fig. 4. Bronze D-ring from San Salvador. No. 4691 (Pb-1493). Length of shank 2.7 cm.

Fig. 5. *Blanca* of Henry IV of Castile (1454-1474) from San Salvador. No. 4693 (Pb-1494). Obverse. Diameter 2.3 cm., thickness (near apex of breakage) 0.20-0.25 mm.

Fig. 6. Same as Figure 5. Reverse.

Fig. 7. Group of billon coins of Henry IV purchased for comparison with No. 4693. From top left to lower right: nos. 4676 (*cuartillo*, Toledo), 4677 (half-*cuartillo*, Toledo), 4678 (half-*cuartillo* Cuenca), and 4679 (Pb-1479) (*blanca*, Seville). Obverse.

Fig. 8. Same as Figure 7. Reverse.

Fig. 9. Two pottery sherds from San Salvador. Left: no. 4697, *melado* ware, with some lead glaze chipped away. Right: no. 4698, white-glazed or "majolica" (?) ware. (Left edge of 4698 measures 1.1 cm.)

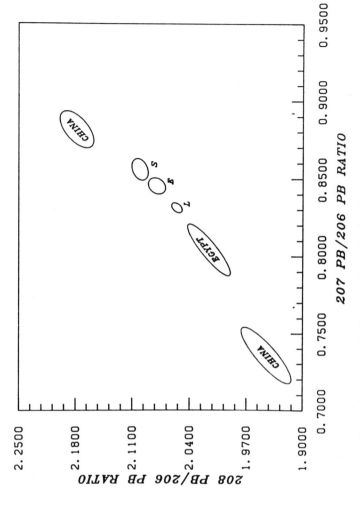

Fig. 10. Summary of lead-isotope ratios for several hundred objects of diverse materials, dates, and proveniences. The leads from the seven San Salvador artifacts all fall in Group S, which is known to contain leads from Spain.

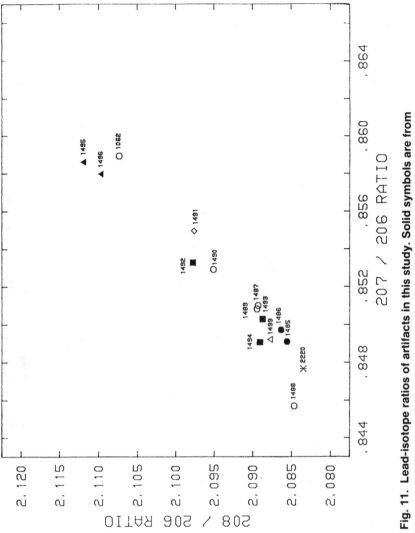

Fig. 11. Lead-isotope ratios of artifacts in this study. Solid symbols are from San Salvador, open symbols from elsewhere. Circles indicate glass; squares metals; triangles glazes; diamond lead metal; * *latticinio* glass.

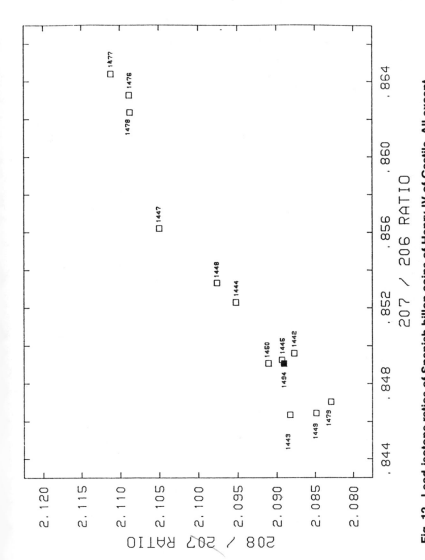

Fig. 12. Lead-isotope ratios of Spanish billon coins of Henry IV of Castile. All except three in upper right are *blancas* minted between 1471-74. Three in upper right are higher denominations. Shaded square is *blanca* from San Salvador.

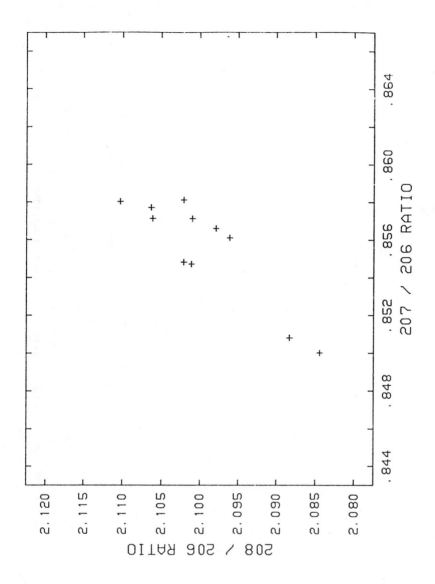

Fig. 13. Lead-isotope ratios of ores and miscellaneous minerals from Spain.

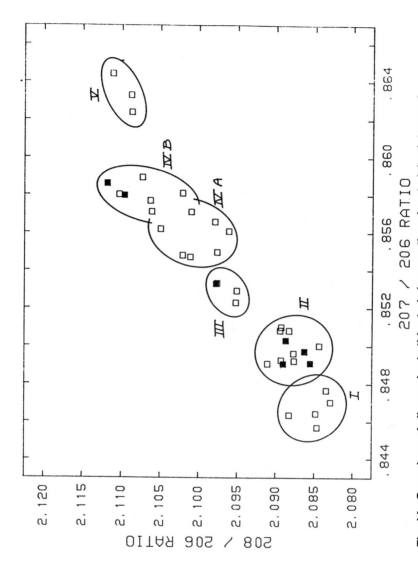

Fig. 14. Groupings of all samples in this study irrespective of materials, dates, and origins. Samples within each group might contain lead from a single mine or mining region.

287

Table 1
Summary of Artifact Analyses

Sample Numbers	Material	Source	Chemical Analysis and Method	Lead Isotope Determination	Physical Properties
5710, Pb-1485	grn. glass	San Sal.	e	+	n
5711, Pb-1486	grn. glass	San Sal.	e	+	n
5700, Pb-1487	grn. glass	Nueva Cadiz	a	+	s
5730, Pb-1490	grn. glass	Peru	a	+	s
5720, Pb-1488	grn. glass	Sinu	a	+	
5721, Pb-1489	ylw. opq. glass	Sinu	a	+	s
5550, Pb-1062	ylw. opq. glass	Igbo-Ukwu		+	s
4092, Pb-2220	latticinio glass	En Bas Saline	e	+	
4692, Pb-1492	bronze	San Sal.	x	+	s
4691, Pb-1493	bronze	San Sal.	a	+	s
4693, Pb-1494	blanca	San Sal.	e	+	
4697, Pb-1495	glaze	San Sal.	e	+	p
4698, Pb-1496	glaze	San Sal.	e	+	p
4699, Pb-1499	glaze	Santo Domingo	x	+	p
--- Pb-1491	lead	3-dog		+	
4694 ---	pottery	San Sal.	a		
4676-79, Pb-1476-79	4 coins	Toledo, Cuenca	a	+	
4742-50, Pb-1442-50	9 blancas	Various mints	a	+	(except Pb-1446)

---

e – electron microprobe

a – atomic absorption and emission spectrography

x – x-ray fluorescence

+ – completed

s – specific gravity

n – refractive index

p – petrography

Table 2
Chemical Analyses of Glass Beads

	San Salvador* br. green 5710	San Salvador* br. green 5711	Nueva Cadiz** em. green 5700	Peru** em. green 5730	Sinu** br. green 5720	Sinu** ylw. opq. 5721
SiO_2	26.7	27.4	19.5	27.5	27.2	20.6
Na_2O	0.01	0.01	1.85	1.32	1.09	2.27
CaO	0.05	0.09	0.063	0.50	0.12	0.12
K_2O	0.14	0.19	0.26	1.15	0.21	0.96
MgO	0.05	0.02	0.50	0.53	0.28	0.61
Al_2O_3	0.40	0.42	1.76	0.60	0.98	1.64
Fe_2O_3	0.47	0.67	0.30	0.21	0.24	0.36
TiO_2	0.05	0.06	0.03	0.03	0.03	0.03
Sb_2O_5	0.05	0.05	0.05	nf	0.03	0.08
MnO	--	--	0.001	0.005	0.005	0.001
CuO	0.51	0.53	0.60	0.60	0.50	0.10
CoO	--	--	nf	nf	nf	nf
SnO_2	--	--	0.03	0.01	0.01	0.77
Ag_2O	--	--	0.008	0.005	0.001	0.001
PbO	72.6	70.9	74.9	67.4	69.2	72.3
B_2O_3	--	--	nf	nf	nf	nf
V_2O_5	--	--	nf	nf	nf	nf
Cr_2O_3	--	--	0.01	0.01	0.01	0.01
NiO	--	--	nf	nf	nf	nf
ZnO	0.07	0.18	0.20	0.17	0.12	0.019
ZrO_2	--	--	nf	nf	nf	nf
Bi_2O_3	--	--	nf	nf	nf	0.15
Sum	101.0	100.5	--	--	--	--
Specific gravity	--	--	5.30	4.77	--	4.96
Refractive index	1.80	1.80	--	--	--	--

* Electron microprobe analyses by Stephen S.C. Tong of Corning Glass Works.

** Combined atomic absorption and emission spectrographic analyses by Brant Rising and Rolando Gonzales of Lucius Pitkin, Inc., New York City. SiO_2 estimated by difference from 100% on these samples.

Na_2O values probably low on microprobe analyses.

nf Sought but not found.

-- Not sought.

Physical properties by Joseph Giardina and Dirk Sears of Corning Glass Works.

Table 3
Chemical Analyses of Metallic Objects

	San Salvador			Castilian Coins of Henry IV					
	D-ring* 4691	Buckle** 4692	Blanca† 4693	Ten blancas* mean ± 90% conf. limits			Three higher denominations* mean ± 90% conf. limits		
Copper	~90	94	95.7 ± 0.59	--	95.4	--	~86	89.0	~92
Silver	nf	0.2	3.78 ± 0.79	2.3	3.41	4.5	6.8	10.1	13.3
Lead	4.98	1.5	0.13 ± 0.08	0.28	0.76	1.2	0.26	0.36	0.46
Tin	2.5	2.5	<0.01	--	0.015	0.04	0.08	0.09	0.10
Antimony	1.34	0.2	0.15 ± 0.04	0.02	0.12	0.22	0.22	0.30	0.38
Nickel	0.26	nf	0.09 ± 0.06	0.002	0.11	0.22	0.01	0.093	0.17
Manganese	--	trace	--	--	0.005	--	--	--	--
Iron	0.58	trace	0.05 ± 0.04	0.004	0.014	0.02	0.01	0.02	0.03
Bismuth	--	--	--	0.006	0.016	0.03	--	0.06	--
Arsenic	--	0.3	--	--	--	--	--	--	--
Magnesium	--	--	--	--	<0.01	--	--	--	--
Gold	--	--	--	0.01	0.03	0.05	--	0.01	--
Silicon	--	--	--	0.02	0.12	0.20	--	--	--
Sum	99.7	98.7	99.90	--	100.0	--	--	--	--
Sp. gravity	8.20	8.43	--	--	--	--	--	--	--

-- Not sought.
* Atomic absorption and emission spectrography by Brant Rising and Rolando Gonzales, Lucius Pitkin, Inc.
** X-ray fluorescence by George J. Reilly and Janice H. Carlson, the Winterthur Museum Laboratory.
† Electron microprobe by Stephen S.C. Tong, Corning Glass Works.
  Also sought but not found: Zn, V, Cr, Mo, Cd, In, Be, Ga, Ge, Co, P, B.
  90% confidence limits = ± 1.69 x std. dev.

Table 4
Lead-Isotope Ratios

Sample No.	NBS No.	$^{208}Pb/^{206}Pb$	$^{207}Pb/^{206}Pb$	$^{204}Pb/^{206}Pb$
Pb- 89	401	2.1021	0.8581	0.05484
Pb- 847	1701	2.10611	0.85712	0.054862
Pb- 848	1702	2.11032	0.85802	0.055019
Pb- 849	1703	2.10097	0.85711	0.054932
Pb-1062	1528	2.10733	0.85892	0.055106
Pb-1442	1674	2.08773	0.84960	0.054433
Pb-1443	1675	2.08827	0.84634	0.054043
Pb-1444	1676	2.09520	0.85228	0.054478
Pb-1445	1677	2.08932	0.84924	0.054329
Pb-1447	1679	2.10496	0.85621	0.054822
Pb-1448	1680	2.09761	0.85331	0.054515
Pb-1449	1681	2.08483	0.84643	0.054122
Pb-1450	1682	2.09106	0.84906	0.054278
Pb-1476	1522	2.10880	0.86328	0.055269
Pb-1477	1523	2.11115	0.86440	0.055312
Pb-1478	1524	2.10870	0.86237	0.055133
Pb-1479	1525	2.08290	0.84703	0.054150
Pb-1485	1387	2.08556	0.84909	0.054402
Pb-1486	1380	2.08632	0.84971	0.054440
Pb-1487	1381	2.08930	0.85099	0.054443
Pb-1488	1382	2.08464	0.84569	0.054030
Pb-1489	1383	2.08944	0.85081	0.054344
Pb-1490	1384	2.09508	0.85291	0.054515
Pb-1491	1385	2.09761	0.85497	0.054639
Pb-1492	1264	2.09776	0.85327	0.054530
Pb-1493	1521	2.08872	0.85028	0.054422
Pb-1494	1386	2.08906	0.84905	0.054201
Pb-1495	1526	2.11184	0.85860	0.055040
Pb-1496	1527	2.10963	0.85797	0.055084
Pb-1499	1683	2.08766	0.84920	0.054368
Pb-2220	1725	2.08346	0.84765	0.054271
--	676	2.1021	0.8548	0.05458
--	677	2.0979	0.8566	0.05496
--	679	2.1063	0.8577	0.05482
--	681	2.1011	0.8547	0.05453
--	691	2.0844	0.8500	0.05673
--	707	2.0883	0.8508	0.05440
--	708	2.0961	0.8561	0.05491

Table 5
Nearest Neighbors in Lead-Isotope Ratios
(Listed in approximate order of increasing values)

Group in Figure	Sample No.	Descriptions, sources	Other leads
I	Pb-1488	Bead, Sinu	Borderline English leads
	1443	Blanca, Toledo	7 Italian, Dutch, and
	1449	Blanca, Avila	Flemish paintings
	1479	Blanca, Seville	
	2220	Latticinio, En Bas Saline	
	*		
II	Pb-1450	Blanca, Cuenca	
	1445	Blanca, Seville	
	1494	Blanca, San Salvador	
	1499	Glaze, Santo Domingo	
	1485	Bead, San Salvador	
	1486	Bead, San Salvador	
	1442	Blanca, Segovia	
	NBS-691	Silver, Almeria	
	1493	D-ring, San Salvador	
	1489	Bead, Sinu	
	1487	Bead, Nueva Cadiz	
	NBS-707	Galena, Albergaria (Port.)	
	*		Lead, Roman, Carteia
III	Pb-1444	Blanca, Cuenca	Italian painting
	1490	Bead, Peru	Jarosite, Rio Tinto
	1492	Buckle, San Salvador	(Ref. .)
	1448	Blanca, Burgos	Lead, Roman, Majorca
	*(?)		
	Pb-1491	Pistol ball, Three-Dog	Italian painting
	*(?)		Italian painting
IV A	NBS-681	Galena, nr. Almeria, Sierra de Gador	Galena, Bottino (Italy)
	NBS-676	Galena, Sierra de Gador	Lead, Roman, Carteia
	NBS-708	Galena, Posadas, Cordova	
	NBS-677	Galena, nr. Granada	
	849	Earthy material, Rio Tinto	3 leads, Roman, Coimbriga
	89	Galena, Rio Tinto	
IV B	1447	Blanca, Toledo	
	847	Lead, Rio Tinto	
	NBS-679	Galena, nr. Linares, Sierra Morena	
	848	Earthy material, Rio Tinto	
	1496	Glaze, San Salvador	
	1495	Glaze, San Salvador	
	1062	Bead, Igbo-Ukwu	
V	Pb-1478	Half cuartillo, Cuenca	
	1476	Cuartillo, Toledo	
	1477	Half cuartillo, Toledo	

*	Small, but significant difference
——	Distinct difference

Note: Other leads include unpublished NBS-CMG analyses some of which were run several years ago and therefore are not known for certain to be in calibration with current analyses. These samples are not plotted in Figure 13.

Origin and Development of the Indians Discovered by Columbus

Irving Rouse[1]
Department of Anthropology
Peabody Museum of Natural History,
Yale University

ABSTRACT

Ethnohistorians have classified the natives of the West Indies into three major groups, Guanahatabey, Taino, and Island-Carib. Columbus met only Tainos during his first voyage. They spoke a single language, also known as Taino, and shared the same culture, which reached its highest development in Hispaniola and Puerto Rico.

Linguists have assigned the Taino language to the Arawakan family and have traced that family back to the middle of the Amazon Basin by reconstructing its ancestral languages. They find that speakers of its proto-Northern language moved into the West Indies from the Guiana coast about the time of Christ. The Proto-Northerners developed the Taino language after reaching the Greater Antilles, and carried it into the Bahamas.

Archaeologists have confirmed the linguists' conclusions. They have assigned the pottery of the Taino Indians to an Ostionoid series of styles and have traced that series back to a Saladoid series, which originated in the Orinoco Valley. They find that the Saladoid potters entered the West Indies about the time of Christ, introducing not only pottery but also agriculture and zemiism, the religion of the Tainos. The Saladoids and their Ostionoid descendants gradually pushed the previous inhabitants of the islands back into western Cuba, where they became the Guanahatabeys. The Ostionoids developed Taino culture after reaching the Greater Antilles, and carried it into the Bahamas.

INTRODUCTION

The islands of the West Indies form a crescent separating the Caribbean Sea from the Gulf of Mexico and the Atlantic Ocean (Fig. 1). Since the natives lacked Columbus' ability to cross large bodies of water, they could only have entered the crescent at the points where it approaches the mainland: by way of the Yucatan Peninsula in Middle America, the Florida Peninsula in North America, or the islands of Trinidad and Tobago at the mouth of the Orinoco River in South America.

The prevailing winds and currents favor entry from South America, as does the outpouring of floodwater from the Orinoco River. Nevertheless, the natives only had to cross 75-125 miles of open sea to reach the island chain from either Middle, North, or South America. Once past this initial barrier, they could easily have spread throughout the archipelago, for almost all of its islands are within sight of each other.

Anthropologists interested in problems of origin have been attracted to the West Indies by these possibilities. They have sought to determine who the natives were, where and when they discovered the island crescent, and how they developed after they arrived there:

The anthropologists who first attempted to answer these questions failed because they were generalists, who did not discriminate between different kinds of data.[2] Today's anthropologists succeed because they have become specialists, using methods adapted to the kinds of data they study. Ethnohistorians work with the documentary evidence; linguists, with the surviving traces of the natives' languages; archaeologists, with the remains of their cultures; and physical anthropologists, with their biological traits.[3] This paper covers only the ethnohistorical, linguistic, and archaeological research; physical anthropology has made too little progress in answering the questions of origin to be included.

ETHNOHISTORICAL RESEARCH

Ethnohistorians proceed in terms of ethnic groups, that is, groups which are mentioned in the documents or can be inferred from them. They recognize three major ethnic groups in the West Indies: the Guanahatabeys, who lived in western Cuba; the Tainos, who occupied the rest of the Greater Antilles and the Bahamas; and the Island-Caribs, in the central and southern parts of the Lesser Antilles (Fig. 2). The affiliation of the Indians in the northern part of the Lesser Antilles is unknown; those islands appear to have been largely depopulated in the time of Columbus.[4]

The three major groups are each defined by a variety of linguistic and cultural traits. They should not be confused with geographically or politically defined ethnic groups, such as the Lucayans in the Bahamas and the chiefdoms in the Greater Antilles. Lesser groups like these are beyond the scope of the present paper.

Guanahatabeys. The Indians of the first major group are also known as Ciboneys. This is a misnomer. The Ciboneys were actually a local group of Taino Indians who lived farther west in Cuba.[5]

The Guanahatabeys became extinct before they could be studied firsthand. They must have had a separate language, since Columbus' Taino interpreters were unable to speak with them. The chroniclers report that they were savages, lived in caves, subsisted by food gathering rather than agriculture, and were organized into bands rather than villages.

The documents tell us nothing about their origin. Ethnohistorians infer from their primitiveness and their remote position that they were descendants of the original inhabitants of the West Indies, pushed back into western Cuba by the next group to be discussed.[6]

Tainos. The Indians of this group had no name for themselves. Ethnohistorians call them Tainos because they used that term, which means "good" or "noble," to indicate to Columbus that they were not Island-Caribs. They are also known as Arawaks, but this is another misnomer. The Indians who called themselves Arawaks were limited to South America; they originated in the Guianas and spread only as far north as the island of Trinidad.[7]

The Tainos must have spoken a single language, for Columbus was able to use the same interpreters throughout their territory. They lived in villages and practiced a relatively advanced form of agriculture. They were ruled by hereditary chiefs, who derived much of their authority from personal deities known as zemis. These so intrigued Columbus that he commissioned Ramn Pan, a friar who accompanied him on his second voyage, to make a study of the religious practices and beliefs on the island of Hispaniola. Pan reports that the Tainos carved statues of their zemis, and portrayed them on their household utensils. Priests conducted ceremonies to the zemis in public places.[8]

The Tainos have left us no origin traditions. It is assumed that they came from South America because they bore resemblances in both language and culture to the Arawak Indians on the mainland. This is the reason for calling them Arawaks, but it is wrong because the Tainos and Arawaks spoke separate languages[9] and lived in different cultures. Only the Tainos had chiefdoms and worshipped zemis.

Island-Caribs. The final group called themselves Caribs or Kalinas. Ethnohistorians have added the prefix in order to distinguish them from an ethnic group in the Guianas that bore the same name but had another language and culture.

The Island-Caribs differed in language and culture from the Tainos as well. Like the latter, they lived in villages and practiced agriculture, but their lives centered around warfare rather than religion. Their men raided the Taino settlements, killing the enemy warriors and consuming bits of their flesh in order to acquire their prowess. (Our word *cannibal* is derived from the Spanish version of their name.) They captured Taino women, brought them back to their villages, and set them up in family houses, apart from the men's houses in which they lived. They had no chiefs except for the leaders of their war parties, who were elected for the purpose.[10]

According to their traditions, they were descended from war parties that came from the Guianas shortly before the time of Columbus and conquered the previous inhabitants, whom they called Igneris. They imposed their own name and their warlike orientation on the Igneris, but appear to have adopted the latters' domestic traits.[11]

295

Linguists proceed in terms of speech communities, each of which had a separate language. Linguists classify the languages into families. They work back within each family from its historic languages to the common ancestor, reconstructing the development of the languages in reverse. They plot the development in the form of a family tree, or phylogeny, which begins at its bottom with the original proto-language and ends at its top with the historical languages. From the phylogeny they are able to infer the origin and development of the family's speech communities and their languages.

Too little is known about the speech of the Guanahatabey Indians to apply this procedure to them. Resemblances have been noted between the Guanahatabey speech and that of the Warao Indians in the Orinoco Delta, which belongs to a Chibchan family, widespread on the western side of the Caribbean Sea.[12] These resemblances may have developed independently, however, or they may be due to trading contacts rather than population movement.

The Taino language is a member of the Arawakan family. Island-Carib was originally assigned to the Cariban family because of its name, but it has also turned out to be Arawakan. Apparently the Island-Carib warriors who conquered the Igneris of the Lesser Antilles adopted the Igneri's language, just as the Norman invaders of England gave up French in favor of English. The Island-Carib men retained only a secondary, pidgin language belonging to the Cariban family, which they spoke in their men's houses.[13]

Working back from the Taino, Island-Carib, and Arawak languages, linguists have constructed the phylogeny of the Arawakan family that is shown in Figure 3. They find that the original, Proto-Arawakan language most probably developed in the middle of the Amazon Basin. The speakers of that language originally expanded upstream to the headwaters of the Amazon, as shown on the right side of the diagram. Other Proto-Arawakan speakers moved up the Negro River, a northern tributary of the Amazon, passed through the Casiquiare Canal, and entered the Orinoco Valley (Fig. 1). Somewhere along that route they developed a new, Proto-Maipuran language, which evolved into Proto-Northern after their arrival in the Orinoco Valley.

The speakers of the Proto-Northern language subsequently spread into the Guianas and the West Indies. The Proto-Northerners who remained in the Guianas intercommunicated primarily among themselves and as a result developed their own Arawak language, which later became Lokono (Fig. 3). The Proto-Northerners who settled in the Lesser Antilles similarly produced their own Igneri language, which they transmitted to their Island-Carib conquerors. The Proto-Northern speakers who continued into the Greater Antilles, intercommunicated among themselves there, developed the Taino language, and carried it into the Bahamas.

The dates along the side of Figure 3 have been obtained by glottochronology, a technique that estimates the length of time since two languages began to diverge by counting the number of differences in their basic vocabularies and dividing that figure by the rate of change known for historic languages. Glottochronology indicates that the Proto-Arawakan language arose about 3500 B.C.; Proto-Maipuran about 1500 B.C.; Proto-Northern during the first millennium B.C.; and Arawak, Island-Carib, and Taino within the Christian era. We may therefore conclude that the ancestors of the Taino speakers entered the West Indies about the time of Christ.[14]

ARCHAEOLOGICAL RESEARCH

Archaeologists proceed in terms of peoples, each of which had its own culture. Archaeologists identify each people by the remnants of its culture. Through study of the protohistoric remains in the West Indies, they have been able to divide Taino culture into three subcultures: Classic Taino in eastern Cuba, Hispaniola, and Puerto Rico, with extensions into the Turks and Caicos and Virgin Islands; Western Sub-Taino in the rest of the Greater Antilles; and Eastern Sub-Taino in the northern part of the Lesser Antilles (Fig. 4). The Classic Tainos have left more elaborate remains than the Sub-Tainos, most notably ball courts, ceremonial plazas, and complex carvings of zemis.

In tracing the origin and development of the Taino people and sub-peoples, archaeologists work primarily in terms of pottery, since it constitutes 95 percent of the artifacts found. They determine the sequence of ceramic styles in each local area and put the local sequences together in the form of regional chronologies. Then they compare the styles in these chronologies and group together those which appear to have developed one from another, like languages within a family. They call the resultant units series of styles, and name each series by adding the suffix -oid to the term for one of its member styles. Following the lead of the late Gary Vescelius,[15] I have recently introduced a distinction between series and subseries, and have named each subseries by adding the suffix -an to the name of a member style.

Chronological charts for the West Indies and the adjacent part of South America are given in Figure 5, *a* and *b* respectively. The original peopling of the region is shown at the bottom of the figure, subsequent prehistoric developments in its center, and the Historic age at its top. The names of the three ethnic groups discussed in the first part of this paper are shown at the beginning of the Historic age, and beneath them are given the names of the subseries and series of styles by means of which the ethnic groups may be identified archeologically. It will be seen that the Tainos are identified by an Ostionoid series of styles. The Classic Tainos had a Chican Ostionoid subseries; the Western Sub-Tainos, a Meillacan Ostionoid subseries; and the Eastern Sub-Tainos, an Elenan Ostionoid subseries. These three subseries can be traced back through an Ostionan Ostionoid subseries to two subseries of a previous Saladoid series: Cedrosan Saladoid in Puerto Rico, the Lesser Antilles, and the coast on either side of the Orinoco Delta; and Ronquinan Saladoid in the Orinoco Valley. Archaeologists have not yet been able to carry the ancestors of the Tainos farther back along the route worked out by the linguists.

Four periods, numbered I to IV, are shown along the sides of Figure 5. Period I is the time when the ancestors of the Guanahatabeys made their first appearance and Period II, the time of arrival of the ancestors of the Tainos. During Period III, the latter advanced at the expense of the former to the position in which Columbus found them. Period IV was the time of arrival of the Island-Caribs in the Lesser Antilles and of the development of Classic Taino culture in the Greater Antilles. The dates given for the four periods are based upon radiocarbon analysis, a technique that estimates the age of organic materials found among the remains by determining the amount of radioactivity the organisms have lost since they died and applying to that figure the rate of decay established by studying the decay in historically dated sites.

The advance of the ancestors of the Tainos into the West Indies cannot be understood without reference to the origin and development of the peoples who stood in their way, the ancestors of the Guanahatabeys. Since the latter peoples lacked pottery, they have had to be defined by their stonework. This is tentatively classified into two series of lithic complexes, Casimiroid and Ortoiroid, as indicated at the bottom of Figure 5.[16] The peoples defined by the Casimiroid complexes appear to have come from Middle America, and the peoples defined by the Ortoiroid complexes, from South America. The Casimiroids discovered the West Indies some 6000 years before Columbus did. They appear to have arrived there while still in the Lithic age, that is, while still making only chipped stone implements. They later began to grind stone tools and thereby advanced into the Archaic age, to which the Ortoiroid peoples also belonged. The two groups presumably gave rise to the Guanahatabey Indians via the lines of development shown for the Archaic age in Figure 5,*a*.

The ancestors of the Tainos were in the Ceramic age. As they advanced at the expense of the Archaic-age peoples, they paused at a series of five frontiers, each of which is indicated by a jog in the boundary between the Ceramic and Archaic ages in Figure 5. The five frontiers are mapped in Figure 6. The last of them is the boundary between the Guanahatabeys and Tainos in the time of Columbus (cf. Figs. 2, 4, and 6).

As already noted, our knowledge of the ancestry of the Tainos begins with the Ronquinan Saladoid potters, who lived in the Orinoco Valley during the first millennia B.C. (Fig. 5,*b*). Their frontier with the Archaic-age peoples was at the head of the Orinoco Delta (Fig. 6, *1*). They were making surprisingly complex pottery, decorated by modeling and incision as well as white-on-red painting (Fig. 7). They were already producing most of the vessel shapes and designs present on any of the later forms of pottery along the route traversed by the ancestors of the Tainos.

During the first millennium B.C., they passed along the right side of the Orinoco Delta and established a new frontier in the Guianas (Fig. 6,2). They seem to have been responding to pressure from another series of potters, the Barrancoids, who developed upstream from them. On the coast, they are assumed to have developed a new, Cedrosan Saladoid subseries, but the transition from Ronquinan to Cedrosan Saladoid pottery remains to be demonstrated (Fig. 5,b).[17]

About the time of Christ, the Cedrosan Saladoid potters expanded westward via Trinidad and the adjacent Venezuelan coast to the island of Margarita, and northward through the Lesser Antilles to Puerto Rico and the eastern tip of Hispaniola, where they established another frontier with the previous Archaic-age population (Fig. 6,3). Again, they appear to have been responding to pressure from the Barrancoid peoples, who expanded to the coast behind them. They brought with them Cedrosan Saladoid pottery, which is characterized by white-on-red painting and zoned-incised crosshatching (Fig. 8,a,b). They made incense burners, which may be the result of Barrancoid influence, and clay griddles, which they used to bake cassava bread (Fig. 8,c,d). They also carved figures of zemis, including pendants and small three-pointed objects (Fig. 9,a,b). Hence, they may be said to have introduced agriculture and the worship of zemis into the Antilles.

After pausing some 500 years at the third frontier on the eastern end of Hispaniola, they moved on to a fourth frontier in eastern Cuba (Fig. 6,4). Meanwhile, they had developed a new form of pottery, Ostionan Ostionoid, which archaeologists use to trace their forward progress along the south coast of Hispaniola to Jamaica and through the valleys of northern Hispaniola to eastern Cuba (Fig. 10,b,c). The transition from Cedrosan Saladoid to Ostionan Ostionoid pottery has been well worked out on the island of Puerto Rico. The local potters gradually abandoned their Cedrosan Saladoid decoration, first its modeledincised designs, and then its white painting. This left only simple modeling and red painting, which has caused archaeologists to refer to the Ostionan Ostionoid pottery as "redware." The reason for the simplification of their pottery is unknown; perhaps they had become isolated in the Greater Antilles, interacted mainly among themselves, and as a result were not exposed to the new developments that were taking place on the mainland.

Around 800 A.D., the Ostionan Ostionoid potters in the northwestern part of the Dominican Republic developed a new, Meillacan Ostionoid subseries, which spread through Haiti, Jamaica, and eastern Cuba. The Meillacan Ostionoid potters then expanded into central Cuba, moving the Ceramic-Archaic age frontier to its position in the time of Columbus. Their pottery had the same materials and shapes as the previous Ostionan Ostionoid pottery but was decorated with rectilinear incised designs that appear to have been borrowed from the Casimiroid peoples on the other side of the frontier (Fig. 10,d,e). In the Bahamas, this pottery degenerated into Palmetto ware, which was largely plain (Fig. 10,f).

Meanwhile, the Ostionan Ostionoid potters in the eastern part of the Dominican Republic developed a Chican Ostionoid subseries, which reached a new height of ceramic art, comparable to the earlier Cedrosan Saladoid climax. Chican Ostionoid pottery spread throughout the territory occupied in the time of Columbus by the Classic Taino people. It is characterized by elaborate modeled-incised designs, many of which appear to be representations of zemis (Fig. 11). The pottery is accompanied by ceremonial plazas in which the public worship of zemis took place, and by the most highly developed carvings used in that religion (Fig. 9,a,d). These features and the rise of heirarchical chiefdoms indicate that the Chican Ostionoid potters had advanced from the Ceramic into the Formative age, that is, into the beginning of civilization (Fig. 5,a).[18]

CONCLUSION

The ethnohistorical, linguistic, and archaeological research all indicate that the ancestors of the Taino Indians, whom Columbus met during his first voyage, came from South America and advanced into the West Indies at the expense of the ancestors of the Guanahatabey Indians, whom the Admiral encountered during his second voyage. If the ethnohistorians' conclusions be regarded as working hypotheses, both the linguistic and the archaeological research may be said to have confirmed these hypotheses. Both have disclosed that the ancestors of the Tainos arrived in the West Indies about the time of Christ by way of the Orinoco Valley and the Guianas, and gradually pushed the ancestors of the Guanahatabeys back into western Cuba where Columbus found them. Linguists have shown that the invaders diverged into speakers of the Island-Carib language in the Lesser Antilles and of the Taino language in the Greater Antilles and the Bahamas. Archaeologists find that these two speech communities also constituted separate peoples, each of which had developed a different culture. Taino culture reached its classic form in the heart of the Greater Antilles, where Columbus established the first European settlements.

NOTES

1. This paper is adapted from the author's *Migrations in Prehistory: Inferring Population Movement from Cultural Remains* (New Haven, 1986), pp. 106-56. Figures 1, 3, and 5-11 come from that book, where they are Figures 21-29 respectively.

2. E. G. Sven Lovén, *Origins of the Tainan Culture, West Indies* (Göteborg, 1935).

3. The Indians encountered by Columbus became extinct before they could be studied by anthropologists who specialize in the study of living populations.

4. Irving Rouse, "Whom Did Columbus Discover in the West Indies?", *American Archaeologist*, in press.

5. Ricardo E. Alegría, *El uso de la terminología etno-histórica para designar les culturas aborígenes de las Antillas* (Valladolid, 1981), pp. 5-6.

6. Sven Lovén, *Origins of the Taino Culture, West Indies* (Göteborg, 1935), pp. 3-5.

7. A. Boomert, "The Arawak Indians of Trinidad and Coastal Guiana, ca. 1500-1600," *The Journal of Caribbean History*, XIX, in press.

8. José J. Arrom, *Mitología y artes prehispánicas de las Antillas* (Mexico City, 1975).

9. D. G. Brinton, "The Arawack Language of Guiana in its Linguistic and Ethnological Relations," *Transactions of the American Philosophical Society*, XIV (1871), 427-44.

10. Irving Rouse, "The West Indies," in *Handbook of South American Indians* (Washington, 1948), vol. 4, pp. 547-65.

11. Louis Allaire, "On the Historicity of Carib Migrations in the Lesser Antilles," *American Antiquity*, XLV (April, 1980), 238-45.

12. Julian Granberry, "West Indian Languages: A Review and Commentary," *Journal of the Virgin Islands Archaeology Society*, X (1986), 51-6.

13. Douglas R. Taylor and Berend J. Hoff, "The Linguistic Repertory of the Island-Carib in the Seventeenth Century: The Men's Language — a Carib Pidgin?", *International Journal of American Linguistics*, XLVI (October, 1980), 301-12.

14. Irving Rouse, *Migrations in Prehistory: Inferring Population Movement from Cultural Remains* (New Haven, 1986), pp. 120-6.

15. Gary S. Vescelius, "A Cultural Taxonomy for West Indian Archaeology," *Journal of the Virgin Islands Archaeological Society*, X (1986), 38-41.

16. Archaeologists have not yet been able to reach agreement about the origin and development of the ancestors of the Guanahatabeys. For an alternative version, see Marcio Veloz Maggiolo, *Las sociedades arcaicas de Santo Domingo* (Santo Domingo, 1980).

17. Irving Rouse, Louis Allaire, and A. Boomert, "Eastern Venezuela, the Guianas, and the West Indies," in *Chronologies in South American Archaeology*, edited by Clement W. Meighan, in press.

18. Irving Rouse, *Migrations in Prehistory: Inferring Population Movement from Cultural Remains* (New Haven, 1986), pp. 147-9.

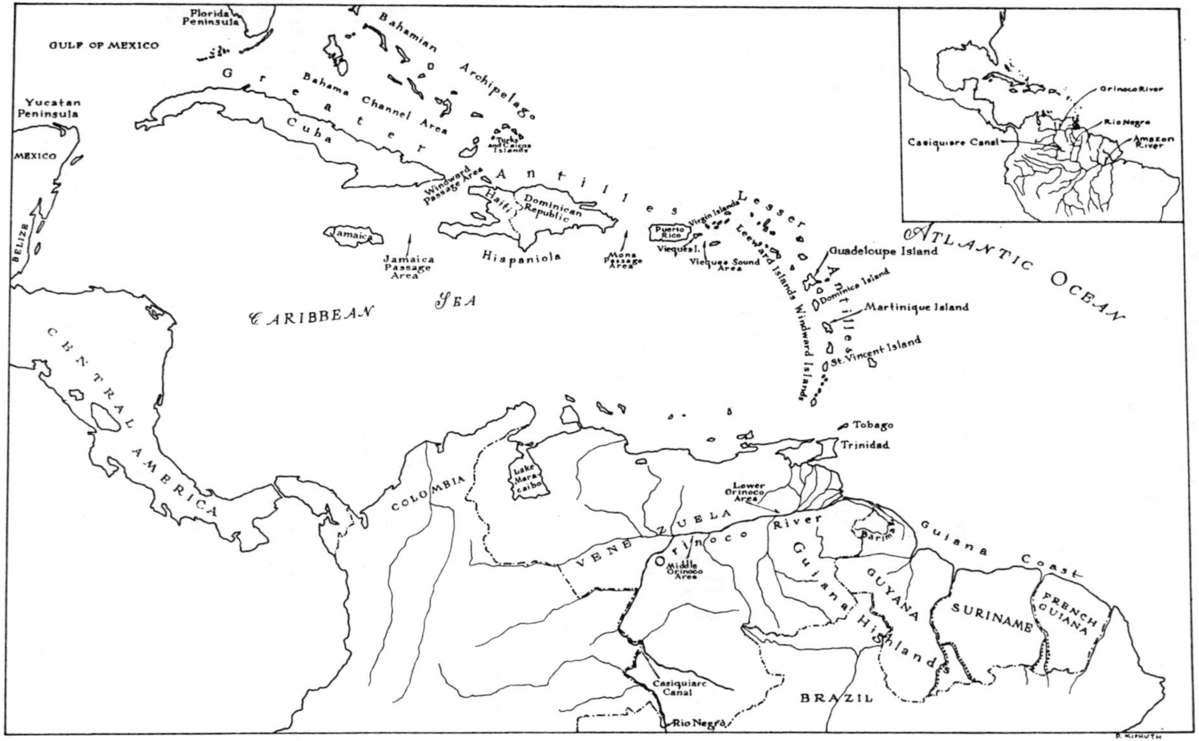

Fig. 1. Map of the Caribbean Area

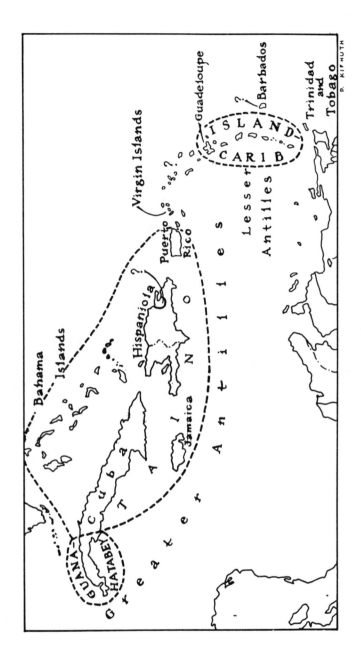

Fig. 2. Ethnic Groups and Languages Encountered by Columbus in the West Indies

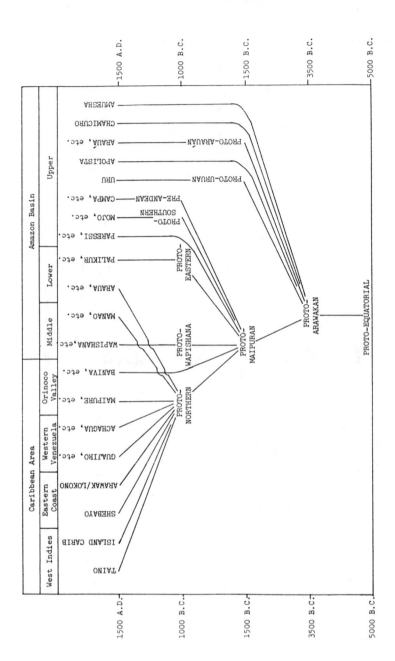

Fig. 3. Phylogeny of the Arawakan Languages

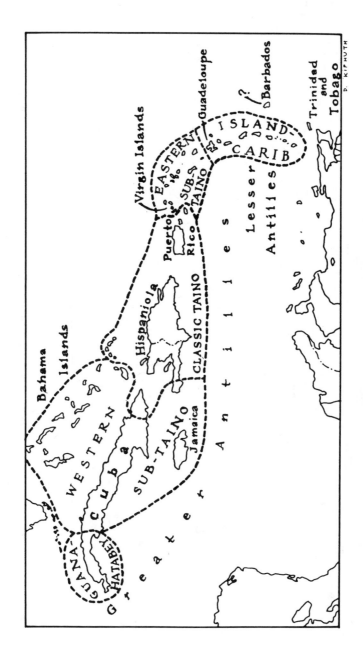

Fig. 4. Peoples and Cultures Encountered by Columbus in the West Indies.

305

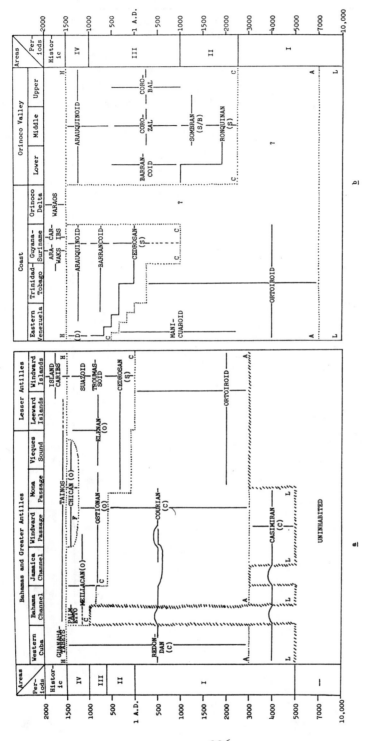

Fig. 5. Chronology of the Peoples and Cultures in the Caribbean Area: (a) West Indies. (b) coast and Orinoco Valley. Ages: L = Lithic, A = Archaic, C = Ceramic, F = Formative, H = Historic. Series of peoples and cultures: (C) = Casimiroid, (S) = Saladoid, (B) = Barrancoid, (O) = Ostionoid, (D) = Dabajuroid

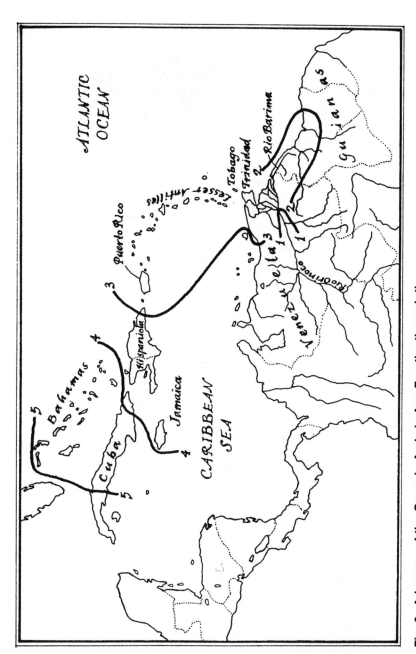

Fig. 6. Advances of the Ceramic-Archaic Age Frontier through the Caribbean Area

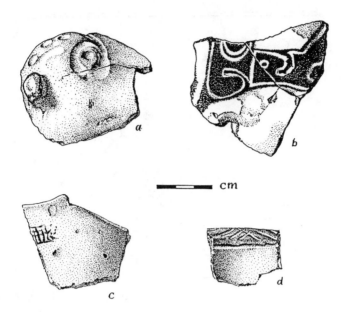

Fig. 7. Ronquinan Saladoid Pottery: *a*, modeled-incised design on vessel wall, La Gruta style; *b*, white-on-red painted sherd, La Gruta style; *c*, red-painted sherd, Saladero style; *d*, incised sherd, Saladero style

Fig. 8. Cedrosan Saladoid Vessels and Utensils: *a*, whiteon-red painted pot, Puerto Rico; *b*, modeled and zoned incised crosshatched pot, Guadeloupe; *c*, incense burner, Martinique; *d*, clay griddle, Martinique

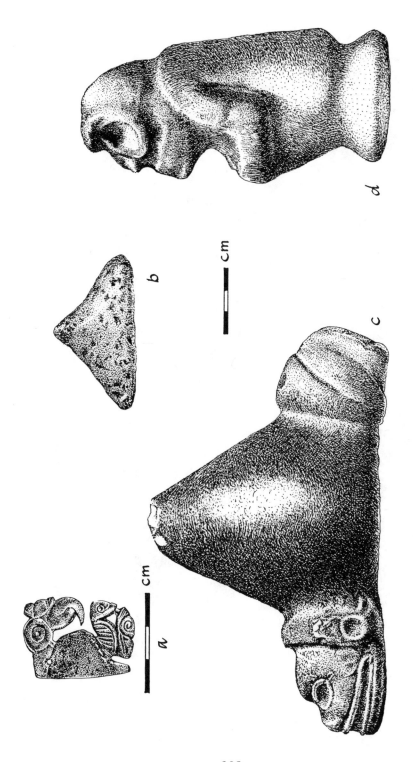

Fig. 9. Artifacts Used in the Worship of Zemis: *a*, bird pendant of stone, Vieques Island; *b*, small, plain three-pointer of stone, Puerto Rico; *c*, large, carved three-pointer of stone, Dominican Republic; *d*, stone statue, Dominican Republic

309

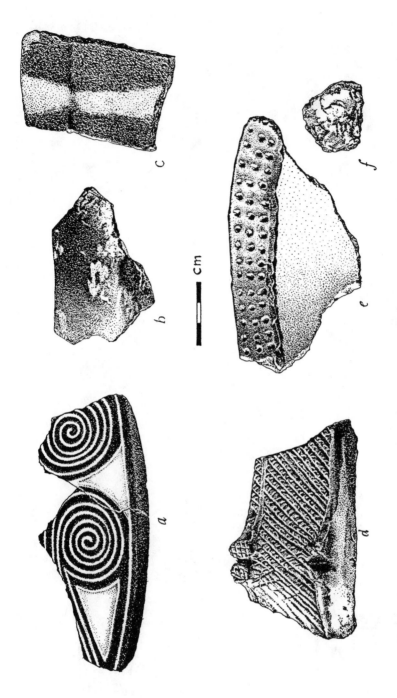

Fig. 10. Markers for the Ceramic Age Repeopling of the Greater Antilles: *a*, Cedrosan Saladoid pottery, Puerto Rico; *b, c*, Ostionan Ostionoid pottery, Puerto Rico, Dominican Republic; *d, e*, Meillacan Ostionoid pottery, Haiti; *f*, Palmetto ware, Bahamas

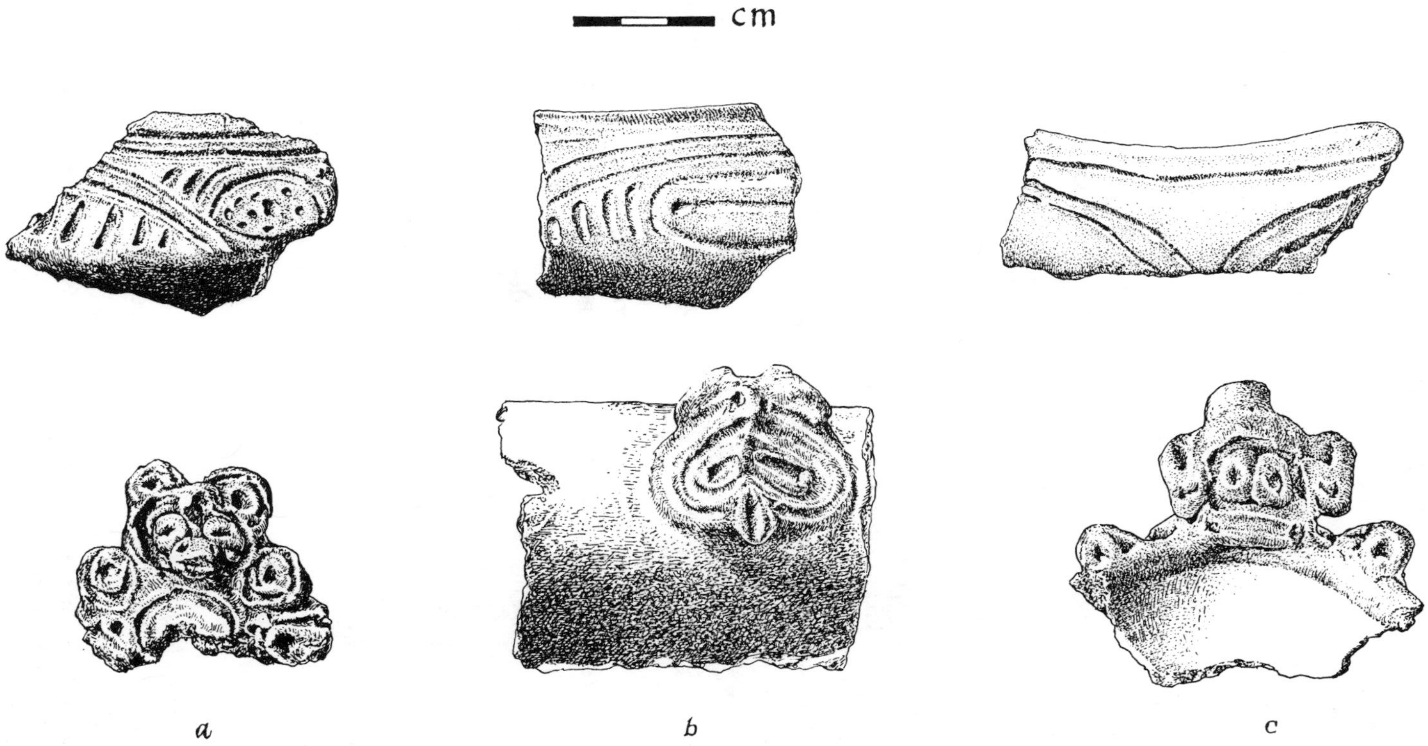

cm

Fig. 11. Chican Ostionoid Pottery: *a*, Cap style, western Puerto Rico; *b*, Boca Chica style, central Puerto Rico; *c*, Esperanza style, eastern Puerto Rico

BIBLIOGRAPHY

Alegría, Ricardo E. *El uso de la terminología etno-histórica para designar las culturas aborígenes de las Antillas*. Valladolid: Seminario de Historia de América, Universidad de Valladolid, 1981.

Allaire, Louis. "On the Historicity of Carib Migrations in the Lesser Antilles." *American Antiquity*, XLV (April, 1980), 238-45.

Arrom, José J. *Mitología y artes prehispánicas de las Antillas*. Mexico City: Siglo Veintiuno Editores, S. A., 1975.

Boomert, A. "The Arawak Indians of Trinidad and Coastal Guiana, ca. 1500-1650." *The Journal of Caribbean History*, XIX, in press.

Brinton, D. G. "The Arawack Language of Guiana in its Linguistic and Ethnological Relations." *Transactions of the American Philosophical Society, Held at Philadelphia, for Promoting Useful Knowledge*, XIV (1871), 427-44.

Granberry, Julian. "West Indian Languages: A Review and Commentary." *Journal of the Virgin Islands Archaeological Society*, X (1980, actually 1986), 51-6.

Lovén, Sven. *Origins of the Tainan Culture, West Indies*. Göteborg: Elanders Bokfryckeri Äkfiebolag, 1935.

Rouse, Irving. "The West Indies." In *Handbook of South American Indians*, edited by Julian H. Steward, vol. 4, pp. 495-565. Washington: Bulletin of the Bureau of American Ethnology, CXLIII, 1948.

——————. *Migrations in Prehistory: Inferring Population Movements from Cultural Remains*. New Haven: Yale University Press, 1986.

——————. "Whom Did Columbus Discover in the West Indies?" In "On the Trail of Columbus," edited by Charles H. Hoffman, *American Archaeologist*, in press.

Rouse, Irving, Louis Allaire, and A. Boomert. "Eastern Venezuela, the Guianas, and the West Indies." In *Chronologies in South American Archaeology*, edited by Clement W. Meighan. Los Angeles: University of California, in press.

Taylor, Douglas R. and Berend J. Hoff. "The Linguistic Repertory of the Island-Carib in the Seventeenth Century: The Men's Language — a Carib Pidgin." *International Journal of American Linguistics*, XLVI (October, 1980), 301-12.

Veloz Maggiolo, Marcio. *Las sociedades arcaicas de Santo Domingo*. Santo Domingo: Museo del Hombre Dominicano and Fundación Garca-Arévalo, Inc., 1980.

Vescelius, Gary S. "A Cultural Taxonomy for West Indian Archaeology." *Journal of the Virgin Islands Archaeological Society*, X (1980, actually 1986), 38-41.

San Salvador in 1492:
Its Geography and Ecology

John Winter
Molloy College
Rockville Centre, NY

ABSTRACT

Christopher Columbus in 1492 could have experienced the climax evergreen woodlands of San Salvador, when he writes of very green trees, fruits, and much water. Unfortunately, since that time all of the woodland has been cleared, burned, and selectively cut at least once. In addition, the coastal topography has undergone several changes through progradation, retrogradation, and sedimentation. This has created an island which is a far different sight from that of Columbus'. A reconstruction of San Salvador is made possible through historical records and environmental processes.

INTRODUCTION

On the 12th October 1492 after 33 days at sea, Christopher Columbus described the geographical conditions of the New World. According to Columbus, his landfall, San Salvador, was an island that was quite large, very flat, and with very green trees. There was a very large lake in the center and many waters. The island did not possess any mountains and all of it was green.[1]

In making these statements, Columbus has been accused of stretching his imagination somewhat. However, one should remember that Columbus was most likely making a comparison with the islands of the Old World, such as the Canary Islands which are mountainous and deforested. In addition, San Salvador probably did have many waters in the form of ponds and tidal creeks, which through time have dried up or turned into inland lakes or salinas. Finally, those who see San Salvador today see only the modern evergreen woodland, which is only a secondary growth woodland, rather than a climax woodland.[2]

Unfortunately, there are no written records dealing with the geography of San Salvador until the Farquarhson journal,[3] which deals with the clearing of the fields and pastures. However, there is ample information regarding general conditions for the Bahamas and other specific islands. These accounts will be used to re-create a possible scenario for San Salvador in 1492.

THE WOODLAND

The evergreen woodland of the Bahamas contains about 40% of the 60 genera which can be found in the southeastern United States. This reveals an historical relationship to that region dating to Eocene times, 40 million years ago.[4] Today, the evergreen woodland is similar to the low limestone environment throughout the New World sub-tropics with trees reaching 10 meters high and 20-30 cm wide, but in the past these same trees may have reached over 20 meters high and 60 cm wide.[5]

The evergreen woodland can be characterized into three habitats: whiteland-consisting of the Holocene dunes and beach ridges; flatland-consisting of the Pleistocene marine plains; and blacklands-consisting of the Pleistocene dunes and beach ridges. Each habitat will evolve through stages of woodland succession until a climax period is reached, if ever. Tables 1, 2, 3 were compiled by Anthony Byrne[6] to indicate the present day stages of woodland succession for each habitat. It is the historical record which should provide additional species so as to produce a more complete picture of the woodland succession.

At the time of Columbus' arrival to the Bahamas, the islands had been inhabited for about 500 years by Amerindian horticulturalists. The Lucayans, the group met by Columbus, appear to have lived in small villages and practiced shifting agriculture through the slash and burn method.[7] Just how much of the primitive evergreen woodland had been cleared with this method prior to Columbus' visit is unknown. It is known, from Columbus' log, that the Lucayans constructed canoes from a single tree trunk and that these canoes could hold 40 to 45 men.[8] The first measurement of a canoe was recorded on the 27th November at Baracoa, Cuba, with the canoe being 95 palms long. The actual length was either 7 meters or 23 meters depending on which palm unit was applied, most likely it was the later. It is believed that this canoe would have held about 150 men.[9] Therefore, if Columbus observed a canoe which held 40 to 45 men on San Salvador, it might be safe to say that it measured less than 95 palms long. Although the Lucayans may have traveled to other islands for trees, it would seem reasonable to state that large local trees were also used in the construction of canoes.

Although not much is known about the Lucayans' deforestation practices, the evergreen woodland could have recovered after the Lucayans left the islands. The European settlers began to work this renewed evergreen woodland in the late 1600's to late 1700's, and it is through the works of Catesby, Schoepf, and Harvey[10] that a clearer picture emerges as to what was contained therein. The evergreen woodland appears to have been manipulated in two ways: by the selective cutting of commercial woods and by the growth of plantations.

The commercial uses of the evergreen woodland were for dyewoods, barks, and timber. The major dyewood trees were the braziletto (*Caesalpinina*) and the yellow wood (*Zanthoxylum flavum*), both can reach to heights of 25 feet today. The major bark trees were the sweet wood (*Croton eluteria*) and the wild cinnamon (*Canella winterana*), both can reach to heights of 20 feet today. The major timber trees were the mahogany (*Swietenia mahogani*), the horseflesh (*Lysiloma sabicu*), the pine (*Pinus caribaea*), and the mastic (*Mastichodendron foetidissmum*), all of which can reach to heights of 50 feet today. Additional timber trees were the lignum vitae (*Guiacum sanctum*), the iron wood (*Krugiodendron ferreum*), the boxwood (*Buxus bahamensis*), and the cedar (*Juniperus lucayana*), all of which can reach to heights of 25 feet today.[11] The previously mentioned historical accounts note that there was a decline in the supply of these commercial trees from the early 1700's to the mid 1800's. This appears to be the result of over exploitation. So that the economically valuable species now became rare in remotely undisturbed areas and perhaps extinct in others.

The growth of the plantation system took its toll on the evergreen woodland when the American loyalists moved into the Bahamas. Between 1780-1800, the American way of clearing larqe stands of woodland to make farmland was accomplished.[12] This technique then exposed the topsoil to the action of wind and rain. In a short time, the topsoil was depleted.[13] This wholesale clearing of the land led to the destruction of additional trees such as gum elemi (*Bursera simaruba*), wild tamarind (*Lysiloma latisiliqua*), pigeon plum (*Coccoloba diversifolia*), manchioneel (*Hippomane mancinella*), and poison wood (*Metopium toxiferum*), all of which can reach to heights of 50 feet today.[14]

After the abandonment of the plantations, the evergreen woodland began to re-build itself with weedy types taking hold first: horsebush (*Gundlachia corymbosa*), greasebush (*Corchorus hirsutus*), white sage (*Lantana involucrata*), grannybush (*Croton linearis*), strongback (*Bourreria ovata*), and the *Pithecellobium*. The continued farming efforts of the present inhabitants, by clearing and burning areas for farming, has helped to keep the islands in their secondary growth conditions.[15] Only in very remote areas is there any indication that the Pre-Columbian woodland may be returning.

THE COASTAL ZONE

The Bahama Islands lie within the northern hemisphere's tradewinds, which produce a northeasterly breeze. The tradewinds are associated with a northward longshore current, which results from the 0.9 knot current of the Old Bahama Channel as it works its way through the islands. Together, the current and wind deposit the white/pink coral sands to form the beaches of these islands.

Although the tradewinds are fairly constant, there are seasonal variations. In the winter months, cold weather fronts are brought across the islands from the North American continent by northwesterly winds. This activity counters the normal longshore current, and now wave and surf action attack the white/pink coral sands from a different direction. In the summer months, the rainy weather is brought up from the Caribbean region by southeasterly winds, creating high rolling waves and strong winds that reshape the beaches. The wind and current then alter the coastline through the processes of progradation and retrogradation creating numerous changes since Columbus' landfall.[16]

Likewise, the tidal creeks, which flowed during Columbus' visit to the Bahamas, have also been changed. The entrances have been silted in by storms and the longshore movement of the white/pink coral sands. In addition, the topsoil run-off from the Loyalist period may have increased the sediment load of the tidal creeks which increased the sedimentation process near the inlets. This has led to the formation of inland lakes and salinas.[17]

There has also been a rise in the mean sea level since the Wisconsin glaciation. This rise in mean sea level has covered and destroyed the coastline. Core samples taken in 3 to 4 meters of ocean water near the shoreline of several islands have revealed peat deposits. These peat samples date from 4,000 to 6,000 B.P. and indicate evidence of former marsh areas now drowned.[18] The average rise of mean sea level for the past 2000 years has been estimated to be 7.5 cm[19] and 15.0 cm[20] per century. So that in 1492, the mean sea level could have been between 37.5 cm and 75 cm lower than the present. The lower mean sea level could have added to or reduced the coastal zone dimensions 50 to 100 meters from the foredune, depending on whether the coast was undergoing progradation or retrogradation.[21] These factors would have definitely created a different picture of the islands from Columbus' time to the present.

SAN SALVADOR

As the previous sections bear out, the islands of the Bahamas appear to have had more extensive evergreen woodlands and coastal zones in the past. It would then seem reasonable to state that this was also the case for San Salvador. Recently, a wooden mortar, made from the trunk of a Yellow wood (*Zanthoxylum flavum*) tree, was recovered from an inland bluehole on the island. The mortar is 63.5 cm in height, 138 cm in circumference and 44 cm in diameter. The interior of the mortar is funnel shaped, measuring 40 cm and 15 cm in diameter from top to bottom respectively. Whether the mortar was used in the processing of manioc or maize is unknown,

316

however a radiocarbon-14 date of 530 ±65 yrs B.P. (Beta 16732) places it prior to the timeframe of Columbus' visit to the island. In addition, I recently discovered a fallen mahogany (*Swietenia mahogani*) tree on the top of a 25 foot high hill near the northeast arm of the Great Lake. The tree was approximately 30.5 cm in diameter and may be between 50 to 100 years old. These could be considered to be good indicators for the size of the trees in 1492.

However, the ecology of San Salvador is not complete until a mention is made towards Columbus' many waters. Without a doubt, one can observe that there is a large lake in the center of the island. Previous mention was made to the tidal creeks, inland lakes and salinas. These large bodies of water can be confirmed back to the late 1700's in the Deeds and Land Grants Books at the Lands and Survey Office in Nassau. These records also reveal the location of ponds, mangroves, and surface freshwater, some of which still exist today. The size of these ponds is often dependent upon the amounts of rainfall during the year. In my travels to the interior of San Salvador, I have located additional surface freshwater areas. It would then seem reasonable to state that there existed many waters in 1492, more so if the rainfall had been abundant during the October rainy season. In addition, there is a large semi-protected area on the north coast called Grahams Harbour. This would appear to be the harbour that Columbus speaks about on the 14th of October,[22] when he and his men rowed the long boats to reach the other side of the island.

CONCLUSIONS

It would appear that Columbus was correct in his description of the landfall. The island had no mountains similar to those of the Old World. There apparently was a variety of water sources, not all fresh but still water, although their appearances today can be misconceiving. There had existed an evergreen woodland, which for the most part has been selectively cut and/or cleared for farming within the past 200 years. This then left the secondary growth woodland of today.

Using the biological, geological, and historical records of the Bahamas, there emerge conditions which can be applied to San Salvador island. These conditions can be used as evidence in stating that the island called San Salvador is indeed Columbus' San Salvador.

ACKNOWLEDGMENTS

I would like to thank Dr. Don and Kathy Gerace of the College Center of the Finger Lakes' Bahamian Field Station, San Salvador for their generous support and encouragement. I would also like to express my gratitude to Dr. Gail Saunders of the Archives Department, Nassau for her help and arrangements during my stay in Nassau, and to the personnel of the Lands and Survey Department, Nassau for providing me with the Deeds and Land Grants Books. Finally, I would like to thank Mr. Georges Charlier for the use of his slides and Dr. Robert Smith of Hartwick College for his analysis of the botanical specimens.

NOTES

1. Eugene Lyon, The Columbus Log of the First Voyage 10-27 October 1492, (Unpublished manuscript, 1986), 48 p.

2. Anthony R. Byrne, Man and the Variable Vulneraility of Island Life: A Study of Recent Vegetation Change in the Bahamas (Unpublished Ph.D. dissertation, University of Wisconsin, 1972), 291 p.

3. A. Dean Peggs, *A Relic of Slavery*, (Nassau, 1957).

4. Anthony R. Byrne, op. cit.

5. *Ibid.*; David G. Campbell, *The Ephemeral Islands: A Natural History of the Bahamas*, (London, 1978), 151 p.

6. Anthony R. Byrne, op cit.

7. J. Winter, J. Granberry, and A. Leibold, "Archaeological Investigations within the Bahmas Archipelago," in Allaire, L., ed., *Proceedings of the 10th International Congress for the Study of Pre-Columian Cultures of the Lesser Antilles* (Montreal, 1985), pp. 83-92.

8. Eugene Lyon, op. cit.

9. Bartolome de Las Casas, *Historie de las Indias* (Madrid, 1875).

10. Anthony R. Byrne, op. cit.; David G. Campbell, *The Ephemeral Islands: A Natural History of the Bahamas* (London, 1978), 151 p.; John D. Schoepf, *Travels in the Confederation*, ed. and translated by Alfred J. Morrison (New York, 1968), pp. 252-319; Thomas Chapman Harvey, *Official Reports of the Out Islands of the Bahamas*, ed. by Peter T. Dalleo (Nassau, no date), 43 p.

11. Anthony R. Byrne, op. cit.; David G. Campbell, op. cit.; J. Patterson and G. Stevenson, *Native Trees of the Bahamas* (Hope Town, Abaco, 1977) 128 p.

12. Anthony R. Byrne, op. cit.

13. J. Winter, et. al., op. cit.

14. Anthony Byrne, op. cit.; J. Patterson and G. Stevenson, op. cit.

15. Anthony R. Byrne, op. cit.

16. John Winter, Speculations on Prehistoric Coastal Topography (Paper presented at 3rd Symposium on the Geology of the Bahamas, San Salvador), 1986.

17. Steven W. Mitchell, "Late Holocene Tidal Creek-Lake Transitions, Long Island, Bahamas", in J. Teeter, Ed., *Addendum to Preceedings of the Second Symposium on the Geology of the Bahamas* (San Salvador, Bahamas, 1985), 1-27.

18. Neil E. Sealey, *Bahamian Landscapes: An Introduction to the Geography of the Bahamas* (London, 1985), 96 p.

19. Ibid.

20. John C. Kraft, "Marine Environments: Paleographic Reconstructions in the Littoral Region" in J. K. Stein and W. R. Farrand, eds., *Archaeological Sediments in Context* (Orono, Maine, 1985), 111-125.

21. Winter, op. cit.

22. Lyons, op. cit.

BIBLIOGRAPHY

Byrne, Anthony R. "Man and the Variable Vulnerability of Island Life: A Study of Recent Vegetation Change in the Bahamas." Ph.D. dissertation, University of Wisconsin, 1972.

Campbell, David G. *The Ephemeral Islands: A Natural History of the Bahamas*. London: Macmillan Education Limited, 1978.

Dean Peggs, A. *A Relic of Slavery*. Nassau, Bahamas: A. Peggs Dean, 1957.

Harvey, Thos. Chapman. "Official Reports of the Out Islands of the Bahamas." Edited by Peter T. Dalleo. Nassau, Bahamas: Dept of Archives, no date.

Kraft, John C. "Marine Environments: Paleographic Reconstructions in the Littoral Region," in Stein, J. K. and W. R. Farrand, eds., *Archaeological Sediments in Context*. Orono, Maine: Center for the Study of Early Man, Univ. of Maine, 1985.

Las Casas, Bartolome de. *Historie de las Indias*. Madrid, Spain, 1875.

Lyon, Eugene. The Columbus Log of the First Voyage 10-27 October 1492. Unpublished manuscript, 1986.

Mitchell, Steven W. "Late Holocene Tidal Creek-Lake Transitions, Long Island, Bahamas," in Teeter, J., ed., *Addendum to Proceedings of the Second Symposium on the Geology of the Bahamas*. San Salvador, Bahamas: College Center of the Finger Lakes Bahamian Field Station, 1985.

Patterson, J. and Stevenson, G. *Native Trees of the Bahamas*. Hope Town, Abaco: Jack Patterson, 1977.

Schoepf, Johann D. *Travels in the Confederation*, edited and translated by Alfred J. Morrison. New York: Bergman Publishers, 1968.

Sealey, Neil E. *Bahamian Landscapes: An Introduction to the Geography of the Bahamas*. London, England: Collins Caribbean, 1985.

Winter, John. "Speculations on Prehistoric Coastal Topography." Paper presented at the 3rd Symposium on the Geology of the Bahamas, College Center of the Finger Lakes Bahamian Field Station, San Salvador, 1986.

Winter, J., Granberry, J., and A. Leibold. "Archaeological Investigations within the Bahamas Archipelago," in Allaire, L., ed., *Proceedings of the 10th International Congress for the Study of Pre-Columbian Cultures of the Lesser Antilles.* Montreal: Centre de Recherches Caraibes, Montreal, p. 83-92.

Lucayan Lifeways at the Time of Columbus

Richard Rose
Department of Anthropology
Rochester Museum & Science Center
Rochester, New York

ABSTRACT

The Lucayan Indians of the Bahamas were the first New World natives encountered by Columbus. Columbus's journal of his sixteen-day journey through the Bahamas archipelago is the only known eyewitness description of the Lucayans who had succumbed to European pestilence, treachery and greed within two decades of the Landfall. Archaeological research conducted at Pigeon Creek, San Salvador, and other prehistoric settlements in the central Bahamas has provided important information on Lucayan origins, subsistence, technology and trade. A reconstruction of Lucayan lifeways at the time of Columbus enables us to better understand these New World natives, as well as to verify certain of Columbus's observations.

INTRODUCTION

"They all go quite naked as their mothers bore them,"[1] said Christopher Columbus of the islanders who had gathered to watch the landing of the Nina, the Pinta and the Santa Maria. Thus began one of the most astonishing encounters of history, the meeting of the Old World and the New. On October 12, 1492, Columbus took possession of a small island at the far reaches of the Ocean Sea and named it San Salvador after the Holy Savior who had guided him safely ashore. To the natives who watched this ceremony without understanding its meaning or comprehending its magnitude, the island already had a name. It was *Guanahaní*. The people of Guanahaní, who Columbus called Indians, are called Lucayans.

Columbus' *Journal of the First Voyage* provides the earliest eyewitness description of the Lucayans. He tells us that they were a gentle people, handsome and of good stature. Their hair was worn down over their eyebrows with a long hank in back which they never cut. They painted their faces and bodies in red, black and white designs which must have been a

321

colorful if disappointing sight to the Europeans who had crossed the ocean in search of gold, spices and the Grand Khan of Cathay. But not riches nor Oriental potentates awaited Columbus on that isolated beach in the Bahamas."They are very poor in everything," was his sad comment. The Lucayans wore little clothing, nothing more than the leaf of a plant or a net of cotton covering their private parts, and except for a few ornaments there was no sign of the gold that Columbus had hoped to find in great abundance.

Columbus' wish was to convert the Indians to Christianity but his arrival was ultimately responsible for their eradication. Only a few years after the landfall the Spanish priest-historian Bartolomé de las Casas was able to comment that to sail to the Lucayan Isles one need only to follow the floating corpses of Indians that marked the way.[2] Although this was likely an exaggeration, the gentle Lucayans were little prepared to deal with the onslaught of Europeans to their island paradise. They had no resistance to the diseases brought by the Europeans; nor were they able to live under the harsh treatment that the Christians imposed upon them. It has been estimated that from 20,000 to 40,000 Indians lived in the Bahamas when Columbus arrived. Their encounter with Europeans, however, was so devastating and so final that within two decades of the landfall the Lucayans were gone, victims of pestilence, treachery and greed. The Lucayans, who had welcomed Columbus to the New World, became to first to succumb to the new social order that was to overwhelm America.

THE LUCAYANS

Who were the Lucayans? When and from where did they come to the islands we call The Bahamas? What was their lifestyle like? Such questions have interested archaeologists and other scholars for close to a century. In 1887, William K. Brooks presented the first scientific paper on the Lucayan Indians.[3] Brooks noted the close resemblance between three Lucayan skulls from New Providence Island and crania known from Haiti and Cuba. By referring to the Lucayan specimens he was also able to dispel the then current myth that a race of giants had once existed in western Florida! Theodoor de Booy conducted an archaeological survey of the Bahamas in 1912, followed by additional surveys and test excavations by Froelich G. Rainey, Herbert W. Krieger, Julian Granberry, John M. Goggin and Ruth Durlacher Wolper.[4] Krieger suggested that a close cultural connection existed between the Lucayans and the Arawaks of Hispaniola. Granberry divided the Bahamas into three cultural-geographical zones and pointed to a close relationship between Lucayan ceramics and the pottery of northern Haiti.

The first systematic excavation of an open coastal midden was conducted in 1965 by Charles A. Hoffman at the Palmetto Grove site on San Salvador Island in the central Bahamas.[5] Hoffman defined the Palmetto

Ware assemblage of Lucayan ceramics and recognized the relationship of Bahamas pottery with that of Haiti and the Virgin Islands. Between 1965 and 1978 sites were excavated on Cat Island, Eleuthera, New Providence, Crooked Island, San Salvador and Middle Caicos.[6] The status of Bahamas prehistory was reviewed in 1978 by William H. Sears and Shaun D. Sullivan.[7]

Since 1978 there has been a flurry of archaeological activity in the Bahamas, much of it encouraged and supported by the CCFL Bahamian Field Station on San Salvador.[8] The Pigeon Creek site on San Salvador has been the focus of an ongoing field research project by the author who has also conducted preliminary excavations on Cat Island.[9] Hoffman has excavated the protohistoric Long Bay site on San Salvador and recently has investigated sites on Samana Cay.[10] Mary Jane Berman and Perry Gnivecki have excavated sites on San Salvador and Long Island.[11] John Winter has conducted site surveys in the central and northern Bahamas, and William F. Keegan and Steven W. Mitchell have investigated sites in the southern and central Bahamas.[12] Now, one hundred years after the first interest in Lucayan archaeology we can begin to summarize and assess our knowledge of the existence, substance and caliber of Lucayan culture in the Bahama Islands.

Lucayan Origins

Columbus observed that the people he met during his journey through the Bahamas spoke the same language and shared the same customs as those he encountered later on the island of Cuba. At the time of Columbus the Tainos had successfully colonized all of the major islands of the Greater Antilles with the exception of western Cuba where the pre-ceramic Guanajatabey (also known as the Ciboney) had managed to retain their non-agricultural lifestyle. In the Lesser Antilles to the south lived the Island-Carib, a bellicose people whose northward intrustion into the Taino heartland was only checked by the arrival of the Spaniards.

The Taino occupation of the West Indies had its beginnings at about the time of Christ when migrants from the Orinoco Delta and Guinea Coast entered the Caribbean by way of Trinidad and Tobago.[13] Using the islands of the Lesser Antilles as stepping stones, these people reached the Greater Antilles by A.D. 600. There they developed a number of chiefdom-level societies, practiced manioc agriculture and the gathering of intertidal and pelagic marine resources, and shared in a religious system based on the worship of "zemis." Another aspect of Taino society, one which is not clearly understood, was their possible role as accomplished traders interacting within an economic network that included the Mesoamerican mainland of the Yucatan and Central America as well as possible contacts with the southeastern United States.

The entry of man into the Bahamas is thought to have occurred between A.D. 800 and 1000, although the exact pattern of island occupation is not yet understood. Three distinct migration routes may be considered based on archaeological and historical evidence. Sears and Sullivan believe that Tainos from Hispaniola and/or Cuba moved into the Caicos region in the southern Bahamas as early as A.D. 800 in order to collect crystalline salt and dried conch.[14] These commodities were sought after by the historic Tainos of Hispaniola but it is not certain that they can account for early settlement in the archipelago.[15] It also is possible that migrants from Cuba colonized the central Bahamas at about A.D. 900. Radiocarbon dates from the Pigeon Creek site on San Salvador indicate that a large village had been established there by A.D. 1100 and perhaps even earlier based on pottery designs which show strong affinities with the Meillacoid ceramic series from eastern Cuba. The ceramic inventory from Pigeon Creek also suggests the possibility of a third migration route emanating from the Magens Bay region of the Virgin Islands as early as A.D. 900.[16]

A more precise determination of the initial route of migration into the Bahamas must await further archaeological research. Indeed, the peopling of the Bahamas may well have been the result of simulatneous migrations from two or more islands in the Greater Antilles leading to the suggestion that the Bahamas may have been a colonial region that was exploited by a number of cultures, or chiefdoms, in the West Indies.

Lucayan Settlement

Well over one hundred prehistoric sites are known in the Bahamas ranging in type from village settlements to cave burials to single activity areas and in size from five hectares to a few square meters. Sites have been found on all of the major islands and many of the smaller ones. Site distribution in the Bahamas seems to correspond closely with climatic conditions. There are relatively few sites in the northern Bahamas, which has been classified as a moist subtropical zone.[17] Whether the low site inventory is due to climatic constraints, distance from the centers of occupation to the south, or the lack of reconnaissance research in the region is not known. The central Bahamas, a moist tropical zone, has the largest number of sites and apparently was the most densely populated zone in prehistoric times. The southern Bahamas, including the Turks and Caicos Islands, have been characterized as a dry tropical zone. Site inventory is relatively low, although a major ceremonial center has been located on Middle Caicos.[18]

It is interesting to note that the islands with the largest number of sites are those which are located closest to the open ocean on the eastern bank of the archipelago. These include Eleuthera, Cat Island, San Salvador, Long Island and Crooked Island, all in the central Bahamas. Site location also appears to follow natural or environmental features. It is not uncommon to find sites on coves, inlets, lagoons or other protected areas. Sites are also more commonly found on the leeward side of islands, and with the exception of cave burials are located adjacent or close to the shoreline. Few sites are known to occur in inland locations.

The Pigeon Creek site on San Salvador has been chosen for our discussion of Lucayan settlement, subsistence and technology. Although larger than other known sites, Pigeon Creek is fairly typical in terms of location, midden deposits and other archaeological and environmental features. We suspect that Pigeon Creek was a *cacique* residence and may have played an important role in the social and economic development of Lucayan culture.

Pigeon Creek is the largest-known Lucayan settlement in the Bahamas, occupying and area of 8.4 hectares (approximately 12 acres) (Fig. 1). The site was probably settled as early as A.D. 1100 or possibly earlier and may have been penecontemporaneous with Columbus' landfall, based on a range of radiocarbon dates from A.D. 1110 to A.D. 1560.[19] The Pigeon Creek settlement was situated in an ideal location. The site covers a long dune ridge along the northeastern shore of the Pigeon Creek estuary in the southern part of San Salvador. It has been said that estuaries have long been a focus of human settlement because of their wide array of living and nonliving resources.[20] The Pigeon Creek village certainly fits this description as its location, large size and inventory of archaeological remains clearly indicate. The site's location on a protected cove on the leeward shore of of an estuary would have provided the inhabitants with a safe bearth for their dugout canoes as well as a convenient access to the rich marine resources of both the shallow waters of the estuary and the nearby ocean. The site has yielded an abundance of clam shells, particularly *Codakia obicularis*, as well as other marine food remains which must have been collected in the vicinity. Bones of grouper (*Epinephelus striatus*), parrot fish (*Sparisoma* sp.) and other ocean species, as well as shells of sea snails (*Strombus* sp., *Cittarium pica*, *Fasciolaria tulip*) and an array of other mollusks attest to a varied marine diet for the Pigeon Creek Lucayans (Fig. 2).

In addition to harvesting the rich bounty of the sea, the people of Pigeon Creek had an agricultural economy. These is evidence that manioc (*Manibot*) was grown and used to make cassava cakes, the staple food of the pre-Columbian Caribbean cultures. It is likely that corn, chili peppers, avocados and other food crops were also utilized. Based on ethnohistoric observations of Taino foodways, the Lucayans probably prepared their meals in large "pepper pots," a kind of slow cooking stew into which any available food was added. The marine and agricultural diet of the Lucayans must have been supplemented with wild plants and animals although we are unsure as to the extent of their utilization. The *hutia*, a rodent-like land animal, as well as iguanas, birds and even the domesticated dog were eaten by the Lucayans. One of Columbus' men, upon tasting dog meat for the first time, pronounced it "none too good."

Excavations at Pigeon Creek have enabled us to reconstruct the prehistoric lifestyle of the Lucayan residents. Archaeological evidence of house floors has shown that houses were built side-by-side along the crest of the dune ridge overlooking the estuary. The house floors consist of an obdurate layer of sand, 15 cm. to 17 cm. thick (Fig. 3). Contained within the hard-packed floors were artifacts, food remains and fragments of charcoal. Artifacts included fish and bird bone needles, dart points of shell and bone, and fragmentary bits of pottery (Fig. 4). Food remains were primarily fish bones and mollusk shells. Pea-size pieces of limestone were distributed throughout the floor layer. Charcoal samples submitted for radiocarbon analysis have given dates of A.D. 1110 ±60 and A.D. 1160 ±70 for the occupation of the house floors. Presumably, locally gathered palm fronds and other plant materials were used in the construction of the Pigeon Creek houses but archaeological evidence of these perishable materials has not been recovered. Nor do we know whether the number of houses at Pigeon Creek corresponds to the observations of Columbus who reported seeing villages of 12 to 15 houses.

Extensive midden deposits of pottery, stone and shell tools, food remains and other debris are located along the eastern slope of the dune ridge between the house floors and the shoreline. More than 95% of the pottery excavated from the Pigeon Creek middens was the red-colored, shell-tempered Palmetto ware which occurs throughout the Bahamas. The dominant shapes of Palmetto vessels are wide-mouthed bowls, carinated bowls, boat-shaped bowls, and discoidal griddles. The pottery bowls were used for food preparation and storage as well as collecting drip water from caves. The flat-bottomed griddles were used for baking cassava cakes made from manioc flour. The abundance of pottery found at Pigeon Creek suggests that the settlement supported a full-time, agriculturally-based population probably over a long period of time.

The analysis of Palmetto ceramics has provided insights into the nature of Lucayan technology. Pottery production in the limestone and coral islands of the Bahamas must not have been an easy task. Deposits of clay are rare and silicates practically nonexistent. The Palmetto potters used crushed *lucina* shells as a tempering agent which resulted in the production of low-fired, thick-walled bowls and griddles. The thickest pottery, often exceeding 20 mm., is represented by the Palmetto griddles. Griddle sherds generally have mat-marked impressions on their bottom surface. Rather than a design, the impressions result from the clay having been modeled on plaited fiber mats. This would have facilitated the handling of the large, heavy griddles which were 12 inches or more in diameter. In addition to fiber-plaited mats, palm leaves were sometimes used to support the griddles as indicated by sherds marked with leaf impressions on their under surface (Fig. 5).

The Lucayans of Pigeon Creek also utilized locally available resources for their tools and utensils. *Strombus* shells were reworked into scrapers, gouges, awls and spoons (Fig. 6). This was the hardest material available to the Lucayans and conch tools would have served a variety of purposes from canoe making and woodworking to agricultural and household needs. Other shells, such as the *Codakia* and *Lucina* clams, were also made into

326

tools. Shells were also used as ornaments. Pendants were made from cowrie, olive and oyster shells and tiny shell beads are commonly found on Lucayan sites. A large *Chama* shell from Pigeon Creek has two drilled holes which were probably threaded with a cotton cord for use as an amulet (Fig. 7).

Coral (*Acropora* sp.) occurs frequently at Pigeon Creek. Coral in its fresh state is naturally abrasive due to the sharp polyps on its surface. As a tool, it would have been an excellent woodworking rasp and could also have been used for grating manioc into flour as well as to card seeds from cotton bolls. Coral tools from Lucayan sites have usually been ground to a smooth surface. Limestone was also utilized by the Lucayans. Limstone slabs and bowls would have had many uses and calcified limestone blades, although brittle, could have been used to cut vegetables or split palm fronds for basket making.

An unique limestone sculpture found in a Pigeon Creek midden gives us a rare glimpse into Lucayan ritual and belief. It is carved in the likeness of a parrot fish on a thin piece of limestone much in the manner of the thin stone heads, or *hachas*, of Mexico and Guatemala (Fig. 8). The carving is probably a "zemi." Zemis were nature spirits or deities represented as idols of stone, wood, clay or cotton fashioned as human or animal effigies. Images of zemis were painted on the body, carved as amulets and modeled onto the rims of pottery bowls. [21] Zemiism can be defined as the personification of spiritual power achieved with the aid of supernatural forces represented as idols. It was a widespread belief system among the Tainos, although when Columbus sailed through the Bahamas he failed to observe any evidence of Lucayan religion and believed that the Indians had none.

LUCAYAN TRADE

A number of tools and ornaments made from materials not indigenous to the Bahamas have been excavated at Pigeon Creek. Polished stone celts and pestles, quartz beads and smooth granite polishing stones could only have been obtained from localities outside of the Lucayan heartland. The utility of such objects and the social prestige of their ownership is obvious, but the implications of their presence at Pigeon Creek must be given close scrutiny. It is suggested that these exotic materials were brought to the islands as trade items in return for products that the Lucayans had to offer.

When Columbus sailed through the Bahamas he witnesses many aspects of native life and economy. One of his first observations on the day of discovery was that of the islanders swimming and canoeing out to his ships with parrots, skeins of cotton thread and darts which were quickly swopped for glass beads, hawks' bells and other European trade goods. The Lucayans appeared not to have been deterred by the strange visitors with their awesome looking ships. According to Columbus they willingly traded everything they had. This suggests that the Lucayans were experienced traders and that trading was indeed an important part of their economy.

The reciprocal movement of goods from one region to another must correspond to the availability of tradable resources in each region. In the coraline islands of the Bahamas where certain natural resources are not available there would have been a need to import non-local commodities such as quartz tempered pottery, stone axes and celts, polished stone pestles and quartz beads, all of which have been found archaeologically. An x-ray diffraction pattern for a jade celt fragment from Pigeon Creek has pointed to the Motagua Valley of Guatemala or the Nicoya region in Nicaragua as likely places of origin thereby demonstrating that long distance trade did indeed occur.[22] The idea that the Lucayans may have taken part in a long distance trading network begs the obvious question: What local resource or resources in the Bahamas were exchanged in return for the imported commodities?

Columbus provides descriptions of at least three commodities that may have been important Lucayan trade items, namely parrots, darts and cotton. Parrots and darts are mentioned only in passing and will not be discussed here. Cotton, however, is mentioned frequently by Columbus and must be seriously considered as a possible Lucayan trade product.

Cotton in the Bahamas

At least two species of cotton were present in the West Indies in pre-Columbian times. *Gossypium barbadense*, also known as Sea Island cotton, reached the West Indies from Peru by way of northern South America. *G. hirsutum* of southern Mexico and Guatemala extended into the Antilles with one of its varieties, *punctatum*, reaching the Bahamas where it is known today.[23]

The distinctive black loam soil and moist tropical climate of the central Bahamas is ideal for growing cotton as the Loyalists learned when they brought their plantations to the islands in the 18th century. In his 1708 description of the Bahamas, John Graves from Carolina mentioned that the islands produced the best cotton in all the Indies,[24] and in 1783 the Loyalist John Wilson gave an optimistic assessment of the potential of the Bahamas black loam for growing Sea Island cotton.[25] By 1875 the Loyalists had planted 2,476 acres to cotton, producing 124 tons. During the next 25 years this amount steadily increased to 602 tons.[26] The eventual collapse of the Bahamas cotton economy was due less to soil depletion than to destructive insects and unstable social conditions.

The Archaeology of Cotton

The archaeology of cotton in the West Indies is yet to be documented and little is known about cotton production in the region prior to Columbus. That cotton was grown in the islands cannot be disputed. Columbus was offered skeins of spun cotton wherever he went. On San Salvador he obtained 16 skeins, or the equivalent of an *arroba* (25 lbs.) of spun cotton thread. "I saw clothes of cotton made like short cloaks," he said upon reaching Fernandina, and went on to describe "beds and furnishings (made) like nets of cotton," or hammocks. The Lucayans are said to have snared parrots with cotton nooses and pigeons with fiber nets. They also caught fish with cotton nets and cotton lines.[27] Cotton cords or nets may also have been used to fasten cargo to canoes and cotton bolls would have made a good caulking material for the wooden dugouts.

Explanation of past lifeways is largely dependent upon the interpretation of the material remains which have survived in the archaeological record. Evidence of a cotton economy among the Lucayans, however, may not be immediately recognizeable in the archaeological record due to the perishable nature of cotton products. Cotton thread, cordage, hammocks, fish nets and the like would not be expected to survive in the damp climate of the Bahamas. Archaeologists, therefore, must look for secondary evidence of Lucayan cotton production. The analysis of fiber impressed pottery may prove to be informative in this regard. We have seen that pottery griddles were formed on basketry mats and occasionally on palm leaves. If cotton cloth was also used in a similar manner the fiber impressions should show up on pot sherds.

Artifacts used in the production of cotton thread should also be present on Lucayan sites. Clay spindle whorls, although not abundant, are known from Long Island,[28] and a possible limestone whorl and perforated shell disk have been found at Pigeon Creek. Non-ceramic whorls may also have been used by the Lucayans. The expectations of finding such artifacts, however, must be understood within the contexts of preindustrial cotton technology. Being a lightweight fiber, cotton is difficult to spin and care must be taken not to put too much force on the thread. The modern Indians of Peru use lightweight wooden or even vegetable whorls on thin wooden spindles which are spun in small pottery or wooden bowls, 4" to 5" in diameter.[29] Clam shells would, of course, serve the same purpose.

In the Lucayan Isles there are a number of materials that could have been used to spin cotton thread. Wooden and vegetable whorls would have been available. Small gourds or calabashes could also have been used as is illustrated by Douglas Taylor's account of spinning by the Caribs of Dominica:

> A band of teased cotton wound around the left wrist is spun onto a long stick or spindle by rolling the latter on the right knee. The upper end of the spindle is crooked. A round disk of calabash, through whose center the stick is passed, acts as a base for the growing spool of thread.[30]

CONCLUSIONS

Columbus' assessment of Lucayan Indian culture was bleak and tinged with disappointment. Archaeological research conducted over the past century has provided a basic knowledge of Lucayan origins, settlement, economy and social life. It is now evident that Lucayan culture was not as stark or impoverished as Columbus reported in his journal. To the contrary, the Lucayans lived in a region of abundant food resources, enjoyed social and economic relationships with other peoples of the Caribbean, and had developed a level of technology that was particularly well adapted to a carbonate island ecology. It appears that the Lucayan lifestyle was enhanced by their participation in an economic interaction sphere that included many islands in the northern Caribbean. Indeed, Lucayan settlement in the Bahamas was surely influenced by and may have depended upon the production and intra-island exchange of cotton and cotton products.

NOTES

1. All quotations from Columbus are from *Journals and Other Documents on the Life and Voyages of Christopher Columbus*, trans. & ed. by S. E. Morison, (New York, 1963).

2. Bartolome de las Casas, *Tears of the Indians*, (1896 ed.).

3. W. K. Brooks, "On the Lucayan Indians," *National Academy of Sciences, Memoirs*, 4 (Philadelphia, 1888), pp. 215-22.

4. T. DeBooy, "Lucayan Remains on the Caicos Islands," *American Anthropologist*, 14 (1912), pp. 81-105; _____, "Lucayan Artifacts from the Bahamas," *American Anthropologist*, 15 (1913), pp. 1-7; F. G. Rainey, "Porto Rican Archaeology," *N. Y. Acad. Sci.* 18 (1940); H. W. Krieger, "The Bahama Islands and Their Prehistoric Population," *Explorations and Field Work of the Smithsonian Inst. in 1936*, (Washington, 1937); J. Granberry, "The Cultural Position of the Bahamas in Caribbean Archaeology," *Amer. Antiq.* 22 (1956), pp. 128-34; J. M. Goggin, "An Anthropological Reconnaissance of Andros Island, Bahamas," *Amer. Antiq.* 5 (1939), pp. 21-6; R. G. D. Wolper, "A New Theory Identifying the Locale of Columbus's Light, Landfall, and Landing," *Smithsonian Misc. Coll.* 148,1 (Washington, 1964), pp. 1-41.

5. C. A. Hoffman, "The Palmetto Grove Site on San Salvador, Bahamas," *Contrib. FL State Mus., Soc. Sci.* 16 (Gainesville, 1970), pp. 1-26.

6. J. C. MacLaury, "Archaeological Investigations on Cat Island, Bahamas," *Contrib. FL State Mus., Soc. Sci.* 16 (Gainesville, 1970), pp. 7-50; S. D. Sullivan, "Archaeological Reconnaissance of Eleuthera, Bahamas," (MA thesis, Florida Atlantic Univ., Boca Raton, 1974); J. H. Winter, "The Clifton Pier Rockshelter, New Providence, Bahamas," *J. Virgin Isl., Arch. Soc.* 6 (St. Croix, 1978), pp. 45-8; _____, "Preliminary Work from the MacKay Site on Crooked Island," *Proc. 7th Inter. Cong. Study of Pre-Col. Cult. of Lesser Antilles*, (1978); M. K. Pratt, "Preliminary Reports (1973 & 1974) Prehistoric Archaeology of San Salvador, Bahamas," *Island Environmental Studies* (Corning, 1974); S. D. Sullivan, "An Overview of the 1976 to 1978 Archaeological Investigations in the Caicos Islands," *The FL Anth.* 33, 3 (1980), pp. 120-142.

7. W. H. Sears and S. D. Sullivan, "Bahamas Prehistory," *Amer. Antiq.* 43 (1978), pp. 3-25.

8. I am indebted to Dr. Donald T. Gerace, Director of the CCFL Bahamian Field Station, and Kathy Gerace for their support, encouragement and hospitality during the past eight years.

9. R. Rose, "The Pigeon Creek Site, San Salvador, Bahamas," *The FL Anth.* 35, 4 (Coral Gables, 1982), p. 45; _____, An Archaeological Reconnaissance of Cat Island, the Bahamas, 1985, Unpubl. report on file, Rochester Museum, (Rochester, 1986).

10. C. A. Hoffman, "The Long Bay Site," Paper presented at Soc. Hist. Arch., (Boston, 1985); R. H. Brill and C. A. Hoffman, "Some Glass Beads Excavated on San Salvador Island in the Bahamas," Paper presented at 10th Cong. Inter. Assn. Hist. Glass, (Madrid, 1985); J. Judge, "Where Columbus Found the New World," *Nat. Geog. Soc.* 170, 5 (Washington, 1986), pp. 566-99.

11. M. J. Berman and P. Gnivecki, personal communication.

12. W. F. Keegan and S. W. Mitchell, "An Archaeological Reconnaissance of Long Island, Bahamas," Report to the Government, (1983).

13. I. Rouse, "Ceramic and Religious Development in the Greater Antilles," *Journal of New World Archaeology* 5, 2 (Los Angeles, 1982), pp. 45-52; _____, "Arawakan Phylogeny, Caribbean Chronology, and Their Implications for the Study of Population Movement," Paper presented at XXXIV Convencion Anual de AsoVAC, (Venezuela, 1984).

14. Sears and Sullivan, *Op. cit.*

15. W. F. Keegan, Personal communication.

16. R. P. Bullen, "Ceramic Periods of St. Thomas and St. John Islands, Virgin Islands," *The William L. Bryant Foundation*, 4 (Gainesville, 1963).

17. Sears and Sullivan, *Op. cit.*

18. Sullivan, *Op. cit.*

19. Beta 17839 (840±60 BP), Beta 17840 (790±70 BP), UM 2274 (620±70 BP), UM 2273 (580±90 BP), UM 2733 (540±60 BP), UM 2738 (480±70 BP), UM 2736 (390±60 BP).

20. G. H. Lauff, ed., *Estuaries*, American Assn. for the Advancement of Science, (1967).

21. I. Rouse, "The Arawak," *HSAI, BAE* 143 (Washington, 1948), pp. 507-46.

22. K. R. Johnson, "Results of Tests to Determine Mineralogy of an Artifact from San Salvador, Bahamas," Paper on file with R. Rose.

23. R. A. Hutchinson, et. al., *The Evolution of Gossypium*, (New York, 1947).

24. M. Craton, *A History of the Bahamas*, (London, 1962).

25. *Ibid.*

26. G. Saunders, *Bahamian Loyalists and Their Slaves*, (Caribbean, 1983).

27. Craton, *Op. cit.*

28. Collections of the National Museum of Natural History, Smithsonian Institution.

29. E. Franquemont, Personal communication.

30. D. Taylor, "The Caribs of Dominica," *BAE Bulletin*, 119 (Washington, 1938), pp. 103-59.

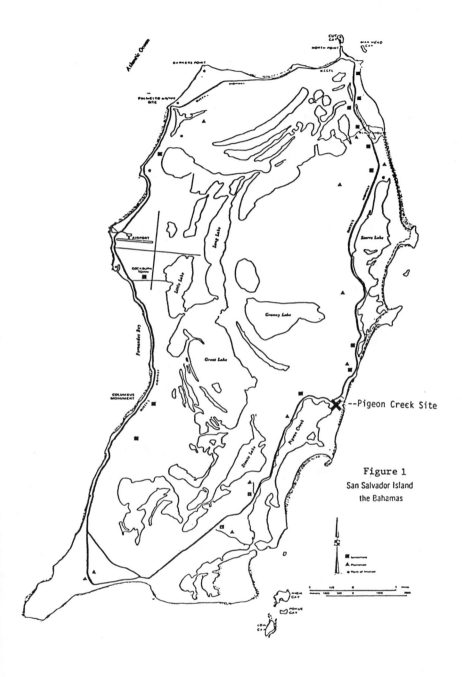

---Pigeon Creek Site

Figure 1
San Salvador Island
the Bahamas

Fig. 1. San Salvador Island, the Bahamas

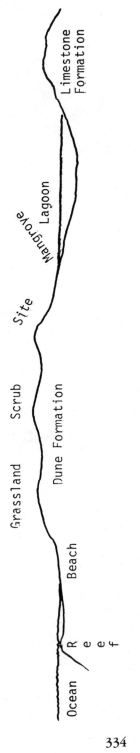

Fig. 2. An Idealized East-West Transection of the Pigeon Creek Site Region

Sandy Black Loam

Sand w/ shell & pottery fragments

Hard-pack Sand Floor [occupation level]

Marl [sterile]

Fig. 3. South Face of Occupation Feature at Pigeon Creek (1 cm = 20 cm)

Fig. 4. Bone Dart Point, 3.5 cm (top left); Shell Dart Point, 2.5 cm (top right); Bird Bone Awl, 10.5 cm (bottom)

Fig. 5. Palmetto Griddle Sherds. Mat-marked (top); Mat-impressed (top); Palm-impressed (bottom); 7.5 cm x 5 cm (bottom right)

Fig. 6. Shell Gouge (*Strombus Gigas*), 11 cm

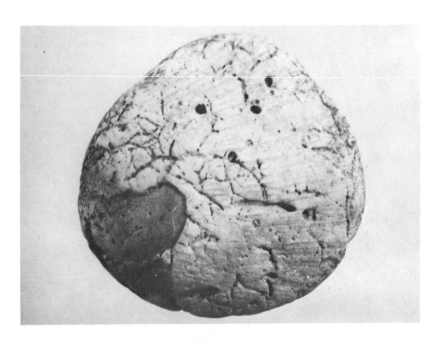

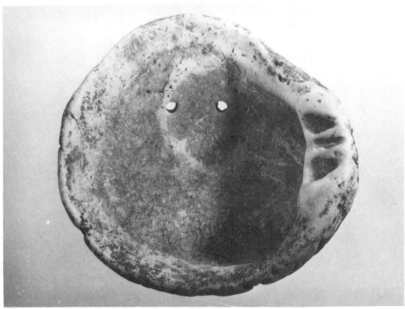

Fig. 7. Shell Pendant (*Chama* sp.), 9 cm

Fig. 8. Limestone Sculpture Depicting a Parrot-Fish, 15 cm

Initial Encounters: Arawak Responses to European Contact at the En Bas Saline Site, Haiti

Kathleen Deagan
Florida State Museum
University of Florida
Gainesville, Florida

ABSTRACT

The En Bas Saline site in Haiti is believed to have been the village of Guacanacaric, the Arawak cassique who assisted Columbus and his men after the wreck of the Santa Maria on December 24, 1492. Columbus subsequently established the tiny colony of La Navidad in Guacanacaric's town, where 39 Spanish men lived in daily contact with the Arawak Indians for nearly nine months. Three years of archaeological research carried out at the site by the University of Florida have verified the very early contact period date of the site, have provided information about Arawak society on the eve of the contact, and have yielded preliminary data on the changes that occurred in the Indian community between 1492 and ca 1515 (when the town was no longer occupied). This paper will summarize these results, and offer suggestions about the nature of changes that occurred in Arawak society as a result of the very earliest European-American interactions in the New World.

INTRODUCTION

The Arawak Indians of the greater Antilles were the first native Americans to experience sustained interaction with European settlers in the New World. They were also the first Amerindian group to disappear as a result of this interaction. Today they are extinct; the victims of disease, enslavement, warfare and severe social and economic disruption. Although many other Amerindian groups were subjected to these pressures as a result of European contact, none succumbed as quickly as, or to the extent of the Arawak, who were not only the first to encounter Europeans, but who were also among the few groups adapted to and restricted to island systems. The Arawak of Hispaniola sustained a population density that was possibly greater than any other pre-state, sedentary society in North America or the

Caribbean.[1] In their island environments they had no hinterland population reserves or areas for retreat, and Spanish policy for dealing with the Indians was initially uncontrolled and based almost exclusively in labor and natural resources exploitation. Under these circumstances, Arawak extinction was effectively ensured by the population declines that had occurred as early as 1520.[2]

Because of this astonishingly rapid post-contact cultural demise and the concomitantly very short period of historical documentation, it falls to the field of archeology to provide detailed documentation of these people and their culture. Of special interest to anthropologists in this undertaking is the opportunity to observe — at least indirectly — the specific mechanisms by which cultures change in response to population decline and disruption.

The search for Columbus has provided us with an unsurpassed opportunity to study these Arawak peoples of Hispaniola in considerable detail, and to trace the changes that occurred in at least one society as a result of contact with Europeans. I refer to the archeological research being conducted at the site of En Bas Saline, Haiti, which is believed to have been the Arawak town of the cassique, Guacanacaric, and in which Christopher Columbus established the small fortified settlement of La Navidad in 1492. It was here that the first sustained interaction between Europeans and Native Americans took place. In the process of searching for La Navidad, a great deal of information about the Arawaks before and after contact is being recovered and applied to questions about Arawak life and culture at the time of contact, and about some of the changes that occurred after contact.

The site of En Bas Saline was discovered in 1976 by Dr. William Hodges, a medical missionary in Haiti who has had a lifelong interest in the history and archeology of the region. The site has been the focus of archeological survey and testing by the University of Florida since 1983, and we have conclusively documented the presence of both prehistoric and very early post-contact period Arawak components.[3]

The En Bas Saline site is located 1 kilometer inland from the north coast of Haiti at Limonade Bord de Mer (Figure 1), about 10 kilometers east of present day Cap Haitian. It is situated in an area of low, alluvial marine soils in a humid subtropical forest life zone, adjacent to an area of dry subtropical forest. The vegetation of the area has been greatly modified since the 15th century, due to deforestation and overcropping, and almost no forest or other original plant communities are extant in the area. The site itself is under cultivation (manioc, corn, bananas, beans, potatoes) and is at the edge of a saline basin (once a river channel connecting the site to the shore) with adjacent stands of mangrove and bayahonda.

Using Columbus' log, coastal conditions and currents, shoreline information and a knowledge of sailing, Samuel Eliot Morison and others determined that the *Santa Maria* went down off the coast of Haiti at the town of Limondade Borde de Mer.[4] By Columbus' accounts, the town of

Guacanacaric was 1.5 leagues (4.3 miles).[5] The site located by Hodges is about 1 kilometer from the shore and 4 miles from the reef, (Figure 2). Aerial photographs reveal that the site was connected at one time with the shore by multiple, now non-navigable river channels. The major of these were tributaries of the Grande Riviere du Norde, which was diverted in the 18th century by French planters for irrigation purposes, resulting in the oxbow lake and present littoral pattern at the site.

With the assistance of Guacanacaric, the *Santa Maria* was offloaded and her goods stored, and the timbers were salvaged to build a small fortified area named La Navidad. We believe from Columbus' own accounts[6] that one or two large houses belonging to the cassique Guacanacaric were fortified with a palisade and possibly a moat. Columbus left 39 men there with instructions to trade with the Indians for gold until he returned. He did, in fact, return some 9 months later, to find all of his men dead and the fortress and surrounding Indian town burned, ostensibly as a result of conflict with Indians from the interior.[7] Columbus abandoned the area and moved westward along the coast to establish the town of La Isabela.

After the demise of La Navidad, the Indians of En Bas Saline were left in relative isolation from Europeans until 1503, when the Spanish town of Puerto Real was established at about 2 kilometers from the Indian settlement. Puerto Real was a ranching community occupied by a Spanish and Indian population that fluctuated between 100 and 15 families.[8]

The Indians of En Bas Saline were undoubtedly and immediately impacted by the settlement of Puerto Real. The Spanish *repartimiento* records of 1514 (developed to allocate the available Indians and Indian labor to the Spanish settlers) is revealing. 942 Indians, including men, women, children and "old people", under 14 cassiques (including three women cassiques) were distributed to the settlers.[9] The Indians were drawn from at least as far away as the Ft. Liberte region (30 km. from Puerto Real), however by this time all of the cassiques had Spanish names and thus are difficult to locate or identify.

What few Indians were left at En Bas Saline were probably further decimated in the smallpox epidemic of 1518-1519.[10] There is some suggestion that the population was already very low by 1508, when the Spaniards began to raid the Lucayan (Bahamas) Islands for Indian slaves to replace the decimated Arawak of Hispaniola.[11] It is unlikely that traditional Arawak culture survived past 1520, when even the Lucayans were decimated and it became necessary to import large numbers of African slaves as a labor source.[12]

The site remained isolated from the early 16th century until the 19th century, when it was partially occupied by the tiny Haitian village of En Bas Saline. No passable road existed until the archeological work began, and the only known cultural activity at the site has been intermittent hoe cultivation of manioc, beans, bananas and potatoes. Today the site is divided into 21 small gardens surrounded by cactus fences and filled with garden crops.

Reconnaissance work began at En Bas Saline in 1983 as part of a long-term archeological study of initial contact and colonization in the region. We had been working at the nearby site of Puerto Real since 1979 in order to investigate Spanish responses and adaptations to the circumstances of Caribbean colonization, and the processes by which a crystallized Hispanic-American cultural tradition emerged.[13]

Thirty-four weeks of fieldwork at En Bas Saline have been conducted over the past three years, much of it devoted to survey and mapping activities. We have completed a 10 cm. interval topographic map of the site; and an electromagnetic survey using an EM31 terrain conductivity meter on a two-meter grid, done to search for anomalies related to a moat or a storage cellar. A complete surface collection was done to take advantage of the clearing required for the survey and the abundant, low-cost labor available in Haiti.

In addition to the survey and surface collection, two series of 25 cm square test pits were excavated at 10-meter intervals across the north-south and east-west extents of the site. These have provided a guide to the general nature of depositional depth and composition, and site structure. We have also excavated areas totalling approximately 93 square meters, selected through topographic, surface and electromagnetic data as potential sites of the fortified structures of La Navidad.[14]

More than seven tons of archeological materials have been recovered from the site, and are analyzed and curated at the Florida State Museum at the University of Florida, eventually to be returned to the Government of Haiti. More than 40,000 artifacts, nine kilos of faunal remains, and 300 kilos of shell have been catalogued.

The only direct evidence for the fort of La Navidad itself will be architectural features from a fortified — and possibly Indian — structure, possibly with a well, moat, palisade and/or cellar. Such features should be burned, and associated with European seeds, fauna and other small items. European artifacts are not necessarily the primary evidence category in the identification of La Navidad, since it is almost certain that any transportable European items — which would have been extremely exotic to the Indian villagers —would have been removed from the immediate area of La Navidad to other loci of use. We expect that only those European items not considered exotic, or too small to be noticed, would enter the archeological record of La Navidad.

Although we have not encountered anything we are willing to unequivocally identify as La Navidad, we have amassed a large body of circumstantial evidence pointing to the identification of the site as Guacanacaric's town. This evidence is based on the interfaces between archeological remains, documentary sources, and chemical-physical analyses of materials.

The size and configuration of the site conforms to the expectation of a substantial chiefly town with a large central plaza, as indicated by documentary accounts. The site is described by a C-shaped, raised earthwork open to the south, and measuring 350 meters north to south and 300 meters east to west. The earthwork itself averages about 20 meters in width, and is about 80 cm high. The test pits across the site suggest that the earthwork is composed largely of midden debris rather than soil elevated to provide montones for farming, although the contour map indicates that borrow pits may be present adjacent to the highest parts of the mound. The southern, open portion of the "C", although not elevated, does have a significant quantity of surface debris in a distribution corresponding to the shape of the raised area. The interior of the site (inside the earthwork) is flat and relatively free of cultural remains except for a mounded area near the center. This is currently hypothesized to represent a plaza and chiefly residence complex, and our excavations to date have concentrated on this area.

Few Arawak towns in the region have been studied to determine the extent and nature of intrasite settlement patterning, and no systematic regional surveys have been done in northern Haiti. Little is specifically known, therefore, about spatial organization on a regional or community level. Ethnohistoric accounts and archeological mapping activities have indicated that some sites were quite large, and were inhabited by as many as 3,000 people.[15] Others were reported to have contained only a few families,[16] possibly in a pattern similar to that described for the southeastern United States Mississippian chiefdoms.[17] These towns were typically organized in a rectangular or oval fashion around a central plaza or ballcourt, on which the cassique's house stood.[18] The sites at Ft. Liberte,[19] Bois Neuf,[20] Yuma,[21] and En Bas Saline, conform to this pattern.

Two major stratigraphic components have been identified at En Bas Saline through the test excavations. These include an upper zone of 10 to 12 cm in depth (A horizon) that has been disturbed by modern hoe cultivation, but that nevertheless contains large quantities of aboriginal material and almost no post-contact material. The densest occupation at the site is represented by the "B" horizon, which ranges from 25 cm in depth in the site center to more than 50 cm on the earthwork. It has been excavated in increments of 10 cm, and these, on the basis of stratigraphy and content analysis can be assigned to three subhorizons (B1, B2, B3). Two charcoal samples from the lowest stratigraphic components at the site have provided radiocarbon dates of AD 1270±80 and AD 1350±70. This is consistent with Rouse's proposed date of ca A.D. 1200 for the appearance of Carrier ceramics and their associated cultural phenomena.[22]

The material from the excavations indicates that the site contains almost exclusively Carrier artifacts,[23] with no evidence of earlier occupation. Analyses of the sub-horizons and their associated features indicates that the A and B1 deposits are of the historic period. Five bones from European fauna (*Rattus rattus* and *Sus scrofa*) and 17 European artifacts (*melado*, Columbia Plain majolica, Olive jar or unglazed coarse earthenware, a nail and latticino glass — all dating typologically to the late 15th century) have been recovered from excavated contexts. One of these contexts was a very large and very unusual feature initiating in the Bl horizon. This feature appears to have no precedent in Hispaniola Indian sites, and has been suggested as a candidate for the well of La Navidad. Radiocarbon dates were calculated on charcoal from the feature's fill, and TL dates on ceramics in association with the charcoal, resulting in a weighted average date of 1450 ± 80 (A.D. 1370-1530). The presence of a rat and a pig bone, however, provide a TPQ of 1492 for the filling in of the feature. The contents are otherwise exclusively aboriginal, including a large number of decorative ceramics. They indicate that a material assemblage consistent with descriptions of late prehistoric Arawak sites was still present at En Bas Saline during the post-contact period, suggesting a very early historic period component.

Stable isotope analyses have been conducted on the pig and rat teeth by Jonathon Ericson of the University of California, Irvine. Ericson's preliminary work indicates very strongly that the pig tooth came from an animal that lived in the vicinity of southwestern Spain during that part of its life when its bones were forming. This will be very significant if evidence that live pigs were a common feature on 15th century ships can be encountered. The fact that the En Bas Saline pig had its origin in Europe is a potentially strong argument for its association with La Navidad.

The well-like feature, the European fauna and evidence for a burned structure are concentrated in one area of the site, the mounded portion of the central plaza believed to have been associated with the Cassique's residence. Analysis of a cinder-like substance found in quantity in that area has been carried out under the direction of Dr. Dow Whitney of the University of Florida Materials Sciences Department. Whitney indicates that the substance is burned clay daub that was subjected to such an intense heat that it formed Cristobalite, a phase of quartz formation that occurs at about $1400°$ C. This conforms to documentary accounts of the burning of La Navidad.

Other structural evidence includes postmolds in the central raised area and a few small circular hearths or fired pits although no complete structure has yet been delineated. Two unusual and adjacent features dating to the pre-contact period have been located at the site. These enormous, straight-sided hearth-like features are filled with food debris, ash and griddle fragments, and occur in the flat central part of the site unassociated with structural evidence. These may represent communal or long-term cooking activities.

Sixty-two percent of the excavated artifacts are from post-contact deposits, and 38% from pre-contact contexts. Certain differences are evident in the pre-and post-contact assemblages, although these should be considered with caution as preliminary samples. The majority of remains from both periods come from a few very large and densely filled features and possibly do not form a representative sample of the range of past activities at the site. We have been unable, for example, to recover a systematic spatial sample, owing to the requirements of the search for La Navidad. We are therefore unable to address questions of settlement and spatial organization. We do, however, believe that the available data provide a general description of changes that occurred from pre- to post-contact times in the material life of the Indians at En Bas Saline.

The most substantial category of evidence is, not unexpectedly, ceramic materials. These ceramic items conform overwhelmingly to the Carrier wares first described by Irving Rouse. Very small amounts of Meillacoid ceramics also occur at the site, comprising 9.3% of the assemblage ceramics in the lowest stratigraphic horizon at the site. This decreases steadily through time to 0.1% in the post-contact horizons. It suggests that the site was initially occupied by Chicoid tradition people who had somewhat stronger involvement in Meillac material culture than did later occupants of the site.

A general trend from pre- to post-contact times is an overall decrease in the proportion of decorated ceramics from 19% to 14% of the assemblage. Certain design motifs also decrease in frequency from early to later times at the site, including rows of double punctation and concentric circles. Only one element, broad-line incising, increases in frequency with time.

The general decrease in decorated wares during post-contact times is accompanied by a significant increase in the proportion of unidentified aboriginal wares (that is, not conforming to any previously recognized or defined types). These wares increase from 4% of the assemblage in pre-contact times to 9% of the assemblage in post-contact times. Varieties include both grit and sand tempered plain wares, and a very thick, coarse low-fired pottery known at Puerto Real as "Colono ware".[24] Such wares are known from other early contact sites occupied by both Indians and Spaniards in the early 16th century Caribbean colonies, including Nueva Cadiz, Venezuela; Puerto Real and Yayal, Cuba. This, along with the appearance of plain, grit-tempered wares, is suspected to have been a material response to the changes brought about by colonization, depopulation and social disintegration. Such a response suggests a general simplification in craft tradition resulting from contact-induced change.

Vessel forms also decrease in number through time (only 6 of the 8 vessel forms noted in the assemblage are found in postcontact contexts). Bottles, jars and ceramic griddles decrease in proportion through time, while platters and shallow bowls increase in frequency. Round and boat-shaped bowls were not represented in post-contact contexts, and carinated bowls are the only form that occurs in roughly the same proportions through the temporal divisions at the site. It is noteworthy that although the artifact assemblages of the pre- and post-contact periods are roughly equivalent in number, the proportion of recognizable vessel forms varies greatly. Eighty-one percent of the sherds exhibiting vessel form occurred in pre-contact proveniences. Although this is certainly in part a function of depth of deposit, we believe that it also reflects a general simplification of form and a reduction in the number of different forms in the post-contact period.

Other, more subtle changes are detectable in the non-ceramic assemblage at the site, most apparently in the lithic category. All of the chipped chert debitage occurs in post-contact proveniences. Stone griddles appear only in post-contact contexts, however stone beads are much more frequent in pre-contact contexts. Nearly all carved bone or shell ornaments (with the exception of a cojoba tube made from a turkey leg bone) occurs only in pre-contact contexts. Very few such items have been recovered to date, however, and their presence primarily in the distinctive features discussed earlier makes it difficult to determine their significance until a larger sample is available.

Preliminary analyses of fauna from the site, done at the Florida State Museum under the direction of Dr. Elizabeth Wing, indicate that an extraordinarily diverse range of animals was exploited at the site during both the pre-contact and the historic period. More than 60 vertebrate species from 47 families, and 57 invertebrate species from 31 families are represented in the faunal assemblage. These reflect a very broad exploitation base centering around estuarine and marine resources, with little emphasis on terrestrial fauna. Habitats include a variety of estuarine shallow coastal waters, freshwater lakes and rivers, coral reefs, mangrove estuaries, and less commonly, deep sea waters.

Diversity and equitability indices were calculated on the pre- and post-contact faunal assemblages to measure the range of diversity in animals used, and the degree to which certain animals were preferred and emphasized at the expense of others in the diet. The overall diversity index for vertebrates in pre-contact times was 4.611, which is very high (4.99 is the maximum value possible). They were also used very evenly, with no single animals heavily selected. This is reflected in the equitability value of 1.027. Both diversity and equitability were reduced somewhat in the historic period, which had a diversity index of 3.822, and an equitability index of 0.839. In both periods, bony fishes were the major food source (78% pre-contact, 82% post-contact), followed by small mammals (8% pre-contact, 6% post-contact), and lizards (5% pre-contact, 4% post-contact).

Patterns of vertebrate fauna exploitation did not change dramatically in the post-contact period, other than the slight increase in diversity. Invertebrate fauna, however, show a marked increase in diversity during the post-contact period, with 90 species used as compared to 83 species in pre-contact times. Shellfish collection requires fewer specialized skills than fishing for vertebrates, particulary open water species. The reduction in diversity of fishes, and the increase in diversity of invertebrates may reflect a more generalized pattern of resources exploitation resulting from a population decrease and concomitant reduction of the labor force performing specialized subsistence tasks. This may also have extended to farming activities, although there is little direct evidence in the archeological record for plant use. Ceramic griddle fragments decline in frequency from 2.8% of the assemblage in pre-contact times to 1.4% of the post-contact assemblage, which may reflect a decreased emphasis on manioc in the diet.

The archeological assemblage from pre-contact to post-contact times at En Bas Saline reflects less change than had been anticipated at the beginning of the project. A general trend toward simplification can be detected, manifested in reductions in both the proportions of decorated ceramics and the number of motifs used; in a reduction in the number of vessel forms used; the appearance of plain grit-tempered wares in the postcontact period; in the reduction of bone, shell and stone ornaments in the post-contact period; and possibly in subsistence activities as discussed above. None of these changes is dramatic, however, and we are left with the possibility that our post-contact sample was extremely early in the historic period, probably representing a very short time period after contact. Certainly no direct evidence of European influence in the native material assemblage can be detected. It is possible that the post-contact deposits at En Bas Saline represent a historic period occupation by Indians who had not yet suffered severe demographic and social disruption, which would be consistent with the hypothesis that it was associated with La Navidad.

We expect to continue our excavations in the summer of 1987, both to continue the search for La Navidad, and to obtain a more representative sample of pre- and post-contact Arawak occupation at the site. We believe that archeological work of this kind is a particularly critical element in the quincentenary effort, not only because of its intellectual content related to Columbus, but also in a more urgent sense as more and more archeological sites are impacted by development activities. The documentation of American Indian culture at the time of contact, and the tracing of the changes these cultures underwent after contact are surely among the most important tasks facing archeologist in the Americas for the remainder of this century.

ACKNOWLEDGMENTS

The research at En Bas Saline is a joint effort of the University of Florida, Florida State Museum (Dr. Peter Bennett, Director) and the Institute for Early Contact Period Studies (Dr. Michael Gannon, Director), and the Bureau National D'Ethnologie D'Haiti (Dr. Max Paul, Director). The work at En Bas Saline was funded by grants from the Organization of American States, the National Endowment for the Humanities, the University of Florida, the National Geographic Society and the Wentworth Foundation.

Maurice Williams of the Florida State Museum supervised the fieldwork at En Bas Saline, and the analysis and computerization of the data. I want to acknowledge also the assistance of Bonnie G. McEwan in preparing the faunal equitability and diversity indices used in this paper, and Mr. Jim Cusick who oversaw analysis and data organization of the En Bas Saline artifacts.

In addition to our regular field crews, we have benefited from the presence in the field at various times of Dr. William Hodges, Dr. Jerry Milanich,

Mr. Clarke Moore, Dr. William Goza, Dr. Michael Gannon, M. Jean Messina, M. Jean-Claude Selime, and M. Abner Septembre.

Faunal remains were analyzed in the Florida State Museum Zooarcheology Lab under the direction of Dr. Elizabeth Wing, and is ongoing as of this date. Thanks also to Dr. Jonathon Ericson of the University of California, Irvine for his analysis of stable isotopes in the pig and rat teeth from the site; to Dr. Dow Whitney and Florida Future Scientist student Susan Strasbourg of the University of Florida Materials Sciences Department for analysis of clay daub composition and to Dr. William Maples the Florida State Museum for looking at human teeth and bone fragments from En Bas Saline. Dr. Robert Brill of the Corning Museum of Glass analyzed the composition of the European glass fragment, and wood from the site (reported elsewhere) has been identified by Ms. Lee Newsome of the University of Florida.

I particularly would like to acknowledge the assistance of Dr. William Hodges of the Hopital le Bon Samaritain, the discoverer of the site, for his support, assistance and advice over the past three years of work at En Bas Saline. It is due to him and to the original vision of M. Albert Mangones of the Institut de Sauvegaurde du Patrimoine National, that the work was initiated. Thanks are also due to Dr. Max Paul of the Bureau National D'Ethnologie D'Haiti who has coordinated and facilitated the project for the Haitian Government, and who has provided assistance of many kinds. M. Ragnar Arnesen of OAS-Haiti has also been a consistent source of help and encouragement during the project.

NOTES

1. Gary Feinman and Jill Neitzel, "Too many types: An overview of sedentary pre-state societies in the Americas," in *Advances in Archeological Method and Theory*, ed. M. Schiffer (1984), 7, 39.

2. Bartolome de Las Casas, *Historia de las Indias* Tomo II, Libro II (Mexico, 1951), p. 154; Sherburne Cook and Woodrow Borah, *Essays in population history, Vol 1: Mexico and the Caribbean* (Berkeley, 1971), pp. 376-398; Kathleen Deagan, "Spanish-Indian interactions in sixteenth century Florida and the Caribbean," in *Cultures in Contact*, ed. W. Fitzhugh (Washington, D. C., 1985), p. 290.

3. Maurice Williams, "Preliminary field report on 1983 survey activities at En Bas Saline," Project report on file, Florida State Museum and Bureau National D'Ethnologie D'Haiti (Port au Prince, 1983); Deagan, op. cit.; Maurice Williams and Kathleen Deagan, "Preliminary field report on excavations at En Bas Saline, 1985-1986," Project report on file, Florida State Museum and Bureau National D'Ethnologie D'Haiti (Port au Prince, 1986).

4. Samuel E. Morison, "The route of Columbus along the north coast of Haiti and the site of La Navidad", *Transactions of the American Society* XXXI, 4 (1940), 239-285; Emilio Paolo Taviani, *I viaggio di Colombo*, 2 vols (Rome, 1983).

350

5. Conversion factor of 2.86 miles = 1 league, provided by Dr. Eugene Lyon, personal communications, St. Augustine, Florida, 1985.

6. Consuelo Varela, *Cristóbal Colón. Textos y documentos completos* (Madrid, 1982), pp. 98-99.

7. Juan Gil y Consuelo Varela, *Cartas de particulares a Colón y relaciones coetaneas* (Madrid, 1984), p. 167.

8. Eugene Lyon, "Puerto Real: Research on a Spanish town on Hispaniola's north coast," Project historian's report on file, Florida State Museum (Gainesville, 1981); William Hodges, "Puerto Real Sources," typescript on file, Musée de Guahábá (Haiti, 1980); Las Casas, vol. 2, ch. 10.

9. Martin Fernandez de Navarette, Compiler, *Coleccion de documentos ineditos relativos al descubrimiento, conquista, y organizacion de las antiguas posesiones espanoles de America y Oceanea* (Madrid, 1864), Tom. 1, pp. 182-290; Hodges, pp. 10-15.

10. Las Casas, book 3, ch. 128.

11. *Ibid.*, book 2, 154-156; Antonio Herrera y Tordesillas, *The General History of the Vast Continent and Islands of America (1725-1726)*, trans. by J. Stevens (London, 1973) I, 325; Hodges, p. 8.

12. Carl O. Sauer, *The Early Spanish Main* (Berkeley, 1969), pp. 206-207.

13. Lyon, op. cit.; Rochell Marrinan, "Report on excavations at Building "B", Puerto Real, Haiti," Project report on file, Florida State Museum (Gainesville, 1982); Raymond Willis, "Empire and Architecture at 16th Century Puerto Real, Hispaniola" (Ph.D. dissertation. University of Florida, 1984); Gary Shapiro, "A soil resistivity survey at 16th century Puerto Real, Haiti," *Journal of Field Archaeology*, 11 (1983), 101-110; Bonnie MacEwan, "Spanish colonial adaptation on Hispaniola: The archeology of Area 35, Puerto Real, Haiti" (MA thesis. University of Florida, 1982); Bonnie MacEwan, "Domestic adaptations at Puerto Real, Haiti," *Historical Archaeology*, 20, (1) (1986), 44-49; Charles Fairbanks and Rochelle Marrinan, "The Puerto Real Project, Haiti," *Proceedings of the Tenth International Congress of the Study of Precolumbian Cultures of the Lesser Antilles* (Santo Domingo, 1981); Elizabeth Reitz, "Early Spanish Subsistence at Puerto Real, Hispaniola," Paper presented at the Eleventh International Congress on Caribbean Archeology (San Juan, 1985); Kathleen Deagan, "La Arqueologia de los Sitios del Primer Contacto Espanol en el Caribe," Paper presented at the conference *Espana y America en la epocha del descubrimiento* (Madrid, 1985); Charles Ewen, "From Spaniard to Creole: 16th Century Hispanic-American Cultural Formation in Hispaniola," Paper presented at the Society for Historical Archaeology (Sacramento, 1986); Greg Smith, "A Study of Colono Ware and Non-European Ceramics from Sixteenth Century Puerto Real, Haiti," Paper presented at the Society for Historical Archaeology (Sacramento, 1986); Maurice Williams and Kathleen Deagan, "Sub-surface Patterning at Puerto Real, a 16th Century Spanish Town on Haiti's North Coast," *Bureau National D'Ethnologie D'Haiti*

Bulletin, 1 (1984), 48-61; Maurice Williams, "Sub-surface Patterning at 16th Century Puerto Real, Haiti," *Journal of Field Archaeology*, in press; Charles Ewen, "In Search of the Spaniards on Haiti's North Coast," *Archaeology*, in press.

14. Maurice Williams, "Preliminary field report on 1983 survey activities at En Bas Saline," Project report on file, Florida State Museum and Bureau National D'Ethnologie D'Haiti (Port au Prince, 1983); Deagan, 1986, op. cit.; Williams and Deagan, 1986, op. cit.

15. Irving Rouse, "The Arawak," in *Handbook of South American Indians, vol. 4, The Circum-Caribbean Tribes*, ed. J. Steward, *Bureau of American Ethnology Bulletin* (1948), 143 (4), 524.

16. *Ibid.*

17. Vincas Steponaitis, "Location theory and complex chiefdoms: A Mississippian example," in *Mississippian Settlement Patterns*, ed. B. Smith (New York, 1978).

18. Ricardo Alegria, "Ball Courts and Ceremonial Plazas in the West Indies," *Yale University Publications in Anthropology* (New Haven, 1985); Rouse, 1948, 524-525.

19. Frolich Rainey, "Excavations at Ft. Liberte Region, Haiti," *Yale University Publications in Anthropology*, 23 (New Haven, 1941); Irving Rouse, "Culture of the Ft. Liberte Region, Haiti," *Yale University Publications in Anthropology*, 24 (New Haven, 1941).

20. Froelich Rainey and Juan Ortiz Aguilu, "Bois Neuf: The Archeological View from West-Central Haiti," Paper presented at the 10th International Congress for the study of Precolumbian Cultures of the Lesser Antilles (Martinique, 1983).

21. Marcio Veloz-Maggiolo, *Medioambiente y Adaptación Humana en la Prehistoria de Santo Domingo*, 2 vols. (Santo Domingo, 1977), p. 87.

22. Irving Rouse, "Ceramic and Religious Development in the Prehistoric Greater Antilles," *Journal of New World Archaeology* (1982), 52.

23. Rouse, 1941, op. cit.

24. Smith, op. cit.

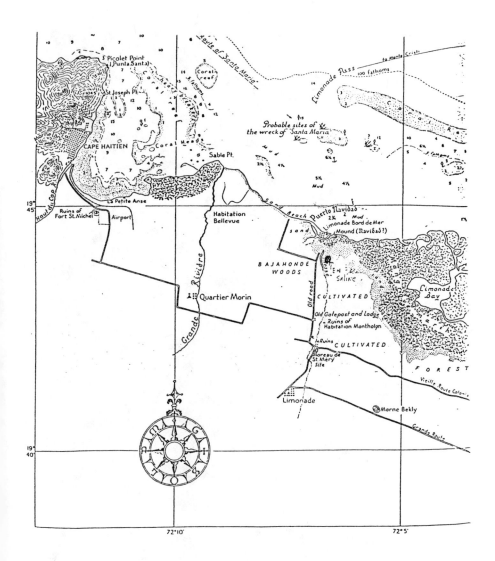

Fig. 1.

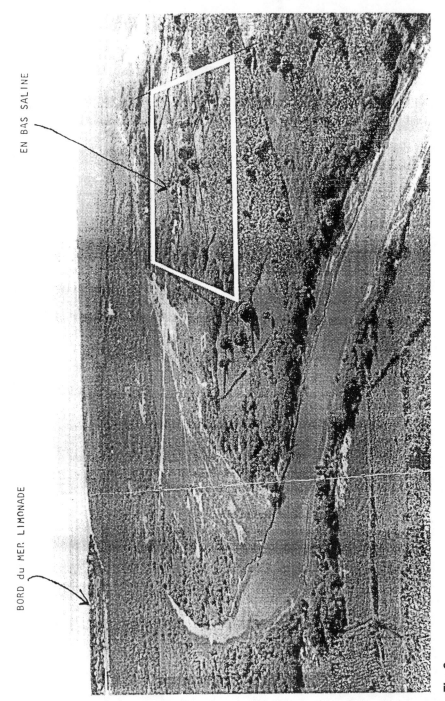

EN BAS SALINE

BORD du MER: LIMONADE

Fig. 2.

BIBLIOGRAPHY

Alegria, Ricardo. "Ball Courts and Ceremonial Plazas in the West Indies." *Yale University Publications in Anthropology* (1985).

_____. "Ethografia Taina y los Conquistadores." *Proceedings of the Eighth International Congress on the Study of Pre-Columbian Cultures of the Lesser Antilles.* Edited by S. Lewenstien. Tempe: Arizona State University, 1980. (Arizona State University Anthropological Papers No. 22.)

Benzoni, Girolamo. *History of the New World (1725).* Translated and edited by W. H. Smyth. London: Haklyut Society Publications 21, 1857.

Boggs, Stanley. "Notes and News." *American Antiquity* 5, 3 (1940), 258.

Cassa, Roberto. *Los Tainos de la Espanola.* Santo Domingo: Universidad Autonoma de Santo Domingo, 1975.

Cook, Sherburne and Woodrow Borah. *Essays in Population History, Vol I: Mexico and the Caribbean.* Berkeley: University of California Press, 1971.

Cummings, George H. "Reefs and Related Sediments of the Cap Haitian Region, Haiti." MA thesis, University of Florida, 1973.

Deagan, Kathleen. "Spanish-Indian Interactions in Sixteenth Century Florida and the Caribbean." In *Culture in Contact.* Edited by W. Fitzhugh. Washington, D. C.: Smithsonian Institution Press-Anthropological Society of Washington, 1985.

_____. "La Arqueologia de los Sitios del Primer Contacto Espanol en el Caribe." Paper presented at the conference Espana y America en la epocha del descubrimiento. Instituto de Cooperacion Ibero-Americano, Madrid, 1985.

_____. "The Search for La Navidad on Haiti's North Coast." Paper presented at the Society for Historical Archaeology Annual Meeting, Sacramento, California, 1986.

Dominguez, Lourdes. "La transculturacion en Cuba (s. XVI-XVII)." *Cuba Arqueologica.* (Havana, 1978), pp. 33-50.

Ericson, Jonathon. "Strontium Isotope Characterization in the Study of Pre-historic Human Ecology." *Journal of Human Evolution,* 14 (1985), 503-514.

Ewen, Charles. "From Spaniard to Creole: 16th Century Hispanic-American Cultural Formation in Hispaniola." Paper presented at the Society for Historical Archeology Meetings, Sacramento, California, 1986. (dissertation in prep, University of Florida).

_____. "In Search of the Spaniards on Haiti's North Coast. *Archaeology* (forthcoming).

Fairbanks, Charles and Rochelle Marinan. "The Puerto Real Project, Haiti." *Proceedings of the Tenth International Congress for the Study of Precolumbian Cultures of the Lesser Antilles.* Santo Domingo: Museo del Hombre Dominicano, 1981.

Feinman, Gary and Jill Neitzel. "Too Many Types: An Overview of Sedentary Pre-state Societies in the Americas." *Advances in Archeological Method and Theory.* Edited by M. Schiffer. Vol. 7. 1984.

Fitzhugh, William. *Cultures in Contact. The European Impact on Native Cultural Institutions in Eastern North America.* Washington, D.C.: Smithsonian Institution Press, 1985.

Gil, Juan y Consuelo Varela. *Cartas de Particulares a Colón y Relaciones Coetaneas.* Madrid: Alianza, 1984.

Herrera y Tordesillas, Antonio. *The General History of the Vast Continent and Islands of America (1725-1726).* Translated by J. Stevens, London. New York: AMS Press, 1973.

Hodges, William. "Puerto Real Sources." Typescript. Limbé, Haiti: Musée de Guahábá, 1980.

Holdridge, L. R. *Carte de l'ecologie de la Republicque d'Haiti.* Washington, D.C.: Bureau of Regional Development, Organization of American States, 1968-70.

Keen, Benjamin, trans. *The Life of the Admiral Christopher Columbus by his Son, Ferdinand.* New Brunswick, N.J.: Rutgers University, 1959.

Las Casas, Bartolome de. *Historia de las Indias.* Edicion de Agustin Millares Carlo. 3 vols. Mexico City: Fondo de Cultura Economica, 1951.

Lyon, Eugene. "Puerto Real: Research on a Spanish Town on Hispaniola's North Coast." Project historian's report on file, Florida State Museum, University of Florida, Gainesville.

MacEwan, Bonnie. *Spanish Colonial Adaptation on Hispaniola: The Archeology of Area 35, Puerto Real, Haiti.* MA thesis, University of Florida, 1982.

_____. "Domestic Adaptations at Puerto Real, Haiti." *Historical Archaeology* 20, 1 (1986), 44-49.

Major, R. H., trans. *Letters of Christopher Columbus with Other Original Documents Relating to his Four Voyages to the New World.* Reprinted 1961. New York: Corinth Books, 1857.

356

Marrinan, Rochelle. "Report on Excavations at Building "B", Puerto Real, Haiti." Project report on file, Florida State Museum, University of Florida, 1982.

Martyr D'Anghiera, Peter. *De Orbe Novo.* Translated by F. A. MacNutt. 2 vols. New York: Burt Franklin, 1970.

Moore, Clark. "Inventaire des Sites Arqueologiques Dans le Peninsule Sud D'Haiti." *Bureau National D'Ethnologie Bulletin,* 2 (1985), 65-83.

Morison, Samuel E. "The Route of Columbus Along the North Coast of Haiti and the Site of La Navidad." *Transactions of the American Society,* XXXI, 4 (1940), 239-285.

Navarette, Martin Fernandez de, compiler. *Coleccion de Documentos Ineditos Relativos al Descubrimiento, Conquista, y Organizacion de las Antiguas Posesiones Espanoles de America y Oceanea.* 42 vols. Madrid: 1864-1884.

Oviedo y Valdes, Gonzalo Fernando de. *Historia General y Natural de las Indias.* Madrid: Biblioteca de Autores Espanoles, 1959.

_____. *Sumario: Historia de la Historia Natural de las Indias.* Mexico: Fondo de la Cultura Economica, 1950.

Rainey, Frolich. "Excavations at Ft. Liberte Region, Haiti." *Yale University Publications in Anthropology,* 23 (New Haven: Yale University Press, 1941.

Rainey, Froelich and Juan Ortiz Aguilu. "Bois Neuf: The Archeological View from West-Central Haiti." Paper presented at the 10th International Congress for the Study of Precolumbian Cultures of the Lesser Antilles. Martinique, 1983.

Reitz, Elizabeth. "Early Spanish Subsistence at Puerto Real, Hispaniola." Paper presented at the Eleventh International Congress on Caribbean Archeology. University of Puerto Rico, San Juan, 1985.

Rosenblatt, Angel. *La Poblacion de America en 1492. Viejos y Nuevos Calculos.* Mexico City: 1954.

Rouse, Irving. "Prehistory in Haiti." *Yale University Publications in Anthropology* 21. New Haven: Yale University Press, 1939.

_____. "Culture of the Ft. Liberte Region, Haiti." *Yale University Publications in Anthropology* 24. New Haven: Yale University Press, 1941.

_____. "The Arawak." in *Handbook of South American Indians, Vol 4, The Circum-Caribbean Tribes.* Edited by J. Steward. *Bureau of American Ethnology Bulletin* 143, 4 (1948), 507-546.

357

_____. "Prehistory of the West Indies." *Science* 144 (1964), 499-513.

_____. "Ceramic and Religious Development in the Prehistoric Greater Antilles." *Journal of New World Archaeology* (1982).

Rouse, I., L. Allaire and A. Boomert. "Eastern Venezuela, Guianas, and the West Indies." in *Chronologies in New World Archeology*. Edited by C. Meighan and R. E. Taylor. Second Edition. New York: Academic Press, in press.

Rouse, Irving and Jose Cruxent. *Venezuelan Archeology*. New Haven: Yale University Press, 1963.

Rouse, Irving and Clark Moore. "Cultural Sequence in Southwestern Haiti. *Bureau National D'Ethnologie Bulletin*. 1 (Port au Prince, 1984), 25-38.

Sauer, Carl O. *The Early Spanish Main*. Berkeley: University of California Press, 1966.

Shapiro, Gary. "A Soil Resistivity Survey at 16th Century Puerto Real, Haiti." *Journal of Field Archeology*, 11 (1983), 101-110.

Smith, Greg. "A Study of Colono Ware and Non-European Ceramics from Sixteenth Century Puerto Real, Haiti." Paper presented at the Society for Historical Archaeology Meetings, Sacramento, 1986.

Steponaitis, Vincas. "Location Theory and Complex Chiefdoms: a Mississippian Example." in *Mississippian Settlement Patterns*. Edited by B. Smith. New York: Academic Press, 1978.

Steward, Julian. "The Circum-Caribbean Tribes." in *Handbook of South American Indians. Vol 4. The Circum-Caribbean Tribes*. Edited by J. Steward. Washington, D. C.: Smithsonian Institution Press, 1948.

St. Mery, Moreau de. *Description Topographique et Politique de la Partie Franccaise de L'isle de St. Domingue*. Philadelphia: 1797.

Sturtevant, William. "Taino Agriculture." in *The Evolution of Horticultural Systems in South America: Causes and Consequences — A Symposium*. Anthropological Supplement #2. Caracas: 1961.

Taviani, Emilio Paolo. *I Viaggio di Colombo*. 2 vols. Rome: Instituto Geografico de Agostini Novaro, 1983.

Varela, Consuelo. *Cristobal Colon. Textos y Documentos Completos*. Madrid: Editorial Alianza, 1982.

Veloz-Maggiolo, Marcio. *Medioambiente y Adaptación humana en la Prehistoria de Santo Domingo*. 2 vols. Santo Domingo: Editorial de la Universidad Autonoma de Santo Domingo, 1976-77.

Williams, Maurice. "Preliminary Field Report on 1983 Survey Activities at En Bas Saline." Project report on file, Florida State Museum and Bureau National D'Ethnologie D'Haiti, Port au Prince, 1983.

_____. "Sub-surface Patterning at 16th Century Puerto Real, Haiti. *Journal of Field Archaeology* (Fall, 1986).

Williams, Maurice and Kathleen Deagan. "Sub-surface Patterning at Puerto Real, a 16th Century Spanish Town on Haiti's North Coast." *Bureau National D'Ethnologie D'Haiti Bulletin*, 1 (Port au Prince, 1984), 48-61.

_____. "Preliminary Field Report on Excavations at En Bas Saline, 1985-1986." Project report on file, Florida State Museum and Bureau National D'Ethnologie D'Haiti, Port au Prince, 1986.

Willis, Raymond. Empire and Architecture at 16th Century Puerto Real, Hispaniola. Ph.D. dissertation, University of Florida, 1984.

Wing, Elizabeth and Elizabeth Reitz. "Prehistoric Fishing Economies of the Caribbean." *Journal of New World Archaeology*, V, 2 (Los Angeles, 1982), 13-32.